CHIMERAS OF FORM

MODERNIST LATITUDES

Modernist Latitudes
Jessica Berman and Paul Saint-Amour, Editors

Modernist Latitudes aims to capture the energy and ferment of modernist studies by continuing to open up the range of forms, locations, temporalities, and theoretical approaches encompassed by the field. The series celebrates the growing latitude ("scope for freedom of action or thought") that this broadening affords scholars of modernism, whether they are investigating little-known works or revisiting canonical ones. Modernist Latitudes will pay particular attention to the texts and contexts of those latitudes (Africa, Latin America, Australia, Asia, Southern Europe, and even the rural United States) that have long been misrecognized as ancillary to the canonical modernisms of the global North.

Barry McCrea, *In the Company of Strangers: Family and Narrative in Dickens, Conan Doyle, Joyce, and Proust*, 2011
Jessica Berman, *Modernist Commitments: Ethics, Politics, and Transnational Modernism*, 2011
Jennifer Scappettone, *Killing the Moonlight: Modernism in Venice*, 2014
Nico Israel, *Spirals: The Whirled Image in Twentieth-Century Literature and Art*, 2015
Carrie Noland, *Voices of Negritude in Modernist Print: Aesthetic Subjectivity, Diaspora, and the Lyric Regime*, 2015
Susan Stanford Friedman, *Planetary Modernisms: Provocations on Modernity Across Time*, 2015
Steven S. Lee, *The Ethnic Avant-Garde: Minority Cultures and World Revolution*, 2015
Thomas S. Davis, *The Extinct Scene: Late Modernism and Everyday Life*, 2016
Carrie J. Preston, *Learning to Kneel: Noh, Modernism, and Journeys in Teaching*, 2016
Gayle Rogers, *Incomparable Empires: Modernism and the Translation of Spanish and American Literature*, 2016
Donal Harris, *On Company Time: American Modernism in the Big Magazines*, 2016
Celia Marshik, *At the Mercy of Their Clothes: Modernism, the Middlebrow, and British Garment Culture*, 2016
Christopher Reed, *Bachelor Japanists: Japanese Aesthetics and Western Masculinities*, 2016
Eric Hayot and Rebecca L. Walkowitz, eds., *A New Vocabulary for Global Modernism*, 2016
Eric Bulson, *Little Magazine, World Form*, 2016

CHIMERAS OF FORM

Modernist Internationalism Beyond Europe, 1914–2016

Aarthi Vadde

COLUMBIA UNIVERSITY PRESS   NEW YORK

Columbia University Press
Publishers Since 1893
New York Chichester, West Sussex
cup.columbia.edu

Library of Congress Cataloging-in-Publication Data

Names: Vadde, Aarthi, author.
Title: Chimeras of form : modernist internationalism beyond Europe, 1914–2016 / Aarthi Vadde.
Description: New York : Columbia University Press, [2016] | Series: Modernist latitudes | Includes bibliographical references and index.
Identifiers: LCCN 2016026231 | ISBN 9780231180245 (cloth : acid-free paper) | ISBN 9780231542562 (e-book)
Subjects: LCSH: Modernism (Literature) | Internationalism in literature.
Classification: LCC PN56.M54 V33 2016 | DDC 809/.9112—dc23
LC record available at https://lccn.loc.gov/2016026231

Columbia University Press books are printed on permanent and durable acid-free paper.
Printed in the United States of America

Cover Image: Rabindranath Tagore, stylized animal, 1920s. The British Museum

For my parents Nirmala and Prasad Vadde
And, of course, Erik and Siddhartha

CONTENTS

Acknowledgments ix

Introduction: Chimeras of Form 1

1. Autotranslations: Rabindranath Tagore's Internationalism in Circulation 37

2. Alternating Asymmetry: International Solidarity and Self-Deception in James Joyce's *Dubliners* and "Cyclops" 74

3. Stories Without Plots: The Nomadic Collectivism of Claude McKay and George Lamming 108

4. Archival Legends: National Myth and Transnational Memory in the Works of Michael Ondaatje 149

5. Root Canals: Zadie Smith's Scales of Injustice 182

Epilogue: *Migritude*—The Re-Mediated Work of Art and Art's Mediating Work 219

Notes 233
Bibliography 265
Index 283

ACKNOWLEDGMENTS

Writing this book has been far from a solitary activity. It is with great pleasure that I thank those who helped me conceive the project, saw me through its many transformations, and now I hope share in the joy of its publication. During my time at the University of Wisconsin–Madison, I encountered extraordinary scholars and thinkers. Rebecca Walkowitz changed the way I approach modernism and understand its potential to shape thought. I thank her for her warm encouragement in all things, professional and personal. Rob Nixon challenged me to substantiate and refine my reflections on the relationship between literary form and political agency. That challenge became a core concern of this book. I remain grateful for his critical insights and generous spirit. I am also indebted to Susan Stanford Friedman, Anne McClintock, and Bala Venkat Mani, who provided valuable advice as well as the inspiration of their own work. Others at Madison deserve thanks as well: Vinay Dharwadker, Theresa Kelley, and Caroline Levine lent their time and wisdom to my scholarly endeavors. Jack Dudley, Claire Falck, Aline Lo, and Cody Reis continue to see me through.

A fellowship at the Harvard Department of English gave me the opportunity to expand my intellectual community and meet new friends in the field. It was especially a delight to exchange ideas with Homi Bhabha, Glenda Carpio, Amanda Claybaugh, David Damrosch, and Nirvana Tanoukhi as I embarked on this book. As I finished it, I enjoyed the company of the wonderful fellows at the Committee on Globalization and Social Change at the CUNY Graduate Center. Special thanks go to Gary Wilder for inviting me into that interdisciplinary group and to David Joselit for leading the conversation on my work-in-progress. Portions of this project have also been presented at the Global Modernism Symposium at Ithaca College, the Modernist Studies Association, the American Comparative Literature Association, the Society for Novel Studies, and the Mods working group at the University of Pennsylvania. I thank

Devorah Fischler, Christopher Holmes, Gayle Rogers, and Jennifer Spitzer for those opportunities. I am also grateful to Thomas Davis and Nathan Hensley for inviting me into their fantastic MSA seminar on "Global Scale and Critical Form." My chapter on Tagore benefitted from a research trip to the Rabindra Bhavana (Institute of Tagore Studies and Research) at Visva-Bharati, in Santiniketan. I am pleased to mention Swapan Majumdar and Manju Rani Singh, whose hospitality there made my visit a delightful and productive experience.

At Duke and beyond, I am fortunate to have the support of colleagues who are as generous as they are intelligent. Srinivas Aravamudan, Nancy Armstrong, Rey Chow, Deborah Jenson, Ranjana Khanna, Jahan Ramazani, Paul Saint-Amour, and Priscilla Wald participated in a manuscript workshop for this book, sponsored by the Franklin Humanities Institute. Discussing my work with such a formidable group was a highlight of my academic career and no doubt improved the manuscript, though any shortcomings remain my own. Paul and Priscilla kept reading, even after the workshop; they model the kind of mentorship I wish to practice. Leela Gandhi, Nathaniel Mackey, and Jessica Namakkal read portions of the book and returned exceedingly helpful comments. For their conversations about this project and warm encouragement along the way, thanks to David Aers, Dominika Baran, Sarah Beckwith, Jessica Berman, Christopher Bush, Ian Baucom, Joe Donahue, Brent Edwards, Thomas Ferraro, Laura Harris, Frances Hasso, Sharon Holland, Priya Joshi, John Marx, Joshua Miller, Rob Mitchell, Michael Valdez Moses, Fred Moten, Sumathi Ramaswamy, Urmila Seshagiri, and Marianna Torgovnick. Nancy Armstrong and Len Tennenhouse have been crucial sources of advice ever since I arrived at Duke. Philip Leventhal, my editor at Columbia University Press, and his assistant, Miriam Grossman, guided me through the stages of book production with assurance and aplomb. The anonymous readers offered astute commentary on the manuscript and useful suggestions for refining it. Ellen Song supplied excellent research support. I am grateful to the Dean's Publication Subsidy Fund at Duke for financially supporting the publication of this book. I also thank the members of my classes at Duke, particularly those in my graduate and undergraduate seminars on modernism, for engaging with me and challenging me to be a better thinker and teacher.

Parts of chapters 2 and 4 have been previously published in different forms: "Putting Foreignness to the Test: Rabindranath Tagore's Babu

English," *Comparative Literature* 65, no. 1 (2013): 15–25; and "National Myth, Transnational Memory: Ondaatje's Archival Method," *Novel: A Forum on Fiction* 45, no. 2 (2012): 257–275. My thanks to Duke University Press for permission to include portions of these pieces.

My mother, Nirmala Vadde, and father, Prasad Vadde, have nurtured my strange endeavors from the very beginning, even when these took me away from vocations readily recognizable to them. I thank them for letting me follow my passions and for enabling me to do so in every way. Kavitha Vadde, Steve Botlagudur, Kirin, and Prem offered lively support, just enough curiosity, and much needed distraction. As did enduring friends: Urvashi Chakravarty, Leigh Goldstein, Julia Kim, Shahirah Majumdar, and Anri Yasuda. I am quite sure that *Chimeras of Form* would not have been written without the patience, love, and intelligence of Erik Larsson. As this book was in its latest stages, Siddhartha Isak Vadde Larsson was in his earliest ones. We are so glad to welcome our little internationalist to the world.

CHIMERAS OF FORM

INTRODUCTION

CHIMERAS OF FORM

> How did one map a country that blew into a new form every day? Such questions made his language too abstract, his imagery too fluid, his metre too inconstant. It led him to create chimeras of form, lionheaded goat-bodied serpentailed impossibilities whose shapes felt obliged to change the moment they were set, so that the demotic forced its way into lines of classical purity and images of love were constantly degraded by the intrusion of elements of farce.
>
> —Salman Rushdie, *The Satanic Verses*

> If Hobbes is right, the idea of global justice without a world government is a chimera.
>
> —Thomas Nagel, "The Problem of Global Justice"

Who gets to decide the range of the possible? How does one remain open to a transformable and politically progressive future while still challenging the ideology of unlimited progress identifiable with modernity itself? Such questions lie at the heart of this book's literary and political investigations into the chimeras of modernist internationalism. I broach them not with a simple response but by yoking them to yet another, equally startling interrogative taken from Salman Rushdie's *The Satanic Verses*: "How did one map a country that blew into a new form every day?" Rushdie's query derives possibility from impossibility. It acknowledges the limitations of aesthetic representation in the face of social upheaval, yet his prose also attempts to overcome those limitations by pushing received styles to their breaking point. The breaking point of language, the point at which the writer produces not form but "chimeras of form," is also the point at which the range of the possible comes into view as a matter of enunciation. By risking illegibility and incomprehensibility in their fictional narratives, Rushdie and the other writers featured here stretch the range of the sayable, and even the thinkable, within political, philosophical, and cultural understandings of global imagination.

The capacity of chimeras of form to at once delimit the range of the possible and exceed it is an epistemological one. It allows them to, in Judith Butler's words, "pose the question of the limits of our most sure ways of knowing."[1] For Thomas Nagel, global justice is surely a chimera, a castle in the air, in the absence of a world state, but for the writers in this study, the unlikelihood of global justice ever being achieved is the occasion for a conversation about the perceived obstacles to international obligation, rather than mere acceptance of such obstacles. I use the phrase "chimeras of form" as conceptual shorthand for pushing the epistemological limits of imagining community and for testing the categories by which social life is rendered coherent and speakable. The chimera is primarily understood in its mythic dimensions, as a monstrous figure of the unclassifiable body ("lionheaded goatbodied serpentailed impossibilities"), but it also can be seen in its botanical and genetic dimensions, as a figure of taxonomic interference and rearrangement that brings newness out of the old, more familiar categories (lion, goat, serpent) that it grafts together.

Chimeras of Form undertakes its own projects of grafting: aesthetic and political categories come together in the titular formation "modernist internationalism"; literatures usually separated by period and geography are sutured together as part of a single body; and collectivities such as nation, federation, and globe are rarely considered apart from one another, though they remain distinct models of political and affective community. By allowing modernist internationalism to subsume a variety of writers working across the twentieth and twenty-first centuries and within colonial and postcolonial contexts, I am not aiming to homogenize a century of literary history under the standard of modernism. Instead, I join the movement to deprovincialize a once exclusively European aesthetic category that has been redeployed in exciting ways beyond Europe and beyond modernism's usual end date of 1940. My reformulation of modernist internationalism speaks foremost to the institution of modernist studies, but it also goes beyond it and into the intellectual history of globalization.

From Rabindranath Tagore to Zadie Smith, the writers featured here have developed and extended modernist theories and practices of literary form in order to contest isolationist understandings of national community and to give shape and substance to matters that press for international and global frames of inquiry. Such matters include transnational migration, human rights interventionism, and the vast economic inequality that separates the Global North from the Global South. In pursuing an unapologetically aesthetic line of inquiry under the title *Chimeras of Form*, this study also shows that literature is an overlooked venue for responding to the presuppositions that would relegate internationalism and global justice to the realm of chimeras—that is, to the realm of illusory pursuits divorced from or insensitive to practical constraints.

Given that literary endeavor is often greeted as an impractical form of political interventionism, it seems an especially fitting starting point from which to explore how categories of poetic and political invention might inflect one another in ways that challenge the prevailing boundaries between "realistic change" and "chimeric fantasy." I am not claiming that poetic inventiveness can directly change the circumstances of political reality, but I do believe that it can sharpen our sense of the thinkable and the sayable in the face of at least preliminarily impossible impasses. Paying close attention to the formal and theoretical complexities of a deprovincialized modernist internationalism, as this book does, invites readers to dwell in those impasses, though it makes no guarantee of getting through them. On the contrary, *Chimeras of Form* asks its readers to stick with chimeras as they lead us into a reengagement with and reconsideration of the facts, values, and frames associated with imagined community, good citizenship, international solidarity, and political agency.

I am interested in the chimera as a site where the line between possibility and impossibility is under dispute and capable of being redrawn. Its knotting together of hopeful illusion and hard reality is one of the reasons I have made it into an emblem of a modernist internationalism attentive to colonial and contemporary histories of inequality. It also gets at why I have retained the keyword *internationalism*, despite the flourishing of much current global theory under the banner of cosmopolitanism. Late twentieth-century turns toward cosmopolitanism have worked hard to rid internationalism of its chimeric taint. Bruce Robbins's foundational work in this field, *Feeling Global*, declares that "internationalism is not a utopian idealism, an infinitely deferred ideal of ultimate justice for all," while Kwame Anthony Appiah has approached cosmopolitanism not as the miracle cure to the world's ills but as a challenge of habitation, a balancing act between maintaining moral norms and respecting cultural difference that is just as pertinent to everyday life as it is to state policy decisions.[2]

The cosmopolitan cultural turn has been deeply important for grounding internationalism in the impure spaces of real-world politics and in the habits and behaviors of ordinary people, but it buries an analytical opportunity by creating an opposition between the idealism of the concept and the reality of the lived situations in which it functions. Rather than retool unachievable internationalisms into achievable cosmopolitanisms, I return to moments in modernist fiction when the line between the unachievable and the achievable is being actively discovered. I approach the unachieved ideal as an opportunity to reflect on the value of the ideal in the first place and to see whether what was accomplished might have something new and interesting to offer in our quest to discover what qualifies as a possible and worthwhile pursuit. Rather than being embarrassed by internationalism's chimeric associations, in *Chimeras of Form* I reflect on standards of judgment as they inflect the art as well as the politics of global thought.

Such standards of judgment are at play in the Rushdie epigraph at the beginning of this chapter. The flummoxed artist of the quote is Baal, a poet in the ancient city of Jahilia, who regards his chimeras of form as "failed art" because they cannot bring aesthetic order to his country's rapid changes.[3] Baal associates literary form with standards of organization that promote harmony, consistency, and unity. His ideal of form prevents him from seeing a countermodel of wholeness in his actually existing sentences. Their mixture of high and low language (classical and demotic) and their conjuncture of paradoxical figures of feeling (images of love and elements of farce) do not negate the discontinuous and discordant movement of history but instead conjure its very real effects through the organized arrangement of literary representation. What Baal perceives as incoherent and therefore vain art, Rushdie promotes as an autoreferential description of his own style. He accordingly turns Baal's failure into a test of his assumptions about art forms as well as communal forms. Baal's intention is not simply to capture or portray his country but quite specifically to "map" it. Mapping a country glazes aesthetic order with cartographic abstraction and evokes a clearly bordered shape on a political map. Chimeras of form, by showing that aesthetic and historical processes overlap, distort this image. Baal's failure to map his country in art conveys the vital truth that the boundaries of collectivity are never as given as a cartographic outline would suggest.[4]

By using Baal's failed art to challenge the containment function of aesthetic form, Rushdie draws out the ideological tension between literary form as a stabilizing force and literary form as a tool for capturing the perpetual motion of communities themselves. This perpetual motion, which Baal experiences as the uncontrollable intensity of change, dovetails with what Jed Esty has identified as "the central contradiction of modernity . . . the state of permanent transition."[5] *Chimeras of Form* takes up the oxymoron of "permanent transition" not only as the unconscious expression of uneven development within the world-system (Esty's primary use) but also as part of the self-conscious anxiety of being modern, of making one's way in the world without recourse to the myth of knowable community.

Raymond Williams famously coined the term "knowable communities" to designate those "traditional" novels that depict social relations in communicable ways, whether as the product of face-to-face encounters or as the outgrowth of transparent forms of connection among characters. By contrast, he associates the modernization of literature with the decline of the knowable:

> Identity and community became more problematic, as a matter of perception and as a matter of valuation, as the scale and complexity of the characteristic social organization increased . . . the increasing division and complexity of labour; the altered and critical relations between and within social classes: in changes like these any assumption of a knowable community—a whole community, wholly knowable—became harder and harder to sustain.[6]

In this passage, Williams is careful to specify the conditions of modernization responsible for puncturing the myth of communities as knowable, but in his larger essay he is equally at pains to address the role of "the observer's position" and "matters of consciousness" in a literary work's production of the knowable. The knowable comes under pressure not just from the modernization of modes of production, exchange, and social organization but also from the organization of literary works that destabilize the conventions of selectivity and social recognition, which produce the security and the allure of the knowable. I refer to such works as modernist, and I maintain that such a definition is of a piece with a less exclusive, more attitudinal turn toward theorizing modernism's relationship to modernity.

Working against the strictures of the knowable, writers and texts representative of modernist internationalism beyond Europe manage to reveal the conflict between imagining community as a stable, idealized entity—such as, for example, the "future heaven" of the postcolonial nation—and capturing nations, colonies, and continents' very real immersion in transitional and transnational regimes of power. Their own experiments in formal dissolution and regeneration suggest that properly contending with the permanent transitions of a globalized modernity demands resituating ideals of communal order and identity within the actual indefiniteness of a "country," a geographic designation that simultaneously, and not incidentally for my purposes, connotes both the nation and a region of undetermined expanse.

Chimeras of Form treats the impossibly restless image of "a country that blows into a new form every day" as a poetic distillation of modernity itself, unfolding under what Pheng Cheah has called "the uneven and shifting force field of the cosmopolitical."[7] For Cheah, the force field is a metaphor for the "mutating" economic, political, and cultural matrices of imperialism and neocolonial globalization whose "material linkages" are the proper focus of cosmopolitical critique. Without disputing the vital importance of analyzing this force field, I find Cheah's way of writing about the cosmopolitical to be more deterministic than historically contingent, despite his many references to the force field's constantly changing patterns.

To elicit the dynamic reading practices for which his theory calls, my own method draws on Caroline Levine's recent defense of formalism. Levine treats the relationship between aesthetic forms and social forms as one of unpredictability, in which no one element dominates the others. She tracks the volatility of these colliding formal types and illustrates how the force fields governing large social orders are actually *form* fields. The shift to thinking about not just art but also political communities and institutions as having formal attributes leads Levine toward a new configuration of the relationship between literature and society in which no forces—even those as powerful as capitalism and colonialism—are left unaltered by their manifestation through multiple orders of form. Levine's formal logic produces a powerfully distributive explanatory model of collective life—one that forgoes "an exclusive focus on ultimate causality" in favor of strategic thinking about "the artificiality and contingency of social arrangements."[8]

How to analyze the social arrangements of a variety of collectivities, empowered and disempowered, enduring and transient, territorialized and deterritorialized, remains a question without a ready answer. Although I do not correlate literary and institutional forms exactly as Levine does, I do follow her distributive approach, and I likewise attempt to break down large-scale processes (in my case, processes of globalization) without getting locked into narratives that evacuate individual agency or absolutely separate literary consciousness from political consciousness. The exemplary chimeras of *literary* form in this book are chosen expressly because they provoke counterintuitive understandings of wholeness, in which forms do not contain contradictions but construct and channel them. Such literary forms are particularly useful for drawing out the artificiality and contingency of *communal* forms, and for making them more susceptible to rethinking within an incompletely knowable global landscape.

Hence, *Chimeras of Form* substitutes a chimeric model of literary form for a containment model in its characterization of modernism, and further theorizes modernist internationalism as doing the kind of cosmopolitical critique that deploys rather than denies epistemological crisis. Such a critique begins not by negating but by engaging the more radical elements within the ideologically mixed-up history of the articulation of modernist internationalism. Instead of dividing radical from pragmatic energies, I consider how idealized dreams of internationalism are staged and situated, restrained or wholeheartedly pursued, such that modernism's chimeras of form reveal the analytical power embedded in aspirations—even, and perhaps especially, when those aspirations face accusations of fantasy, triviality, or misguided illusion. Though the writers and works I feature stretch the usual parameters of canonical modernism, they are accurately called modernist because they do not look to literature to overcome the real illegibilities, distortions, and affective conflicts that pervade attempts to think through collectivity or to do cosmopolitical critique. Rather, they allow those irregularities room to flourish, and reveal surprising arenas in which anticolonial and global thought converge.

The case studies in this book, which exemplify chimeras of form, include autotranslations, alternating asymmetry, stories without plots, archival legends, and root canals. With the exception of autotranslations, which are a known mode of writing, I have opted for enigmatic titles that, in the cases of alternating asymmetry (James Joyce), stories without plots (Claude McKay and George Lamming), and the root canal (Zadie Smith), bring famously gnomic formal innovations of the authors out for interpretation. These forms of writing reveal the many dimensions of a chimeric modernism because, taken together, they mediate disputes about the real and the unreal (as well as the realistic and the unrealistic); they undermine a strong division between trivial fancies and heroic vision; and they challenge aesthetic and communal categories of success denoted by organic wholeness and self-sufficiency. Chimeras of form are not examples of what Rushdie's Baal called "failed art," in the evaluative sense of a review or self-appraisal, but they are forms that demonstrate devalued or unappreciated forms of creativity (such as translation) and that foreground amputation and incompletion (such as in stories without plots) as strategies for rethinking definitions of the work of art built on originality, wholeness, cohesion, and autonomy.

In reading chimeras of form as figures of modernist internationalism, I propose that rethinking such unifying principles of aesthetic form, as the writers in this study do, enables them to question how those same principles (originality, wholeness, cohesion, and autonomy) operate as measures of the identity and health of communities, particularly national ones. Anti-internationalist principles of nationhood stress the value of homogeneity, isolation, and even exceptionalism in the creation of the nation's cultural fabric, which itself is often presented as the organic outgrowth of tradition. The works in this study reveal how concerns with the mechanics of form, medium, and compositional methods—the tools of art—led their authors not only to think about nations as contingent constructions but also to imagine what kinds of national constructions might be continuous with or even dependent upon the critical valuing of international and supranational solidarities. By distinguishing between state sovereignty and national autarky (Tagore), by preserving the distinctions of nationality through the arousal of shared regional and diasporic affiliations (McKay and Lamming), and by discerning the provisionality of communal scales in producing local and global narratives of inequality (Smith), the writers examined in *Chimeras of Form* contribute to the political imagination of internationalism. They rethink the exclusivity of national loyalty and explore the impact of global forces on alternative and less codified forms of collective life. With them as my guides, I show how strategies of breaking down, reassembling, and generally testing the wholeness of the work of art become essential to the analysis of cosmopolitical conflicts.

Internationalism: Utopia and Reality

The chimera: a mythological monster of disparate parts; a biological creature containing within it two or more genetically distinct types of cells; an implausible dream that nonetheless lives on. Chimeras of form: attempts to graft together theoretically separate spheres such as art and politics, nature and culture, but also attempts of a particularly wary kind in which the writer's agency in the world is a matter of self-reflection and debate rather than a fait accompli. At its broadest level, *Chimeras of Form* takes to the borderlands of impossibility and possibility, fracture and assembly, artistic agency and self-doubt. It shows how modernist writers' analytic work in these borderlands participates in philosophical and cultural debates about internationalism that have persisted since the early twentieth century. The chimera's knotting together of threatening change and harmless fantasy makes it a powerful symbolic figure for internationalism, a discourse punctuated, on the one hand, by dramatic calls for transformation in the loyalties of ordinary people and the realpolitik of states, and, on the other hand, by recurring doubts about its efficacy in affecting either ordinary people or state policy.

Internationalism's battle for legitimacy is observable across the ideological spectrum. Liberal philosopher Thomas Nagel has described cosmopolitan internationalism and its attendant "chimera" of global justice as a moral aspiration without political teeth, whereas Marxian cultural critic Fredric Jameson has famously remarked that, in the wake of socialist internationalism's failure, "it is easier to imagine the end of the world than a world without capitalism."[9] Calls for internationalism on the extreme ends of liberal and socialist thought have tended toward normative universalisms that evacuate cultural specificity. Strong cosmopolitans, such as Martha Nussbaum, will demand that a citizen of the United States should care as much about a person in a country they have never visited as they would about their fellow Americans; whereas strong socialists, such as the conveners of the 2013 World Social Forum, will declare that, in their efforts to end historically situated and diverse forms of discrimination and oppression, "there is no solution within the capitalist system!"[10]

Such blanket statements certainly can be judged naive and unrealistic, in light of the differential ties that bind people and the differential effects of the varieties of systems that comprise global capitalism, but the demands for change that their chimeras impose can also serve what Sianne Ngai calls a "diagnostic function"; that is, they can help us make sense of "representational predicaments" that connect the psychic desire for a different kind of world to the material constraints of social and political life.[11] Although Ngai's claim pertains to ugly or weak feelings, unsuitable to taking political action, my claim for the diagnostic power of chimeras pertains to the way they (and the literary forms they animate) reveal the tacit terms of ideality and reality operating within our notions of what separates powerful illusions from vain ones.

Nationalism, as many have argued, is a powerful illusion, one with traction over the hearts and minds of people and connectedness to the institutions of state that give it a concrete political apparatus.[12] Internationalism, if we adopt Nagel's view, is a vain illusion, unless it eventually paves the way for "global sovereignty"—in others words, for the existence of some kind of world state whose political form will attain the concreteness that nation-states now enjoy. The aspiration toward a global sovereign, qualitatively different from empire, was debated by H. G. Wells and Rabindranath Tagore in 1930 as part of an event sponsored by the League of Nations' International Committee on Intellectual Cooperation. Wells was for and Tagore was against, and the reasons for their differences will be addressed in chapter 1. But Nagel envisions a state-centered theory of justice in action: justice depends upon the existence of a sovereign government, which can coordinate and control the collective self-interest of its people and set the parameters by which justice is judged. Outside of states, the rules of justice do not apply.

Nagel arrives at the conclusion that international relations are anarchic and global justice is chimeric via Thomas Hobbes, but a more immediately relevant intellectual ancestor is E. H. Carr. Carr's book *The Twenty Years' Crisis* (1939), which he originally wished to title *Utopia and Reality*, set the theoretical vocabulary for what would become the academic discipline of international relations. Carr is known in that discipline for shaping and propounding the "realist" view to which Nagel subscribes and for discrediting the "utopian" strategies of Wilsonian internationalism to foster cooperation across nations. Although Carr was derisive of Wilsonian internationalism for taking up a set of positions that took morality rather than self-interest as the starting point for its policies, what he really condemned were its hypocrisies, the ways in which organizations like the League of Nations would sponsor cultural internationalism while perpetuating economic imperialism within and beyond Europe. The shortcomings of Wilsonian internationalism's specific utopianism are well known, but Carr's muted defense of utopianism's place in international politics is not so well known, particularly because of his reputation in the discipline of International Relations as the resolute political realist.[13]

In *The Twenty Years' Crisis*, Carr regarded international politics as an "infant science," and he saw it, like other infant sciences, as "markedly and frankly utopian . . . in the initial stage in which wishing prevails over thinking." Wilsonian internationalism was based on wishing, and it was the job of international political scientists to correct the balance of aspiration with analysis. Indeed, achieving a balance of utopia and reality, as opposed to just siding with realism, was for Carr the hallmark of mature thought:

> There is a stage where realism is the necessary corrective to the exuberance of utopianism, just as in other periods utopianism must be invoked to counteract the barrenness of realism. Immature thought is predominantly purposive and utopian. Thought which rejects purpose altogether is the thought of old age. Mature thought combines purpose with observation and analysis.

Carr's definition of maturity in the science of international politics, much as in the story of Goldilocks, is about finding out what kind of thought is "just right." An immoderate realism, beholden to "what was and what is" is "impotent to alter the course of events." Moderated by utopianism, mature thought recognizes that "theory, as it develops out of practice and develops into practice, plays its own transforming role in the process."[14]

Despite my reservations about Carr's rhetoric of youth and maturity, which imply developmental stages that the literature in this study challenges, his statement about theory and practice resonates strongly with my reading of the Rushdie epigraph. Rushdie combines Baal's idealist desire for form with his written chimeras of form to revise literary form's theoretical association with order and containment. Combining utopianism with realism in the self-consciousness of chimeras (wishes that know themselves in some way to be false) allows Rushdie to give form to the dynamism of historical processes that Baal sets out to freeze.

The chimeras of form underpinning modernist internationalism are thus not moves toward formlessness but literary attempts to redirect and diffuse the existing frameworks through which international attachment and global justice might be recognized. If a state-centric view of politics views international relations as anarchic, a more cosmopolitical view would strive to develop frameworks that target the relationships between groups and theorize accountability across different kinds of collectivities. The writers in this study, like Carr, attempt to bring shape and form to the "formless" space of international politics; however, they are not interested in turning that project into a science or erasing the imbalances of utopianism and realism that would have us wonder whether internationalism is visionary or just laughter in the dark. Their uncertainties about their own artistic agency play into their efforts to push the limits of aesthetic and social representation. By breaking down literary forms but also rebuilding them, they explore how political communities of various scales (nations, empires, and federations) create the lines between order and disorder, alien and citizen, which states claim only to police. From Tagore to Smith, these writers also try to reshape, if not the borders of political communities, at least the borders of reader consciousness, so that the idea of justice may more readily extend from the national to the global.

In 1939, Carr wrote, "Frank acceptance of the subordination of economic advantage to social ends, and the recognition that what is economically good is not always morally good, must be extended from the national to the international sphere."[15] In 2016, even though progress has been made ("fair trade" is part of the vernacular now), we are not at the level of frank acceptance for global social justice. The story that *Chimeras of Form* tells thus has a purpose that goes beyond academic endeavor; my own chimera, or "genial illusion," to quote Joyce, is that a study that helps internationalism to gain acceptance in the domains of sentiment and culture will ease its acceptance into the domain of politics.

Although there is no guarantee that increasing the cultural acceptance of internationalism will breed political change—or global economic redistribution, which is even tougher—there is something to be said for taking stock of an ideal like global justice, the debate of which lends insight into the intellectual history of globalization. Samuel Moyn, who is, like Nagel, a firm skeptic of global justice's ability to translate its formation as a "scholarly movement" into "real-world outcomes," has nonetheless historicized the philosophical emergence of the ideal, to fascinating effect.[16] Moyn recovers the disavowed conjuncture between cosmopolitan theories of global justice, rooted in the foundational work of political philosopher Charles Beitz, and the alliance-based Third-Worldism of developing countries in the New International Economic Order (NIEO) of the 1970s. The NIEO brought the values of Third-Worldism to the United Nations Conference on Trade and Development in 1974, where its proponents pressed for the protection of postcolonial national economies (including the nationalization of resources), restitution for resources exploited under colonialism, and special measures to ensure the development of the world's poorest countries.[17] In an essay entitled "Justice and International Relations" (1975), Beitz supported the NIEO platform as consistent with the goal of global justice, but he later backed away from that position in his 1979 book *Political Theory and International Relations*, which argued for a more liberal conception of global justice rooted in the rights of the individual over the self-determination of states.

In tracing the course of Beitz's "deradicalization" and his eventual distancing from NIEO positions, Moyn nonetheless finds in those positions an "alternative version of global justice" built around policy prescriptions for restructuring trade rather than expanding sovereign power over larger and larger state formations.[18] Whereas state-centered theories of justice, such as that of John Rawls or Nagel, abstractly disentangled states, both Third-Worldist and cosmopolitan theories acknowledged the history of economic and political interdependencies that make such disentangling impossible, even if cosmopolitan theories ultimately softened the revolutionary edge of Third-Worldism's collectivist demands.

Like Moyn, I examine the often occluded interface between anticolonial and liberal theories of internationalism, though I am less interested in chronicling anticolonialism's containment by liberalism than I am in examining how these dueling-yet-imbricated discourses might be mediated and illuminated by literary works irreducible to ideological agendas. If the scholarly concept of global justice is grounded in very real historical demands still waiting to be met, then the chimeras of literary form brought forth by modernist internationalism take us into the mix of intimate experiences, disappointed expectations, and recalcitrant aspirations that lend immediacy and embodiment to historical reckonings.

Deprovincializing Modernism

The subtitle of my study, *Modernist Internationalism Beyond Europe*, demands some explanation, especially because the version of modernist internationalism I am offering is remarkably different from the European formulation that came to be institutionalized in the 1950s and 1960s. In his introduction to *Modernism: An Anthology*, Lawrence Rainey recalls several early approaches to accounting for modernism, which constitute possible origin stories for the movement's incorporation into the academy. Most influential of these early forays was Harry Levin's 1956 essay "What Was Modernism?," which proceeded to define the category by populating it with specific writers. Building a canon, which this essay did, was thus key to establishing the definition of modernism, and Levin's selections and pedagogy played a profound role in shaping modernism's association with elitism and gatekeeping.

To reinforce this point, Rainey recalls a legendary Harvard course taught by Levin entitled simply "Joyce, Proust, and Mann," in which students were required to read the complete *À la recherche*, *Ulysses*, and one or more novels by Thomas Mann, with either Proust or Mann being read in the original language. This syllabus contributed to the formidable image of modernism and to its further definition as a "pan-European and cosmopolitan phenomenon, one promulgated by an international community effectively removed from the contingencies of time and place."[19]

Other early accounts of modernism include that of Graham Hough, who inadvertently suggested Anglo-American modernism's first period boundaries when he claimed that "the years between 1910 and the Second World War saw a revolution in the literature of the English language."[20] Though Hough oriented modernism around the relationship of T. S. Eliot and Ezra Pound, Rainey classifies his and Levin's early definitions of modernism as "neoclassicist." They conceived of modernism not just as rebelling against romantic and Victorian conceptions of art but also as searching for deep symbolic structures of order that might serve as a refuge from the chaos of contemporary history.

Anyone privy to debates in modernist studies since the early 2000s will know that this neoclassicist vision of modernist internationalism, centered on politically disinterested expatriates in Western European nations has come under profound pressure from all sides. A 2001 essay by Susan Stanford Friedman entitled "Definitional Excursions: The Meanings of Modern/Modernity/Modernism" revisits the task of field definition begun by Levin, but in a less positivist, more excursive vein. Her essay's conjunctural approach to the modern, modernism, and modernity as well as its tendency to produce, in the language of jazz, variations on their definitions, shows how much scholarly accounts of modernism have migrated away from the early nominal accounts of Levin and Hough, and even from the later gatekeeping practices of Hugh Kenner, who in 1984 also defined modernism as an international phenomena and, by that criteria, excluded Virginia Woolf, William Faulkner, and William Carlos Williams as "provincial" writers.[21] Such selectivity prompts Friedman to assert, "If he [Kenner] had included these writers [Woolf, Faulkner, Williams] in his pool of modernists to begin with, his generalizations about modernism would have been different. So might his concept of the internationalism of modernism if his pool had included writers from Africa, South America, and Asia."[22] Jahan Ramazani has also called attention to the discrepancy between modernism's "vaunted internationalism" and its critical history of circumscription, arguing for the traversal of disciplinary boundaries separating modernist and postcolonial studies.[23] Friedman's and Ramazani's important reappraisals of modernist internationalism made the paradigm's own provinciality hard to ignore, as did the flourishing of scholarly studies in the 2000s under the rubric of what Douglas Mao and Rebecca Walkowitz called the "new modernist studies."[24]

So why return to the fusty category of modernist internationalism when so much rich work has been done within a new set of vocabularies emphasizing the transnational networks, material contexts, and medial variety of modernism? Because I want to generate friction between the term's initial institutionalizing function and the revisionary account on offer in the present work. Modernist internationalism is not a theoretically abstract principle but a historically articulated category open to infiltration and rearticulation precisely because we maintain a record of its past associations. Whereas modernist internationalism has, with the hindsight of postcolonial and transnational methods, become associated with Eurocentric aestheticism and an exclusive politics of literariness, my account begins by recontextualizing modernist internationalism within the historically specific milieu of the interwar years, when multiple internationalisms—political and aesthetic, European and non-European—commingled. By taking modernist internationalism beyond Europe, I aim to deprovincialize the category rather than supersede or supplant it. This means exposing the assumptions at work within the making of an exclusivist modernist canon and illustrating how the concept of modernist internationalism grows and changes when we consider literary texts from across multiple continents, and internationalisms from across a variety of ideologies.

To be clear, I am not suggesting that deprovincializing modernism is something particularly unprecedented. Far from it; the archive I assemble in this book may be entertained as modernist thanks in great part to the conceptual pressure and stretch that previous studies in the field have already placed on the category. Laura Doyle and Laura Winkiel's prescient collection *Geomodernisms* rewrites the modernism of Anglo-American New Criticism by taking a "locational approach" to modernism's diverse geographies and historical contexts.[25] Their formulation of modernism as "geocultural" and plural laid early groundwork for rethinking modernism through a global lens.

Pamela Caughie's collection *Disciplining Modernism* frontally addresses the difficulties of rendering modernist studies interdisciplinary, especially when definitions of modernism and modernity vary dramatically across the arts, philosophy, and the social sciences. By channeling our understanding of modernism through these disciplinary realms, Caughie's collection yields an important insight for deprovincializing modernism: that clarifying confusion about definitional terms may ultimately matter less than explaining with precision the "divergent perspectives and motives" that create such confusion.[26] I take to this to mean that, although standardizing terms such as "modernism" and "modernity" is important for critical dialogue, it cannot tell us as much about those terms as can understanding their splintering through actual use.

The differential ways in which modernism and modernity have been invoked by writers across nations and periods inflect my work in *Chimeras of Form*. My tendency toward multiplying strains of modernist internationalism rather than homogenizing them is also anticipated by Mark Wollaeger's *Oxford Handbook of Global Modernisms*, which offers a large-scale vision of modernist study that replaces positivist, panoramic definitions of modernism with hermeneutical reflection on the methods by which scholars identify works as modernist across a variety of regions and languages.[27]

Paul Saint-Amour has retrospectively labeled such collective efforts to rethink modernism as a form of descriptively weak theory in which the definition of modernism has become increasingly associative and probabilistic as opposed to nominal and binary (e.g., defining works as either modernist or not modernist).[28] The waning of a strong theory of modernism, with its exclusivist notions and gatekeeping functions, has led to the waxing of modernist studies as a field. Like descriptive weakening, deprovincializing modernism (as I use the phrase) is meant to draw out and name preexisting currents within modernist studies that may not have been parsed in such terms before. It is also intended, perhaps surprisingly, given the "beyond Europe" of my subtitle, to use the momentum gained from the project of provincializing Europe to rethink Europe's symbolic function in scholarship on modernism and modernity.

Since the publication of Dipesh Chakrabarty's seminal book *Provincializing Europe*, the titular idea has guided progressivist critics looking to understand experiences of modernity outside of European geographies and chronologies.[29] "Beyond Europe" has meant not only abandoning the restricted vision that metonymically took European thought for universal thought (Eurocentrism) but also questioning the use of European categories of cultural history to explain the cultural production of non-Europeans. The endeavors within modernist studies to address non-European literatures have certainly overcome the restricted vision of modernist internationalism's earlier institutional history, but the question of whether they have overcome diffusionist or assimilationist paradigms of knowledge production remains a contentious one, often depending on whether scholars view the categories of modernism and modernity as "incontestably European in origin."[30] Proponents of alternative modernities have, on the face of it, eschewed such a claim in order to point to the intellectual and creative autonomy of non-European cultures, whereas proponents of a singular modernity have embraced its Europeanness in order to emphasize the undeniable economic differentials that separate the metropoles and peripheries of former European empires.[31]

Despite the opposition of these positions, the structures of the debate they have provoked have, sometimes purposefully and sometimes unwittingly, reinforced Europe's position as agent of empire and a standard of modernity, with alternatives arrayed around it. Such a narrative leaves something to be desired for many different parties. For those who work on the internal power structures of Europe (for example, in colonial Ireland, Eastern Europe, or Scandinavia), it leaves a reductive view of the continent unexamined. For those who study non-European cultures' contributions to modernism and modernity, it yields a relativism that leaves the power structures of economic and cultural development unaddressed.

The move toward deprovincializing epistemological categories avoids some of the impasses of the modernity debates by shifting their terrain away from origins to encounters. An emphasis on encounters shows that orienting conversations about modernity around singularity and plurality cedes too much to Europe from the outset. As Gary Wilder has argued:

> Modern, concrete universalizing processes (like capitalism) were not confined to Europe. Nor were concepts of universality (or concepts that became universal) simply imposed by Europeans or imitated by non-Europeans. They were elaborated relationally and assumed a range of meanings that crystallized concretely through use.[32]

To alight on the origins of modernity, whether European, Asian, or multiple, is not the only way to study historical power relations or to overcome ongoing epistemological inequities. Rather, we should question the foundation of originality itself and, moreover, be wary of confirming provenance as a measure of thought's identity or natural belonging to a certain territory. Wilder builds on Susan Buck-Morss's notion of "the communism of the idea" when he argues that "supposedly European categories of political modernity . . . self-determination, emancipation, equality, justice, and freedom" are not the property of Europe but part of the shared legacy of modernity.[33] Tracing the history of concepts like modernism and decolonizing them by exposing the power relationships embedded in their making is one way in which scholars of modernism and modernity can ensure they are deprovincializing their fields, as opposed to simply expanding them.[34]

Chimeras of Form returns to the first half of the twentieth century to recover a series of colonial encounters that brings peripheral European (specifically Irish) and non-European (specifically South Asian and Caribbean) experiences of modernity to the core of modernist internationalism's aesthetic and communal experimentation. By doing so, the book reveals modernist literature's engagement with the international as an emergent scale of analysis in the interwar era.[35] The idea of an interconnected and securitized world was already a salient concept in the early twentieth century. Technologies such as international standard time contributed to an increased awareness of the global simultaneity of collective existence, while the institution of passport requirements for travel across European empires and their colonies following World War I created discrepancies in raced and gendered groups' experiences of transnational mobility that were hard to miss.[36] Modernist internationalism beyond Europe addresses itself to such globalizing processes of modernity. It coheres around artistic efforts to rethink notions of autonomy and organicism in literary form and attends to how a subset of modernist formal experimentation contributed to intellectual projects of evaluating internationalisms of diverse political persuasions. All the writers in this study inject perspectivism, collage, and revision not only into their literary forms and compositional methods but also into their political theories of collective membership, affiliation, and action.[37] Rethinking autonomy probably does not sound traditionally modernist; perspectivism and collage no doubt do. Although it is undeniable that many of this study's featured works meet the threshold of "modernist" established by preceding typologies of modernist form and periodizing rubrics, it is not my aim, as should be apparent by now, to shore up a strict prototype of modernism against those who would use the term even more flexibly than I have here.[38] I support undertakings that theorize modernism differently, provisionally rather than definitively, and with an eye for the discrepancies between the literary institutionalization of modernist internationalism and the lived encounters of a one and unequal global modernity.

Such latitude is reasonably met with certain questions and criticisms—some particular to this study and some more far-reaching: Aren't there other writers and works—say, W. E. B. Du Bois's *The Souls of Black Folk* and Virginia Woolf's *Three Guineas*—that have been historically marginalized from the modernist canon and are directly concerned with matters of international solidarity? Doesn't using the largeness and vagueness of global modernity as an index for modernism flatten out the distinctiveness of the "high modernism" that occupies a solid and orienting place within European and Anglo-American narratives of literary history?[39]

My answer to both these questions is yes. I cannot claim that *Chimeras of Form* is an exhaustive study of the kind of modernist internationalism it outlines. Its case studies are exemplary and not all-inclusive of efforts to come to terms with the growing unknowability of communities. The geographic spread of the project purposefully troubles teleological paradigms of literary history, which tend to favor evolutionary stories of literary development and to prize the strict causalities that are more possible to assert when working within a bounded territory.[40]

In offering a sampling of writers who have been traditionally divvied up into different primary groups (Indian literature, in the case of Tagore; international modernism or Irish literature for Joyce; the Harlem Renaissance for McKay; Caribbean literature for Lamming; Canadian for Michael Ondaatje; British for Smith), I am arguing for what sociologist Mark Granovetter calls "the cohesive power of weak ties."[41] Such ties lend insight into relationships across groups and illuminate elements of social structure that are obscured by attention to intragroup dynamics. My principle of selection is thus native to the critical challenge set by internationalism and cosmopolitics themselves. To understand the relationships between different identity groups, as well as the thicker and thinner bonds that comprise what Bruce Robbins calls "attachment at a distance," we must be willing to pursue more diffuse configurations of literary culture, especially when diffuseness enables us to target the eccentricities of national literature traditions.[42] Such eccentricities might include translated works, such as Tagore's, whose English autotranslations of his Bengali writings internalized the demand of writing for multiple audiences; works composed outside the author's country of birth and with no particular national audience yet in existence, as with McKay's *Banjo* or Lamming's *The Emigrants*; or works that thematize and theorize supranational state formations, such as Zadie Smith's "The Embassy of Cambodia," a short story that ties the fate of its characters more to the European Union than to England.

When I deploy modernist internationalism as a category to be interrogated as well as remade, I am allowing the chimeras of form that populate this study to affect the book's own methodological self-understanding. Rather than divide modernism, postcolonialism, and globalism into discrete and datable periods of literary history, *Chimeras of Form* treats them as analytical apertures onto the concurrent and unfinishable projects of modernity, decolonization, and internationalism. In the suffix shift from unfinish*ed* projects to unfinish*able* projects, I declare my difference from philosophers of modernity such as Jürgen Habermas, who retain faith in the Enlightenment precepts of progress.[43] Whereas "unfinished" embeds a telos of liberation and accomplishment that defines Habermasian optimism, "unfinishable" acknowledges the intractability of economic inequality, neocolonialism, racism, and various other kinds of oppression, the structural parameters of which have shifted but not disappeared across a globalized modernity.

The sustaining mood of *Chimeras of Form* is thus, apropos of modern-day usages of the word *chimera*, pessoptimism.[44] An ambivalent mixture of innocence and experience, hope and doubt, pessoptimism invites in some of the negativity that utopianism usually keeps at bay. The chimeras collected in this book capture the elements of dispute and disbelief at work in determining the conditions of possibility for social transformation. They yield a modernist internationalism in which the historical experiences of colonial dependency, racial exclusion, peripheralness, and various other forms of economic and cultural subordination are neither simply overcome nor left behind.

Artificial Life: Chimeric Form and the Modernist Grotesque

The taint of negativity that accompanies the chimera, its designation as everything from a monstrous body to a foolish dream, lends perverse insight into the received norms governing our definitions of proper bodies and wise ambitions. Although the task of tracing a full genealogy of such received norms of body and mind is beyond the scope of the present project, it is useful to consider how the chimera, long held as an exemplary figure of the irrational and the grotesque, has functioned within theories of imaginative writing and the imagination in general. By examining the role the chimera has historically played in determining imaginative and aesthetic value, we gain a better sense of the literary and communal assumptions that are disturbed by the formal experiments highlighted in this book.

In his classic work of criticism *The Mirror and the Lamp* (1953), M. H. Abrams argued that eighteenth-century empirical theories of the mind, as represented by David Hume and Alexander Gerard among others, often invoked "mythological grotesques" to exemplify the action of the imagination and its grounding in, even subordination to, sensation. Abrams cited Gerard's *Essay on Genius* (1774), which used the chimera to illustrate the empiricist principle that the imagination's claims to novelty are always a product of its reassembly of sensible perception: "When Homer formed the idea of the *Chimera*, he only joined into one animal, parts which belonged to different animals; the head of a lion, the body of a goat, and the tail of a serpent." The chimera is a product of mental processes that Abrams classifies under "the mechanical theory of literary invention," which, contrary to what he calls genius, relies on the "less perfect energies of art" to assemble a new object out of existing materials, rather than on the more perfect energies of nature, which does not just assemble but converts extrinsic material into that which is intrinsically essential. Gerard compares genius to a plant converting "moisture from the earth" into "nourishment." With that metaphor, he offers a protoromantic organic theory of literary invention that looks forward to the "full development of the organism as aesthetic model."[45]

The chimera, as an example of what, in the wake of romanticism, would be described as "mere" mechanical invention, thus provides a degraded figure of invention, the impurity of which is specifically linked to its alignment with the less perfect processes of art rather than the more perfect processes of nature. In "Of Simplicity and Refinement in Writing" (1742), Hume also adduces the chimera to explain inferior forms of imaginative invention, but unlike Gerard, he restricts himself to the more narrow field of writing and distinguishing that which is "fine writing" from that which is crude. Quite interestingly, the chimera is an example of the crudeness that arises not as the opposite of refinement but as an excess of it:

> On the other hand, productions, which are merely surprising, without being natural, can never give any lasting entertainment to the mind. To draw chimeras is not, properly speaking, to copy or imitate. The justness of the representation is lost, and the mind is displeased to find a picture, which bears no resemblance to any original. Nor are such excessive refinements more agreeable in the

> epistolary or philosophic style, than in the epic or tragic. Too much ornament is a fault in every kind of production. Uncommon expressions, strong flashes of wit, pointed similes, and epigrammatic turns, especially when they recur too frequently, are a disfigurement, rather than any embellishment of discourse.[46]

Copying and imitating do not connote a dull mimeticism to Hume; they are methods by which the writer achieves a balance, a "just medium" between simplicity and refinement, so that the grace of the natural is perceived and preserved. The chimera's excessive refinement (note how the word *refinement* lends to artistry the mechanical connotations of a refinery) renders it a "disfigurement" rather than an "embellishment" of discourse, although it may be more accurate to say the embellishment is what disfigures this organic wholeness of fine writing for Hume: "As the eye, in surveying a Gothic building, is distracted by the multiplicity of ornaments, *and loses the whole by its minute attention to the parts*; so the mind, in perusing a work overstocked with wit, is fatigued and disgusted with the constant endeavour to shine and surprize" (italics mine). The chimera is both an example of denaturalizing stylistic extravagance and a symbol of the dangers of the grotesque as it evolves from Homeric epic to Gothic architecture.

The chimera's association with excessive refinement and disorientation of the eye makes it symbolic of a grotesque whose aesthetic effects overlap with the aesthetic effects that modernists in this study are interested in creating. They reconceptualize the empiricist rejection of extravagant stylistic experimentation as the necessary courting of literary difficulty and even illegibility. Such aesthetic values opposed the achievement of simplicity in an effort to push the boundaries of reader identification and to question the self-confirmations of universality and particularity as principles of reading and writing across cultures. In *Nationalism*, for example, Tagore situated himself between two rejected paths: "the colourless vagueness of cosmopolitanism," on one side, and the "self-idolatry of nation-worship," on the other.[47] For him, autotranslation offered a third way between the polarities of cultural indistinction and cultural autarky—a linguistic vehicle through which to explore the dynamic interplay of illegibility and translatability as initially a condition and later a principle of international exchange.

McKay, in turn, embraced embellishment and disorientation of the eye as of way of stymieing surveillance, both biographically and literarily. Take this anecdote from his autobiography, *A Long Way from Home*:

> For the first time in my life [in Morocco] I felt myself singularly free of color-consciousness. I experienced a feeling that must be akin to the physical well-being of a dumb animal among kindred animals, who lives instinctively and by sensations only, without thinking. But suddenly I found myself right up against European intervention and proscription.
>
> A *chaoush* (native doorman and messenger) from the British Consulate had accosted me in a *souk* one day and asked whether I was American. I said I was born in the West Indies and lived in the United States and that I was an American, even though I was a British subject, but I preferred to think of myself as an internationalist. The *chaoush* said he didn't understand what was an internationalist. I laughed and said that an internationalist was a bad nationalist. He replied gravely: "All the Moors call you an American, and if you are British, you should come and register at the Consulate." I was amused at his gravity, reinforced by that African dignity which is so impressive in Morocco, especially as I had said I was an internationalist just by way of a joke and without thinking of its radical implications. But I wasn't aware then how everybody in Morocco (European and native) was looking for hidden meanings in the simplest phrases. The natives imagine (and rightly enough) that all Europeans are agents of their respective countries with designs upon their own, and the European colonists are suspicious and censorious of visitors who become too sympathetic and friendly with the natives.[48]

I quote McKay at length because his recollection, as it unfolds, puts a privileged idea of disembodied, if not universal, experience within the context of imperial surveillance, where his jokes are inescapably politicized by the paranoid milieu of the French protectorate. He discovers that simplicity is not a feature of such climates where "everybody . . . (European and native) was looking for hidden meanings." Misunderstanding, tonal dissonance (between McKay's levity and the *chaoush*'s gravity), and mutual suspicion are the historical conditions of McKay's internationalism, but they are transformed into formal strategies (puns, syntactical ambiguities, plotlessness) in *Banjo* (1929), the novel that he was revising while in Morocco. In fiction, McKay explored playfulness and elusiveness as the survival tactics of migrants without papers or paths to citizenship. To claim the identity of an internationalist—because it was comical, but also because it was inscrutable—illustrates a chimerical kind of unknowability; it interferes with and repurposes categorical language to push against external attempts at classification.

McKay's internationalism is of an entirely different order from the proposed plans and institutional forms of Wilsonian internationalism that E. H. Carr called utopian. Indeed, his experiences and his transformation of those experiences into art offer a certain kind of historical truth about the dark side of liberal internationalism, lost to the once "infant" and now grown science of international politics. In showing how McKay and other writers contribute to the analysis of international conditions, I am making a case for literature's contribution to the intellectual history of globalization. Intellectual history, as I invoke it here, refers less to a subdiscipline of history, itself rife with self-definitional and methodological debates, than to a multidisciplinary humanistic project of understanding—in Stefan Collini's words, "those ideas, thoughts, arguments, beliefs, assumptions, attitudes, and preoccupations that together made up the intellectual or reflective life of previous societies."[49] Such a project is necessarily interdisciplinary in scope, but, Collini continues, it benefits from a variety of what may be seen as discipline-specific skills: "the trained sensibilities of the literary critic, alert to all forms of affective and non-literal writing, or the analytical skills of the philosopher, probing the reasoning that ostensibly connects premises and conclusions."

In attributing to literary works the capability of, if not exactly arguments, their own forms of analytical intervention into global thought, I am hybridizing the "trained sensibilities" of the literary critic with the "analytical skills" of the philosopher. I suspect few literary critics would object to this approach, but those outside the field of literary studies may find it more surprising. Reading literature not just for the lived experience of those who came before us or exist alongside us (albeit in very different ways) but also for the ways in which literary works stage the interaction of ideas with feelings, action, and embodiment in fact addresses one of the old but recurring criticisms of intellectual history: that it is too willing to grant autonomy to ideas (as opposed to human actors or systems) as the engine of history.[50] Although self-identified intellectual historians have developed multiple ways of addressing the social context and material distribution of ideas, fiction is often overlooked as a space capable of grounding ideas. It is my contention that it epitomizes a milieu in which the history of thought and the history of writing become inseparable.

The works featured in *Chimeras of Form* lend specific insight into the affective and analytical predicaments of globalization by inviting readers to think about the scale of knowledge and how the boundaries we draw around communities play a role in determining what or who we perceive as unknowable or more difficult to know. A chimeric modernism, informed by the grotesque, grapples with the conjunctures of the known and the unknown, of bounded communities and unbounded forces. Ideologically speaking, it lacks "the encapsulating and enclosing sense" of what Raymond Williams would call, in the wake of *The Country and the City*, the "regional" novel. The regional novel refers to a variety of subgenres that produce knowable communities by imagining their settings as self-contained. Such genres of "provincial" fiction include

> the *rentier* novel, the corporation novel, the university novel—in which absorption in the details of an essentially local life depends, ultimately, on not seeing its relations with a more general life: the work which is at the source of rentier income; the market and power relations which are the true source of the corporation's internal operations and maneuvers; the wider process of learning and resources and access which constitute a particular kind of university.[51]

Williams is performing a materialist critique of the regional novel's holistic qualities, which has now grown quite familiar, but his interpretation also bears some forgotten insights. He argues that, in projecting the region as "organic" (that is, as an "internal whole"), the regional novel creates the region as an autonomous entity either divorced from external sources of income and labor, in the case of privileged regions, or subject to damaging external forces, in the case of disempowered or endangered regions. In either case, organicism becomes a synonym for the "autonomy" of the community's formation, which is expressed in spatial terms. The community's "internal processes" existed prior to and independent of whatever forces now threaten it from the spatial position of "wholly external."

Williams's understanding of so-called regional novels helps us to understand what happens when ideologies of organicism go beyond theories of literary inventiveness and start applying to the representation of a variety of actually existing collectivities. They cultivate a sense of wholeness by naturalizing a sense of boundedness. An organic definition of communal form proceeds by retrospectively erasing the history of intersection that enables its existence and reframing it as the history of distinct internal and external forces.

Such communal organicism, which Williams identifies with the corporation and the university, arguably took its most influential and far-reaching form in romantic theories of nationalism, which as Étienne Balibar argued, created "a people" from diverse populations by devising a model of unity, "an internal collective personality," that was imagined as *anticipating* the constitution of the state.[52] National unity was so powerful not because it utterly subordinated the internal differences of populations but because it allowed the state to minimize those differences while making the difference between "citizens" and "foreigners" of absolute symbolic value. For Balibar, the organicism of "the nation form," historically speaking, facilitated isolationism and even racism shaped by the nation's ruling interests. His argument represents a foil to Pheng Cheah's, which, prizing intention over effect, explains the philosophical motivations behind the organicist positions of German romantic thinkers such as Schlegel, Novalis, or Schleiermacher: to realize "the harmonious unity of individuals in a society that preserves their autonomy" from a "paternalistic state-machine."[53] Aligning the nation against the state, Cheah argues, the romantics metaphorized the nation as a living, breathing organism, while the state became a machine inimical to freedom.

The tension between the Balibar argument, which accentuates the xenophobic tendencies within national organicism, and the Cheah argument, which accentuates the liberationist values intrinsic to it, captures some of the tensions that exist between cosmopolitan and postcolonial approaches to the nation under globalization. Cosmopolitan accounts prioritize the movements of people and see strong nationalist sympathies, particularly in Europe and North America, as obstacles to instituting more egalitarian and just forms of belonging; postcolonial accounts prioritize the continuing domination of weaker nations by neoliberal policies and see national uprising (where the nation is proximate to the popular) as the best avenue of resistance to them. Given the power differentials between the Global North and Global South, it makes sense that the critique of nationalism would register differently across these geographies. Yet, it does not seem right to leave the divide as one of irreconcilable differences, in which cosmopolitanism is allied with neoliberal apologia and postcolonialism with a reductionist suspicion of the supranational. Cheah himself proposes that organicism and liberation are dubiously linked in the aftermath of decolonization's failure to produce genuine emancipation and economic freedom: "the most apposite metaphor for freedom today is not the organism but the haunted nation."[54]

Drawing on Derrida, Cheah argues that haunting or spectrality is "the inscription of *techne* within the living body: it opens up every proper organic body to the supplementation of artifice." This supplementation insinuates the presence of death and thus the possibility of a kind of mechanical failure into the organism; however, it also is what conditions the realization of the national ideal in the concrete form of the nation-state. The national spirit, in other words, must struggle to transform the "inorganic prosthesis" of the state into an organic form of popular sovereignty, yet the state's susceptibility to the deadening forces of global capital renders the national spirit inevitably spectral—a ghostly reminder of the possibility of popular resistance to global capital, but also of the historical failure of that resistance. Although he never uses the term, Cheah's language renders the actually existing nation-state a chimera in the biotechnological sense: a body that is both born and made, organic and artificial. Spectrality is the result of postcolonial nationalism's failed idealism, and Cheah is quite explicit about associating the "nation-people" with life, and "global capital" with death.[55]

While I do not share this logic because it ontologizes the division between the national and the global, heroizing the former by irreducibly connecting it to the people and vilifying the latter by irreducibly connecting it to capital, Cheah is right to seek a rapprochement between organism and machine in his metaphorics of the nation-state. However, rather than seeing their imperfect fusion as the corruption of the national ideal by state appropriation, I would use the fusion as a reminder that all real collectivities are prosthetic bodies in which natural and artificial elements are not so easily separated out and judged life-giving or deadening. Indeed, as Cheah himself knows when he aligns spectrality with *techne*, artifice (and not organicism) is what enables his retheorization of the nation as always already haunted by its contamination.

One final purpose the chimera serves in *Chimeras of Form* is to provide a new metaphor for actually existing societies—societies shaped by division, hierarchies of power, and the compulsion to construct and reconstruct their identities in ritualized ways. In using the chimera, an example of what the empiricists dubbed mechanical invention and a figure for what Cheah dubs "the contamination of political organicism," to highlight the constructedness of collective bonds, I am not suggesting that societies are best understood as lifeless machines instead of living organisms, but rather that they should be viewed, analogically speaking, as hybrid forms of artificial life.[56]

The biotechnological connotation of chimera, familiar now if not in the eighteenth century, helps move beyond the opposition between the organic society that incarnates life and the mechanical society that deadens it, and points to the artifices by which collective feeling comes to seem more spontaneous (i.e., organic) at some scales, such as the national, and more forced (i.e., mechanistic) at other scales, such as the global. Devising new metaphors for collectivity is important because such language organizes our understanding of how, to paraphrase Bruno Latour, the social is assembled and might be reassembled, at least epistemologically, through projects of redescription.[57] The chimeras of form that populate this book participate in the project of redescribing the cosmopolitical landscape. They learn from, but also challenge, the powerful legacy of organicism over literary and communal theories of form, and, most importantly, present modernist grotesques of artful and artificial life as alternatives to it.

The Chimeras (Chapter Organization)

Each chapter in *Chimeras of Form* is organized around a different genre of writing or formal conceit that establishes the relationship between modernist literary practices and internationalist imagination. These "chimeras" take illegibility, distortion, disproportion, and even unboundedness as techniques for analyzing imperial power, transnational mobility, and supranational collective affiliations. They can be understood as grotesque (disfigured or embellished) literary forms in the sense that they fail to meet aesthetic standards of value based on organicism, and, consistent with the vernacular understanding of a chimeric pursuit, they reflect desires and yield insights that sometimes fail to meet political standards of vision based on rational and heroic action.

As Geoffrey Galt Harpham has argued, the grotesque designates a "species of confusion" that reminds us that disorganization can be as constitutive and purposive a feature of art as organization. Indeed, in Harpham's definition, the grotesque comes to stand in for the self-reflexivity of an art "that recognizes its own incongruities and paradoxes."[58] By reflecting on and harnessing the contradictions of their art, the writers examined here not only register their experiences of a globalizing modernity but also reinterpret those experiences as the basis for specific conceptual interventions into debates on national and transnational belonging.

In designing my exposition around a more continuous twentieth and twenty-first century than the usual narratives of rupture around 1945 (the end of World War II and the beginning of decolonization) or 1989 (the end of the Cold War) would imply, I am also arguing for the persistence of premises, articulated under the early twentieth-century umbrella of internationalism, within premises articulated under the late twentieth-century banner of global consciousness.[59] Rather than assert that globally oriented analytical terms such as *transnationalism*, *cosmopolitanism*, *planetary*, and *world-system* supersede older terms such as *empire*, *anticolonialism*, and *internationalism*, I contend that they sublate them—that is, absorb their lessons in the process of claiming to move past them.[60] As I cut across the divides of the twentieth century, my goal is to make clearer the terms of that sublation, which affects multiple disciplines beyond literary studies.[61] This is not to say that nothing changes in the aftermath of great historical events but that reenergizing the relationship between early and late twentieth-century thought furnishes contemporary "globalization talk" with a richer understanding of its own world-making vocabularies.

I begin my account of modernist internationalism with Tagore, whose autotranslations stand as examples of degraded art for two reasons: first, because translations have traditionally failed to meet the criteria of aesthetic originality and autonomy required of art; and second, because the critical consensus around Tagore's English works is that they fail to transmit the beauty and flair of their Bengali originals. Rather than discount Tagore's translations, my first chapter centralizes them. It shows how he turned unglamorous, second-order acts of literary production, such as compilation, translation, and editing, into modernist strategies for preserving linguistic difference and defending partial unintelligibility as a necessary feature of transnational communication across imperial lines of power.

Through my close readings of *Nationalism* and *The Home and the World*, I demonstrate how Tagore treated his Bengali originals not as hermetically sealed, finished works but rather as repositories of material. The circulation and translation of these works into English allowed him to mediate between utopian internationalisms that dreamed of perfect communication between nations and autarkic nationalisms that argued for the cultural self-sufficiency of the nation as a marker of its readiness for sovereignty. Against both these more absolutist positions of globalism and nationalism, Tagore's autotranslations offer a model of national autonomy that precludes cultural organicism and a model of internationalism that makes imperfect communication a topic of conversation rather than an obstacle to overcome.

Up next is James Joyce's famed modernist internationalism, which though long understood in terms of his radical break from collective ties and his move to mainland Europe, is reappraised in chapter 2. Since the 1990s, postcolonial and cosmopolitan approaches to Joyce have challenged his reputation as an apolitical aesthete by examining the relationship between his formal innovations and the colonial conditions of Ireland. Chapter 2 builds on such approaches, but it also reconfigures the opposition between modernism's aesthetic individualism and postcolonialism's political collectivism by analyzing what I call, borrowing from Walter Benjamin, Joyce's mediated solidarity with the Irish people. Mediated solidarity entails a serious critique but not an outright rejection of solidarity, whether national or international, particularly when expressions of solidarity rely on rather than contest practices of self-deception.

Joyce treated the self-deceptions embedded within individual ambitions and collective nationalist fantasies as chimeras with the potential to deflate the grandiose comparative claims of Irish cultural revivalism. In a rejoinder to revivalism's politically powerful but specious comparisons, Joyce developed his own critical comparativism, which I trace under the title of "alternating asymmetry." This chimera of form addresses the material inequalities that persisted beneath well-intentioned but overstated claims to both Irish and European solidarity. Connecting various formal figures of uneven comparison, from *Dubliners* (1914) to the "Cyclops" episode of *Ulysses* (1922), this chapter shows how Joyce plunged into rather than glided over the necessary costs of political unification in his efforts to dispel the self-deceptions internal to the operations of both colonial underdevelopment and anticolonial nationalism.

The third chapter brings together Caribbean-born migrant writers Claude McKay and George Lamming and forms a bridge across the divides of period and national literature that usually assign McKay to the Harlem Renaissance and Lamming either to the category of postwar black British literature or to Caribbean literature. In allowing these two writers to converge, I argue that a paranational version of modernist internationalism emerges in their mutual formal and theoretical engagement with plotlessness. The lack of a plot—understood in the polysemic sense of a planned-out heteronormative life, a collective political program, and a patch of land to call home—becomes the common ground from which McKay's *Banjo: A Story Without a Plot* and Lamming's *The Emigrants* explore the fugitive life and fantasies of colonial black subjects within securitized Europe. In deforming plot and finding an alternative idiom, rhythm, and structure for the mobility of stigmatized populations, McKay and Lamming become unlikely guides to contemporary theorists of cosmopolitics and international law (namely, Étienne Balibar, Seyla Benhabib, and Nicolae Gheorghe) who have argued for the accommodation of transience within territorialized models of belonging and citizenship.

The chimera of form featured in my fourth chapter is the archival legend, which is how I classify Billy the Kid from Ondaatje's *The Collected Works of Billy the Kid* and Sailor from his *Anil's Ghost*. Combining theories of the archive as a space of material collection and artifactual remains, and theories of the legend as a genre of storytelling that cultivates the unreal and the unknowable, I argue that Ondaatje uses archival legends to broach the tensions between isolationism and internationalism, cultural particularity and universal norms of justice. Although some critics have argued that Ondaatje's collage aesthetics are irresponsible and compound injustice because they obscure the cause and effect of historicist narratives (a criticism that will recall, for many, Georg Lukács's famous disregard for modernism), this chapter shows that Ondaatje subjects the norms of both international justice and historicist causality to criticism for being inadequately sensitive to cultural memory. Rejecting both the disembodying abstractions of human rights dicta and the embodying practices of historical identification, he uses archival legends as figures of semi-embodiment brought into being by formal strategies of artifact collection, fragment accretion, and loose assembly. These legends situate universal norms and historical facts within the foggier but no less real realms of national myth and transnational memory. Ondaatje suggests that internationalism must attend to these domains of sentimental remembrance or risk becoming tone deaf to the cosmological gaps that persist in how members of "strong" versus "weak" nations view the effect of colonialism on the global present.

The fifth chapter follows Zadie Smith's "root canals," a metaphor and a narrative form she developed in her first novel *White Teeth*, to describe the transnational historical networks obscured by nation-centered accounts of the past. Like Ondaatje, Smith develops forms of unboundedness like the root canal in order to entwine different groups' collective memories; unlike him, she uses that strategy to address head-on the topic of causality within a global framework. Smith asks what economic, political, and personal conditions bring migrants to Europe and the United Kingdom and, in turn, how residents in these regions might be implicated in stories of migration, distant violence, and global economic inequality that they see as irrelevant to the scope of their everyday lives.

Focusing specifically on Smith's northwest London fictions, I show how her strategies of formal division (sectioning, chapter construction, and unsynthesized narrative remainders) address the problem of drawing boundaries around accounts of both personal attention and structural inequality. Although drawing boundaries enables political positioning, it also risks blindness to the scales of such positioning—as, for example, when Smith considers what it means to defend a local neighborhood from gentrification while also remaining hospitable to migrants who are drawn to Europe's prosperous cities for work. Smith uses the dyads of form and matter, parts and wholes, in her fiction to bring ongoing (and sometimes competing) stories of uneven global development to bear on tarnished dreams of upward mobility. One of the most acute observers of fiction's ambiguously political work in the world, she asks how literature today might contribute to leftist projects of demanding transnational accountability and fighting the privatization of public resources.

Finally, an epilogue brings *Chimeras of Form* up to the very moment of its publication, amid what is being called the global migrant crisis. The years 2014 to 2016 have seen the highest levels of mass displacement in recorded history—higher than in the aftermath of World War II. The difference today is that most refugees come from beyond Europe and are subject to vulnerability and vilification, largely due to their racialized and religious otherness. The epilogue turns to Kenyan writer Shailja Patel's *Migritude* (2010) to show how this experimental work of art transforms the figure of the migrant from an object of knowledge into a subject of it.

Migritude is a one-woman theatrical show that Patel "re-mediated" into a book, combining the script of the show with a poetic account of the production of both the show and the book. The book version is the epilogue's focus and the final chimera of form with which to reflect on the major principles of modernist internationalism as I outline them. This re-mediated work does more than simply give voice to an oppressed and precarious collective; from within its conjuncture of performance and print, it contemplates the medium dependency of voice, the indirect political agency of art, and the always incomplete nature of cosmopolitical knowledge. The eponymous migritude emerges as a powerfully contemporary "public feeling" for modernist internationalism—one that is conducive to analyzing and surviving the violence of forced displacement.[62]

As these chapter descriptions show, chimeras of form both diffuse and reassemble totalities (suturing fragments, deforming plots, rendering off-balance the part–whole relationships of a work of art) to give expression to internationalisms that have incorporated rather than rejected strategies of illegibility, fantasy, myth, and epistemological self-reflexivity. The combination of the chimera's dueling definitions as monstrous body, hybrid life form, and discredited ambition creates the perfect storm from which to deprovincialize modernist internationalism not only as an institutional knowledge formation but also as an aspirational and analytical pursuit.

Such deprovincializing begins with the writers themselves—those who have innovated by falling through the cracks of organized politics and ratified forms of resistance. To emblematize their efforts, I offer as the unofficial mascot for this study the genetically engineered FutureMouse from Smith's *White Teeth*. FutureMouse is a product of Marcus Chalfen's scientific research, a biological chimera made in the lab by grafting together tissues of different genetic constitution. Like their mythological predecessors, biotech chimeras blur the line between organic and mechanistic creation, a unified whole and sutured-together parts. However, in their physical existence, they also speak to history's stretching of the field of possibility such that, over time, "chimera" as a signifier of impossibility might become a signifier of possibility, in all its exciting and dangerous potential.

Smith initially renders FutureMouse as the grotesque creation of Chalfen's techno-utopian imagination ("On his chin the tumors hung like big droplets of dirty rain"), but the last lines of the novel depict the chimera escaping its cage ("the getaway of a small brown rebel mouse").[63] A darkly comic image of freedom, FutureMouse is more fugitive than hero, but it is Smith's sense of vulnerability, irony, and absurdity that allows her to comment on the occlusion of visions that are too certain, too driven, and too faithful to their own precepts (what the novel dubs "Chalfenism"). FutureMouse, embattled chimera, is a kind of spirit animal for modernity's absconders, for those who have faced the butt end of civilizing progress narratives and have devised ways of moving forward that entail going backwards and sideways as well.

A wariness of purity and perfectibility consequently unites all the writers in *Chimeras of Form*, even as they pursue hopes of a more egalitarian world order. Their wariness marks an important distinction between majorly utopian strains of modernism, such as those Boris Groys attributes to the Russian avant-garde, and the minorly utopian, "chimeric" strains of modernism featured in this book.[64] Groys has argued for the conceptual complementariness of avant-garde aesthetics and Stalinist politics on the basis of a utopian constructivism. According to his account, both the artistic movement and the political program sought to "overcome the resistance" of their materials, be it a specific artistic medium or the "economic, social, and everyday life of the nation," and to remake them into their "desired form." Treating the will to power as an inescapable facet of artistic identity, Groys suggests that "the Stalin Era satisfied the fundamental avant-garde demand that art cease representing life and begin transforming it by means of a total aesthetic-political project" in which the success of the state was measured by the aesthetic imperative to create "impenetrable, autonomous artistic worlds."[65]

Groys's emphasis on autonomy and hermeticism is an example of how the Russian avant-garde ideology of autonomy came to inflect the Stalinist political imagination, in which the state is conceptualized as a bounded and policed work of art. Although Stalinism no doubt represents the extremities of such a constructivist approach, the writers discussed here come perilously close to the aestheticist impulse to fashion societies according to the rules of art as they think through the relationships between literary forms and communal forms. Indeed, the dangers of aesthetic projection haunt Tagore's protagonist Nikhil in *The Home and the World*, when he aligns despotism with the molding of social relations into "a hard, clear-cut, perfect form."[66]

The chimeras of form discussed here—autotranslations, alternating asymmetry, stories without plots, archival legends, and root canals—guard against that despotism by contesting theories of the ideal work of art, the work that achieves transcendence, autonomy, succession, and coherence. They develop instead their own theories of the material work of art that, by embracing immanence, subordination, medium dependency, and mechanical acts of construction, continually engage with rather than transcend the resistance of their materials. *Chimeras of Form* makes a virtue of literary forms that, like mythological and biological chimeras, test received understandings of coherence rather than affirming them. It allows the *working* of art, as in the labor of creating art, to come into view so that the task of reconstellating collective solidarities internationally might, through the very qualities we call "chimeric," enter into our poetic and political imaginations as something real, long-standing, and urgent.

1

AUTOTRANSLATIONS

Rabindranath Tagore's Internationalism in Circulation

H. G. WELLS: We are gradually thinking now of one human civilization on the foundation of which individualities will have great chance of fulfillment. The individual, as we take him, has suffered from the fact that civilization has been split up into separate units, instead of being merged into a universal whole, which seems to be the natural destiny of mankind.

RABINDRANATH TAGORE: I believe the unity of human civilization can be better maintained by linking up in fellowship and cooperation of the different civilizations of the world. Do you think there is a tendency to have one common language for humanity?

WELLS: One common language will probably be forced upon mankind whether we like it or not. Previously, a community of fine minds created a new dialect. Now it is necessity that will compel us to adopt a universal language.

TAGORE: I quite agree. The time for five-mile dialects is fast vanishing. Rapid communication makes for a common language. Yet, this common language would probably not exclude national languages. There is again the curious fact that just now, along with the growing unities of the human mind, the development of national self-consciousness is leading to the formation or rather the revival of national languages everywhere. Don't you think that in America, in spite of constant touch between America and England, the English language is tending toward a definite modification and change?

WELLS: I wonder if that is the case now. Forty or fifty years ago this would have been the case, but now in literature and in common speech it becomes increasingly difficult to distinguish between English and American. There seems to be much more repercussion in the other direction. Today we are elaborating and perfecting physical methods of transmitting words. Translation is a bother. Take your poems—do they not lose much by that process? If you had a method of making

> them intelligible to all people at the same time, it would be really wonderful.
>
> TAGORE: Music of different nations has a common psychological foundation, and yet that does not mean that national music should not exist. The same thing is, in my opinion, probably true for literature.
>
> —Rabindranath Tagore and H. G. Wells, "Tagore and Wells"

At the heart of conversations about internationalism in the early twentieth century lay a conflict over the teleology of the global and the desirability of communicative difference. Did increasing contact across nations and languages ultimately lead toward the homogeneity of mankind, as H. G. Wells suspected and advocated? Or, as Tagore contended, did transnational contact proliferate linguistic and cultural differences, the recognition and examination of which were never to be superseded? Wells and Tagore's dialogue, though staged in 1930, engages questions about the social dynamics and collective effects of internationalism that are very much alive today in debates about globalization's standardizing and diversifying force, its tendency to exacerbate inequalities but also to elicit creative forms of resistance and expression. Although both Wells and Tagore are avowedly internationalist in outlook, their odd-couple disagreements about the persistence of national culture and linguistic particularity within global formulations of collectivity betray significant differences in each man's relationship to universality and utopianism. Whereas Wells promotes a strongly unified vision of civilization in which translation is viewed as an obstacle to be made obsolete, Tagore offers the tempered and ambiguous universal of a "common language" that "would probably not exclude national languages."

For Tagore, achieving a common language entailed not transcending translation but negotiating it. His approach to universality did not favor the consolidation of a world language spoken by everyone, but rather the widespread development of common tools for mediating uncommonness. More than the simple transfer of content from one language to another, translation connoted such an analytical tool. It was necessary for navigating stark linguistic differences (between, say, English and Tagore's native Bengali) but also for identifying the subtle variations within seemingly uniform tongues (such as British versus American English).

If Wells and Tagore agreed that technological advances were delocalizing languages ("the time for five-mile dialects is fast vanishing"), they disagreed about the value and uses of linguistic pluralism within the arena of international cooperation that their very dialogue was intended to symbolize.[1]

Throughout various phases of his polymathic career, Tagore treated translation as an imperfect but necessary tool for mediating the uncommon and for broaching the topic of illegibility as central to pursuits of an anti-imperial internationalism. Tagore's investment in the particularity of national languages and literatures is clear in the above excerpt from his dialogue with Wells, but his deep awareness of translation's obscurities becomes explicit as the conversation shifts to music—what Wells calls the "most international" of mediums, because it would seem to obviate translation. Tagore counters: "May I add something? I have composed over three hundred pieces of music. They are all sealed from the West because they cannot properly be given to you in your own notation. Perhaps they would not be intelligible to your people even if I could get them written down in European notation."[2]

Where Wells looks to extract translation from internationalism, Tagore reintroduces translation by calling attention to discrepancies across notation systems and contingencies of taste. Through his experience with translating his own work in different mediums, Tagore came up close and personal with intelligibility's rootedness in cultural conventions, while simultaneously acknowledging the always-shifting ground of such conventions. By interjecting the inscrutabilities of translation into Wells's utopian universalism, Tagore inaugurates the chimeric tradition of internationalism chronicled here.

Tagore self- or autotranslated several of his poetry collections, including the Nobel Prize–winning *Gitanjali* (1912), and he collaboratively translated his novel *The Home and the World* (1919) with his nephew Surendranath.[3] His early poetry was widely celebrated and sponsored by canonical modernists such as W. B. Yeats and Ezra Pound; however, his prose works, including *The Home and the World* and the partially translated *Nationalism*, hurt his reputation in the West. By the time he sat down with Wells in 1930, Tagore's artistic star was fading in Europe and his political reputation as a critic of nationalism was growing more controversial.

Although several scholars have attributed Tagore's short-lived aesthetic appreciation among modernists to orientalist fads, I try to break away from such a narrative because it paints Tagore as a pawn of the modernist milieu rather than as a strategic participant within it, whose translation practices enable us to revisit and diversify the attitudes and techniques associated with modernism.[4] Tagore's English idiom in poetry and prose may not resemble the imagistic poetry of Pound and T. S. Eliot or the ironic detachment of Joseph Conrad. Yet Tagore's interest in the inscrutable and the unintelligible, fragmentation and synthesis, persists at levels of literary composition usually ignored or devalued by a New Critical legacy of formalism that aligns the integrity of the work with its autonomy from the specificities of print cultural practices like excerption, reprinting, anthologization, and, of course, translation.

Contemporary scholars of modernism, including Stephen G. Yao and Rebecca Beasley, have worked to rectify the imbalance between studies of modernist aesthetic form and modernist editorial and translation methods by attending to the ways in which unorthodox translation practices helped shape the works and styles we now take for granted as modernist. However, as Beasley notes, "modernist critical values worked against the appreciation of literature in translation, especially literature that claimed to be innovative in style, when the translation could not be tested against the source text."[5] With my analysis of Tagore's translation and editing methods and reference to his Bengali source texts, I aim to widen the gap between "modernist critical values," derived from the early institutionalization of modernism, and modernist aesthetic innovation, derived from my transnational and bilingual appraisal of Tagore's place in the global modernist milieu.

Tagore treated his Bengali originals not as autotelic, autonomous works, but rather as strategically reproducible and changeable repositories of material ("common-wealths") whose translation and reconfiguration brought cryptic allusion, assemblage, and collage into his Anglophone writings. His recombinatory strategies in *Nationalism* and *Home and the World*, the two works on which this chapter focuses, served the particular purpose evoked by his dialogue with Wells: to disclose the entanglement of translatability and illegibility in cross-cultural discourse and to affirm the particularity of national languages and literatures while challenging the myth of their purity and self-sufficiency. Pushing against the equation of the work of art with an organic whole, Tagore's English writings thematize the story of their own transmission from Bengali. In doing so, they allow Tagore to reflect upon the colonial contexts of international address, to identify the practices of recombination at the heart of nation building, and to mediate uncommon experiences of common modernist reference points, such as the Great War and industrialization, for a diverse English-speaking readership.

Building processes of circulation and translation back into an account of Tagore's style and politics redresses a tendency in scholarship about the polymath writer, painter, and musician to settle along universalist or particularist lines.[6] In the 1990s, which saw the beginning of cosmopolitanism's resurgence as a philosophy for thinking beyond the nation, Tagore, too, experienced a resurgence in popularity—not so much among literary scholars as among philosophers and historians.[7] Martha Nussbaum and Isaiah Berlin identified Tagore's antinationalism with a universal humanism, arguing that it rightfully placed human loyalty over and above national loyalty. Ranajit Guha, Dipesh Chakrabarty, Ashis Nandy, and Amartya Sen, in turn, framed Tagore's critique of nationalism as a higher form of patriotism that rightly questioned loyalty to a Hinducentric Swadeshi movement.[8]

In truth, both sides have ample evidence with which to justify their constructions of a "cosmopolitan" Tagore or a "patriotic" Tagore, despite Tagore's ambivalence about both cosmopolitanism and patriotism. Yet the division rests on an untying of Tagore's own knots, specifically the way in which he connected intra-Indian political disputes to the wider geopolitical frameworks of world war and anticolonial dissent. That the philosophical divide among contemporary scholars is also a linguistic divide is crucial to understanding the evolution of two different Tagores. By focusing on translation in my formal analysis of Tagore's works, I reconnect the "English-language" Tagore encountered by Nussbaum and Berlin to the "Bengali-language" Tagore encountered by the subaltern school historians and scholars of Bengali literature. In my account, the internationalist Tagore is necessarily a bilingual Tagore. The demands of autotranslation enabled him to undermine metropolitan expectations of Indian literature while also refuting anticolonial nationalist principles of cultural isolationism and homogenization. In short, his innovative approach to what are usually considered second-order acts of literary production (compilation, translation, and editing) multiplies the number and scale of collectivities to which he belonged, rather than reducing them to simply the world or the nation.

Compiling *Nationalism*

Prior to the publication of *Nationalism*, poetry collections like *Gitanjali*, *The Gardener*, and *The Crescent Moon*, which Tagore also autotranslated, had created the image of a mystic poet, an orientalist construction that was perpetuated by reviews of his work in the British press. The London *Athenaeum* referred to *Gitanjali* as having "trance-like beauty"; the *Nation* suggested that *The Gardener* allowed English readers to "see love and death through the mystic's eyes."[9] In *Nationalism*, however, Tagore's English writings turned away from peaceful idylls and scenes of spiritual contemplation to address nationalism as a world-historical phenomenon. Its publication recast Tagore as a political polemicist and a colonial subject whose "wisdom" was far from transhistorical.

Nationalism, though undoubtedly a work that strains classification, is fruitfully read as a modernist anthology, a genre that has become of increasing interest for the way it vivifies formal and sociological mediation. Jeremy Braddock places the anthology at the center of modernist collecting practices and describes its form as a "system" with its own internal logic. The anthology's logic makes the social positioning and material circulation of literature difficult to separate from its aesthetic and epistemological interventions.[10] For Rebecca Walkowitz, what makes an anthology specifically modernist is its disruption, and at times its undermining, of the practices of social grouping and comparative analysis employed in the making of a traditional anthology.[11]

My argument builds on Walkowitz's in that it considers traditional anthologies to be cultural totems, hefty objects that embody the weight of the cultural tradition they encapsulate—think of the Norton anthologies of American literature, women's literature, or African American literature. Tagore's modernist anthology breaks down that totemic structure by blurring the line between itself as an object (a book) and as a product of the uncontainable institutional and geopolitical networks that shaped its production. The form (or system, to borrow Braddock's term) of *Nationalism* reveals the overlaps between aesthetic object and social field through its strategies of rhetorical self-presentation, framing, and compilation.

Nationalism is an anthology that contains three lectures on nationalism in different locations (the West, Japan, and India) and one poem by Tagore entitled "The Sunset of the Century." The entries attack rather than reaffirm their master category. Tagore understood that nationalism in all parts of the world derived its power from its perceived autochthony, and consequently, he aimed to discredit its organicism by treating it as a political abstraction of the Western imagination. *Nationalism* reconstructs nationalism as an imperial ideology that claims to affirm diverse, culturally contained groups but can do this only by disavowing its universalizing spread as a European method of political organization. To point out the globally standardizing architecture behind nationalism, Tagore redirects anthological strategies designed to affirm tradition making to the opposite project: exposing the contours of nation-based traditions. Nationalism consequently emerges in the anthology not as the unique expression of individual countries but as a global contagion of political feeling that threatens to extinguish authentic cultural differences across the non-Western world.

Despite Tagore's stringent antinationalism, it is important not to confuse his polemic with a stance against sovereignty, or even against national community. Tagore saw intranational social reform as inseparable from international collaboration. For him, a national consciousness that disavowed outside influence endangered the collective models he most valued. He therefore used the anthology, so often the genre used to confirm literary and cultural nationalism, to contest the worst tendencies, within particular nationalisms, toward belligerent self-interest, competition, and xenophobic violence. Treating nationalism as an imperial abstraction rather than a spiritual emanation (*Volkgeist*) led Tagore to privilege analyses of its transmission over analyses of its origination.

The focus in *Nationalism* on the power dynamics of cultural contact within an increasingly integrated world makes it an early twentieth-century account of globalization. It combines anticolonial politics with a desire for transnational solidarities, which includes saving Europe from itself. On one hand, Tagore asserts that "the world-flood has swept over our country [India]" (*Nationalism*, 16), in order to identify the power imbalances upon which empires flourish and colonies drown. On the other, he writes, "The whole world is becoming one country through scientific facility. And the moment is arriving when you also must find a basis for unity which is not political" (119). This second statement is far more conciliatory, and it searches for an ethical spirit that might balance autonomy with cooperation.

Ironically, this is the statement that compelled more vitriol. The *Detroit Journal*, critical of the timing of the publication of *Nationalism* (the same year the United States entered World War I) warned readers against Tagore's internationalist aspirations, which it deemed the "sickly saccharine mental poison with which Tagore would corrupt the mind of the youth of our great United States."[12] The *Times Literary Supplement* and the *New Statesman* reviewed the anthology with more equanimity but, in light of its wartime appearance, rued the inefficacy of any moral appeal without an army to back it up. What stands out particularly to the *Times Literary Supplement* reviewer is Tagore's equal-opportunity critical eye. Indicting Indian nationalists and British imperialists alike, Tagore spoke on behalf of no side.[13] The British could not claim him for the Raj, despite his criticism of nationalist campaigns in India, and, as Gauri Viswanathan has shown, Indian nationalists considered his public criticism of *swadeshi* tantamount to imperial collaboration.[14] Tagore's internationalist protest ironically left him without any nation to call home.

Tagore's nonpartisanship may have earned him enemies across both Asia and Europe, but his neutrality—that is, his refusal to be claimed by any one nation—was useful for analyzing collective identities in lieu of conforming to them. Tagore displays and manipulates his affiliations to multiple groups in *Nationalism*. The anthology's paratexts provide evidence for this claim, for they are the spaces in which Tagore's national identity (and the collective identity of *Nationalism*) are most in flux. As Samuel Kinser has argued, "paratexts indicate the forces that have shaped the text: they show how contexts invade the text. But they are also an arena in which the author can, more or less openly, combat such forces."[15] Kinser assumes a rivalry between literary text and historical context that the paratextual arena formalizes and exploits. Paratexts become thresholds from which authors can intervene in the reception of the text, but also places from which their authorial personae may be constructed in ways outside their control.

The paratexts of *Nationalism* show both possibilities for Tagore's collective identity. The title page introduces Tagore in Anglicized fashion as "Sir Rabindranath Tagore, author of 'Gitanjali,' 'The Crescent Moon,' Etc."[16] It emphasizes Tagore's Britishness by pointing to his knighthood and previous English-language poetry collections, framing *Nationalism* as continuous with works that had been uncontroversial in England due to their apolitical content and spiritual thrust. The opening preface, however, downplays Tagore's association with Britain by referring to India as his country of origin. In the main text, Tagore aligns himself with the nonnational category of the colonially dispossessed, the "we, who are no nation ourselves" (*Nationalism*, 19).

Comparing Tagore's shifting affiliations across various paratexts and the main text reveals an authorial identity deeply implicated in overlapping traditions: British, Indian, and colonial. Tagore courted these overlaps rather than denying them, to render a single category of belonging not only untenable but also inaccurate with regard to the ways in which collective identities are formed. He uses the anthology to track the history of his own self-translation and to push back against rigid notions of national partisanship on behalf of either himself or his anthology.

His status as an autotranslator capable of revealing the multiple cultural and political contexts of his work is clear from the anthology's opening preface. It elaborates the many sites of production from which the anthology emerges as a coherent object and thus refuses to reduce the location of *Nationalism* to any one national tradition. If context invades text through the paratext, then Tagore's prefaces are the book's major contact zones: the places where the stories of the anthology's making intervene in its reading experience. Mary Louise Pratt coined the term "contact zone" to denote the "social spaces where cultures meet, clash, and grapple with each other, often in highly asymmetrical relations of power."[17] The prefaces of *Nationalism* remind us that such spaces include the literary and that reading itself creates a kind of historical encounter. Reading *Nationalism*, we encounter history in two forms: the material circumstances of East–West relationships in the midst of World War I, and the material circumstances of the anthology's own making as it reflects upon its achievement of objecthood (in the form of a printed book). The latter form of historical engagement is key to understanding the former.

There are two prefaces in *Nationalism*: the opening preface and the preface to its last entry, a poem entitled "The Sunset of the Century," which I will refer to as the second preface. The opening preface reminds the reader of the work's medium specificity as a book, its geographic specificity as a work that was written across multiple countries, and its period specificity. It lists the contents of the anthology in relation to these contexts:

> "Nationalism in the West" [the first entry in the anthology] is one of a series of lectures delivered throughout the United States during the winter of 1916–1917. "Nationalism in Japan" is based on two

> lectures delivered in Japan before the Imperial University and the Keio Gijuku University in June and July 1916. "Nationalism in India," written in the United States late in 1916, is the poet's reflection on the state of his own country, and gives world-wide completeness to the discussion of Nationalism. The poem at the conclusion of the book, "The Sunset of the Century," was written on the last day of the last century.
>
> (*Nationalism*, 7)

The preface discloses the contradictory nature of the anthology. It simultaneously reflects its generic aspirations to totality ("world-wide completeness") and reveals the inevitable impossibility of achieving such a goal through its apparatus of selectivity, which must make choices not only about representative regions but also about the final form of representative entries. *Nationalism* depicts the anthology's animating tension as a battle between method and content. Method—which regions are chosen and how their entries arrive in printed form—complicates the equation of added content (including more countries like India) with more coverage (worldwide completeness). The first two entries, the preface tells us, are versions or composites of unseen materials—either one lecture in a series of lectures ("Nationalism in the West") or a composite of previously distinct lectures ("Nationalism in Japan"). They are printed renditions of verbal performances originating across two continents. As a framing device, then, the preface stages re-mediation (from a series of live performances to a printed book) as a synthesizing process in which the totalizing aspiration of comparison rests on a definitive statement of loss. Despite adding more nations to its list of contents, the anthology's methods of compilation will always demand the reduction of information and the stabilization of versions of a text into a standardized entry. The anthology's enunciation of completeness is belied by its corollary enunciation of compilation; the genre is rhetorically split between claiming totality at the level of content and declaring such totality to be, always already, a record of loss at the level of literary production.

The second preface introduces new information to supplement the opening preface. It makes translation a mediator of the anthology's contents when it reveals that "The Sunset of the Century" was "written in the Bengali on the last day of last century" (*Nationalism*, 157). The lack of a calendar date echoes the language of the first preface, but the addition of the fact of translation from Bengali invites readers to consider the bilingual history behind the seemingly monolingual Anglophone work. We pick up the anthology in medias res—in the thick of several media and geographic contexts, two languages, and at least two calendar systems: the Gregorian and the Bengali. When these contexts invade the text, they become part of its story.

The prefaces put pressure on the boundaries created by the anthology's principles of selection and remind us that selectivity operates at unexpected levels that include the languages and media of circulation. The paratexts in *Nationalism* accordingly turn framing into a device for insinuating the anthology's network into the definition of its objecthood. They tell us that that the further inside *Nationalism* we read, the further outside the anthology we will have to go to understand its contents.

In evoking its transnational and translational formation, *Nationalism* pits its own heterodox worldliness against what Tagore saw as nationalism's growing orthodoxy as the only imaginable ideology of political organization within Europe, the United States, and most recently, Asia. In his anthology's entries and organization, he portrays nationalism as a political ideology that asserts claims to autarky while unwittingly perpetuating homogenizing forms of comparison among nations. The *Oxford English Dictionary* defines *autarky* simply as "self-sufficiency" and, in specialist circles, as a policy of "economic self-sufficiency in a political unit." Not to be confused with *autarchy*, which can refer to both self-government and despotism, autarky, in denoting self-sufficiency above all, also connotes isolationism. Autarkic societies followed a logic of enclosure that understandably appealed to Japanese and Indian nationalists striving to maintain or achieve autonomy from powerful Western nations. Yet Tagore contested autarkic nationalisms as misguided from the start because, he argued, they uncritically substituted political enclosure for epistemological autonomy. One cannot paint the nation as a community of cultural and economic self-sufficiency without acknowledging the borrowed character of nationalist discourse. Even more importantly, one cannot advocate national autarky without sacrificing an internationalist collective imagination rooted in nonautarkic principles such as cooperation and interdependence.[18]

Tagore reproduces nationalism's global epistemological dominance in the anthology's formal architecture. Whereas the genre of the anthology usually presupposes the distinctiveness of each individual entry, the case studies in *Nationalism* are arranged like a series of Russian dolls in which less politically powerful regions become embedded in more politically powerful ones. One region's version of nationalism emerges as a less powerful derivative of the previous one's as Tagore appraises nationalism in the West, Japan, and India. This mise en abyme effect reinforces Tagore's description of the ideology in sweeping terms as a "world-flood" (*Nationalism*, 16) or "tidal wave" (105) enveloping Asian countries within a Western structure of thought and behavior.

In structurally connecting nationalization with Westernization, *Nationalism* anticipates Partha Chatterjee's diagnosis of anticolonial nationalism as a derivative discourse. In his seminal formulation, Chatterjee argued that it is impossible to conceive of colonial nationalisms as autonomous discourses. Rather, they were constituted in the paradoxical crucible of accepting and rejecting the "dominance, both epistemic and moral, of an alien culture."[19] In assuming the mantle of nationalism in a world order without viable political alternatives for statehood, anticolonial nationalists accede to a system in which they will continue to occupy subject positions not only militarily or industrially but also philosophically. Chatterjee focuses on how "thought itself can dominate and subjugate," and situates the colonial effort to become "modern" within a discursive framework that a priori counteracts autonomy. Yes, as Chatterjee argues in a later work, Indian nationalists would manage this impasse by creating their own "domain of sovereignty" within the cultural sphere of society.[20] Their tactics, in other words, reflected the displacement of the dream of autarky onto the making of a private sphere rooted in the gendered practices of domesticity, vernacular language, and tradition keeping, while the public sphere accommodated the material and technological accomplishments of the West. The outcome would be the creation of "a 'modern' national culture that is nevertheless not Western."

Nationalism uses its anthological structure to show that the demand for cultural autarky is a symptom of epistemological colonization rather than an emancipation from it. Nationalism, as its chapter titles make clear, is the standard that conditions the comparison of Japan and India not with other actually existing nations but with an epistemological edifice known as "the West." Tagore's "West" is the preeminent setter of standards. To adopt its standards without critically examining them is to entrench European epistemology even more insidiously within the construction of Asian nations. To be clear, Tagore's lament against the spread of nationalism was not a lament against epistemological influence or cultural appropriation but against the misrecognition and anxious vilification of these processes in nationalist rhetoric of autonomy and sovereignty. Rather than participate in the "separate spheres" theory of tradition and modernization, which informed the structure of anticolonial nationalism, he scrutinized the process by which these polarities came into being.

"Nationalism in Japan" addresses the logic of borrowing that Tagore found endemic to nationalism's importation within Asia. He argues that nationalist feeling rests on problematic ways of seeing the selectivity of adaptation:

> You can borrow knowledge from others, but you cannot borrow temperament.
>
> But at the imitative stage of our schooling we cannot distinguish between the essential and the non-essential, between what is transferable and what is not. It is something like the faith of the primitive mind in the magical properties of the accidents of outward forms which accompany some real truth. We are afraid of leaving out something valuable and efficacious by not swallowing the husk with the kernel. But while our greed delights in wholesale appropriation, it is the function of our vital nature to assimilate, which is the only true appropriation for a living organism . . .
>
> Japan cannot altogether lose and merge herself in the scientific paraphernalia she has acquired from the West and be turned into a mere borrowed machine.
>
> (*Nationalism*, 70–71)

It is easy to be put off by Tagore's statements, particularly for their evocation of old historicist tropes of Asian immaturity ("at the imitative stage of our schooling"). Yet to equate Tagore's perspective with a pro-Empire stance is to misconstrue the thrust of his argument. Tagore is not against Japanese attempts to preserve autonomy; he is against their strategies of military escalation, which he regards as symptomatic of a "wholesale appropriation" of Western militarism. Warning against the devolution of Japan, he argues that the Japanese undermine their own claims to autonomy if they do not adequately reflect upon the conditions under which they cultivate values coded as national.

Distinguishing, transferring, discarding: these are the transnational processes of selection, which prefigure collective identity formation and which Tagore asked the Japanese—and now all readers of *Nationalism*—to examine closely as operations in the cohering of culture. They are also the processes by which *Nationalism*, as a modernist anthology, connects the bound book to the unbound network of lectures, poetry, and performances that Tagore produced prior to it. Those who do not see these processes of selection out of which both national identities and world books emerge become, via Tagore's analogy, less selective themselves. They are the indiscriminate consumers who "are afraid of leaving out something valuable and efficacious by not swallowing the husk with the kernel."

If the prefaces to *Nationalism* remind us of what the anthology leaves out, the main text suggests that leaving things out is not always a bad thing. Selection is a skill worth cultivating as an expression of autonomy superior to autarky. By describing Asian nationalisms as movements insufficiently self-critical of their selectiveness, Tagore struck at the core of national anxieties of influence. To offset those anxieties, he speaks of preserving "our vital nature to assimilate." The pun on *vital*, connoting both importance and aliveness, reflects his desire to link the modern values of progress, transformation, and freedom to substantive social reform within Asian countries and not to the political reproduction of nations as "borrowed machines" from Europe.

Tagore differentiates the selectivity of assimilation from "wholesale appropriation" to emphasize the critical examination of Western influence over the instrumental exploitation of Western tools. His description of Japanese society as a vital organism muddies the distinctions between an autochthonic idea of tradition and an external idea of modernity. Outside or "Western" influence becomes a force with which organic identity must negotiate; consequently, Japan's vitality—that is, its ability to grow and change in response to environmental pressures—counteracts the Herderian essentialism that would make the nation the repository of some primordial Japaneseness. By choosing assimilation over appropriation in the negotiation of Europe–Asia encounters, Tagore advocates critically incorporating ideas (assimilation) before putting the ideas of others to one's own use (appropriation).

This distinction matters, because it vivifies the processes of editing, synthesis, and encoding (selectivity) that enable any oppositional politics of appropriation. In Tagore's usage, tradition is defined not through imitation and insulation but through the discourse of editing on display in

Nationalism. Only when Asian nations dilate and examine transnational processes of cultural contact can they arrive on even epistemological ground with the West: "In your voice [Japan's] Asia shall answer the questions that Europe has submitted to the conference of Man. In your land the experiments will be carried on by which the East will change the aspects of the modern civilization, infusing life in it where it is a machine" (*Nationalism*, 75).

As is evident in "Nationalism in Japan," Tagore disables national categories while reaffirming civilizational ones. "East" and West" come to represent ontologically different spheres of vitalism and mechanism, respectively. Tagore asserts these differences to promote a distinctly spiritual and pacifist role for Asian countries in international politics. Rather than disregard this essentialism, one must understand its function within Tagore's internationalism. The persistence of an "East" in Tagore's rhetoric facilitates his argument for Asia's importance within the universalizing processes of modernity. An East capable of retaining its alterity from the normalizing regime of nationhood retains, in its countries of "nonation" (*Nationalism*, 19, 33, 37, 45), an ability to circulate and translate its own concepts back toward the West.

Tagore shifts the location of knowledge categories from Europe to India in his treatment of intranational discrimination. Against the subordinating comparison of regional units (the West, Japan, and India), Tagore poses questions that break down such collective units through the alignment of their social practices. In his third entry, "Nationalism in India," he writes:

> Many people in this country [the United States] ask me what is happening as to the caste distinctions in India. But when this question is asked me, it is usually done with a superior air. And I feel tempted to put the same question to our American critics with a slight modification, "What have you done with the Red Indian and the Negro?" For you have not got over your attitude of caste toward them.
>
> (*Nationalism*, 118)

Tagore does not deny discrimination in India, but he suggests that the caste system functions shallowly as a synecdoche for a peculiarly "Indian" category of discrimination. Like apartheid, which would function through the second half of the twentieth century as a synecdoche for the uniqueness of South African racism, the caste system functions internationally to isolate India from the rest of the world rather than bring it into a mutual dialogue on discrimination and the status of minorities. Tagore uses comparison to resist his imagined interlocutor's tendentious singularities. By reframing caste as an "attitude," he turns an indictment of India based on its distinctiveness into a provocation to reexamine American progress.

Tagore's analogy produces likeness across caste and race/class hierarchies in the name of creating a commensurability that the metropolitan reader had previously denied. Such rhetoric sacrifices historical specificity in order to reveal the double standards of those who set the standards. It also exposes the assumption behind their questions: that the United States' history of race relations moves forward while India's remains static. In rejecting the particularism to which the imagined American subjects India, Tagore's strategic analogy exposes the power relations that govern when comparison takes place and when it does not; which countries are judged progressive and which are judged regressive by the terms of international dialogue.

Most obviously, then, what *Nationalism* arrives at is what Rey Chow calls a "post-European" perspective on comparison.[21] Such a perspective does not perform a comparison without analyzing the process of comparison itself—its acts of selection, its instantiation of standards, and its consequent valuations. Tagore shows how European standards circulate, how they shape Japanese and Indian nationalisms alike, and how appropriation (without vital assimilation) leaves unexamined ambiguities and blindspots within anticolonial nationalist discourses of autonomy. Tagore's anthology, with its mise en abyme structure, formalizes comparison as what Chow calls a "discursive situation, involuntarily brought into play by and inextricable from the conditions of modern world politics."[22] However, it also brings local and voluntary acts of comparison, such as Tagore's comparison of caste and minority politics, to bear on the overarching colonial regime that Chow so powerfully diagnoses.

When Tagore compares nations, it is not to create a hierarchy of value but to analyze the hierarchies of value embedded in decisions to compare or not to compare. In turn, his prefaces perform their own kind of metatextual reflection upon the anthology's arrival in book form and its distribution to multiple reading audiences across the Anglophone world. In each preface, *Nationalism* invokes the history of its movement into legibility as a work of world literature, and reminds us that such legibility would not be possible without compilation and translation. These processes are vital parts of the "common language" of internationalism that Tagore proposed to Wells, yet they are also processes that create insides and outsides—material incorporated into the book and material excluded from it.

The uncommon remainders of *Nationalism*, the material relegated to the outside of the book, persist in the anthology's paratexts. I think of them as what H. D. Harootunian calls "the ghosts of an unremembered history."[23] For Harootunian, such ghosts represent those stories, experiences, and pasts that modern epistemologies render "mere excess." The phrase is compelling because it lends insight into the way in which remembered or official histories create unremembered ones: not through overt silencing but through the innocuous claims of superfluity. The anthology, a genre defined by selectivity, exemplifies this operational procedure particularly well, but the modernist anthology's self-reflexivity about selection makes redress possible.

Recall the second preface, which introduced the fact of translation into the anthology's production. By signaling the Bengali origins of the translated poem "The Sunset of the Century," the preface creates a bridge between the historical present of the publication of *Nationalism* (during World War I) and the historical past of the poem's initial occasion—the 1899 Boer War. The poem offers a trajectory back into a source language and source history that do not enjoy the same privileges of circulation or attention as English or World War I do. The anthology's allusions to the peripheral language of Bengali and the peripheral past ("the last day of last century") suggest that scholars of *Nationalism* have reading responsibilities that go beyond the covers of the printed book. Although we cannot recover the oral performances lost by the re-mediation of Tagore's lectures into print, we can recover the Bengali source material from which Tagore translated "Sunset" and make it part of the remembered past of *Nationalism*.[24]

Following the trajectory of "Sunset" back to its Bengali origins is revealing but not for the reasons one would expect. The original language and original context of the poem do not provide some firmament that the translated poem lacks; rather, they reveal that origin points are sites of synthesis as well. By any conventional standard of translation, the English "Sunset" has no Bengali original because no corresponding poem exists! "Sunset" is a composite of poems 64 through 68 in Tagore's *Naibedya*. Published in 1901, the collection consists of mostly devotional poetry; however, poems 64 through 68 also address the destructiveness of *jatiprem*, or "nationalism," and contain warnings to India that national pride must not supplant devotion to God.[25]

These poems reflect Tagore's response to the Boer War, which heightened anti-imperial sentiment across India when news spread about Britain's terrifyingly violent tactics (such as the use of concentration camps and scorched-earth policies). The Bengal–South Africa connection that Tagore pursues in *Naibedya* represents some of his earliest indictments in poetry of imperial nationalism. They also offer a rare glimpse into a moment of transcolonial solidarity in which intense preoccupation with the Anglo-Boer War, evident in Indian journalism and print culture of the time, created a "shared public world between India and South Africa" without the intervention of a mediating metropolitan English center.[26] When Tagore selects the *Naibedya* poems and recontextualizes them within *Nationalism*, he is using translation and transposition to generate continuities out of empire's disjunctions. His strategies of reprinting draw a connection between colonial and metropolitan history and situate the national rivalries of World War I within a longer trajectory of imperial competition to divide up the non-Western world.

Tagore frames "Sunset" as a translation that is part and parcel of an *elsewhere* in order to honor origins but not to stabilize them. Yet there is no way of knowing this from the second preface alone. Readers must actually return to the poem's Bengali originals to find out that they are not what we think they are—that is, a single poem. To modify Emily Apter's phrase for a pseudotranslation ("a translation without an original"), "Sunset" is a translation without an equivalent, insofar as no corresponding Bengali-language poem exists. What "Sunset" does have is fragmented antecedents that belie the sanctification of the original work.

This has implications for translation theory. For instance, it tells us that actually existing originals are not always a stabilizing heuristic against which translations can be measured. Far from being an intact work, Tagore's originals are shards of unexpected discovery that nullify any boundary between the life of an original work and the afterlife of its translation. Doing away with such before-and-after sequences, Tagore shows no piety toward his Bengali poems' formal coherence, their wholeness, or their timelessness. His autotranslations readily subject his originals to history by turning finished poems into unfinished storehouses of raw materials to be refashioned and recontextualized by the demands of the present.

Combining poems was a frequent practice of Tagore's in his autotranslations, one that begins at least as early as *Gitanjali* (1912). He describes his unorthodox approach in a 1913 letter to Ajit Kumar Chakravarty as follows: "What I try to capture in my English translation is the heart and core of my original Bengali. That is bound to make for a fairly wide deviation. If I were not there to help you out, you might probably find it impossible to identify the original in the translation." In a later letter, dated May 12, 1913, he further explains, "The forms and features of the original become difficult in my translations—the way I do them these days. My translations are more a reflection than an exact replica of the original image."[27]

Tagore's infidelity to poetic form is the basis for the critical consensus that his translations are "degraded" versions of his Bengali originals. This consensus takes Tagore's recombinatory technique as a corruption of the originals rather than as an aesthetic choice. I take it to be an innovation of translation rather than a perversion of literary form. Tagore's autotranslations contest an autotelic idea of the poem in order to contest an autarkic or self-sufficient idea of national literature more generally. He facilitates the travel of his poetry in new forms and languages to multiply the situations and traditions to which it can speak. In turn, by making the history of translation visible in *Nationalism*, poems like "Sunset" allow otherwise unremembered or insufficiently remembered occasions to speak through them.

When Tagore calls his translations "reflections" as opposed to "replicas," he makes their complex temporal dimensions easier to see. Forgoing an emphasis on replication or mechanical reproducibility, in which translation becomes aligned with seriality (an equivalent series of copies), he stresses the uniqueness of the translation as marking an encounter between the present moment and the ghostly past moment that it conjures up and reshapes. The etymological roots of *reflection* in the Middle French *reflexion* and the Latin *reflectere* suggest "to bend back, bend backwards, turn away." Though the Latin origins of *replica* in *replicare* can also mean to bend back, Tagore's understanding of a replica's serial quality is more aligned with *replicare*'s postclassical denotation: "to repeat or recount again."

Translations that work like reflections, for Tagore, do not simply repeat or recount the past; they bend backwards or turn away from the present moment as a way of speaking to it. They stage a resuscitation of the past rather than a replication of it, and make that staging part of their story. This is exactly the theory of translation that Tagore puts into practice in *Nationalism* when he weaves 1899 back into 1917. "Sunset" disorients the time-space unities framing World War I and consequently creates room for colonial voices and geographies to enter into the war's community of fate.

"Sunset" is an apocalyptic poem that blurs organic and geopolitical imagery. Its opening line declares, "The last sun of the century sets amidst the blood-red clouds of the West and the whirlwind of hatred" (*Nationalism*, 157). Tagore puns on "West," as a geographic marker and civilizational construct with destructive powers that masquerade as the natural cycles of the sun. Beneath its shadow, supposedly civilized nations are personified as "dancing to the clash of steel and the howling verses of vengeance." Tagore's latent comparison of nations to savages recasts nationalism as a modern form of tribalism that substitutes self-interest and material wealth for cooperative ideals.

As the poem unfolds, we discover that Tagore witnesses both the decadence and the degeneration of Europe from within India. Positioned at the crossroads of West and East, India occupies the unique position of witnessing the world becoming one—first through catastrophic destruction and then, possibly, through redemptive salvation:

> The crimson glow of light on the horizon is not the
> light of thy dawn of peace, my Motherland.
> It is the glimmer of the funeral pyre burning to
> ashes the vast flesh,—the self-love of the
> Nation,—dead under its own excess.
> Thy morning waits behind the patient dark of the
> East,
> Meek and silent.
>
> (158)

Tagore places India at an interregnum, which he describes both spatially (between the mythic regimes of East and West) and temporally (between dusk and dawn). In the void created by the death of "the Nation" stands an opportunity either for more catastrophe or for a new kind of communal order to emerge—one that would measure membership not by self-love but by the spiritual principles that Tagore held dear: patience, humility, and simplicity.

Although it is difficult to imagine Tagore's spiritual humanism supplanting nationalism, it is worth considering his attempts to alter the definition of national collectivity. India's fate is bound up in the world's collective fate. Tagore's apostrophe to his motherland demands that she not think like a nation with an eye only toward her own self-interest. Such a perspective, in the above stanza, leads to a dangerous misidentification of "the light of the funeral pyre" as "the dawn of peace" and promises to make good on the destruction threatened in the poem's title.

For Tagore, assuming the mantle of the nation-state without an understanding of international interdependence would never amount to more than a capitulation to the most destructive forces of modernity. His spiritual embrace of passivity and even meekness is not so easily dismissed if we understand these qualities as part of the dissection of belligerent nationalisms during the height of a world war. Rather than reject the nation tout court, he tried to imagine it without the core principles of ethnic homogeneity and economic competition.

Tagore's apostrophes in "Sunset" reflect his ideals. They recompose the collectivity of the poem so that the boundaries of Indian society become difficult to distinguish from the boundaries of the anthology's global audience. In the last quarter of the poem, the subject of Tagore's address shifts quickly from "Motherland" to "India" to the more ambiguously universal "my brothers." Certainly, this shift could be read within the contours of a solely Indian collectivity. However, when addressing India in a translated English poem targeted to non-Indians, "my brothers" likely carves out a wider field of fraternity. Tagore's closing apostrophe aggregates India and the world "as one country"—transcendently in the poet's spiritual vision and immanently in the apocalypse of war.

In the opening pages of *Nationalism*, Tagore states that the world's oneness is a function of scientific facility; in its closing pages, he contemplates the implications of such oneness and roughens it through poetic facility. Tagore's autotranslated "Sunset" registers the history of its transmission across languages, places, and dates. In drawing together discontinuous contextual formations, it does not transcend a location but multiplies the geographies through which it can and should be read. Such works demand a postnational approach to literary study—one that David Porter argues does away with the "Herderian assumption that every text incarnates the culture of its origin," and instead treats a text as "always already a hybrid product of multiple origins . . . on its way to someplace else."[28]

"Sunset" is a poem that concretely illustrates Porter's more abstract claim. Born of the fragments of five Bengali poems arranged and translated into a single English one, its very wholeness testifies to the idea of a literature—national and worldly—made in translation. The poem violates the idea of an autarkic national literature by violating the ideal of a hermetically sealed text. These are important violations that the prefaces in *Nationalism* make visible as traces of a network that exceeds the printed book. Such traces mitigate the various acts of unexamined forgetting that mark the formation of both enclosed national traditions and open world literature trajectories. Tagore's internationalism, then, is best described as one that balances trace against trajectory. Its modernist strategies of compilation and translation draw the English-language reader into an encounter with the untranslatable, the excess of the anthology's synthesis.

India Unbound: Translating *The Home and the World*

In separating Tagore's translation process from his final product, Tagore scholars miss an opportunity to account for the writer's creative acts of self-mediation within a global literary marketplace. Tagore scholars have traditionally considered Tagore's brief popularity in the West a side effect of orientalist fads that were themselves symptomatic of a consumer-driven imagination of and appetite for the East. In dismissing his English translations as pale copies of Bengali originals, they paradoxically uphold sociological values in the international sphere and aesthetic values in the local sphere. The story goes: Tagore's English writings gained popularity in Europe and North America not because of their quality but because of a literary field that assigned value to them for confirming certain images of the Indian poet.

His Bengali writings, however, with their innovative forms and meters, are of transhistorical literary value. In fact, neither the local nor the global sides of Tagore's reception can be described as purely sociological or purely aesthetic. We know of Ezra Pound's attempts to place Tagore's English poetics within a comparative pantheon of formal styles, and we understand Tagore's own deeply privileged place within the Bengali world of letters, where he sponsored many of the most prominent literary magazines and was a major arbiter of aesthetic value in his own right.[29]

Thus, what is most interesting to consider is how Tagore, in the double role of author and translator, balances the sociological with the aesthetic by yoking formal innovation to the historical practices of reprinting, excerption, and recontextualization that marked the circulation of his works across languages and traditions. Tagore brings the historicity of literary production into the literary work, and his English translations register the changes that come with transmission across languages and audiences. More reflection than replica, as he put it, translations desacralize but do not deny origins. Indeed, Tagore tells us that we cannot adequately record the growth and alteration of texts without knowing something about the language and location in which they began. A literary and editorial analysis of the production of *Nationalism* shows that a work's transformation serves as an important record of the diverse political histories and communities it can address.

Tagore's collaborative translation of *Ghare Baire* (literally, *Inside/Outside*) as *The Home and the World* picks up on the themes of circulation, reception, and selectivity that *Nationalism* broached in its examination of nationalist ideology's homogenizing force and autarkic definition of autonomy.[30] If, at the level of method, Tagore's autotranslations disregard the notion of an enclosed work of literature, at the level of form and theme they explore the impossibility and, moreover, the undesirability of an enclosed culture. Like *Nationalism*, *The Home and the World* opens up bounded political forms, such as the nation, by binding together different editions and translations of a "single" literary work. However, by shifting from political argument to a fictional tale of domestic and political strife, Tagore is able to situate the analysis of boundaries within a deeper exploration of various interiorities: those of individual consciousness, household design, and national belonging. He also is able to juxtapose different kinds of consumption: those of the novel's English-language readership and the daily consumer practices and tastes of his protagonists, which become politicized during Swadeshi campaigns for Indian independence.

Tagore's emphasis on the circulation of goods, including his own novel, across borders pushed back at prevailing nationalist discourses within colonial India that equated autonomy with the imagination of a territorially bounded state insulated from the vagaries and coercions of the world market. The pursuit of sovereignty, as Manu Goswami has shown, was framed within a peculiar logic of comparison:

> Nationalist movements and nationalizing states presented themselves as universalistic within the spatial confines of a particularized national community, but as particularistic without, that is, in relation to other nations. . . . The doubled character of the nation form mirrored, in this respect, the spatial partitioning of the modern state system into a series of mutually exclusive, formally equivalent, sovereign states.[31]

Only by defining clear borders between inside and outside the national community can the nation-state declare its distinct identity—both its difference from other nations and its equivalence to them as states. As Hannah Arendt and many others after her have argued, claims to national distinction come from organic appeals to a common race or ethnicity, which ultimately compromise a liberal definition of the state as a legal and political unit uncircumscribed by ethnic or cultural affiliations.[32] Although such organicism is a familiar modus operandi of nationalist discourse, what is noteworthy about Goswami's explanation is her diagnosis of "the doubled character of the nation": "universalistic within" and "particularistic without," Swadeshi nationalism is a discourse grounded in "the spatial partitioning of the modern state system." Premised not just on a Herderian cultural or racial commonality, the Swadeshi movement distinguishes itself from older European nationalisms by adopting a specifically "territorial nativism."[33] Proponents could only imagine India as a nation by first constructing it as a cartographically bounded territorial unit aligned within the world's political geography.

The production of the Indian nation as first and foremost a bounded space took place through a variety of vernacular genres—such as novels, folk songs, and history and geography textbooks, to name a few—which displaced Mughal conceptions of geography with the positivist, cartographic imagination inherited from the colonial state apparatus. Despite deriving the borders of a future sovereign state from the territorial borders of the colony, Swadeshi nationalists attributed their geographic delimitations to the Puranas, sacred texts of Hinduism, whose citation forged a link between national territory and Hindu cultural identity. By retrieving the Indian nation as an artifact of the pre-Mughal and pre-British "Vedic era," Swadeshi nationalism assumed an organic character that rendered Hinduism synonymous with Indianness and relegated Islam and Englishness to the status of foreign pollutants.[34] Swadeshi campaigns to boycott foreign goods reinforced territorial nativism by touting the disjunctive presence of foreign, colonial capital within a newly imagined national territory. By promoting indigenous industry over and against imported commodities, these campaigns aligned political autonomy not just with economic protection from the inequalities of an imperially mediated global market but also with a vision of national coherence defined by the isomorphism of territory, economy, and identity. In simpler terms, the need for economic insulation begot the desire for cultural insularity as well. Regulating domestic consumption made it easier to separate the nation's insiders from its outsiders, rightful inhabitants from foreign intruders.

Against the Swadeshi movement's historical closing down and homogenizing of the national community, *The Home and the World* offers a narrative decisively about the production of India as an unbounded nation forged by the history of multiple colonialisms (particularly that of the Mughals and the British). In his nonfiction and his pursuits of institutional reform, Tagore would call this vision of India *Visva-Bharati* ("World-India"). It proffered a rhetorical alternative to the nationalist slogans "*Bharat Mata*" ("Mother India") and "*Bande Mataram*" ("Hail, Mother"), the latter a patriotic song taken from Bankim Chandra Chatterjee's Bengali novel *Anandamath* (1882). Whereas Bankim, widely recognized as the father of the Bengali novel, indigenized the genre as a vehicle for promoting national feeling,[35] in *Ghare Baire*, Tagore disrupts the association between novels and nationalism by recontextualizing Bankim's patriotic song as a mantra of unthinking obeisance. *Bande Mataram* and *swadeshi* are among the few untranslated words in *Home and the World*, and their untranslatability carries the effect of aligning nationalist language with the particularism that it promoted to the world beyond India. The rest of the novel, however, unmoors the steady division of home and world, nationalism and internationalism. Like Tagore's coined phrase "*Visva-Bharati*," *Home and the World* suggests, in both theme and translated form, that "India" is produced in its encounter with that which is thought to be outside it.

When *Ghare Baire* entered into the realm of world literature as *The Home and the World*, the contact zone of India and "world" registered in the play of text and paratexts. Rabindranath and Surendranath footnoted their translation for foreign readers, but as *Home and the World* has been reprinted—for instance, in both the Penguin Classics and Macmillan India editions—these footnotes have survived as part of the original translation and consequently as part of the original text, with subsequent translators' notes becoming the new paratexts.[36] The Tagores' footnotes are simultaneously textual and paratextual. As the life of *Home and the World* lengthens and widens, these footnotes become more firmly entrenched within the main text and build the Tagores' metatextual awareness of audience and reception into the diegesis of *Home and the World* itself.

This awareness asserts itself in the first line of the novel: "Mother, today there comes back to mind the vermillion mark[1] at the parting of your hair, the *sari*[2] which you used to wear, with its wide red border, and those wonderful eyes of yours, full of depth and peace" (italics in the text). Footnote 1 glosses "the vermillion mark" as "the mark of Hindu wifehood and the symbol of all the devotion that it implies." Footnote 2 glosses "sari," a Sanskrit word, as "the dress of the Hindu woman."[37] The footnotes assume a Western reader unfamiliar with Hindu culture and dress, and inject an ethnographic dimension into Bimala's first-person interior monologue about her struggle to reconcile traditional wifely devotion with the desire of her husband, Nikhil, for a "modern" companionate marriage based on equality and romantic love. The footnoted opening line turns a domestic conflict, privately contemplated, into a scene of translation in which interiority and ethnography disrupt one another. Such a crossing of first-person intimacy with third-person detachment destabilizes the location of readers to the character whose mind we both inhabit and find glossed. The mixture of text and paratext produces an effect akin to free indirect discourse in that it introduces ambiguities of perspective and proximity into the narrative's exposition.

The double gesture of offering the reader access to its characters' interiorities and then preemptively contextualizing those interiorities as culturally foreign situates the English-language reader of *Home and the World* as both inside and outside the community of the novel. A helpful term for describing this relation is James Clifford's "participant analyst."[38] In defining the participant analyst, Clifford speaks of a subject position that both engages an existing cultural tradition and has a hand in constructing it. That construction, in order to be recognized as a construction, requires the participant analyst's negotiation of her proximity to her object of study, and further, her awareness of her own position as constructed through that proximity rather than prior to it. The Tagores' footnotes create their reader as a textual insider and a cultural outsider to India, regardless of who the reader is before encountering the novel. To occupy the reader identity constructed by *Home and the World* is to participate in and analyze the novel's theory of international belonging. The construction of the imagined reader as a textual insider and a cultural outsider illustrates how the territories of "home" and "world" overlap and coconstitute one another.

Of course, the novel's real readers are not the same as its imagined ones, and the tepid reception of *Home and the World* in Europe speaks to that disjunction. Georg Lukács's famously negative review condemned the novel on political grounds, wrongly accusing Tagore of collaborating with Britain by caricaturing Gandhi through the figure of Sandip.[39] In oppositional times, the complexity of Tagore's political vision did not meet Lukács's standards of anticolonial dissent. E. M. Forster, though more generous, also found the novel lacking:

> When a writer of Tagore's genius produces such a sentence as "Passion is beautiful and pure—pure as the lily that comes out of the slimy soil; it rises superior to its defilement and needs no Pears' soap to wash it clean"—he raises some interesting questions. The sentence is not attractive—in fact, it is a Babu sentence—and what does Tagore, generally so attractive, intend by it? Is he being dramatic, and providing a Babu of his creation with appropriate English, or is he being satirical, or was there some rococo charm that had vanished in the translation, or is it an experiment that has not quite come off? Probably an experiment, for throughout the book one is puzzled by bad tastes that verge upon bad taste.[40]

Whereas Lukács dismisses Tagore's novel on the grounds of politics, Forster dismisses it on the grounds of style. His account is revealing as a metropolitan indictment of Indian English and as a reflection of the colonial stereotype it conjures. Forster's distaste for Tagore's "Babu sentences" has as much to do with Forster's orientalized desire for India as it does with Tagore's idiom and sentence structure. In the course of switching genres (from poetry to the novel) and themes (from religious devotion to earthly love and nationalist politics), Tagore, the lyrical mystic of *Gitanjali*, recasts himself, in Forster's eyes, as a prosaic babu. His sentences are rebuffed as vessels of a derogatory colonial stereotype, an illustration of the obsequious failure of the Bengali novelist to imitate an English literary form.

Forster's lackluster reception of *The Home and the World* as a "babu" novel reminds us of the field of social relations in which something as aspiringly disinterested as literary value operates. As a work of world literature, *Home and the World* does not circulate easily into another language or literary culture. Instead, it generates an aesthetic distaste ("bad tastes that verge upon bad taste") that is inseparable from its dubious nationalism (for Lukács) and nationality (for Forster). When the novel, like a colonial subject, cannot be neatly categorized as either "Indian" or "English," utterly exotic or fully assimilated, at least two of its more renowned readers are confused and even repulsed by the indistinction.

My point here is not to defend *Home and the World* by attacking Lukács's and Forster's culturally hegemonic standards. Rather, I am interested in using the terms of the novel's negative reception, particularly Forster's yoking of taste and ethnic stereotype, to bring into relief the novel's own analyses of consumption and display and the relationship of these to the production of identity. If the translated idiom of *Home and the World* offended the sensibilities of British English, it felicitously illustrated at least one message of the novel: taste is conditioned by nationality (Forster's Englishness shapes his dislike of *Home and the World*), but nationality, or the destabilization of it, also can be conditioned by taste (*Home and the World*'s "babuness" is an effect of its bad taste, not of its country of origin).

Tagore establishes the link between taste and the production of identity in the novel through his protagonists' interior monologues, which recall and reflect upon disputes about the distribution, consumption, and display of commodities. One such scene, recollected by Sandip, focuses on obstacles to his Swadeshi campaign's goal of spreading the boycott of foreign-made goods. His disciple Amulya reports how Hindu campaigners burned a Muslim trader's ornate and colorful "German-made shawls." He then raises doubts about the ethics and effectiveness of such tactics: "Should we be so rigorous in our boycott of foreign flannels and merinos" given that "there is no such thing as cheap and gaudy Indian woolen stuff" (*Home and the World* [*HW*], 113)? Amulya sees German shawls as reflective of consumer tastes in general; however, Sandip responds by separating Hindus from Muslims through distinctions in taste. A love of country, which Hindus have, conflicts with a love for "gaily coloured" shawls.

Sandip's version of *swadeshi* thus replicates imperialism's divide-and-conquer tactics by obscuring the messy details of class-based consumption beneath a religious divide. Buying foreign, which was in fact cheaper and therefore appealing to many in the lower classes, ossifies into a stereotype of Muslim decadence, whereas locally made woolens become synonymous with a righteous Hinduism. When Sandip responds that revolution is "not the time to think of looks," the novel indicates that "looks" is exactly what tests overly coherent constructions of patriotism along ethnic lines.

Looks, or artful display, play an equally significant role when we move from Sandip's discussion of cloth to the drawing room of Bimala and Nikhil, wherein foreign and domestically made goods exist side by side. Bimala prefers ornate English-style goods and rues her husband's taste for the minimal:

> My husband still sharpens his Indian-made pencils with his Indian-made knife, does his writing with reed pens, drinks his water out of a ball-metal vessel, and works at night in the light of an old-fashioned castor-oil lamp. . . . We had always felt ashamed of the inelegant, unfashionable furniture of his reception-rooms.
>
> (*HW*, 95)

Bimala goes on to say that when European guests came, she often would replace Nikhil's brass pots with European-made crystal vases, leading Nikhil to respond "that brass pot is as unconscious of itself as those blossoms are; but this thing [the vase] protests its purpose so loudly, it is only fit for artificial flowers."

Despite Nikhil's claims to guilelessness and moderation, Bimala's description suggests that his tastes are equally affected and constitute, perversely, a form of ostentatious asceticism. Nikhil objects to a crystal vase on the grounds of loudness, yet to prefer a brass pot, "unconscious of itself," shows how self-conscious he is about the connection between taste and political affiliation. Taste thus determines what is domestic or foreign to the household, rather than the material fact of where the object was made—whether England, India, Germany, or anywhere else.

In detailing how a gaudy cloth becomes Muslim, a brass pot becomes Hindu, and a crystal vase becomes English, Tagore shows how aesthetic preference, usually a feature of one's individuality, becomes an index of national character and ethnic stereotype. His descriptions of "reception-rooms," threshold spaces within the architecture of the home, establish how processes of domestication and foreignization work: Although several kinds of foreign objects exist within every domestic setting, some become more visible than others. As characters establish what is glaring within the home and what is unassuming, they reproduce and consolidate the ethnic stereotypes of outsiders (Muslim and English) and insiders (Hindu).

By focusing on material objects and the rhetoric of their display, Tagore refuses to vilify Indians' shared vanities as Muslim luxuries or to promulgate Hindu identity as synonymous with the sacrifice of luxury. Swadeshi campaigns may have objected to what they deemed foreign capital, but they had no problems with capital itself. Indeed, the Swadeshi movement defined autonomy through capital accumulation. For Tagore, such an anticolonial strategy shored up inequality rather than restructuring Indian society, and thus it allowed the dream of the nation to mask the hegemonic practices of Hindu nationalism and elide the social reform to which he committed himself.

We see this if we return to the excerpt of *The Home and the World* that Forster quoted—not for its reflection upon the reviewer but for the subject that it treats. The line "Passion is beautiful and pure—pure as the lily that comes out of the slimy soil; it rises superior to its defilement and needs no Pears' soap to wash it clean" (*HW*, 81) is from Sandip's interior monologue, and it expresses his wish to liberate India not only from English rule but also from English taste. That taste is registered literally and symbolically in Pears soap. Sandip's invocation of Pears shows the extent to which Swadeshi nationalist sentiment (metaphorized by the lily) organized itself around an economic and cultural emancipation from English commodities, yet the larger declaration reveals his internalization of the discourses of purity and dirt that English ideologies of domesticity perpetuate.

The distinct mention of the Pears brand is no accident on Tagore's part, for it emphasizes the Englishness of the product and its concomitant imperial associations. Indeed, he and Surendranath changed the brand of soap for the English edition, from Vinolia, in *Ghare Baire*, to the more iconic Pears. As Anne McClintock has shown, Pears's advertising campaign was infamous for framing the imperial project as a civilizing mission enhanced by the rituals of cleanliness and purity. Writing in reference to how Pears soap helped consolidate English national identity, McClintock also points to its pivotal role in imperialism's "cult of domesticity," which spread far beyond the traditionally feminized space of the home to the colonial peripheries.[41] Sandip's allusion to Pears enables Tagore to comment on domesticity—in McClintock's enlarged sense of the term—as a relation of power predicated on disciplining colonized peoples.

Sandip's rejection of Pears for its English iconicity initially makes sense as a resistance to such disciplining, yet Tagore suggests that Sandip's thought process only reinforces his "wholesale appropriation" (to recall that key phrase from *Nationalism*) of a Western-style militarism and materialism. He wants to expel the product, but he accepts and even admires the market and social logic that makes it available. Whereas Sandip uses Pears to clarify distinctions between an invasive Englishness (the soap) and an organically rooted Indianness (the lily), Tagore shows that Sandip's inward identification with capitalist modernity translates imperial values into his nationalist campaign:

> Life is indefinite—a bundle of contradictions. We men, with our ideas, strive to give it a particular shape by melting it into a particular mould—into the definiteness of success. All the world conquerors, from Alexander down to American millionaires, mould themselves into a sword or a mint, and thus find the distinct image of themselves which is the source of their success.
>
> (*HW*, 80)

This passage ironically reveals Sandip's nationalism to be as outward looking as Nikhil's appreciation of an English education and companionate marriage. Sandip values definiteness and distinction as a model of personal and national selfhood, and he looks to insert himself into the pantheon of world conquerors, from Alexander to American millionaires. Although he never praises the British directly, he aspires to imperial might and cleaves to the clarity of "a sword or a mint" to alleviate the "hideous confusion" (*HW*, 81) that marks life in the colony. Fittingly enough, Tagore's placement of Pears soap within Sandip's corrupted logic muddies rather than cleanses, increasing the instability of icons of domesticity at a time when the Swadeshi movement sought to clarify the definition of domestic goods and domestic partnerships (i.e., marriage) as a way of clarifying definitions of the proper way to be Indian.[42]

The Home and the World shows that the economic expulsion of English goods does not solve the larger problems posed by *swadeshi*'s redirection (not rejection) of consumption to indigenous goods. As capital is de-Anglicized and made a property of national identity, the hideous confusion of colonial modernity gives way to the clear vision of an Indian state with Indian goods. Yet this clarity, Tagore suggests, comes at the cost of coercion when regulating taste consolidates ethnocentric paradigms of national culture. Rather than avoid confusion, he amplifies it in his depiction of the Bengali home's interiors. Describing the drawing room in particular as "a thing amphibious—half women's apartment, half men's" (*HW*, 36)—Tagore uses the liminal spaces of the traditional household to push back against the pull of definiteness. If the drawing room is the threshold between *ghare* (inside) and *baire* (outside), Tagore uses its "amphibiousness," its quality of occupying two states of being at once, to model an attitude toward cultural habitation that is different from that of any of his protagonists. The changing patterns of the drawing room as both a designed and an actively lived-in space become an index of the vernacular processes that disrupt the partitions of ethnic and gender identity.

In the amphibious room, as in the translated novel, cultural settings are not found but are made through the activities of their occupants (recall my classification of the reader as a participant analyst). The characters' strategies of decoration and design reveal a lifestyle that cannot be described as Indian without first constructing an "elsewhere"—what the Bengali novel calls "outside" and the English translation calls "the world." Tagore draws on the amphibious reality of colonial culture for the historical grounding of his internationalism. He asks that the confusion of everyday life in the colony, however hideous or anxiety inducing, be written into the definition of the Indian nation rather than disavowed beneath the atavistic rhetoric of a motherland.

Accounting for Taste

Given that taste plays such a vital role in the articulation (and frustration) of collective identity in both the plot of *The Home and the World* and its international reception, it seems right to consider the faculty of taste in more detail. Arendt, drawing on Immanuel Kant, argues that taste exerts an unexpectedly political force because it is a faculty of judgment that is not strictly private. Rather, it requires the judging person to anticipate a public realm in which taste will guide communion with others. The notion that taste might be primarily thought of as a collective impulse is counterintuitive, given conventional understandings of taste as a marker of the personal and even idiosyncratic. Against the popular adage "There is no accounting for taste," Arendt argues, it is precisely the accounting that creates taste as a political judgment and makes it an arbiter of collectivity:

> To classify taste, the chief cultural activity, among man's political abilities sounds so strange that I may add another much more familiar but theoretically little-regarded fact to these considerations. We know very well how quickly people recognize each other, and how unequivocally they can feel they belong to each other, when they discover a kinship in questions of what pleases and displeases. From the viewpoint of this common experience, it is as though taste not only decides how the world is to look, but also who belongs together in it.[43]

When Sandip and Nikhil attribute gaudy tastes to Muslims and reserved tastes to Hindus, they are deciding how India is to look and who belongs together in it. Both make their claims for taste in the presence of others—most notably Bimala—in an effort to "woo the consent" of their interlocutors.[44] Kant's language of love, quoted by Arendt here, aptly reminds us that persuasion is a gentle art that requires romance as well as rational argument. This captures, in a nutshell, the double plot of *The Home and the World*: it is a love triangle that is also a competition in persuasion. Sandip and Nikhil both desire that Bimala will share his taste, which is a reflection of the ethical and political values of each man. Sandip emerges as corrupt in the novel not because he is a nationalist but because he deceives, manipulates, and eventually coerces in order to persuade; Nikhil retains his nobility not because he is cosmopolitan, as Martha Nussbaum has argued,[45] but because he wishes for Bimala to choose him freely, to consent to his judgment in both politics and love.

Yet, as Bruce Robbins has observed, Nikhil's attempts to liberate Bimala from the position of worshipping wife and transform her into a consenting partner only end up reflecting the patriarchal structure of their marriage, in which Nikhil hopes Bimala will freely choose wifehood rather than assume it as a fait accompli.[46] Nikhil is a more ethical wooer, but even he cannot change the social conditions that make persuasion in the novel an imperfect expression of Kant's and Arendt's ideal of a freely aggregated collectivity based on shared taste. In asking readers to understand taste as a bridge between the individual and the collective, and between the vernacular practices of the drawing room and the strategic politics of nationalism, Tagore is also asking us to see ethnic distinctions as artifacts of aesthetic judgment. But that aesthetic judgment is always subject to sociological factors beyond a single person's control.

The case of *The Home and the World* clarifies how Tagore's interest in the circulation of material objects, including his own books, shapes his theory of aesthetic judgment's role in forging collective identities. Bimala and Nikhil's and Sandip and Amulya's disputes over the distribution and display of commodities turn those products into cultural objects that signify autochthony or foreignness—or, in the novel's parlance, home or world. By displaying their strategies of appraisal in *Home and the World*, Tagore undermines the topologies of *swadeshi*'s territorial nativism. The categorical distinctions of "Hindu," "Muslim," and "English" become the results rather than the conditions of taste.

Maulana Mohamed Ali, the editor of the Calcutta newspaper the *Comrade* and later president of both the Indian National Congress and the Muslim League, helps us to see the importance of Tagore's meditations on taste for the ethnically conflicted milieu of colonial India. His 1912 article "The Communal Patriot" posits the rise of communalism as an aporetic feature of the desire for a nation-state, or what he calls "territorial nationality":

> [The Hindu communal patriot] refuses to give quarter to the Muslims unless the latter quietly shuffles off his individuality and becomes completely Hinduised. He knows, of course, the words "India" and "territorial nationality" and they form an important part of his vocabulary. But the Muslims weigh on his consciousness . . . and he would thank his stars if some great exodus or even a geological cataclysm could give him riddance.
>
> The Muslim "communal patriot" owes his origin to a very different set of circumstances. . . . The spectacle of a go-ahead Hinduism, dreaming of self-government and playing with its ancient gods clad in the vesture of democracy, dazed the conservative Muslim who was just shaking himself free from the paralyzing grip of the past. . . . He felt as if he were being treated as an alien, as a meddlesome freak, who had wantonly interfered with the course of Indian History.[47]

In describing patriotism as "communal," Ali suggests there are always competing versions of it. Nationalist unity reveals itself as a pseudouniversality rather than a genuine one, and territorial nationality promises to give form to an exclusivist Hindu spirit. The desire for a Muslim exodus, which Ali attributes to the Hindu communal patriot, is a desire that Tagore would explain, in that same year, as symptomatic of Hindu nationalism's "idolatry of geography."[48] Tagore argued that, by fueling a longing for an organic connection in which a people would become identical with a territory, Hindu nationalism rendered "Indian" spirit into a dangerous and inflexible spatial abstraction that demanded both closed borders and a homogeneous population.

Indeed, communal patriotism's language of formal abstraction returns at the end of *The Home and the World*, when Nikhil, guilty over Bimala's thefts on behalf of the Swadeshi movement, blames himself for her actions: "There was a despotism in my desire to mould my relations with Bimala in a hard, clear-cut, perfect form. But man's life was not meant to be cast in a mould. And if we try to shape the good, as so much mere material, it takes a terrible revenge by losing its life" (*HW*, 197). When Nikhil detects "despotism" within his attempts to persuade Bimala, he couches his guilt in the language of a rigid spatial abstraction that haunts the conclusion of the novel. Nikhil speaks these words before rushing, possibly fatally, to stop a Muslim riot that has broken out on his land in response to Sandip's fostering of communal tensions.

The novel's tragic ending is significant because it suggests the bleak but still undetermined future of a colony seeking sovereignty on the basis of territorial nativism. The specter of a "hard, clear-cut, perfect form" transposes the breakdown of Nikhil and Bimala's marriage onto the breakdown of Hindu–Muslim relations in the novel. Although Tagore could not have known what his novel presaged, his use of formal abstraction foreshadows the crucible of partition, in which hard, clear-cut forms drawn on maps would result in the destruction of families in so much real-world violence.

Though *The Home and the World* remains suspicious of the definiteness and distinction that aesthetic and communal form confers, the ending of the book does not abandon the potential for meaning embedded in most notions of form. Rather, it solicits a new, more chimeric theory of form—one that, in altering perceptions about the perfection of an aesthetic object, might also change expectations for the unity and cohesion of a political community. More powerfully, *Home and the World* exemplifies the theory of form it promotes. The translated novel grafts together what look like firm oppositions—home and world, Bengali and English, the aesthetic and the sociological, creation and reception—in order to tell a story of nationalist politics in an internationalist way.

Visva-Bharati

Tagore's writings contest the sorts of cohesion that he understood nationalism to demand, both within India and beyond it, as the dominant ideology of political self-definition throughout the world. As *Nationalism* and *The Home and the World* show, Tagore was unwilling to suspend inconvenient truths about militarized nationalism, communalism, and marriage in the name of revolutionary goals. Such a legacy makes Tagore himself an inconvenient figure within Indian colonial history; many would rather remember him as the composer of two national anthems (India's and Bangladesh's) than as a fervent critic of the nation.

Nonetheless, Tagore's theories and practices of translation are especially worth remembering as part of an anticolonial cosmopolitics, because they show the limits of partition and autarky as solutions to questions of power and inequality at several scales (local, national, and global) and of several types (ethnic/religious, linguistic, metropolitan versus colonial). Rather than isolate Indian literature and culture in the name of a national organicism, Tagore developed a style of translation that, in defying aesthetic presumptions about the boundaries of a literary work, enabled him to defy political presumptions about the boundaries of a community's identity.

More than simply representing the material conditions by which his works circulate, translation, compilation, and editing, in Tagore's hands, become modernist strategies of collage and defamiliarization. He used them to dispute not only the self-sufficiency of national literature but also the frictionless exchangeability of a Wellsian world literature propelled by the utopian dream of a universal language. Tagore's collaborative translations and autotranslations suture together disparate ideas about production (i.e., authorship and translation) and location (i.e., nationality and worldliness) to puncture utopian internationalist equations of commonality with universality.

Yet they do not back away from promoting their own impossible vision of collective life, in which translatability and illegibility coincide as reciprocal features of global consciousness. The paradoxical communication of opacity in Tagore's translations lends analytical force and perhaps even modest material existence to his aspirational abstraction of *Visva-Bharati* (World-India). They illustrate that national-cultural difference is not a stage to be transcended in a progressivist view of political transition but a density to be achieved through continuous traffic with a wider world.

Beginning with the translations of his Bengali poems, Tagore found himself privileging theories of literary networks and versioning over theories of the singular and auratic work of art. Chafing against hermetic ideas of literary form and national tradition, he devised editorial and translated forms that would address multiple audiences and draw those audiences into the analysis of cross-cultural dialogue. For Tagore, modernist acts of transfer brought definition to an Indian internationalism in which the dream of postcolonial sovereignty would not preclude the circulation of mixed cultures or the diffusion of political solidarities beyond the nation. It would require them.

2

ALTERNATING ASYMMETRY

International Solidarity and Self-Deception in James Joyce's *Dubliners* and "Cyclops"

> If an artist courts the favour of the multitude he cannot escape the contagion of its fetishism and deliberate self-deception, and if he joins in a popular movement he does so at his own risk.
>
> —James Joyce, "The Day of the Rabblement"

> I want to show you that the political tendency of a work can only be politically correct if it is also literarily correct. That means that the correct political tendency *includes* a literary tendency. For, just to clarify things right away, this literary tendency, which is implicitly or explicitly contained in every *correct* political tendency—that, and nothing else constitutes the quality of a work. The correct political tendency of a work includes its literary quality *because* it includes its literary *tendency*.
>
> —Walter Benjamin, "The Author as Producer"

> The cabin door opened and he saw the Hungarian standing in a shaft of grey light: "Daybreak, gentlemen!"
>
> —James Joyce, "After the Race"

James Joyce stands out among the writers assembled here for being the most likely to divest himself of social ties and the least likely to place his faith in the efficacy of collective projects. In that sense, it is not surprising that he stands as the interface between older paradigms of modernist internationalism and the newer one on offer in the present book. Whereas classic accounts established Joyce's "European" aesthetic credentials by divorcing him from Ireland, I will be considering how Joyce's distrust of glorified accounts of European fellowship returned him to the scene of Irish politics.[1] Specifically, it provoked a critical dissection of the rhetoric of Irish solidarity with European nations on "the Continent," a moniker that stood not only for cosmopolitan sophistication but also for a supranational model of solidarity much more desirable than that of imperial Britain.

It is precisely because of Joyce's suspicion of solidarity that his fiction makes it possible to conceive of internationalism not just as an indefinitely deferred dream of universal cooperation but also as an internally combative and competitive discourse in which the tensions between national interests and cosmopolitan identifications rarely resolve themselves. Joyce, as is well known, was deeply critical of such nationalist projects as the Irish Literary Revival, the Gaelic League, and Sinn Féin; however, the dominant narrative behind his modernist persona is that he rejected them on the grounds of their nativist insularity rather than for their methods of international comparison.[2] As I show in this chapter, the infamous cultural insularity of Irish revivalism was not so much a product of willful isolation from other cultural traditions as it was a symptom of a particular kind of engagement with the histories and traditions of other countries, in which international solidarity became a mechanism for asserting both Ireland's singularity and its parity with the sovereign nations of the world. In other words, revivalist expressions of international solidarity hinged on what Declan Kiberd, drawing on the work of Seán de Fréine, calls "the ingenious device of national parallelism."[3]

National parallelism was an epistemological procedure as much as a cultural one, and it worked by exorcising the unevenness of colonial history from the rhetoric of international comparative space. Rather than incorporate the conditions of underdevelopment that would complicate comparison across the Irish colony and European nations, proponents of parallelism pursued comparative equivalences that would participate in liberating Ireland by, at least rhetorically, elevating it from colony to nation. Joyce objected to such inflation and to what he perceived to be the exaggerated national and international solidarities proffered by revivalism in general. Yet he was not immune to revivalism's implicit claim that cultural production was intrinsic to the liberatory politics of decolonization. He accepted the premise that art had a role to play in achieving collective freedom, but he refused to adopt strategies of historical reclamation and aesthetic representation that would prioritize cultural pride over cultural confrontation.[4] Instead, he developed his own techniques of international comparison in his fiction—techniques I gather under the heading "alternating asymmetry." Some readers will no doubt recognize the phrase as Joyce's own, taken from his description of "Cyclops" in the Linati schema. I use it more expansively here to encompass literary techniques and affective tendencies that connect his early work in *Dubliners* to his masterwork, *Ulysses*.

Joyce developed strategies of uneven and disproportionate comparison in order to explore the psychological and material effects of colonialism on ordinary Irish people and, further, to propose that the reassurances of collective solidarity might not always constitute an adequate solution to the challenges facing downtrodden communities. Eschewing narratives of progress and social acceptance for those of underdeveloped pathways, failed unions, and betrayed friendships, Joyce turns the negative sociability of everyday life—its subtle hierarchies and not-so-subtle power plays—toward an analysis of the aggressions and disparities sustained by the conviviality of peers. The focus on finding formal arrangements that capture the asymmetries of actually existing collectivities leads Joyce's fiction into oblique and direct criticisms of parallelism as the comparative tool for forging national unity and international standing.

Joyce's boundary pushing at the level of literary form is of a piece with his overall trajectory of pushing the boundaries of fiction's social content toward both the ordinary and the indelicate. Joyce prized unsheltered styles of writing—writing unafraid to divulge coarse thoughts and deeds, accumulate unflattering impressions, or memorialize its characters through their sustained subjection to ignobility. In reorienting narration from the ennobling to the bathetic, he created affective predicaments in which the awakening of sympathy and pathos for his characters is rarely isolated from the evocation of disgust and disidentification. Such emotional paradoxes, coupled with the strategies of satire and excess that characterize *Ulysses*, reflect how the grotesque permeates Joyce's fiction to become the dominant literary and political tendency of his work. The travestying of previous and concurrent forms of writing, coupled with his relentless mixture of pathos and bathos, suggests a fondness for the lowly as a site of genuinely disturbing feeling and communal questioning.

As a form of social critique, the grotesque worked through involution; it mandated an internal reckoning with oneself in which Dubliners came face-to-face with the very stuff of life—material goods, romantic love, peer recognition—that threatened to destroy their aspirations while also claiming to fulfill them. Joyce's fiction thus draws out the tragicomedy of what Lauren Berlant has called cruel optimism, an attitude whose cruelty derives from its attachment to objects that cannot sustain the weight of their promises. For Berlant, optimism is a pleasure that can "induce conventionality, that place where appetites find a shape in the predictable comforts of the good-life genres that a person or world has seen fit to formulate."[5] Optimism generates pleasure by reproducing received aesthetic as well as social norms. Further, its cruelty lies in the sense of pleasure that such reproduction creates. Brought into relief by such a counterintuitive affective relation as cruel optimism, Joyce's pessimism appears newly kind. His grotesquerie emerges as an attempt to intervene in the reproduction of destructive appetites through the creation of newer and odder literary shapes. He subjects ideals of collective attachment and solidarity—the national past but also a supranational European future—to scrutiny within the historical present.

Joyce's attraction to the degraded and the unpalatable as overlooked sources of regenerative discovery resonates with an older understanding of the grotesque, which Mikhail Bakhtin derived from the poetics of Rabelais: "Degradation here means coming down to earth, the contact with the earth as an element that swallows up and gives birth at the same time. To degrade is to bury, to sew, and to kill simultaneously, in order to bring forth something new and better." For Bakhtin, lowering the spiritual and the cerebral to the realms of the material and bodily did not vitiate the former but revitalized them, so that the energy of "folk humor" in Renaissance literature might combat the aridity of authoritative or official culture.[6] For Joyce, the grotesque inflects the modernist literary project of cultural renewal in a distinctly darker way: it brings out the private humiliations informing corporeal humor and the socioeconomic cruelties that yield obscene or embarrassing displays. As I will show, his asymmetrical comparative forms condense degradation and regeneration into simultaneously apprehensible moments of insight—epiphanies that yoke psychic pain to the process of spiritual recovery.

Kind pessimism may seem a strange and even grudging relation for Joyce to assume. Why withhold the kinds of solidarities that would imbue an occupied territory with a sense of cultural pride and political agency? As the first epigraph to this chapter attests, Joyce feared art's legitimation of self-deception, its indirect ratification of people's tendencies to adopt narratives, however flawed, that confirm their hopes and dreams. The role of the artist, in his reckoning, was to act as a check against such tendencies, even and especially when those tendencies informed crucial efforts at popular mobilization and political unification. This is why he was so critical of the Irish Literary Theatre for staging plays that capitulated to "the forces that dictate public judgment" rather than those that "calmly confronted" it.[7]

Joyce's readiness to confront, startle, and defamiliarize, despite embedding collective ends, demonstrated an autonomy and elitism that placed early critics' "modernist" versions of Joyce in opposition to "postcolonial" recuperations of Joyce as an Irish writer. Joyce's avowed distance from the "multitude" has led critics like Joseph Valente to construe him as self-divided—caught between identification with "the conquerors and the conquered."[8] Such self-division, for Emer Nolan, is a property both of Joyce's individual psychology and of the psychology of his writings: "Their very ambiguities and hesitations testify to the uncertain, divided consciousness of the colonial subject."[9]

Although Valente and Nolan are no doubt correct to identify the psychology of the colonial subject as one of the most interesting aspects of Joyce's work, their identification of that psychology with self-division rather than self-deception limits the sources of his fiction's psychological complexity to the agon between colonizer and colonized and misrecognizes Joyce's efforts to register colonial resistances uncaptured by self-conscious collective projects. Self-division also tends to participate in a logic of selfhood in which the unification of one's loyalties connotes the health of the subject. By focusing on self-deception in this chapter, I might seem equally guilty of instantiating a simplified logic of selfhood in which the realization that one's "effective motives" differ from one's "avowed intentions" comes to be equated with liberation itself—the emancipation of the Irish people from myths of colonial inferiority and national aggrandizement.[10] Certainly, Joyce advanced a version of this argument himself when he was fighting the censorship of *Dubliners*.

However, I will be departing from this line of reasoning to argue for something different: that Joyce's work remains so enduring, and his sense of vocation so controversial, not because he frees his characters or his readers from their chimeras but because he uses those chimeras willfully and analytically. Chimeras, understood here as both individual and collective forms of self-deception, become gateways into the unexamined foundations of colonial stagnation and social recovery. Joyce probes these foundations to better understand the conditions under which the Irish have been pathologized and have themselves internalized assumptions of colonial inferiority. The literary tendency of his fiction toward affective aloofness and formal techniques of grotesquerie sometimes makes it difficult to separate his criticism of pathology from the reproduction of it. Yet walking that fine line is a crucial part of its perversely correct political tendency to question not just the false promises of imperial development but also the grandiose rhetoric of anticolonialism. By juxtaposing the rousing promises of such rhetoric with the small yet staggering setbacks of everyday life, Joyce melts into air all that is solid about solidarity.

Testing National Parallelism

Joyce's distance from, and even disdain for, the collective projects embraced by his Irish literary contemporaries led him to redirect the national and mythic parallels guiding both popular art and popular sentiment. Perhaps the most obvious mythic parallel was the Moses–Parnell comparison pervasive within the political climate of the late nineteenth and early twentieth centuries and, in Robert Spoo's words, indicative of the colony's "*sensus communis*."[11] The common sense that enshrined Charles Stewart Parnell as the guiding light of the Irish people was reproduced and reinforced by elegiac literature like W. B. Yeats's "Mourn—and then Onward!" (1891) and Lady Gregory's play *The Deliverer* (1911). These overtly patriotic works partook in the project of imagining a specifically Irish identity and national destiny not by turning inward into the treasure trove of Celtic legends but by reaching outward into the origin stories of other peoples. The Moses–Parnell typology also gave birth to more collective comparisons between the Irish and Jewish peoples, such as in John F. Taylor's speech promoting the Irish language (a speech that Joyce attended). Taylor, a supporter of the Gaelic League, deployed the familiar trope of an independent Ireland as the promised land, and he developed an extended parallel between the "outlaw languages" of Irish and Hebrew under contemporary English and ancient Egyptian rule.[12] The analogies organizing his speech, which are recalled and recited by Professor MacHugh in "Aeolus," point to the larger milieu of international and interracial comparisons in which revivalism operated.[13]

Indeed, it is important to note that the Irish–Jewish parallel was not the only comparison used to articulate the stakes of Ireland's present via recourse to another nation's past. Nor was it the only one to infiltrate the symbolic designs of Joyce's fiction. The "Hungarian parallel" stands out among national comparisons for its longevity and influence within Irish politics. To those unfamiliar with the history of Irish nationalism, the Irish fascination with Hungary will sound odd, yet the Hungarian parallel was a recurring device of anticolonial discourse from the mid-nineteenth century onward. Thomas Kabdebó offers a history of the parallel, tracing its strategic comparisons back through the writings of such revolutionaries as Thomas Davis, William Smith O'Brien, Michael Doheny, and John Mitchel.[14] O'Brien, Doheny, and Mitchel were members of the Young Irelander Rebellion of 1848, which was inspired in part by the momentum of other revolutions across Europe in the year known as the Spring of Nations. (The twenty-first-century moniker "Arab Spring" plays on this name and the contagion of revolution associated with the events of 1848). Although most of the rebellions (in Belgium, Switzerland, Italy, Denmark, and the Netherlands) failed, some produced lasting changes. France, of course, became a republic, and the Hungarians initially won sovereignty from Austria. However, Austrian rule was restored in 1850, and a compromise was not reached until 1867, when the empire became a dual monarchy known as the Austro-Hungarian Empire.

This last Hungarian victory, after prolonged constraint, became the basis for the Hungarian parallel in its fullest and most popular articulation by Arthur Griffith, in his political work *The Resurrection of Hungary: A Parallel for Ireland*.[15] The work was serialized in the *United Irishman* from January to July of 1904 before being published in book form. Griffith's book constructed Hungary not just as a parallel for Ireland but also as a heroic model of an equally marginalized European country whose political trajectory from Austrian colony to corulers of the Austro-Hungarian Empire presented an antecedent for Ireland's own political aspirations. Griffith advocated for a similar British–Irish dual monarchy, in 1904, as part of the platform of his newly founded Sinn Féin party—an option that would seem viable until the Easter Rising of 1916, the aftermath of which saw the consolidation of republicanism.

Griffith's parallels not only pointed out the similarities structuring Ireland's and Hungary's historical marginalization within Europe but also illuminated the comparative history of negative racialization to which both nations were subjected by their respective colonizers:

> In the Austrian beer-gardens—the equivalent of the English music halls—vulgar beings clad in grotesque imitation of the Hungarian costume, who sang songs reflecting on the Hungarian character, were popular buffoons. The Austrians called them "Magyar Miska" or "Hungarian Michaels"—Michael being the popular peasant-name in Hungary as the English call their music-hall Irishmen "Irish Micks" or "Irish Paddies." Nor was there at one time wanting in Hungary the equivalent of the Irish seoinini—debased Hungarians who, anxious to conciliate the strong ones, applauded the libels on their race, affected to despise the customs, traditions, history, and language of their country, to consider everything Hungarian vulgar and all things Austrian polite.[16]

Griffith's equivalences in this passage situate Ireland and Hungary as internal colonies within Europe and thus subject to similar forms of cultural oppression and self-alienation. They focus particularly on the forms of minstrelsy that helped create and consolidate racial stereotypes—"Magyar Miskas" and "Irish Micks"—while claiming to document and imitate the fixed racial characteristics of subject peoples. In drawing Irish–Hungarian solidarity out of the shared memory of racial subjection, Griffith employs strategies of comparative racialization that might uplift the Irish people by setting up a cross-colonial field of identification with Hungary.

Diana Fuss has theorized identification as a "detour through the other that defines the self." Such a "psychical mechanism" enables self-recognition by allowing "self-difference"—that is, the process by which the self comes into consciousness of itself as a self.[17] Griffith uses the Hungarian parallel to effect this kind of self-recognition at the national scale, wherein Ireland would solidify its own identity through solidarity with Hungary. Such a lateral connection with a now sovereign nation would, Griffith argued, inspire Irish anticolonialism and exorcise disabling vertical comparisons with the English, whose culture, language, and tradition had already been internalized as superior.

In the process of stoking the passions of positive racial consciousness, however, Griffith leaves unquestioned and thus reproduces colonial comparativism's own tightly policed racial binaries of Irishness and Englishness, Hungarianness and Austrianness. These binaries in turn yield their own troubling caricatures: "debased Hungarians" become the equivalent of the "Irish seoinini." *Seoinini* is the Gaelic word for "shoneen," or West Briton, meaning an Irishman who imitates English tastes and manners and who might be compared to a babu in the Indian colonial context. The proliferation of such types shows how imperial taxonomies permeated nationalist campaigns, which, as was seen in the previous chapter on Tagore, derived strength and influence from aligning political principles with the policing of cultural preferences and tastes.

Through its own policing of identity, the Hungarian parallel facilitated a mode of collective self-recognition that was also a manner of self-deception. Rather than keeping the example of Hungary embedded within Ireland's anticolonial cultural imaginary, Griffith allows for its ejection by suggesting that overcoming colonial debasement would best be achieved by turning inward toward an autochthonous past. This move paradoxically disavows the infiltration of Hungarian otherness into Irish self-definition by transforming the unruly field of colonial identification into a stable ground for the comparison of separate-but-equal national cultures.

Griffith's publication was one of the most influential disseminators of such national parallelism, relying on a set of strategies also deployed by the Gaelic League and other revivalists. Such strategies, according to Kiberd, engineered Irish culture as an "apophatic construct"; that is, it defined Irishness as, first and foremost, a negation of Englishness, and it used cultural invention to devise Irish counterparts (and counterpoints) to English law, activities, and dress. For example, Brehon law paralleled English law, Irish hurling became the analog of English hockey, and the kilt corresponded to trousers, regardless of whether such artifacts of heritage "had a secure place in Irish history."[18]

Such modes of revivalist invention surely bordered on the fetishistic, but that is not the sole reason Joyce criticized them. He objected to their internalization of the comparative methods disseminated by the British Empire. By defining Irish culture against English culture, point for point, the revivalists derived cultural specificity even as they assimilated colonial standards of measurement and value. As such, the English standard, even when reviled, remained the unacknowledged gold standard. Opposition to it licensed all sorts of inaccuracies and "deliberate self-deceptions" with respect to the histories and solidarities that revivalism invoked. For example, the nationalist internationalism, of which Griffith's *Resurrection of Hungary* was paradigmatic, conveniently ignored the effects of Hungary's changed status within Europe—from internal colony to colonial power—on its figuration as an oppressed nation.

Deflating as they were, Joyce's stories in the *Irish Homestead* ("The Sisters," "Eveline," and "After the Race"), and later *Dubliners*, corrected for what his *Stephen Hero* would, in a more didactic vein, call the "political absurdities" of revivalism. His criticism bears quoting at length for the echoes that arise among Joyce's words, Griffith's, and Kiberd's:

> He [Stephen] saw that many political absurdities arose from the lack of a just sense of comparison in public men. The orators of this patriotic party were not ashamed to cite the precedents of Switzerland and France. The intelligent centers of the movement were so scantily supplied that the analogies they gave out as exact and potent were really analogies built haphazard upon very inexact knowledge. The cry of a solitary Frenchman (A bas l'Angleterre!) at a Celtic re-union in Paris would be made by these enthusiasts the subject of a leading article in which would be shown the imminence of aid for Ireland from the French Government. A glowing example was to be found for Ireland in the case of Hungary, an example, as these patriots imagined, of a long-suffering minority, entitled by every right of race and justice to a separate freedom, finally emancipating itself. In emulation of that achievement bodies of young Gaels conflicted murderously in the Phoenix Park with whacking hurley-sticks, thrice armed in their just quarrel since their revolution had been blessed for them by the Anointed, and the same bodies were set aflame with indignation [at] by the unwelcome presence of any young sceptic who was aware of the capable aggressions of the Magyars upon the Latin and Slav and Teutonic populations.[19]

Joyce predicates his indictment of revivalism on the tone and style of its comparisons: rousingly general rather than historically meticulous. He picks up on the rhetoric and semiotics of revivalism in the phrases "a glowing example" and "young Gaels . . . whacking hurley-sticks." He also shows how Stephen risks the epithet of *seoinini*, a self-divided rather than "united" Irishman, for being "a young sceptic" in response to representations of Hungarians as a "long-suffering minority." Such representations occlude their contemporary status as sovereigns dominating other populations within the Austro-Hungarian Empire.

For Joyce, the rhetorical strategies of redress and aggrandizement only go so far before elevating the pride of a subject race detracts from its self-knowledge or, worse, its historical understanding of the present. The specter of self-deception was crucial to his aesthetic and political differences with the Irish Literary Revival and went beyond any simple preference for the high culture of Europe. Idolizing Henrik Ibsen, another searingly truthful artist from the so-called margins of Europe, Joyce was not above making his own parallels as he imagined his artistic trajectory from colony to continent. However, it was the ends those parallels served and the kinds of awakenings they inspired that made all the difference in Joyce's cultivation of a "just sense of comparison" among his readers.

Joyce subverts the national parallelisms of revivalism by reworking them in "After the Race," and he achieves a critique of overstated solidarity that is more epiphanic than expository—"exact and potent" in a way that the meandering *Stephen Hero* is not. Published by the *Irish Homestead* in December 1904 (several months after the serialization of Griffith's *Resurrection of Hungary*), and reprinted in slightly revised form in *Dubliners* (1914), the short story was the last to be accepted by the periodical because of the large number of reader complaints regarding the bleakness of "The Sisters" and "Eveline." Comparing "Eveline" and "After the Race" to Yeats's *The Countess Cathleen* and "Red Hanrahan," Richard Ellmann stresses the departure of Joyce's "Irish" stories from Yeats's "Celtic" ones. The "Celtic" stories are "melancholy and warm" and draw upon folklore and legend to extol the nationalist virtues of "self-sacrifice." Joyce's "Irish" stories, by contrast, are "meticulous" and extol the virtue of "self-realization."[20]

Ellmann's classifications differentiate the ethnolinguistic (Celtic) from the national (Irish), and not so subtly attribute romance and idealism to the former, reality and naturalism to the latter. Although such distinctions rightly reflect Joyce's artistic differences with Irish Literary Revival writers, their sharpness belies the ways in which the cultural values of "Celtic" nationalism overlapped with the political calls for economic and legal sovereignty associated with "Irish" nationalism. "After the Race," in particular, picks up on the cultural-political strategies of revivalist rhetoric and responds to the elevating revivalist narratives of racial romance and international solidarity with a debasing one of its own.

The main revivalist strategy that Joyce unsettlingly redeploys in "After the Race" is comparison with Hungary. The short story begins, eponymously enough, as a motor derby is ending. It immediately establishes power differentials among the Irish, Hungarian, and continental characters through well-placed adjectives that judge as much as they describe. The Hungarian Villona is "huge" and implicitly out of place within the "trimly built" French car in which he, along with the protagonist, "the neatly groomed" Jimmy Doyle, is a backseat passenger. Coupled together from the start, and foils throughout the story, the Hungarian and the Irishmen share high spirits that "seemed to be at present well above the level of successful Gallicism." Outside the car, Joyce continues to establish relations of power between drivers and spectators: "The cars came scudding in towards Dublin, running evenly like pellets in the groove of Naas Road. At the crest of the hill at Inchicore sightseers had gathered in clumps to watch the cars careering homeward and through this channel of poverty and inaction the Continent sped its wealth and industry."[21]

The cars, which are French and German, evince a casual superiority born of their speed and perfect alignment, while the image of "Inchicore sightseers . . . gathered in clumps" exacerbates the inertness of watching from the sidelines. By juxtaposing images of Irish lumpenness and Hungarian disproportion with those of continental precision and amplitude, Joyce insinuates strategies of asymmetry into his famed style of scrupulous meanness in *Dubliners*. These strategies turn the Irish into "sightseers" within their own home and draw out, from the specificities of physical place, the colony's sociological place within the symbolic landscape of Europe. They also, by exploiting the resources of the grotesque (descriptive distortion; the arousal of both empathy and disgust) subtly undermine Villona and Jimmy's exuberant "Gallicism." Joyce's invocation of gallicism as a linguistic sign of both cosmopolitan sophistication and social pretension signals that Jimmy and Villona's need for speed may also be a need for borrowed prestige. Their pairing foretells a tale in which ambition and composure, or the lack thereof, become pivotal to exploring the colonial fissures within displays of international camaraderie.

It would be an understatement to suggest that spatial arrangements encode the colonial and continental hierarchies that render solidarity so fragile in "After the Race." Jimmy contrasts the "profane" world of spectatorship with the sacred world of riding inside the French race car, yet the interior of the car is thick with an uneasily shared insouciance. In the front seats, the driver and de facto leader of the group, Charles Ségouin, and his French-Canadian cousin, André Rivière, "[fling] their laughter and light words over their shoulders" while Jimmy must "strain forward to catch the quick phrase" (*Dubliners*, 51). Next to him, Villona hums a melody that, coupled with the noise of the car, blurs the Frenchmen's speech into indecipherable sounds.

Previous readings of "After the Race" have interpreted Jimmy's fascination with the fast lane—expensive cars, gambling, and carousing—as reflective of a *seoinini* upbringing, enabled by a father who traded in his nationalist politics for wealth and status in business.[22] Jimmy's adoration of Ségouin's aristocratic ease would suggest that the young man unwittingly shares the same mind-set as those clumpy Irish the narrative marks as "gratefully oppressed" (*Dubliners*, 49). Although it is not wrong to treat Jimmy's ambitions as symptomatic of a colonial subject's false consciousness, such readings tend to schematize the story's social relations as indexes of political identity rather than attending to how Jimmy's affiliations waver and change across dynamic fields of identification. Consequently, these readings represent their own forms of lumping together: the French with the British in the abstract category of "colonizer"; Villona absorbed into the wealthy and cosmopolitan crowd, despite his characterization as hungry and "unfortunately, very poor" (51).[23]

Rather than create clear factions and alliances, "After the Race" refines our understanding of geopolitical dynamics by exploiting the subtle dynamism of friend groups. A powerful example of this strategy comes when Ségouin welcomes a new addition to the party, an Englishman named Routh, and Jimmy imagines their friendship trumping his own with the Frenchman. Conviviality turns to rivalry, and, "under generous influences," an intoxicated Jimmy reveals to Routh "the buried zeal of his father." Ségouin quickly defuses the tension by toasting to "Humanity" (*Dubliners*, 54–55).

Although the narrative does not contain the words *nationalism* or *empire*, Ségouin's ceremonious neutrality bespeaks the political betrayal of an imagined Irish–French alliance. Irish spectators may have rooted for French drivers, but it is a colonial stereotype, a "Gaelicism" that shatters the beautiful illusions of gallicism and elicits hard realities. Jimmy's unguarded drunkenness and political bluntness close the door on French solidarity but open the window of kinship with Villona. Villona's hunger and Jimmy's drunkenness are analogous examples of bodily expression that rub against the sophisticated impressions both characters wish to create. They are signs of the grotesque surfacing through the genteel. Moreover, they signal that, despite Joyce's critique of the Hungarian parallel in *Stephen Hero*, he actually reworked rather than rejected it in his published fiction.

Joyce creates his own Hungarian parallel by casting Jimmy and Villona as foils—a comparative relation that is also an asymmetrical one, given the unequal value of "major" and "minor" characters. Jimmy and Villona's implicit and unequal comparison undoes the equivalencies Griffith draws between the Irish and Hungarian situations. Nonetheless, it still allows for a similitude that prevents these racialized subjects from the internal peripheries of Europe from being absorbed into the homogenizing solidarity of gallicism.[24] Villona, a Hungarian with a French surname, may seem fully ensconced within the sophisticated illusion of high Europeanism, and perhaps is even part of a larger deception happening at Jimmy's expense.[25] Such a reading, however, fails to account for Villona's poverty or for the odd fact that Joyce portrays him through representational conventions reserved for servants. He provides musical entertainment while the others play cards; he affirms other gentlemen's speech while rarely giving his own opinions.

Andrew Goldstone has argued that servants in aestheticist literature display the attributes of aesthetes, capable and indeed charged with becoming what Oscar Wilde called "a mask with a manner." The overlap between the servant's labor of performance and the aesthete's luxury of performance elicits the contradictions of aesthetic autonomy, whereby its dependence upon material labor and the servant's suppressed individuality becomes evident.[26] Throughout "After the Race," Villona blurs the boundaries between friend and valet, racial other (a "huge Hungarian") and cosmopolite (a "brilliant pianist"). Precisely because he is not officially a domestic worker, his racial character subsumes and conveys his subordination as the material difference that cannot be transcended by his elective affinities. As an example of what Griffith might call a "debased Hungarian," for his French affectations, the sophisticated but impoverished Villona embodies the world of labor, debt, and servitude that Jimmy is trying to escape but that Joyce is aiming to confront as part of his larger literary commitment to combating individual and collective forms of self-deception.

In the final lines of "After the Race," Joyce consequently returns to the collective language of race to give the story its mythic and political dimension. "The Hungarian," rather than the particular character Villona, stands in the iconographic "shaft of grey light" as the angelic messenger of absent authority. His announcement "Daybreak, gentlemen!" occasions the story's epiphany. This epiphany, for Jimmy and readers alike, is not that Jimmy has lost all his money at cards and is now in debt (that, he and we already know) but that the time for avoidance has run out: "He knew that he would regret in the morning but at present he was glad of the rest, glad of the dark stupor that would cover up his folly" (*Dubliners*, 57). Adding insult to injury, the speed that once made Jimmy "too excited to be genuinely happy" (50) truncates his period of permissible stupor/stupidity and hence makes the story genuinely sad. Joyce's ending debases Jimmy but also disabuses him of the false hopes of international solidarity—namely, the promise that having friends in high places can erase the history of belonging to a place and a people lowered by colonialism. Villona's Hungarianness foils Jimmy's Irishness and establishes racialization as a process that cannot be wished away. It is through these characters' lateral friendship that Joyce levels his critique of a hegemonic European internationalism, without altogether giving up on the possibility of international solidarity.

Joyce's positioning of excitement as the antithesis to genuine happiness in "After the Race" places his indictment of colonial paralysis and provinciality, so associated with *Dubliners*, in a new light. Far from reinforcing the disparity between Irish stagnancy and European energy, Joyce's depiction of the motor race and its aftermath suggests that speed is a comparative relation of empire rather than an emanation of racial character. More than a motif of metropolitan splendor, speed becomes the device by which to negate the standardized comparisons of imperial historicism and their concomitant constructions of "belated" or "backward" races failing to develop as rapidly as "civilized" ones.[27]

Joyce threads racializing markers throughout the social rituals of "After the Race" so that the epiphanic sting of belatedness becomes more than a reflection of Jimmy's self-deception. It becomes the collective byproduct of imperial rule, rather than the justification for it, and it removes the overeager identification with ruling powers as a solution to the paralysis of underdevelopment. Rather than reclaim or transvalue the racial negativity ascribed to Irishness or Hungarianness, Joyce's Hungarian parallel confronts asymmetries of power by drawing Villona and Jimmy into humiliating kinship with one other. Villona is the bearer of a debasing truth—

the vessel and vassal of racial conscience that renews the gentleman Jimmy's own buried sense of colonial marginality in a dysphoric way. There is harshness, even cruelty, to this final inverted tableau of international solidarity in which no one stands on equal ground, but Joyce's epiphanies are not without care or collective purpose. They move to decolonize consciousness by turning characters' thwarted aspirations into chimeras to be felt and analyzed by readers.

To experience a chimera in *Dubliners* is to come face-to-face with the most familiar definition of the term as a misguided and hopeless illusion. It is not surprising that Joyce's early stories drew angry letters from readers of the *United Irishman* and that his collection *Dubliners* would later draw the ire of censors. Yet, for Joyce, the desolation of the chimera was always half the story; the rejuvenation to which it would lead was the occulted other half. To be exposed to chimeras in fiction through formal devices such as the epiphany was to take the first step toward liberation from self-deception in life. This, anyway, was the rationale Joyce gave his publisher Grant Richards when he was asked to remove two stories ("An Encounter" and "Two Gallants") from *Dubliners* in response to censors' identification of morally objectionable material:

> If I eliminate them what becomes of the chapter of the moral history of my country? I fight to retain them because I believe that in composing *my chapter of moral history* in exactly the way I have composed it I have taken the first step towards the spiritual liberation of my country. Reflect for a moment on the history of the literature of Ireland as it stands at present written in the English language before you condemn this genial illusion of mine which, after all, has at least served me in the office of a candlestick during the writing of the book.[28]
>
> (Emphasis mine)

For Joyce, writing fiction was a way of contributing to the "spiritual liberation of [his] country," a solitary artistic project, as he conceived it, but one with undoubtedly social ends. His contribution to Irish liberation was conditioned by his fiction's quarrel with the concerted production of a national literature that would affirm the self-image of the multitude and hence deny them the painful but necessary encounter with literature as a revelatory form of reflection. Writing about Irish people from outside cultural nationalism (in an affective and not just geographic sense) gave Joyce the "genial illusion" that we are used to calling modernist autonomy but that may be more specifically theorized, via Walter Benjamin as a mediated solidarity. In Joyce's formulation, autonomy is more than an expression of individualist self-quartering; it is a sustaining principle of asymmetry that reflects upon the special skills of the artist, and the place they afford him within the undeniable hierarchies of society.

As Benjamin wrote in the context of class, the bourgeois artist's background, education, and technical skill furnish him with the "privilege of culture" and "makes him solidary with it [the bourgeois class]."[29] Writing in the context of the nation, Joyce's declaration of autonomy from Ireland does not deny that he is solidary with it, in the sense of being yoked to it by virtue of his formation. But, like Benjamin's imagined author, who must betray his class despite being solidary with it, Joyce must betray the guiding institutions of the nation ("the nets of nationality, language, and religion," as it is stated in *A Portrait of the Artist as a Young Man*) in order to commit himself to spiritually liberating his country from them.[30] That his artistic endeavors might induce social transformation was the enabling chimera under which Joyce labored—an illusion that he recognizes and defends as such. There is certainly irony in the fact that Joyce wishes to preserve his own genial illusions while puncturing those of his imagined readership, but at the heart of Joyce's fiction is the conviction that one must learn to discriminate between enabling and disabling chimeras. The demand for such judgment, and the cultivation of the reader's faculties of judgment, is at stake when he seeks convergence between *Dubliners*, which he subjectively calls his own "moral history," and the actual, presumably objective "moral history of my country," which he laments is lost beneath censorship.

To call *Dubliners* "my chapter of moral history" is to assert that modernist autonomy enfolds back into a project of collective self-knowledge—one that is achieved through a heretical kind of spiritual counsel and a mediated form of solidarity that reflect on the process of forging and forgoing bonds. This process is not always a pleasant one in *Dubliners*, whose epiphanies crystallize social bonds variously as constraints that cannot be overcome (as, for example, in "Eveline" and "A Little Cloud," where the protagonists cannot abandon family for new prospects) or as support systems that prove insufficient, as in "After the Race." The dysphoric epiphanies that punctuate *Dubliners* are rooted in tactics of what David Kurnick calls "social exposure" similar to those in the early sketches that Joyce collected under the title *Epiphanies*. Starting with these sketches, Kurnick identifies a "shaming impulse" within the arc of Joyce's oeuvre that acknowledges the frankly negative and even degrading character of the illuminating device.[31] Overcoming self-deception through the epiphany required Joyce to be not only the angel of revelation but also an artist of betrayal—one who catches Dubliners out at moments of weakness and failure and makes examples of their chimeras.

The epiphanies in *Dubliners*, to draw on an idea from Ernst Bloch, disappoint hope, but the chimeras they yield are key to their spiritually secular counsel.[32] They sacralize profane material rather than purifying it through aesthetic form. Recent reinterpretations of the Joycean epiphany through the lens of colonial modernity have questioned the materialism–spiritualism dichotomy animating its theorization. Accordingly, they have moved away from treating the epiphany as a device that, in Seamus Deane's words, transforms "something solid into something spectral."[33] Saikat Majumdar would instead have us see how the epiphany derives radiance from ordinary objects, phrases, or gestures by accentuating rather than erasing their banality. Encoding the epiphany with the resistance of banal materials of the world to the grand form of art, Majumdar identifies in Joyce's aesthetics a critical refusal to replicate in literature the "epistemological dominance" of imperial historicisms.[34]

I would add that, for Joyce's fiction to rise to the status of moral history, it also would have to be epistemologically decolonizing in the sense of refusing to produce a transactional portrait of Ireland—a portrait that could be exchanged with other national portraits as proof of Ireland's equivalent cultural capital. This is why Joyce's modernist category of moral history is in so much tension with the revival category of national literature, though both can be regarded as anticolonial. In operating according to the logic of parallelism, revivalism imagined Irish culture as unique, but, in doing so, also made it fungible within the international arena (hurling for hockey; kilts for trousers). Joyce, in dredging up the paralyzing effects of colonialism throughout *Dubliners*, disconnects from such principles of equivalence by connecting the epiphany with unabstracted materiality. His stories "epiphanize" the material conditions of colonialism not to spiritualize them away but to come as close as possible to turning them into art objects that exude the decomposition of the colony. As Joyce writes to Richards, "It is not my fault that the odour of ashpits and old weeds and offal hangs round my stories."[35]

David Lloyd has noted how the "odor" of epiphanies in *Dubliners* contrasts with the "aura" retained by Stephen's theory of the epiphany in *Stephen Hero*. That theory, says Lloyd, advanced the *symbolic* character of the epiphany by treating it as the moment in which the particular event or object undergoes a transubstantiation into "an illumination of the transcendent." The epiphanies of *Dubliners*, however, reflect not so much a transubstantiation as an "internal intensification" of the moment, one that becomes so powerfully set off from its surroundings that it forsakes the symbolic terrain of embodiment for the metonymic one of substitution. The metonymic character of such epiphanies prevents *quidditas* (the essential "whatness" of the thing brought forth) from becoming the auratic symbol of something other than itself and thus make the epiphany inert for what Lloyd calls "a nationalist aesthetics with its emphasis on the representative function of the symbol."[36] Instead, in turning inward (and I would argue downward toward chimeras rather than upward toward transcendence), the epiphany releases *quidditas* as an odorous metonym more akin to the once essential, still-nourishing waste material of afterbirth than to the radiant promise of an afterlife in heaven or the nation's memory.

Supplementing Lloyd's distinction between aura and odor with the distinction between afterbirth and afterlife calls attention to the temporalities at work in Joyce's epiphanic chimeras. These temporalities compel us to revisit the causes and effects of Dublin's infamous paralysis. Caused not by the stopping of time in the colony but by the splitting of it into metropolitan speed and colonial slowness, paralysis inheres in the smoothness of imperial wealth extraction and in the consequent steadiness of the colony's decay. This devastating structural relation manifests itself affectively in the epiphanic chimera when Joyce's protagonists suddenly realize that they cannot but be too slow.

This is the paralytic experience of Jimmy Doyle, Eveline, Little Chandler, and the other Dubliners who populate Joyce's collection. It is apparent in the first-person narrative of "Araby," when the young boy overstays the bazaar's hours to give the illusion of purchasing power—an illusion that takes shape through "lingering" and ultimately fails; in "Eveline," where

Eveline's countenance becomes ghostly and stony at once ("her white face . . . passive . . . gave him no sign of love or farewell or recognition"); and even in "Clay," where partygoers avoid explaining to Maria the symbolic implications of her blindfolded choice (that is, that clay equals death) but the forgotten verse of her song, "I Dream that I Dwelt," imparts a latent knowledge of mortality.[37] Even if Maria's conscious realization remains in doubt, her musical repetition of the song's first verse performs its own realization of paralysis.

Although the memorialization of such failures to progress is not without the shaming impulses of social exposure, it also can be seen as writing the debilitating effects of colonialism on the body. The grotesquerie of Joyce's characters registers the bodily refusal that precedes political agency and that would become pathologized as the consolidation of national consciousness supplanted less instrumental forms of resistance. To liberate his country spiritually, Joyce needed to preserve that defective material as part of what Stephen Dedalus would call "the uncreated conscience" of his race.[38]

In turning away from sanctioned forms of oppositional expression such as parallelism, Joyce's fiction consequently awakens solidarity with those forms of bodily refusal that emerge as waste material in the eyes of an increasingly politicized race. They are the race's afterbirth, revealed in their literary solidity to have been sources of nourishment all along. More than symptoms of colonial pathology, Joyce's chimeric epiphanies mobilize immobilization by orienting readers to various kinds of belatedness and slowed time. They take his characters' inner protests (the *quidditas* of colonial paralysis) as far they can go without converting them into triumphal energy. Such restraint is an aesthetic choice, but it also is a political one because it stops shorts of guaranteeing the social renewal that revivalism promised and that even Joyce himself labored under as a "genial illusion."

Lacking such illusions, *Dubliners* can only solicit us to keep better track of time ourselves, to recognize the role it plays in distinguishing races and pitting nations against one another. Sotto voce, the collection asks us to be privy to how anticolonial resistance begins before national consciousness is tasked with setting the terms of political agency and freedom. Such recognition involves trading proud national parallelisms for painful literary ones that dwell in feelings of inequality, paralysis, and shameful exposure. In opposing his asymmetrical internationalism to revivalist internationalism, Joyce suggests that purveying dreams of a glorious past and buoyant future, however emboldening and politically necessary, is not enough. One also must analyze the quiet chimeras of everyday life—the fantasies that come to nothing ("Araby" and "A Little Cloud"), the cravings that produce profligacy and embarrassment ("After the Race" and "Clay"), the reasonable ambitions upon which no action can be taken ("Eveline"). These unremarkable defeats, in true chiaroscuro, bring out the half-light of day in the colony where spiritual liberation is irreducible to the achievement of national sovereignty and international fellowship, if also unimaginable without them.

Imbalancing Acts

The self-deceptions and attenuated solidarities of *Dubliners*, particularly those of "After the Race," alert us to several contradictions animating the homosocial and political landscape of *Ulysses*: how the desire for group acceptance crosses with the suspicion of group solidarity; how displays of gentility are often enabled by conditions of humiliation and hostility; and how individual gestures of camaraderie, animosity, and exclusion become entangled in collective rituals of national definition and international relation. Such contradictions unfold across many episodes. We see them in "Telemachus," when Haines (the English guest who overstays his welcome) imagines collecting Stephen's witticisms into a book of sayings and Stephen wonders whether he will profit from it or become another casualty of colonial wealth extraction. In "Hades," Martin Cunningham excludes Bloom from commiseration about personal debt and moneylending because of Bloom's Jewish lineage, leading Bloom to tell an anti-Semitic story ("an awfully good one") to assert his Irish credentials. In "Scylla and Charybdis," there is even a subtle allusion to Joyce's disputes with revival writers John Eglinton, who in real life declined to publish *Portrait*, and George William Russell, who in the novel leaves Stephen out of an anthology of young Irish poets. Upon being so excluded, Stephen is described as "nookshotten," a vernacular English word describing an object or place of irregular form, full of angles, corners, or projections.[39] To be pushed outside the acceptable parameters of Irish literature, the word suggests, is to be pushed into the decomposed zone beyond the nation's harmoniously imagined form.

Stephen's nookshotten state alludes to Joyce's own insecurity at being distanced from Irish cultural movements and metafictionally names the aesthetic path he took to harnessing that insecurity, especially in the "monster-novel" *Ulysses*.[40] The simmering tensions of these early episodes boil over in "Cyclops," where matters of racial difference and national belonging, trespassing and territorialism, become focal points of the work. They occasion Joyce's meditation on linguistic and social patterns of collective self-deception and continue to expose the limits of revivalism's national parallelism as a strategy for collective awakening.

"Cyclops" revisits *The Resurrection of Hungary*, but from a different vantage point than that of *Stephen Hero*. Whereas *Stephen Hero*, in progress during the publication of Griffith's pamphlet, laments the influence of its "haphazard" analogies over the public, "Cyclops," drafted in 1919, treats the pamphlet by Sinn Féin's founder as a joke dismissed by its target audience, including the citizen, a Sinn Féiner himself. Andrew Gibson suggests that the failed reception of *Resurrection of Hungary* in "Cyclops" reflects Joyce's own derision for the work, but it seems equally plausible that Joyce's later allusion would embed the more strident attitudes of those who, post–Easter Rising and the founding of the Irish Republican Brotherhood, had moved so far beyond the Hungarian parallel as to find it suspicious.[41] As Gibson rightly argues, Griffith's rhetorical techniques in *Resurrection of Hungary* resembled those of the revivalists in that he oversimplified situations by omitting inconvenient facts; minimized distinctions of class, party, and religion within Ireland; and generally stressed "unity rather than conflict and division."[42]

Ironically, in smoothing over the conflicts of Ireland's internal heterogeneity in the name of political unity, Griffith's *Resurrection* created the conditions by which its own invocation of Hungary, a foreign country, connoted a threat to Irish unity and autarkic self-definition. At least, this is how Joyce's satire shows the pamphlet backfiring when the patrons of Barney Kiernan's tavern declare it to be the miscegenated brainchild of Griffith and the Hungarian-Jewish Bloom:

> —He's a perverted Jew, says Martin [Cunningham], from a place in Hungary and it was he drew up all the plans [for Sinn Féin] according to the Hungarian system. We know that in the castle.
>
> —Isn't he a cousin of Bloom the dentist? says Jack Power.

—Not at all, says Martin. Only namesakes. His name was Virag, the father's name that poisoned himself. He changed it by deedpoll, the father did.[43]

To assume that someone of Hungarian origin had to be responsible for the Hungarian parallel is to have already imbibed the logic of autochthony Griffith deploys in the pamphlet. Although Griffith drew Irish nationalism into conversation and comparison with other anticolonial movements, his comparative strategies reinforced the link between racial continuity and national revival, couched in terms of resurrection—the renewal of the already latent rather than the introduction of an outside presence. Cunningham reiterates that linkage to discredit the Irishness of Griffith's pamphlet by attributing it to Bloom, a man who, despite his legally acquired name and Protestant mother, is regarded as having no direct filiation with Ireland.

Joyce's recontextualization of *The Resurrection of Hungary* suggests that Griffith's Hungary provided a revolutionary political model for Ireland only by perpetuating the racially conservative image of discrete peoples achieving their own destinies in isolation from one another—a sentiment on full display at the tavern. In the episode, however, Joyce explodes such racialized unanimity by again turning to the grotesque, specifically to the formally discombobulating "technics" that he calls "gigantism" in the Gilbert schema and "alternating asymmetry" in the Linati schema. Both stylistic principles emphasize incongruity as a way of skewering the self-deceiving discourses informing pub paranoia, foremost among them revivalism's triumphal reconstruction of Ireland's past.

In a less-pointedly antirevival manner, though, this episode also divulges the stake all societies have in finding ways to ignore the self-serving nature of their communal narratives—whether through historical simplification or mythic aggrandizement. Gigantism, in particular, reflects Joyce's stylistic parody of inflated rhetoric, which goes beyond wickedly mimicking specific revivalist writers to addressing the everyday genres of public writing that collectively comprise the "anonymous voice" of "Irish consciousness."[44] Karen Lawrence has read this anonymous voice in terms of Barthesian myths that codify the culture's received norms. Joyce's parody reveals rather than perpetuates that codification, and in doing so, clarifies the vast scale and discursive diversity through which such a collective voice operates. His concerted effort to cluster parodies of revivalism (a conscious project of national self-fashioning) with parodies of politically unmotivated discourse (expressions of Dublin's anonymous voice) contextualizes revival styles within the larger milieu that permitted their flourishing. The effect is a wide-ranging critique of the hypocrisy and evasions of public language culture as it inflects and ironizes the arguments among Bloom, the citizen, and others at the tavern about national belonging and historical injustice.

Alternating asymmetry, the second technique and the eponymous one for the present chapter, calls attention to the overall pattern of the episode, which treats the reader to abrupt and inane discrepancies of style as a way of stymying the cultural streamlining necessary to proceed with national parallelism as a mode of self-defining/deceiving comparison. As mentioned, for such parallelism to work, one must view nations as internally homogeneous and discrete social units whose unique identities, oddly enough, derive from their symmetries with other nations. In other words, cultural distinctiveness derives from a nation's ability to generate a set of one-to-one correspondences (tit for tat) with the cultural and political spheres of other nations.

In "Cyclops," alternating asymmetry makes such correspondence impossible by endlessly diversifying the discursive modes available to the writing of culture. Such proliferation works against transforming cultural practices into the countable attributes of a nation, and thus reveals the impoverishment of parallelism's positivist logic. Similar to the more famous Joycean strategy of parallax, alternating asymmetry draws attention to the role of perception in mediating the external reality of events. But whereas parallax requires a common ground for measuring perception (the prism of character, for example, as we compare Bloom's, Stephen's, and Molly's versions of events), asymmetry withdraws that ground. Instead, it alternates among incompatible orders of storytelling—most identifiably, between the nameless narrator's first-person account and the discontinuous parodies of public writing—while allowing those orders to signify upon one another in ways that violate the coherence of any single unit of narration. In other words, alternating asymmetry is Joyce's formal solution to rendering the internal incommensurability of Ireland's private citizens and public cultures (street, folk, legal, journalistic, to name a few). Rather than resolve such incommensurability into the common ground of a national culture, he altogether undoes the division between figure and ground.

This is why labeling the parodies as interpolations or interruptions, which is common in criticism on the episode, is problematic. It unwittingly instantiates a narrative hierarchy that privileges the anonymous speaker's narration as the continuous thread of the episode, with the parodies modifying and ornamenting it.[45] Such an account mischaracterizes the major stylistic accomplishment of the episode, which is to create a single differential field through which the narrative, like an alternating electrical current, generates energy by reversing directions at short intervals.

Joyce's retraction of a consistent stylistic or temporal ground in "Cyclops" allows him to compare discursive registers without making them equivalent or discrete. He thus literarily counteracts the overstated alignments and divisions of national parallelism as he saw them performed in revivalist historiography's overlap with everyday patriotic sentiment. The tendency of parallelism to bring disparate groups or historical situations into excessive modularity is precisely what Joyce condemns through his mockery of certain characters, such as the citizen, who imagine Ireland going head to head with any country in the world: "We'll put force against force," he declares, against any nation (most immediately England) that threatens Ireland's return to its former glory (*Ulysses*, 270). The citizen notably has a penchant for speaking in symmetries and tautologies, particularly when sidestepping requests for further explanation or clarification. Take the following exchange:

> —Pity about her, says the citizen. Or any other woman marries a half and half.
>
> —How half and half? says Bloom. Do you mean he . . .
>
> —Half and half I mean, says the citizen. A fellow that's neither fish nor flesh.
>
> —Nor good red herring, says Joe.
>
> —That what's I mean, says the citizen.
>
> (263)

The citizen's speech patterns reproduce a binary evenness but obstruct reasonable interrogation. He initially repeats his exact words ("Half and half I mean") in response to Bloom's desire for clarification ("How half and half?"). He then repeats the same idea in different words while retaining the grammatical structure of equivalence in his speech ("neither fish nor flesh"). The citizen is suspicious of those who violate categorization, yet he is incapable of explaining why; his repetitions are both acts of self-confirmation ("that what's I mean") and gestures of exclusion. Joe, who completes the citizen's idiom, reinforces their bond through shared linguistic reference, while Bloom, not already in the know, remains perpetually outside the solidarity of the pub.

The citizen prefers the stability of balanced phrases to the instabilities that questioning categories of collective identity might produce. An aversion to such reflection and analysis is a recurring theme in the symbolically named "Cyclops" and is expressed through motifs of blindness, such as the anonymous narrator's near eye-gouging at the start of the chapter, and his inability to find the pub's exit later. The pub-goers repeatedly express impatience with Bloom's interest in causalities and complexities, especially when they threaten the pride to be gained from circulating the patriotic mythos of resistance martyr Joe Brady's defiant erection. Bloom's pedantry, additionally, constitutes its own form of social blindness, as does his refusal to drink or treat others to drinks. His erudite but moralistic citation of the biblical phrase "Some people can see the mote in others' eyes but they can't see the beam in their own" is directed at J. J. Molloy and the citizen, yet it could reasonably be said to include himself.[46] The biblical allusion's growing applicability throughout the episode suggests that self-deception is a collective attribute of the pub and that any hope of overcoming it lies not in taking sides but in developing new arrangements.

This is what Joyce does in "Cyclops" when he manipulates literary forms of balance and imbalance to analyze solidarity rather than profess it. He understands solidarity's political potential to be double-edged, especially when imagining a national community means misguiding individuals within it. He thus assumes the role of the artist in mediated solidarity with a people by *actually* mediating solidarity—putting the trade-offs of politicians and partisans on display and deriving truths that would otherwise go unobserved. His parodies skewer a host of self-serving, shallow, and even inadvertently cruel assertions of friendship and cooperation across different occasions. He mocks revivalism's revisionist internationalism when he claims a variety of world figures (for example, Dante, Shakespeare, Herodotus, and the Buddha) as part of a catalog of Irish heroes (*Ulysses*, 244). He redirects the citizen's proportionate rallying cry of "*Sinn Fein amhain!* The friends we love are by our side and the foes we hate before us" (251) toward a disproportionate scene of thousands gathered to watch the execution of a single man.

Joyce also lampoons the simultaneously pompous and fawning style in which newspapers covered public events, such as the official visit of a "picturesque foreign delegation" by the name of Friends of the Emerald Isle, aka F.O.T.E.I. Joyce deflates the affair by encrypting bawdy puns into delegation members' names and depicting them acting like buffoons at ceremonial occasions. Such obvious bathos embeds more subtle jabs at the cursory nature of official sympathy: "All the delegates without exception expressed themselves in the strongest possible heterogeneous terms concerning the nameless barbarity which they had been called upon to witness" (252). Here, Joyce portrays international solidarity as little more than an empty rhetorical gesture in which "nameless" barbarities are habitually decried but rarely interrogated. Bearing witness to such hollow professions of solidarity becomes Joyce's way of evidencing the need for more acute forms of transnational understanding. His debasing parodies capture the abuse of demonstrative emotion in expressions of sympathy and moral outrage, and he shows these to be a woefully insufficient substitute for historical scrutiny and thoughtful dissent.

Instead of smoothing over serious differences in the name of political unity, Joyce uses the acrimonious atmosphere and asymmetrical form of "Cyclops" to air them. This is nowhere more evident than in the escalating conflict between the citizen and Bloom, who, as Enda Duffy has argued, are structurally figured as the episode's dual and dueling antagonists.[47] However, whereas Duffy's argument restricts the relationship between the citizen and Bloom to an Irish context in which both embody colonial subjectivities—the resistant ire of Caliban and the respectable civility of Ariel, respectively—my argument treats their head-to-head matchup as bringing Irish colonial subjectivity into relief through comparison with other sites of racial oppression not entirely explained by the representational regime of the British Empire. This comparison does not arise from the opposition of the citizen's and Bloom's own positions on the subject of Irish nationhood, but rather from their *apposition* or mutual modification of one another's positions.

David Kazanjian, building on the work of Fred Moten, has theorized apposition from its grammatical roots in equivalence to its rhetorical effect as a modulating device that insinuates tension into comparisons that insinuate equivalence. Grammatically, *apposition* refers to noun phrases that accrete information but share the same referent and syntactical relationship to the words around them. For example, in the sentence, "My friend James Joyce the writer loves puns," the noun phrases "friend," "James Joyce," and "the writer" are all in apposition because they modify one another and are syntactically parallel. Yet Kazanjian suggests that, rhetorically, the substitution of apposition for stabilizing connectors such as linking verbs or relative pronouns (in other words, "My friend James Joyce is the writer who loves puns") creates "a potential break or rupture between the linked terms, an uncoordinated gap" by which ambiguities of emphasis and contingencies of meaning can emerge.[48] In other words, the convergences of apposition do not lock terms down but open them up to paths of divergence.

When Joyce brings the citizen and Bloom into dialogue, he not only is staging a disputatious argument but also is creating opportunities for both characters to appose one another—to parallel, interrupt, and recontextualize one another's claims. The effect might seem cacophonous, but an important echo ripples through the latter half of the episode. It serves to link the Irish and Jewish diasporas without claiming a neat parallel or equivalence between them, thus rearticulating the Irish–Jewish parallel of anticolonial Irish discourse, but in a less complimentary register. The first articulation of diasporic mourning is that of the citizen, who laments, "Where are our missing twenty millions of Irish should be here today instead of four, our lost tribes?" (*Ulysses*, 267). Although the citizen professes no kinship with the Jews, his language suggests that he cannot help but make sense of the Irish experience of forced emigration by appealing to the narrative of Jewish forced emigration from ancient Israel after the Assyrian conquest. Joyce's sentence structure, which syntactically dislocates the Jewish allusion "our lost tribes" from "our missing twenty millions of Irish," captures both the conscious severance of which the citizen speaks and the unconscious similarity that Irish and Jewish self-definitions assume, once displacement becomes central to both their histories. The citizen's unwitting imbrications of the Irish and the Israelites continue when he declares that "those who came to the land of the free remember the land of bondage" (270). Here, "the land of bondage" blends the British Empire with Egypt, as again the language through which the citizen conveys his sentiments ripples beyond them.[49]

The citizen's xenophobic nationalism lays the groundwork for Bloom's equally problematic universalism, in which he flattens out disparate histories of persecution into a kind of universal law of civilization ("Perpetuating national hatred among nations"). While their opposing philosophies take center stage in a pub debate, the adulterations and redundancies of their apposing speech arguably adds some substance to Bloom's infamously vacuous definition of a nation as "the same people living in the same place. . . . Or also living in different places" (*Ulysses*, 271–272). Although Bloom manages to say very little with this definition, in the context of the conversation, the repetition and oscillation over place further crosshatch the diasporic scattering of the Jews and the Irish begun by the citizen's speech patterns. In other words, Joyce's rhetorical flourishes, by undermining his characters, also prevent them from just recapitulating the logic of national parallels and universal histories. Rather, their speech reminds us how specific histories intersect and how that might lead actual people to intersect, in a very concrete sense, in a fight over politics at Kiernan's tavern:

> —And I belong to a race too, says Bloom, that is hated and persecuted. Also now. This very moment. This very instant.
>
> Gob, he near burnt his fingers with the butt of his old cigar.
>
> —Robbed, says he. Plundered. Insulted. Persecuted. Taking what belongs to us by right. At this very moment, says he, putting up his fist, sold by auction off in Morocco like slaves or cattle.
>
> —Are you talking about the new Jerusalem? says the citizen.
>
> —I'm talking about injustice, says Bloom.
>
> (273)

Given the progression of this passage, it is easy to think that Bloom's anger is intense, but primarily vicarious, as he bears witness to the distant suffering of his fellows. However, Bloom's insistence on the presentness of the persecution hints at a more immediate context—the pub itself, in which he has been repeatedly subjected to anti-Semitic barbs and in which his expression of Jewish solidarity is itself an agitated displacement of his previously uncountenanced Irish solidarity. The redundancy of "This very moment. This very instant . . . this very moment" ties near and far sites of Jewish persecution together to establish a diasporic *meanwhile* that traverses the diasporic *meanwhile* of the citizen's "greater Ireland beyond the sea" (270).

Although the patrons refuse to entertain the possibility that the Irish and the Jews are overlapping peoples, it is the unexpected resonance between the citizen's and Bloom's mourning of their missing tribes that allows Joyce to reveal the pub as much more than a place of convivial solidarity or bullying consensus, depending on your cast of mind. It is a place of circulating claims, where feelings might be shared and yet certain kinds of shared feeling go unacknowledged because they do not reproduce the polarities of distinct national and racial identities. The airing of these feelings through apposition furnishes the uneven ground upon which an inchoate Irish–Jewish solidarity might be founded, though Joyce forecloses such hope with the chapter's escalating violence and juvenile race-baiting (evidenced through citizen's anti-Semitic epithets and Bloom's pro-Semitic taunts).

Nonetheless, as with the chimeras of *Dubliners*, the impossibility of a détente between Bloom and the citizen does not invalidate the possibility that Joyce's unsparing displays of fractiousness might function as an antidote to the characters' self-deception or to the parodies' spurious displays of gentility and grandeur. By setting Bloom and the citizen up as antagonists, Joyce makes members of different racial groups palpably a part of the same time and the same place—they share a historically specific present, which revival-style parallels previously had denied to those peoples whose narratives were appropriated to illustrate the Irish plight. Joyce trades a state-centered view of international solidarity, with all its inflated pageantry, for a street-centered view of the local animosities that were, at best, unaddressed and, at worst, fomented by the impulse to claim likeness too quickly. Such a strategy of debasement exposes the hostilities that solidarity conceals, not in order to humiliate a fledgling Irish nation but to regenerate it through a sharp portrait of what it has concealed from itself.

George Bernard Shaw recognized unflinching portraiture and bitter revelation as defining features of *Ulysses*. Though he was not exactly an admirer of the Joycean aesthetic project, he understood its strategies of social reckoning and did not mince words in describing them. In a letter to Sylvia Beach, he wrote:

> I have read several fragments of *Ulysses* in its serial form. It is a revolting record of a disgusting phase of civilization; but it is a truthful one; and I should like to put a cordon round Dublin; round up every male person in it between the ages of 15 and 30; force them to

> read it; and ask them whether on reflection they could see anything amusing in all that foul mouthed foul minded derision and obscenity. To you possibly *Ulysses* may appeal as art; you are probably (you see I don't know you) a young barbarian beglamoured by the excitements and enthusiasms that art stirs up in passionate material; but to me it is all hideously real: I have walked those streets and known those shops and have heard and taken part in those conversations. . . . It is, however, some consolation to find that at last somebody has felt deeply enough about it to face the horror of writing it all down and using his literary genius to force people to face it. In Ireland they try to make a cat cleanly by rubbing its nose in its own filth. Mr. Joyce has tried the same treatment on the human subject. I hope it may prove successful.[50]

For Shaw, there is a stark line between appealing art and the "revolting record" of Dublin that *Ulysses* provides. Indeed, it seems as though Shaw refuses to see art in the "hideously real," despite acknowledging the "literary genius" required to evoke it. Shaw is right about Joyce's penchant for confrontation, but he is wrong to characterize him as a joyless disciplinarian of "the human subject." Joycean obscenity and derision lampoon social pieties more than they enforce them. Unable to look fondly upon the "foul mouthed foul minded," Shaw sees only rebuke in *Ulysses*, but Joyce clearly derives humor, sensitivity, and pathos from the cruelty of his characters' many failed social interactions.

This is evident in the conclusion to "Cyclops," when Bloom, fleeing from the escalating threat of physical violence, ascends to "the glory of the brightness . . . like a shot off a shovel" (*Ulysses*, 282). The prospect that "even Him, ben Bloom Elijah" could rise above the melee beneath is emotionally as well as literally uplifting. Readers experience Bloom's escape, however silly, as a triumph, and yet, in sharing Bloom's triumph, we cannot quite make peace with its terms. This is not only because Bloom transcends conflict in ridiculous fashion; it is because the conflict at the heart of the episode remains unreconciled. Suspicion and misunderstanding among individuals devolves into explicit hatred between groups. To think that Bloom's ascension could solve the problems that "Cyclops" raises is wishful thinking at best.

The chimeric ending to "Cyclops" is both comic and tragic; it pursues transcendence while poking fun at it and leaves unanswered the violence in its wake. Such irresolution, though, is not entirely obscure. The incongruities of "Cyclops" resurface in subsequent episodes and cast light upon the major failed friendship of the book—between Bloom and Stephen. "Eumaeus" and "Ithaca" join Bloom and Stephen in symbolic, even cosmic, filiation; however, they mar that long-awaited filiation with scenes of social awkwardness and antagonism. Miscommunication, condescension, boredom, and anti-Semitic insult punctuate Bloom and Stephen's encounter. Their relationship (though not nearly as hostile as that of Bloom and the citizen) thus reprises some of the social and moral blindness of "Cyclops."

"Eumaeus" features Bloom at his most pedantic and socially obtuse as he continually makes overtures to a demonstrably recalcitrant Stephen. The episode revisits the violence at Barney Kiernan's pub as Bloom remembers his fight with the citizen and his declaration, in response to the anti-Semitic remarks hurled against him, that Christ was a Jew. Bloom tells Stephen this story to advertise his own cool forbearance, but the episode's description of him reveals an aching vulnerability: "He turned a long you are wrong gaze on Stephen of timorous dark pride . . . with a glance also of entreaty for he seemed to glean in a kind of way that it wasn't all exactly" (*Ulysses*, 525).

What the infelicitous narrative voice tropes here is "the meaningful glance," the look that expresses Bloom's need for Stephen's friendship. Unfortunately, Stephen remains "noncommittal," withholding the recognition and consensus for which Bloom yearns. As Margot Norris has argued, Bloom chooses Stephen as his only confidante, recounting the story of his persecution to him in "Eumaeus" while omitting it in his nighttime conversation with Molly in "Ithaca." Nonetheless, as Norris rightly points out, the much-anticipated encounter of "Eumaeus" culminates in the failure of reciprocity between the two men: the conversation between Stephen and Bloom "has clearly been asymmetrical with Stephen barely listening and consequently unresponsive."[51] The memory of the altercation in "Cyclops" serves to deflate readers' hopes that the climactic meeting of Bloom and Stephen will be a communion of souls. Instead of showing us the mutuality of friendship, Joyce gives us the asymmetry of Bloom's overeagerness and Stephen's aloofness.

As "Eumaeus" gives way to "Ithaca," Bloom's longing for mutuality permeates the episode's literary form and seems to become the driving wish of the episode itself. The opening to "Ithaca" presents Bloom and Stephen as a duumvirate, an alliance of two people sharing power and authority equally. The balance of this relation is compounded by the catechistic form of the episode, with its neat pairings of questions and answers. "Ithaca," in contradistinction to "Cyclops," emphasizes symmetry over asymmetry, correspondence over deviation, consummation over irresolution. The Linati schema lists its technics as "dialogue, pacified style, fusion," but the pacified style of "Ithaca" tries to engineer a friendship where a foundation for it does not really exist. Bloom's and Stephen's pas de deux is summarily halted by Stephen's singing of the anti-Semitic ballad "Little Harry Hughes." Not only is the song, in which a Jewish girl beheads a Christian boy, an abuse of Bloom's hospitality, but also its singing interrupts the generous exchange of Irish and Hebrew lessons that leads up to it. Just as visions of Irish and Jewish diaspora come together only to drive individuals apart in "Cyclops," the brief linguistic accord of "Ithaca" conjures a Hebraic–Hibernian bond only to dismiss it. When Stephen's chant of "Little Harry Hughes" meets Bloom's chant of the Hebrew anthem "Hatikvah" ("The Hope"), the catechistic structure of "Ithaca" becomes catechrestic. Stephen responds to Bloom's call improperly. In place of a song of solidarity, he substitutes one of unexpected and disturbing cruelty. This turn of events is profoundly unsentimental and illustrates Joyce's refusal of filial unification despite the symbolic design of *Ulysses*.

Homosocial hostilities, broken bonds, and derailed friendships lie at the core of *Ulysses*. They tie personal wounds to collective ones and are the primary motifs through which Joyce expresses his distrust of solidarity's healing powers. "Cyclops" is well known as the episode in which Joyce criticizes the exclusivist construction of national bonds, but it is also the episode in which he rejects the overweening pretensions of the "European family" and "universal love" (*Ulysses*, 267, 273). Such anticommunitarianism, seemingly as politically inert as the barely articulated protests punctuating *Dubliners*, nonetheless has a role to play in the cultivation of modernist internationalism—if not always as a mode of cooperation, then as a mode of inquiry into the available vocabularies of political agency and self-assertion.

As Joyce sought to achieve a "just sense of comparison" in his fiction, he arrived at alternating strategies of asymmetry that splintered and reaggregated the kinds of conflict in which Irish people were implicated. He also diversified the language of opposition available to them. His formal satire diminishes the uplifting claims of national parallelism, but the force of his dark comedy and light tragedy is far from nihilistic. It stems from the serious conviction that supplying the social coherence one claims to rediscover bypasses the difficult confrontations necessary for mediating as well as professing solidarity with others.

Joyce's scrutiny of nationalist and internationalist myths and his exacting attention to the forms of self-deception and self-knowledge they produce are of enduring value to the work of dissecting narratives of political unification. Such narratives prioritize the development of common ground, either through the invention of tradition, civilizational principles, or racialized continuity, in order to unite disparate peoples in a common cause. Nonetheless, a common cause does not always entail common sacrifice or common profit, nor does it guarantee similar rates of advancement to those who pledge themselves to it. The odd angles of Joyce's "nookshotten" fiction—the unequal foils, chimeric epiphanies, tropes of disproportion, and appositional arrangements—lend comparative perspective to the residual inequalities and exclusions haunting nationalist and transnationalist projects of unification, from postcolonial Ireland to the new Europe. Their mix of insurgent emotion and meticulous questioning anticipates the work of later writers, such as Michael Ondaatje and Zadie Smith, whose own chimeras of form will distinguish the ambivalent ties that bind specific collectivities from the facile connectivity that marks a triumphal globalism.

3

STORIES WITHOUT PLOTS

The Nomadic Collectivism of Claude McKay and George Lamming

> Banjo had no plan, no set purpose, no single object in coming to Marseilles. It was the port that seamen talked about—the marvelous, dangerous, attractive, big, wide-open port. And he wanted only to get there.
> —Claude McKay, *Banjo: A Story Without a Plot*

> Someone had posted me a book called *The Living Novel* and I read it as though by habit, page after page, for several hours. The Novel was alive, though dead. This freedom was simply dead.
> —George Lamming, *The Emigrants*

The August 17, 2013, issue of the *Economist* contained an obituary for Nicolae Gheorghe, sociologist and human rights advocate for the Roma people. Faced with summing up a life, the obituary strings together a number of possible identities:

> "Nomad" was a good word for Nicolae Gheorghe. He was always on the move, with his worldly goods strapped to his back. . . . "Cosmopolitan" would have suited him, too. He could perch happily in Geneva, Helsinki, Warsaw or Washington. . . . Or you could call him "gypsy." After all, that was what he called himself, when pushed to give an identity. There was no denying it: both his parents were gypsies; you could see it, he admitted, in his slightly darker skin and thick lips, which his schoolmates mocked him for.[1]

Gheorghe's itinerancy suffuses the article and highlights the disjunctions of privilege associated with individuals on the move (cosmopolitans) and collectives on the move (gypsies). Gheorghe's life's work was to close that gap. His filiation with the gypsies, a racial inheritance marked on the body in early life, became an embraced affiliation later on, a chosen identity. The Roma's nomadism, their deracination, for Gheorghe, was a feature of their collective identity that defied national paradigms of citizenship and demanded new ways of thinking about international political community.

The European Union has been one such experiment in concrete international citizenship, even if it has proven difficult to substantiate the still-fledging category of belonging known as "European" with collective feeling, much less with rights and protection for a deracinated population such as the Roma. A 1995 resolution by the European Council declared the Roma a "transnational people," a phrase that could well be taken as a romanticized version of statelessness but that I think confronts us with a conceptual category worth exploring.[2] How can we adapt prevailing notions of belonging to a transnational people? How do nonnormative, nomadic subjects—the Roma, guest workers, refugees—test normative conceptions of citizenry?

Philosophers, political scientists, and activists for a more democratic internationalism readily admit that nation-based models of citizenship cannot accommodate migratory groups without conceiving of them as a crisis or a threat, because migration is tacitly understood as a right of the individual, not of groups. Étienne Balibar calls this phenomenon "international individualism" and argues that it is enshrined in the assumptions and declarations of international law. Citing the Universal Declaration of Human Rights, Balibar argues that the institutionalization of human rights relied on a feedback loop between individuals and collectives, wherein one pole, the individual, became the bearer of rights and the other pole, the collective, became the political body that must recognize rights. This body is the state, which in practical terms, reduces more diverse kinds of collectivity (for example, diasporic or continental) to the nation. International individualism creates the common-sense logic that associates travel or circulation with the individual, and immobility or permanence with collective membership in a nation. No matter where an individual goes, he cannot change his national citizenship without extreme effort and often long-term residence in the country of choice.

Balibar's theorization of transnational citizenship begins by contesting the national equation of community with the territorialization of groups. It proposes a counterlogic, *civitas vaga*, "a citizenship of the roads and the changing places," which takes *movement*, *wandering*, and *circulation* as the keywords for rethinking "the philosophical character of the citizen."[3]

These are also the words that must be conceived of as rights—for example, the right to circulate—if "a transnational people" is to be more than a euphemism for (nation-)statelessness.

Though the novel is not the arena in which rights are invented or distributed, it is certainly the one in which the bearer of those rights, the individual, was created and given character. As Joseph Slaughter has argued, the bildungsroman and human rights law are symbiotic narrative forms in which the former creates and refines a model of the individual's relationship to the collective, which the law in turn ratifies and redeploys. The classic or realist bildungsroman "novelizes" citizenship through a particular organizational model: plot. Plot, ideologically speaking, is a technology of social incorporation in which potentially problematic individuals are reformed and absorbed into a society that is representative of the nation-state.

"Constitutive, rather than derivative," of character, plot designates the series of events over which the novel's protagonist matures into adulthood and develops the capacity for rational self-government.[4] Such a capacity, as Nancy Armstrong has argued, is defined by the simultaneous assertion and restraint of individuality. The problematic individual, or what she calls (via Louis Althusser) the "bad subject," becomes the "good citizen" by subordinating his passions and self-interest to the common good of a society. He does this by internalizing "bourgeois morality," namely those qualities of sincerity and cooperation that we have to come to associate with authentic personhood. Once the bad subject has learned the self-restraint of the good citizen, he is also ready to be a good subject of the state. He gladly trades freedom and mobility for property and protection. As Armstrong puts it, "an individual's willingness to stay in his place is what gives him moral value" in the eyes of the state.[5]

Armstrong's idiomatic formulation of discipline not only explains the origin of the citizen-subject's place within a state apparatus; it also discloses the role of territoriality in producing the citizen. Part of "staying in his place" requires staying in place. To set down roots and to own property become essential to expressing an innate spirit of communal responsibility. These classical characteristics of liberal individualism gel well with the nation-state's territorial norms, and their residual effects are what make residence rather than border crossing seem like the necessary basis of belonging itself. However, if we understand this theory of belonging as ideologically national rather than universally true, then it becomes possible to see alternatives to liberal nationalist models of belonging that precede and support Balibar's *civitas vaga.* Such alternatives, to which Balibar has not linked his own work but which deserve mention, have been richly theorized by scholars working under the rubrics of African diaspora studies and transnational blackness.

Paul Gilroy and Carole Boyce Davies were among the first scholars to note the limitation of nation-centered paradigms for theorizing black collectivity, and they have offered concepts such as the Black Atlantic and migratory subjectivity as tools for identifying forms of diasporic belonging in the face of systematic political exclusion from the nation-state.[6] In the groundbreaking *The Practice of Diaspora,* Brent Edwards extends their work by tracing diaspora through the material linkages of print culture. His focus on the mobility not just of peoples but also of texts reminds us that ties to the African diaspora, far from being static and consistent, are forged through mobility and, often, mistranslation. He coins the term *décalage* to capture the unevenness that haunts all attempts to articulate a unified racial belonging.[7] Such approaches supply a refined vocabulary for theorizing collectivity out of the crucible of fugivity and deterritorialization.

Though scholars such as Gilroy, Davies, and Edwards refrain from endorsing a normative model of transnational citizenship, I build on their critical insights as part of the ongoing project of bridging divides between black cultural studies and modernist studies.[8] Studies of transnational blackness and black internationalism have, given their object of study, tended to affirm a specifically racial solidarity even as they acknowledge the discrepant histories and linguistic differences that fissure the African diaspora.[9] Black thought forms a countercurrent to European narratives of modernity, and the oppositional potential of blackness derives from its exteriority to European epistemologies.

In bringing the lessons of black internationalism to bear on my own conception of modernist internationalism, I argue that experimental black writing actually anticipates cosmopolitical models of European belonging, rather than remaining perpetually outside them. If such writing is regarded as speaking only to or for the African diaspora, its susceptibility to routine marginalization or, worse, absorption into universal theories without awareness or acknowledgment, increases. In an effort to work against such patterns of intellectual separatism, I show that twenty-first-century theories of transnational citizenship, like Balibar's *civitas vaga,* find their own symbiotic literary form in the "plotless" novels of Claude McKay and George Lamming. These novels rejected the politics and style of realism for creating illusions of order, which they perceived to be disjunctive with modern black experience. Instead, these authors used the material of linguistic idiom and, in particular, narrative organization to redesign the novel around those racialized practices of nomadism—vagabondage and emigration—that stymied liberal-national models of individuality and territorialized belonging. McKay's vagabonds and Lamming's emigrants are "inter-national" subjects in the sense of "between nations, belonging nowhere." Unable to integrate into Europe's national communities, their exclusion becomes the ground from which they both disrupt and make their claim upon the philosophical character of the citizen. Depicting belonging under transient conditions and drawing out the double standards of imperial versus national citizenship, McKay and Lamming move the novel away from international individualism and toward the expression of nomadic collectivism. They do this by using stories without plots to address vagabondage and emigration not just as the activities of characters but also as the activities of narrative form.

Claude McKay and George Lamming are rarely read together. Their migratory paths (McKay arrived in New York in 1914, after a brief residence in Charleston; Lamming went to London in 1950) and age differences (McKay died in 1948, five years before Lamming published his first novel) have led critics to view them as part of different national traditions and literary periods, despite their common ancestry in the British Caribbean. McKay is more often discussed as a Harlem Renaissance writer than as a colonial writer. In turn, Lamming's post-1950s production has resulted in his canonization as a postcolonial writer, despite the fact that his most well-received early novels were written in Britain in the decade before decolonization.[10] However, the separation of McKay and Lamming into separate national traditions (American versus West Indian) and historical moments (colonial versus postcolonial) misses, first, the ways in which these writers' careers traversed multiple geographies, and, second, the role that colonial deracination played in both writers' turns toward international socialism, their breaks from official political organizations, and their elaboration of experimental aesthetics explicitly founded on modernist notions of the artist in exile.

The McKay and Lamming who emerge in this chapter are both migrant writers who contest the conflation of bourgeois morality with the capacity to self-govern and who reject the partitioning of citizenship from deracination as fundamentally overlooking the historical experience of British imperial citizenship for subjects of color. Their generational differences do not fundamentally separate their aesthetic projects, even if they inflect their sense of political possibility. McKay, writing in the 1920s and 1930s, did not yet identify colonial emancipation with national sovereignty, as Lamming would in the 1950s.[11] Yet McKay's fascination with the ephemeral and pointedly derelict collectivities of Harlem and Marseilles lays the groundwork for emancipation from the prefabrications of plot, understood as both a conventional literary form and a conservative social attitude. His desultory style dismantles the dyad of self-governing individuality and territorially enclosed community, which casts the citizen in both a liberal and national mold. Lamming's novels of the 1950s, particularly *The Emigrants*, need to be understood as inheritors of McKay's "plotless" modernism, even if Lamming is not known to be especially influenced by McKay's works. Both understand the cancellation of plot as a literary path toward rethinking the structure of social ties across geographic and political boundaries. Their stories without plots are thus also stories about internationalizing citizenship.

Deviant Plotlessness

Heather Love has described "modernity's others" as those rendered ineligible or perpetually behind Kantian progress narratives that culminate in the birth of a rational-critical citizen.[12] By turning away from the heteronormative development plot of the bildungsroman, these "others" refuse to abide by the stable order of time that it creates. Rather, they call attention to the simultaneity of modernism's tropes of pastness, such as primitivism, tradition, and folklore, with its tropes of futurism, such as technology, progress, and civilization. McKay's commitment to stories without plots reflects his commitment to the modernism of modernity's others, and he uses the novel as a vehicle for turning that which is marked as both primitive and deviant (blackness) toward the pursuit of aesthetic and political novelty. In McKay's novels, the formal device of plotlessness serves the intellectual purpose of rethinking the attitudes associated with political responsibility and communal belonging within the racialized context of political exclusion and spiritual statelessness.

Claude McKay became an American citizen in 1940, but his most creative periods are characterized by peripatetic wandering from Jamaica to the United States to Europe and finally to North Africa, where he finished writing *Banjo*. Critics have disputed McKay's identity as a Jamaican or American writer, but it is rarely noted that he spent much of his life under the technical legal status of a British subject. To paraphrase a line from *Banjo*, describing the immigration status of the vagabonds, his affective status was "nationality doubtful." McKay, like Joyce, was more likely to fly by the nets of communal belonging than to get tied up within them. Yet, unlike Joyce, who left Ireland in the name of artistic exile, McKay imagined himself doubly exiled by the "deracinated ancestry" of New World black communities in the Caribbean and United States.[13] McKay felt deracinated at birth, and this paradoxical sense of uprooted nativity led him to define home as a site of changeable affinities rather than filial piety. *Home to Harlem* (1928) establishes this motif in his work, but rather than following a model of incorporation typical of both the classic bildungsroman and the coming-to-America tale, the novel defines artistic maturity through his protagonist's continued flight beyond the community that would inspire him.

Home to Harlem, much like Joyce's *A Portrait of the Artist as a Young Man*, presents itself as a *Künstlerroman*, a splinter genre of the bildungsroman in which artistic readiness is at odds with communal subordination. Refusing the constraints of bourgeois morality and the carrots of institutional success, Stephen, in book IV of *Portrait*, decides to fall, to fall utterly. The biblical connotations of the word *fall* align Stephen with the devil, but the downward trajectory also suggests that artistic maturity might rest on a commitment to immaturity by the standards of polite society. *Home to Harlem* takes the notion of a fall into artistry even further than *Portrait* does, as its protagonist, the immigrant-artist Ray, finds succor in Harlem's underworld.

Home to Harlem aligns artistic flowering not just with aesthetic individualism but also with the ignobly decadent and antisocial figures of the Harlem underworld—the pimps, sex workers, drug addicts, and impoverished members of society who fail to meet the requirements of bourgeois morality or responsible citizenship. Indeed, the novel vacillates between aligning Ray with Harlem's great unwashed and separating him into a pantheon of cosmopolitan artists:

> Dreams of patterns of words achieving form. What would he [Ray] ever do with the words he had acquired? Were they adequate to tell the thoughts he felt, describe the impressions that reached him vividly? What were men making of words now? During the war he had been startled by James Joyce in *The Little Review.* Sherwood Anderson had reached him with *Winesburg, Ohio.* He had read, fascinated, all that D. H. Lawrence published. And wondered if there was not a great Lawrence reservoir of words too terrible and too terrifying for nice printing. Henri Barbusse's *Le Feu* burnt like a flame in his memory. Ray loved the book because it was such a grand, anti-romantic presentation of mind and behavior in that hell-pit of life. And literature, story-telling, had little interest for him now if thought and feeling did not wrestle and sprawl with appetite and dark desire all over the pages.[14]

In this passage, Ray encodes biographical anxieties about growing up into the universal aesthetic language of "achieving form." Attaining mature reason and retaining immature "appetite" are allegorized as in the distinction between achieved form and the ongoing "wrestle and sprawl" of dispersed "patterns."

It is significant that McKay's description of Ray's artistic ambition as "patterns of words achieving form" ironizes his dream of maturation by presenting itself in the grammatically incomplete form of a sentence fragment. McKay's syntactic contradiction suggests that the energy of Ray's art will come from the overturning of a progressive temporal narrative in which patterns coalesce into forms. Rather, he must recognize patterns as always already formed, signs of the modes of organization that reside within the putatively formless. "Patterns," syntactically and socially, signals something extra that the future promise of "form" threatens to extinguish. Not quite whole and not quite assimilated into Ray's maturation plot, it marks an excess order that asserts itself before the proper time. One might call such aesthetic order underdeveloped or immature, but as with McKay's precursors Joyce and Lawrence, it is the pursuit of experience in the absence of maturity that characterizes the artist's defiant heroism and his self-doubt.

While Ray reflects on the risks of pursuing art that is only half-formed, McKay turns the novel into a genre for the promotion of a deliberately immature aesthetics that can capture the energy and vigor of black lifeworlds that do not aspire to cultural assimilation. Michael North has written vividly of McKay's poetry as the genre in which his own drama of assimilation and estrangement played out. Made famous by the dialect poems *Songs of Jamaica* (1912) and *Constab Ballads* (1912), McKay saw the pernicious effects of writing in Jamaican dialect. The poems were received not as art but the spontaneous expression of a primitive voice. In attempts to move away from such ethnographic definition, McKay turned to conventional forms and standard English in his later collections *Spring in New Hampshire* (1920) and *Harlem Shadows* (1922), which, despite their profusion of traditional English sonnets, still resulted in his presentation as a "stuffed exhibit" for white readers.[15]

If the turn to highly regulated forms in poetry had no effect on shattering stereotypes of black primitivism, McKay's turn to prose suggests a change in the attitude of the author. No longer interested in meeting or defying white expectations, McKay saw prose as affording possibilities different from those of poetry. In *Home to Harlem* and *Banjo: A Story Without a Plot* he experimented with the dyad of form and formlessness that he found particular to the medium. The attractions of prose lay in the vagueness of its form and the precision of its idiom. This lack of alignment allowed it to elude the developmental scale from primitivism to modernity—or, in biographical time, childishness to adulthood—that McKay's poetic trajectory from dialect to sonnet had come to illustrate. The contradictions of "a story without a plot" further captured the double meaning of deracination, as McKay's novels focused on characters without loyalty to a physical territory (i.e., a plot of land) or lives scripted by the expectations of others.

A negative theory of literary form makes explicit in its perversity what North calls "the spiritual truancy" of modernist expatriate writing.[16] Unlike North, though, McKay yokes that truancy to the pursuit of black collectivity outside the political structures and confinements of the nation-state. McKay makes deracination the property of a group rather than the dream of the individual. In turn, he reinvents the modernist artist not as a heroic iconoclast in solitary flight from the collective but as a kind of Moses, leading his collective into exile from the nation.

Spiritual truancy looked like juvenile irresponsibility to McKay's critics. W. E. B. Du Bois saw in McKay something of the Pied Piper, and his famously negative review of *Home to Harlem* made no separation between the novel's immature aesthetics and its immoral politics. That Du Bois judged McKay's novels to be immoral for their uninhibited content is common knowledge; that he regarded them corrupt because of their form, or supposed lack thereof, is less often observed. Du Bois feared that McKay's depiction of the Harlem underworld pandered to "that prurient demand on the part of white folk for a portrayal in Negroes of that utter licentiousness which conventional civilization holds white folk back from enjoying."[17]

Du Bois's review, steeped in the politics of positive imagery, expressed a fear that the novel's examination of decadence and vice would only reaffirm stereotypes of black irrationality and excess. This danger was compounded by what Du Bois perceived to be the formal grotesqueness of *Home to Harlem*, which he describes as both "padded" and deprived of "any artistic unity." By organizing his criticisms of worldly excess in the language of formal excess, Du Bois articulates a conservative politics of style that understands aesthetic conventions as vehicles of racial integration and uplift. His demand for temperance from a future project is expressed in terms of a desire not just for proper content but also for proper form. He desires from McKay a novel with a "strong, well-knit as well as beautiful theme." In other words, a novel streamlined by plot.

McKay's riposte to Du Bois is now as well known as the review of *Home to Harlem* itself. In it, he embraces his own "utter absence of restraint" and defends excess as a tactic of social critique aimed not at pleasing the white world but at defying the need for their recognition. Whereas Du Bois and other black reviewers demanded a homogenized and sanitizing portrait of the black community in the name of fostering racial uplift, McKay sought out its diversity, its rivalries, and its internal spectrum of skin colors and nationalities in the service of a more cosmopolitan, less ascetic socialism. Despite having broken with various socialist organizations and the international communist movement by the time of its publication, McKay cited *Home to Harlem* as a "real proletarian novel."[18] In addition, as Shane Vogel notes, McKay used the novel to pursue solidarities across working-class and "submerged tenth" lines, rather than incorporating the lower classes into the bourgeois morality of upward mobility.[19]

I agree with Vogel that McKay deviated from the assimilationist policy of the black bourgeoisie in the name of more flexible definitions of racial and sexual identity; however, I would add that such deviation also arose from a fundamental questioning of the structures of collective consciousness. If McKay was committed to race as a category that the individual could not transcend, he was equally committed to testing race as the grounds for an obligatory solidarity. In an essay for the *New York Herald-Tribune* entitled "A Negro Writer to His Critics" (1932), he speaks of political consciousness as paralyzing: "From all this I should say we are floundering in a mass of race, color, national consciousness and all the correlative consciousnesses. Besides, many of us who are trying to see and live tolerantly and temperately are worried of a guilty conscience. White and colored."[20] Tolerance and temperance, McKay goes on to argue, are virtues that black uplift narratives demand but that depend upon the castigation of the most poor and vulnerable within a society. Imagining and indulging in decadence is McKay's way of contesting a social ladder that denigrates those who have not yet or may never climb it: "poor minorities, especially the colored who often find it rubbed into them that their state is due to their lack of 'white' virtues." McKay does not envision minorities transcending the markers of group identity, but he does object to Du Bois's amalgamation of collectivity and morality because it contributes to the fiction of "'white' virtue" that he is out to explode.

Banjo doubles down on McKay's project of unsanitized representation and plotless form, as it shifts settings from Harlem, New York, to the Ditch, a bohemian neighborhood in Marseilles, France, which, as James Smethurst notes, becomes "for McKay the true international capital of the modern Negro World that [Alain] Locke claimed Harlem to be." Like *Home to Harlem*, *Banjo* rejects a racial consciousness modeled on virtue and cleansed of the "wrestle and sprawl" of submerged life-worlds. Its formal design produced another round of reviews, this time in English and French, that linked its immorality to its perceived formlessness. Dewey Jones, in a *Chicago Defender* review entitled "Dirt," declared the novel's protagonists to be enrapt with laziness: "a group of tramp sailors who prefer loafing and bumming to working and earning an honest dime." André Levinson, for the French periodical *Nouvelles Littéraires*, portrayed the vagabonds as free riders in the "land of plenty," whose unstructured lives are reflected by McKay's unstructured tale: "*Banjo* is not properly a novel; it is a suite of episodes haphazardly arranged [alignés au hasard]" to offer a "literal reproduction" of black sociability.[21]

Because Levinson sees *Banjo* as a transcription of black life rather than an artful re-creation, he does not think to array McKay's "invertebrate tale" with other modernist novels accused of indecency and plotlessness, such as, for example, Joyce's *Ulysses*. At times, however, Levinson observes the richness of McKay's idiom and the difficulty of its style, in a language redolent of modernism: "The verbal material is dense and colorful. But the language in which these new black novels [les nouveaux romans nègres] are written becomes an obstacle to their diffusion. . . . The phonetic transcription of speech, with its curious deformations, turns out an illegible scrawl [*grimoire*] that one can hardly decipher."[22]

Levinson's choice of words in the French is felicitous not for the opinions it expresses but for the exclusive politics of literariness that it reveals. The innovations of "les nouveaux romans nègres" are recoded as sociological transcription, and their aesthetic difficulty is recoded as *grimoire*, or utter illegibility, with a primitivist subtext. In French, *grimoire* functions as a figure of speech connoting incomprehensibility; its meaning derives from the standard definition of a grimoire as a magician's manual for practicing spells, invoking demons, and contacting the dead. Charles Baudelaire invoked the grimoire as a metaphor for poetry's enchantments,[23] yet Levinson uses it to reinforce the distance between black writing and deliberate formal experimentation.

Still, Levinson unwittingly furnishes a modernist vocabulary for understanding McKay's pursuit of calculated illegibility. The etymological roots of *grimoire* lie in the Old French *gramaire*, or "grammar." Its dynamic semantic history reminds us that even the most devalued and debased forms of knowledge carry within them a system of rules governing their composition. McKay's novel may have featured the "illegible scrawl" of an unfamiliar black vernacular, but its real foreignness arose in its negative structural grammar for organizing the sprawl of the African diaspora. A story without a plot, *Banjo* foregrounds *lack* as the common ground of an international collectivity characterized by its dispersal and deterritorialization.

Finding a new grammar for the novel is no easy task, especially when plot is understood as interchangeable with grammar itself. Peter Brooks has defined plot as the novel's "syntax," the way in which its events are ordered and arranged to produce its constituent parts. This syntax further conveys a "certain way of speaking our understanding of the world," meaning that a novel's plot does not just tell a fictional story.[24] It denotes a formal organization that is always already an interpretive process. Although particular plots may vary in complexity, the need for plot, according to Brooks, reflects a human need for the kind of meaning that can only be achieved through narrative.

Brooks's argument depends on the meanings that narrative generates and connects to the finite structure of plot—its identifiable beginnings, middles, and ends. Indeed, the "subterranean logic" that Brooks claims unifies plot's heterogeneous definitions as physical territory and literary design is the "idea of boundedness, demarcation, the drawing of lines to mark off and order. . . . From the organized space, plot becomes the organizing line, demarcating and diagramming that which was previously undifferentiated."[25] Brooks's spatial geometry helps to explain plot's power as a cognitive tool that both produces divisions and makes those divisions easier to see. In constantly differentiating space over time, plot brings the world of the novel into being. The movement of plots toward their meaningful completion is what leads Brooks to call them "not simply organizing structures" but "intentional structures, goal-oriented and forward-moving."

Although Brooks does not use the term, his understanding of plot is dialectical in that the novel emerges as the totality of plot's developmental process. Plot's movement sublates any elements of disorder within its larger structure, and it arrives at meaning through achieving the "idea of boundedness" that spurred its movement. The dialectical engine of plot is precisely what *Banjo* sets out to disable with its promise of plotless storytelling. Its grammar is not dialectical but anecdotal, not progressive and conserving in its narrative momentum but pulsating and expending in its exposition.

Levinson recognizes these attributes of *Banjo*, but he is obviously mystified by their implications when he describes the novel as "not a novel, but a suite of episodes aligned at random, of detached chapters that one by one crumble away into anecdotal dust."[26] As Levinson oscillates between "n'est pas proprement un roman" (not properly a novel) and "nouveau roman nègre" (new black novel), we see how *Banjo* reactivates definitional debates about the novel by transforming the propulsions of narrative desire into the disintegration of narrative structure. What Levinson reads as the novel's random and crumbling architecture, McKay uses to display the subject formation of the vagabond, whose vagrancy furnishes the novel with a new spatial and temporal scheme. In the opening pages of *Banjo*, McKay introduces the vagabond as a vital, if overlooked, painter of modern life:

> Banjo was a great vagabond of lowly life. He was a child of the Cotton Belt, but he had wandered all over America. His life was a dream of vagabondage that he was perpetually pursuing and realizing in odd ways, always incomplete but never unsatisfactory. He had worked at all the easily-picked-up jobs—longshoreman, porter, factory worker, farm hand, seaman. Seized by the old restlessness for a sea change while he was working in an industrial plant, he hit upon the unique plan of getting himself deported.
>
> (*Banjo*, 11)

The sensation of restlessness in the face of a monotonous and mechanical industrial modernity is one of the most commonly identified affective states of modernist literature. Deportation is without doubt one of the rarer solutions. Unlike Stephen's exile in *A Portrait of the Artist as a Young Man* or the expatriation of so many modernist writers, deportation fully and openly implicates the state in the direction of a person's life. Banjo, like his author McKay, understands the intimate association of international wandering with border policing and turns it to his advantage. Not having the financial means to wander, Banjo criminalizes himself, ascending to greatness as a vagabond by willfully descending into statelessness.

Pursuing a life "always incomplete but never unsatisfactory" clearly differentiates the restless vagabond from the proto-citizen-subject of the realist bildungsroman, for whom achieving one's destiny is bound up in finding an appropriate resting place or niche within their community. More surprisingly, it also revises what Jed Esty has defined as the distended or frozen youth of the modernist bildungsroman. Whereas, for Esty, a modernist protagonist's prolonged youth is a symptomatic condition of imperial modernity's failed progress narrative, for McKay, youthfulness is a dispositional politics of survival in the face of perpetually adverse conditions.

Banjo is organized not around endless youth but around an internationalism of endless youthfulness. Vagabond conviviality consists of dancing, drinking, and debating—practices of energy expenditure rather than of conservation. As these open-ended practices accumulate, their "anecdotal dust" establishes the vagabond as both a product of state surveillance and a subject position decidedly indifferent to the state's disciplinary mechanisms. The novel's plotless structure asserts the value of unconserved, unsynthesized time. It heeds those interactions and experiences that, in their ephemerality and triviality, test the norms of continuity, seriousness, and growth that align plot development with the birth of the bourgeois individual. In disrupting the temporality of maturation, *Banjo* adapts the novel form to those motley and heterogeneous others who persevere on the other side of citizenship. Far from a series of "random adventures,"[27] it generates patterns of banding and disbanding that furnish the rhythm of illegality to what Du Bois called, in his more positive review of *Banjo*, McKay's "international philosophy of the Negro."[28]

McKay's decision to embrace vagabondage as a portmanteau internationalist identity privileges a set of behaviors (vagabonding) as a response to the historical conditions of deracination and dispossession (bondage). The subject position, in refusing to be race-specific, brought black internationalism into conversation with the broader anticolonialism of the non-European world. Further, in refusing to be heroically oppositional, vagabondage provides insight into the ramshackle subcultures of capitalist modernity:

> Commerce! Of all words the most magical. The timbre, color, form, the strength and grandeur of it. Triumphant over all human and natural obstacles, sublime yet forever going hand in hand with the bitch, Bawdy. In all relationships, between nations, between individuals, between little peoples and big peoples, progressive and primitive, the two lovers spread and flourish together as if one were the inevitable complement of the other.
>
> (*Banjo*, 307)

The unbreakable compact between commerce and bawdiness, capitalism and vagabondage, is central to McKay's international philosophy. The shameless "Bawdy," unlike Du Bois's dignified "Negro," personifies a counterculture immorality that is structural rather than racial and residual rather than reabsorbed into capitalism's ruthless cycles of accumulation. Like gadflies, bawds and vagabonds encapsulate the ambiguous agency of subcultural others. More irritating than threatening, their power lies not in revolutionizing or overturning Western civilization but in bearing accurate witness to it. By flourishing alongside modernity as its seamy underside, McKay's vagabonds remain unconsumed by it. They are its shadow class rather than its aspirants.

McKay ties his broad critique of capitalist modernity to legal regimes of imperial nation-states in which immorality is defined not by wasting time but by wasting space. Nomadic existences are both guaranteed and punished by state apparatuses that deny transient populations the right to claim nationality without documentation:

> Colored seamen who had lived their lives in the great careless tradition, and had lost their papers in low-down places to touts, hold-up men, and passport fabricators, and were unable or too ignorant to show exact proof of their birthplace, were furnished with new "Nationality Doubtful" papers. West Africans, East Africans, South Africans, West Indians, Arabs, and Indians—they were all mixed up together. . . . They were agreed that the British authorities were using every device to get all the colored seamen out of Britain and keep them out, so that white men should have their jobs.
>
> (*Banjo*, 312)

The passage clarifies the institutional racism informing Banjo's preference for deportation. Europe's immigration laws reclassify "colored seaman" as stateless men. With their nationalities stripped away, vagabondage becomes a form of what William J. Maxwell wryly calls "state-sponsored transnationalism," in which enforced transience replaces national belonging as a site of shared culture.[29] Vagabondage produces paracollectivities of amorphous nationalities and races whose documented illegibility McKay builds into the novel as grimoire form. *Banjo* renders itself a dubious document in the course of refashioning the novel's syntax to speak in the idiom of the detained.

Diversionary Tactics

In treating vagabondage as an escape bred of constraint, McKay refrains from romanticizing a precarious internationalism while also stopping short of subordinating diverse existences to militant projects of political transformation. McKay's embrace of vagabondage is often seen as continuous with his break from the organized politics of international socialism in the early 1920s, but the substitution of vagabond for activist operates under the tacit assumption that his literary projects supplanted political ones. An anecdote from McKay's correspondence corrects this misperception and establishes an important political motivation for advertising *Banjo* as a story without a plot.

While in Russia attending the fourth congress of the Communist International, McKay was drafting a collection of essays entitled *Negroes in America*, which criticized American radicals' marginalization of race within the class struggle. His friend and patron Max Eastman responded that McKay's qualms were both overblown and blind to the larger strategic picture of socialism. He asked if McKay were living in "the practical 'scientific' era of Lenin or the age of Thomas Paine." McKay replied, "If you had in your whole body an ounce of the vitality that Paine had in his little finger, you with your wonderful opportunities, would not have missed the chances for great leadership in the class struggle that was yours in America."[30]

McKay's defense of Paine's implied utopianism as "vitality" tells us something about the enervation and closed-mindedness he associated with the institutions of international socialism. What Eastman saw as a dispute only about race, McKay saw as exemplary of a larger dispute about outlook. Eastman subordinated diverse identities to one goal, whereas McKay argued that diverting attention to those marginalized by radical internationalism's drive had the potential to change the political goals of that movement for the better. McKay was willing to divert the plot of Marxist politics in the name of addressing the heterogeneous concerns of those who comprised its constituency.[31]

As Leela Gandhi has argued, the divide between scientific and utopian socialism was often articulated through a rhetoric of maturity. When Eastman accused McKay of impracticality, he was following in the footsteps of a scientific socialism that rebranded the ideology as one of discipline and unity rather than of pleasure and promiscuity. Whereas Edward Carpenter once argued for "the wealth and variety of affectional possibilities" within socialism, influential leaders such as Henry Hyndman, Friedrich Engels, and Vladimir Lenin dismissed such logic as chaotically trivial and eclectic.[32] Their "scientific" approach replaced such juvenile and consequently chimeric utopianism with strategies of centralization and a consistent definition of the proletariat. Hyndman, leader of the Social Democrat Federation (Britain's first socialist political party), observed that socialism could no longer be a "depository of odd cranks: humanitarians, vegetarians, anti-vivisectionists, anti-vaccinationists, arty-crafties . . . sentimentalists. They confuse the story."[33] Hyndman's phrasing reminds us that socialism is a story, and that disputes over that story's protagonists and plot reflect disputes over the achievement of its ends. When McKay faced continued membership in a movement that coded race as trivial and multiple loyalties as immature, he chose to articulate an alternative socialist internationalism in a modernist idiom that courted confusion (a story without a plot) and enabled the profusion of vagabond protagonists who are nothing if not contradictory and changeable in their affections.

Banjo turns to vagabondage out of a principled refusal to delimit the discourse of the political by the extant categories of the utopian and scientific. Although it may be tempting to read the novel as immature or naive in its fondness for transitory communities, I (like Brent Edwards) understand the novel's restlessness as immanent to the institutions of modernity—commerce, labor, immigration law—that would deform black existence in the process of regulating it. Edwards persuasively argues that "vagabond internationalism" illustrates the author's suspicion of any clear-cut attempts to promote a consistent racial consciousness across the various divides of nationality, language, accent, or shades of color. He sees the novel as mounting, on the one hand, a "radical critique of black internationalism" and, on the other, a chimeric renovation of it in which the novel's one model of collective possibility—the orchestra—becomes a paradoxically anti-institutional vision of the "dream to institutionalize black internationalism." The dream of an orchestra remains a chimera because Banjo fails to assemble a group with any permanent members or profit potential, yet his "obliviousness to wage and profit seems to be not just absentmindedness but actually inherent in the aesthetic" of vagabond life. The peripatetic nature of vagabondage—its intrinsic impermanence—would seem to exclude characters like Banjo and his friends from any kind of recognizable political community, but their exclusion activates another model of community, in which casual musical collaborations or "jam sessions" reveal music as one of the ways in which "community is performed."[34]

Edwards's reading of *Banjo* derives the alternative collective potential of music from its spiritual dimensions—its ability to cut through the prevailing logic of territorialized community while also signifying a kind of transcendental resting place beyond the strictures of institutionalized group membership. Building on this reading, it would seem that the presence of music in the novel is representative of more than just an escapist fantasy; its chimeras are tactical mediums of diversion. By playing music (and talking about playing music), McKay's vagabonds are able to rethink the affects, dispositions, and persons associated with normative political belonging and action. They introduce elements of friendly dispute, confusion, and vagrancy into black internationalism's somber conversations about class conflict, racial uplift, and positive imagery. As a result, they challenge respectability politics and scientific socialist discipline as the only indexes of political seriousness.

Banjo partners music and narrative in ways that show the discomfiting proximity between taking apart a stereotype and participating in its perpetuation. Broad allegory tempts us to read the central friendship of the novel, between the musically nicknamed Banjo (whose legal name is Lincoln Agrippa Daily) and the writer Ray (the same character as in *Home to Harlem*), as a display of opposites, lyric and narrative, attracting. Yet McKay uses Banjo's ambition of forming an orchestra to complicate the friendship by setting up a chiastic relationship between his central characters. The usually free-spirited, "prepolitical" Banjo displays premeditation and focus: "Banjo dreamed constantly of forming an orchestra, and the boys listened incredulously when he talked about it. He had many ideas of beginning" (*Banjo*, 19). Meanwhile, the agonized, intellectual Ray displays spontaneity and distraction:

> "But you're interested in race—I mean race advancement aren't you?" Goosey asked Ray.
>
> "Sure, but right now there's nothing in the world so interesting to me as Banjo and his orchestra."
>
> (92)

In the last lines of a chapter called "The Flute-Boy," Ray avoids a conversation about race to pursue a conversation about music, building on Banjo's earlier dismissal of Goosey's suggestion that a black band needs a stereotype-defying flute to replace the stereotype-affirming banjo. Ray's and Banjo's politically disrespectable decisions become critical diversions for McKay, who, in suspending the exhausting (and exhausted) conversation about racial imagery and advancement, refreshes its logic by following his protagonists' lead. He brings focus to a practice all about diversion: partying.[35]

One of the best-known chapters from *Banjo*, "Jelly Roll," couples some of McKay's more primitivist and ethnographic writing with his depictions of revelry and carousing, giving rise to the commonplace notion that he is partaking in stereotypes of African peoples as wilder and more passionate than their restrained and consequently more civilized European counterparts. Yet the atmosphere of "wildin' out" that he creates is deeply structured by narrative and syntactical diversions that entangle music and money, racial mixture and commercial mixture, into a sly commentary on the symmetries of civilization and savagery. When McKay ends "The Flute-Boy" with a diversion from race to music, he guides readers back to the beginning of "Jelly Roll," which diverts us from jazz to money:

> Shake That Thing. The opening of the Café African by a Senegalese had brought all the joy-lovers of the darkest color together to shake that thing. Never was there such a big black-throated guzzling of red wine, white wine, and close, indiscriminate jazzing of all the Negroes of Marseilles.
>
> For the Negro-Negroid population of the town divides sharply into two groups. The Martiniquans and the Guadeloupans, regarding themselves as constituting the dark flower of all Marianne's blacks, make a little aristocracy of themselves. The Madagascans with their cousins from the little dots of islands around their big island and the North African Negroes, whom the pure Arabs despise, fall somewhere between the Martiniquans and the Senegalese, who are the savages. Senegalese is the geographically inaccurate term generally used to designate all the Negroes from the different parts of French West Africa.
>
> The magic thing had brought all shades and grades of Negroes together. Money.
>
> (*Banjo*, 45)

The major diversion in this passage is executed through a bait-and-switch of jazz for money, made possible by the ambiguity of the phrase "the magic thing." Yet there are minor diversions as well: the presence of a second paragraph, which slows the movement from jazz to money, and, within that paragraph, a meeting up of inconsistent sensibilities. The declarative fixities of sociology ("For the Negro-Negroid population of the town divides sharply into two groups") mix with the anecdotal editorializing of a neighborhood gossip ("make a little aristocracy of themselves" and "whom the pure Arabs despise") to make the line between sincere and parodic ethnography quite blurry.

The paragraph's jostling tones suggest that the party is underway in McKay's narrative voice before the music officially starts. The purpose of their diversion is to infiltrate and make flexible the fixities and hierarchies of black society, not to abandon them, as "indiscriminate jazzing" would suggest. Jostling tones connect jousting currencies: sociology and anecdote; the jazzing that levels social distinctions and the money that creates them. Layering diversion upon diversion, *Banjo* makes music of narrative, and narrative of music. Its blending of mediums reveals primitivism to be an artifact of modernity and black "vitality" to be an expression of the felt mortality of a precarious existence in a commerce-driven world.

That mortality is pervasive in the chapter's repeated, increasingly agitated refrain of "Shake That Thing." As the vagabond party moves from the café to what seems to be a brothel, described as "a showy love shop," Banjo and his makeshift band replay the song, a version of the hit "Jelly Roll Blues." Its lyrics occasionally interrupt the narrative, initially complementing the action and then delving into its more painful motivations. They start cheerfully in the vein of sex ("Old Uncle Jack, the jelly-roll king / Just got back from shaking that thing!") and wandering ("Dry land will nevah be my land, / Gimme a wet wide-open land for mine"), but then quickly darken, in a shift from adventurous virility to sickness and death ("Old Brother Mose is sick in bed / Doctor says he is almost dead"). The song's story ends with a shift back to cheer, this time in a clear display of bravado ("dead / from shaking that thing") (*Banjo*, 49–52).

Although first and foremost a euphemism for sex, it is worth pointing out the history of black objectification and forced labor is very much present in the imperative "Shake that thing!" The double meaning bundles the opposing tendencies toward freedom and manipulation that Sianne Ngai has identified with the racialized affect animation. Animation, closely associated with the stereotype of hyperexpressivity (a stereotype that McKay was thought to be reproducing), conjures complex notions of agency by fusing "signs of the body's subjection to power with signs of its ostensive freedom."[36] The lyrics to "Shake That Thing" are a reminder of the "thingification" of black bodies and the diversions—sex and migration—that rejuvenate them. The reclaiming of "thingness" in song reminds us of the circumscribed freedom of the vagabonds, whose hypermobility is conditioned by the history of black subjection and forced labor.

Banjo conveys the pressures of inter-national nomadism through various kinds of compressed syntactical and orthographical innovations, achieving the grimoire, or modernist idiom that Levinson called merely transcription and utterly illegible. Puns like "youse sure one eggsigirating spade" (*Banjo*, 55) play on the homophonic nearness of *exaggerate* and *gyrate*, as well as the double meaning of *spade* as a tool and as a derogatory signifier of blackness. The sentence spoken in response to speculations about violent crime in the Ditch conjures the double vision of salacious dancing and the coiled sensation of being under constant threat. A reduction of the song's lyrics to "Back . . . thing . . . bed . . . black . . . dead . . . Oh, shake that thing . . . Jelly-r-o-o-o-o-oll!" (54) summons a nightmarish vision of objecthood's return—"back . . . thing; black . . . dead"—and a plea for recreation as a form of re-creation in response. The braiding of black vitality with black mortality becomes even more explicit at the end of the chapter, when McKay allows the song lyrics to permeate the main narrative as a series of commands: "Shake down Death and forget his commerce, his purpose, his haunting presence in a great shaking orgy. Dance down the Death of these days, the Death of these ways in jungle jazzing, Orient wriggling, civilized stepping" (57). In these lines, frenzy clearly has a both an existential and a political purpose. Far from a return to savage instinct or regression away from modernity, it is a strategy immanent to the modern, a way of surviving "these days, these ways."

What looks like primitivism in McKay can be read as a riposte to the logic of civilization—one shared by avant-garde philosophers such as George Bataille. Bataille's interest in jazz in the interwar years arose out of his reading of it as an "excretion," a sound for those elements that would not or could not be assimilated into metropolitan narratives of idealism or progress.[37] Bataille assigned to black music the dissident work of decomposing civilization from within:

> To the extent that blacks participate in revolutionary emancipation, the attainment of socialism will bring them the possibility of all

> kinds of exchanges with white people, but in conditions radically different from those experienced by the civilized blacks of America. Now black communities, once liberated from all superstition as from all oppression, represent in relation to heterology [Bataille's philosophical doctrine] not only the possibility but the necessity of an adequate organization. All organizations that have ecstasy and frenzy as their goal (the spectacular death of animals, partial tortures, orgiastic dances, etc.) will have no reason to disappear when a heterological conception of human life is substituted for the primitive conception; they can only transform themselves while they spread, under the violent impetus of a moral doctrine of white origin, taught to blacks by all those whites who have become aware of the abominable inhibitions governing their race's communities. It is only starting from this collusion of European scientific theory with black practice that institutions can develop which will serve as the final outlets (with no other limitations than those of human strength) for the urges required today by worldwide society's fiery and bloody Revolution.[38]

Bataille's critique of capitalist civilization is undoubtedly couched in all sorts of troubling assumptions and essentialisms, beginning with the notion that "ecstasy and frenzy" are the "goals" of black "organization." Yet he is worth hearing out for the ways in which he interiorizes and embodies external and structural oppressions. Note the odd use of the word *inhibitions* to characterize the exploitation and restriction of black communities worldwide, and the transposition of an ideological goal, "the attainment of socialism," into the domain of "urge" fulfillment. The porousness between individual repression and collective oppression is clear within Bataille's reasoning, and it is useful for mediating McKay's own understanding of musical ecstasy as a form of interior experience and exterior organization that must be shared among the vagabonds of the Ditch before more politically legible kinds of internationalism can be imagined.

What makes Bataille and McKay so interesting together is their shared conviction that "ecstasy and frenzy" constitute affective states that are also forms of communication among strangers. For Bataille, the communication that takes place in a state of ecstasy is paradoxically one of shared anguish in which the rational-critical self is shattered by the suffering of another. As Amy Hollywood argues, in Bataille's controversial meditation on a photograph of a Chinese man being tortured, the philosopher seeks communion with the object of his gaze so that he might obliterate the subject–object relationship altogether in a state of ecstasy that he calls "inner experience."[39] In this case, Bataille's inner experience comes with certain costs that should not be dismissed lightly: the erasure of the Chinese man's historical difference and the annexation of his suffering for Bataille's own ends. In seeking a communication that veers dangerously toward a perceived communion, Bataille's ecstasy obliterates strangeness.

For McKay, ecstasy temporarily levels hierarchies, but it does not absorb intraracial and international differences. It arises from their friction. Even as McKay uses ecstasy to confront ongoing historical anguish with a "great shaking orgy," he does not pretend that such a confrontation will breed the strong bonds of a black cultural nationalism. Rather, ecstasy complicates black nationalist or Pan-African desires for a unifying origin story, because it generates not just a loss of individual consciousness but also a collective self-shattering of racial consciousness. Such uplifting and politically progressive phrases as "the race" and "race man" give way to the syntactic shattering of "Back . . . thing . . . bed . . . black . . . dead." The subjectless anguish of ecstasy communicates the horrors of black mortality across "all shades and grades" of international difference.

The ecstasy of internationalism for McKay, then, lies in the proliferation and sustenance of insubordinate difference, even in proximity to that most universal condition: death. His impulse not to eradicate difference but to extend it invites a solidarity that goes beyond racial unity. "Jungle jazzing, Orient wriggling, [and] civilized stepping" all become ways of maneuvering within modernity's confinements and, on an existential level, confronting finitude itself: "Sweet dancing thing of primitive joy, perverse pleasure, prostitute ways, many-colored variations of the rhythm, savage, barbaric, refined—eternal rhythm of the mysterious, magical, magnificent—the dance divine of life" (*Banjo*, 57–58).

In the closing lines of the chapter "Jelly Roll," the collective aggregation and self-shattering of ecstasy gives way to the birth of a new kind of language in the novel, rooted in the reorganization of parallel structures. The perfect parallelism of racialized dances ("jungle jazzing, Orient wriggling, civilized stepping") leads into the blurred and irregular division of particularized and universal abstractions. "Sweet dancing thing of primitive joy, perverse pleasure, prostitute ways" bleeds into "many-colored variations of the rhythm, savage, barbaric, refined" and "eternal rhythm of the mysterious, magical, magnificent." The shift from the ethnographic classifications of dance to the antimimetic culmination of "the dance divine of life" invites the reader into the experience of ecstasy as a kind of rebirth through which it becomes easier to see the interpenetration of word, movement, and world. Fixed classifications like "jungle jazzing" are neither innate nor mapped onto a preexisting material world. They are fictions, which are also variations on civilization's rhythm of development. McKay searches for an alternative rhythm in ecstasy by replacing the mystery of God or an imagined other with the mystery of survival, "the dance divine of life."

Beyond the experience of ecstasy in music and dance, the lasting record of an alternative rhythm within black internationalism is the grimoire form of *Banjo* itself. McKay writes without an ideal community, a utopia, on the horizon—no nation, no Pan-African continent, no territorialized place can contain the African diaspora or the even more differentiated collectivity of "colored seamen" that populate a commerce-driven world. Even ideational categories such as "blackness" or "colored," which would try to establish the foundational unities for such being, become undesirable as the novel veers further away from recognizable modes of political organization. In the absence of knowing or believing in an object of desire, the novel runs on without a plot. It also runs away from domestication of any kind.

The final conversation of the novel, between Banjo and Ray, makes the evasion of heteronormative maturity and the pursuit of fugitivity explicit: "Don't get soft ovah any one wimmens, pardner. Tha's you' big weakness. A woman is a conjunction. . . . Come on pardner. Wese got enough between us to beat it a long ways from here" (*Banjo*, 326). A partnership built on subjunctive possibility and sustained by desire without rest is, McKay suggests, both a chimeric alternative to the territorialization of modernity's shadow classes and a description of their actually existing internationalism. The unlikely partnership affords unique purchase on the monstrosities of modernity and on the nomadic strategies of sociability used to survive them. McKay's grimoire is no doubt a gendered grammar, in which women are not merely excluded but definitive of the entire system of values that Ray and Banjo wish to escape. Nonetheless, the partnership born within the novel might also be extended to the reader. The final line's direct address asks the reader to "Come on pardner," makes explicit an invitation that has been present all along. It is the perfect textual stopping point for a vagabond novel that promises to continue onward without end.

Banjo is a story without a plot because it teaches us to understand desire differently. No longer the expression of a rational-critical subject motivated by the pursuit of an object (the kind of desire that shapes the bourgeois individual), the desire of the vagabond subject is without limit and without achievement. Something is missing, to invoke the dialogue that Ernst Bloch and Theodor Adorno staged on the concept of utopia, but it is precisely the missing part—the amputation of plot—that produces hope.[40] The ending of *Banjo* delays Ray's dream in *Home to Harlem* of "achieving form," via its open-ended invitation to the reader and its refusal of the consummations implied by the double meaning of *conjunction* (first, as a stabilizing form of connection, and second, more obscurely, as a state of union in marriage). Discounting both the household and the territorialized homeland as sites of black incorporation and liberation, McKay replaces the equilibrium of a marriage plot with the unspoken possibilities of transnational male friendship.[41]

McKay's conviction that one might articulate a bond while remaining in motion is a key insight for building deracination and circulation into the citizen's philosophical character. Rather than preserve the citizenship norm that every person must be born into and thus have a single country, *Banjo* uses the inter-national character of the vagabond to bring the lives of others to bear on what Seyla Benhabib, in her study of the modern institutions that produce certain categories of people only to make them into outcasts, calls "the rights of others."[42] "Others," in its deliberate amorphousness, refers to aliens, refugees, and deportees who, in having no country and residing across many, are written into illegibility by border-policing regimes. *Banjo* converts that enforced illegibility into a principle of internationalist expression. It shows that narratives of good citizenship rely on notions of individual responsibility that can be destructive in their self-righteousness and tone-deafness to the needs of pariah populations. By articulating a rhythm, order, and idiom for paranational life, *Banjo* holds out the possibility that vagabond culture might challenge the plot of citizenship to encompass habitation without roots.

Plotless Suspense—Waiting in *The Emigrants*

Banjo introduces the reader to the dark conditions of global illegality, and, through them, articulates a denationalized ethos necessary for conceiving solidarity in more deterritorialized terms. George Lamming's *The Emigrants* continues McKay's project of finding a narrative form for the perpetual deracination of black subjects, and it takes us a step closer to incorporating the restlessness of the vagabond into a renovated philosophy of the citizen. Lamming's emigrant occupies an intermediary subject position between the vagabond and the citizen—one that does not altogether reject the liberal development plot but instead radically distends and disorients it to produce a thoroughgoing criticism of the bourgeois individual as model citizen. His protagonists, who literally are West Indian migrants on their way to England, figuratively represent colonial subjects' paralysis within the waiting room of history. Lamming uses the space of the novel to dramatize their confrontation with time, and, like McKay, he uses the fundamentally unstable dwellings of black transient life as generative grounds for thinking beyond colonialism's authorized categories of being and behavior.

McKay, writing in 1928, did not yet foresee the possibility of Caribbean decolonization, but Lamming saw the realization of an independent West Indies Federation as a concrete way of bringing the negative history of black deracination back into the positive production of West Indian citizens. Whereas McKay's experimentations in plot negation accompany a rejection of sedentary, nationalized belonging, Lamming's dismantling of plot reflects an attempt to make readers more comfortable with discontinuous and uprooted forms of connection. Adapting to such connections enabled Lamming to reclaim the traumatic history of the African diaspora as the basis for a regional sense of belonging that was crucial to the exceptional geographic space of the Caribbean.

Lamming knew that the greatest challenge a future West Indian nation would face was its members' refusal to put the federated islands' needs above the interests of any one particular island. He saw literature, particularly the novel, as a unique space in which to transform the anxieties of the waiting room of history into opportunities for imagining a new kind of nation populated by an unprecedented kind of citizenry. Composed not of international individuals (recall Balibar's argument about individualism) but of a transnational people, Lamming's ideal citizenry would refuse to take territorial rootedness as the most natural criterion for communal belonging.

The challenge of reconciling deracination with populism is not easily overcome, especially because Lamming, like McKay, strove to circumvent the individualism of the liberal cosmopolitan tradition. Yet he found a way, by restructuring the novel around collective protagonists: the village in his first novel, *In the Castle of My Skin*, and the emigrants in *The Emigrants*. In his 1983 introduction to *Castle*, Lamming wrote that collectivism was what made Caribbean writing distinct:

> The book is crowded with names and people, and although each character is accorded a most vivid presence and force of personality, we are rarely concerned with the prolonged exploration of an individual consciousness. It is the collective human substance of the Village itself which commands our attention. The Village, you might say, is the central character . . .
>
> Where community, and not person, is the central character, things are never so tidy as critics would like. There is often no discernible plot, no coherent line of events with a clear, causal connection. Nor is there a central individual consciousness where we focus attention, and through which we can be guided reliably by a logical succession of events.[43]

Lamming's retrospective theorization of the techniques in *Castle* speaks just as well, if not better, to *The Emigrants*, which lacks a central character to rival G and represents a stronger incarnation of the ambition articulated above. Lamming's narrative collectivism sought to alter the novel form dramatically by subordinating the maturation of any individual character to the life cycle of the group. The result is a story without a plot and without legible centers of consciousness, but it is also a new kind of novel, which judges the contours of life differently from the European novel. Rather than capturing life through a series of developmental stages or through the pattern of impressions on the mind, Lamming makes the novel live (to paraphrase the present chapter's second epigraph) by dispersing its faculties of attention and timekeeping to account for a community's emergence in the absence of an omniscient narrator or overseer. The result is a paratactic and disjunctive narrative form that, in withholding the unities of time and space, subjects even the most localized examples of community, whether the Village or the emigrant ship, to radical disruption.

Lamming's commitment to delocalizing Caribbean aesthetics allows him to inscribe into group identity alienation—a negative attribute, by most standards of collective consciousness, but an important one for releasing the West Indian novelist from what he calls "peasant" writing:

> Writers like [Sam] Selvon and Vic Reid—key novelists for understanding the literacy and social situation in the West Indies—are essentially peasant. I don't care what jobs they did before; what kind or grade of education they got in their different islands; they never really left the land that once claimed their ancestors like trees. That's a great difference between the West Indian novelist and his contemporary in England. For peasants simply don't respond and see like middle-class people. The peasant tongue has its own rhythms which are Selvon's and Reid's rhythms; and no artifice of technique, no sophisticated gimmicks leading to the mutilation of form, can achieve the specific taste and sound of Selvon's prose.[44]

One may disagree with Lamming's assessment of Selvon and Reid, but what is important to note is how his definition of "peasant" shapes his antipathy to it. For Lamming, being a peasant is not simply a condition of birth; it is marked by imperviousness to rupture. Such imperviousness may insulate West Indian writing from the pain of migration, but in failing to allow migration to alter the novel's structures of feeling, it misses an opportunity to challenge island provincialism. The "peasant tongue" is defined by emotional sedentariness ("they never really left the land") and organic similes ("claimed their ancestors like trees"). Its feeling of rootedness, which may indeed be a misapprehension, is nonetheless what Lamming's own version of populist consciousness sets out to deracinate.

Despite the hint of negativity toward formal experimentation here ("no artifice of technique, no sophisticated gimmicks"), Lamming pursues his own version of grimoire aesthetics through "the mutilation of form" in *The Emigrants*. Mutilation serves as a way of asserting national consciousness in the face of island provincialism. In order to imagine a West Indianness that could compete with the micronational loyalties of a Jamaican, a Barbadian, an Antiguan, etc., Lamming had to think transnationally about nationhood. Like the European Union today, the West Indies Federation demanded an alignment of multiple loyalties. Even more challenging, however, was the fractured geography of the Caribbean archipelago. The island's geographic boundaries presented physical enclosures that could easily give way to affective enclosures. "Mutilation," with its etymological origins in the cutting or breaking off of a body part, proved a rich metaphor for retrieving a history of the Caribbean that island localism had repressed.

The Emigrants formalizes mutilation by replacing the cause-and-effect sequencing of plot, in which a "pleasant voyage" leads to a "safe arrival," with narrative dead zones or black holes that signal the danger of the emigrants' journey in terms of voided understanding transplanting a desired illumination.[45] The novel's tripartite structure grafts together three sections. Section I, "The Voyage," chronicles the emigrants' journey from the Caribbean archipelago to the shores of England. This portion of the novel is almost the same length as section II ("Rooms and Residents") and section III ("Another Time") combined. The latter sections trace the alienation of the emigrants in London and the ultimate breakdown of their relationships and senses of self. Between each section, an unspecified amount of time passes and the narrative changes centers of consciousness, from an unidentifiable "I" narrator to a third-person external narrator and back again. These blatantly textual effects effectively translate the emigrants' disorientation to the reader, who is invited to experience the resonance of voyage and void, the passage of time and paralysis, that is essential to the temporality of migration. They also disrupt the illusion of psychic wholeness that the pronoun *I* has come to represent through the tradition of the novel.

Unabashedly critical of the liberal fiction of an autonomous, coherent self, the novel dispenses with its first-person narrator as the first condition of narrating the deracinated "we" of West Indian identity. The "I," who is invested with no backstory or biographical markers, is a placeholder for individuality rather than a psychologically fleshed-out person. Upon observing a Good Friday Mass, "I" martyrs himself in a speech act that sets up a guiding tension in the novel between abstract personhood and embodied being: "I understood the mourning of this day's death, but the resurrection which was not a pure assertion of spirit but an equal ascension of blood and bones had given the *body* a new meaning. . . . Father Into Thy *Hands* I Commend My *Spirit*" (*Emigrants*, 24; emphasis his).

Lamming's dissolution of "I" alongside the ceremony of the Good Friday Mass suggests that he wants to rewrite the abstractions of subjectivity through the concreteness of the body. The narrator suggests that the Crucifixion is a ritual whose value lies in restoring corporeality to spirituality ("an equal ascension of blood and bones"; "hands" cupping "spirit"). Lamming uses religion to blur the spirit–body distinction. Christian ritual contests liberal rationalism and draws attention to the body as the expelled remainder of abstract individuality.

Wilson Harris, another Caribbean modernist, helps to explain the poetics implicit within Lamming's crucified "I" when he reminds us of the material body animating any spiritual metaphor of black existence. Where Lamming featured a Christian ritual, Harris calls forth specifically African rituals that put Lamming's mutilations into the wider context of black Atlantic history: "*Limbo* and *vodun* are variables of an underworld imagination—variables of phantom *limb* and *void* and a nucleus of strategems in which *limb* is a legitimate pun on *limbo*, *void* on *vodun*" (emphasis his).[46] The slightly imperfect homophonic pun of *void* and *vodun* and homographic pun of *limb* and *limbo* become "legitimate" because each shares a common genealogy or, to continue in the vein of Harris's punning, a common route/root. The Middle Passage serves as the ancestral zone in which the slave's bodily dismemberment ("the phantom limb") and heritage loss ("void") yield cultural reassembly in forms of bodily innovation (limbo) and translated ritual (vodun).

Harris's theory of puns asserts the materiality of language as crucial to expressing the corporeal, physical traumas often judged more "real" or "worldly" than literary experimentation. It also invites, as Nathaniel Mackey argues, a renewed appraisal of diasporic deracination. Rather than attempting to regain African origins lost in the Middle Passage, Harris looks on the black Atlantic past as an "opportune disinheritance" in which the "insularity of various African peoples brought to the New World—the Ibo, Arada, Nago, Congo, and so on—was broken or dislocated."[47] Harris asks us to see the potential for beauty and cultural synthesis in his images of bodily and tribal dismemberment. Lamming takes this deracinated outlook as the bedrock of a West Indian archipelagic national consciousness and uses the transatlantic voyage to awaken the "underworld imagination" of the Middle Passage. The separate islanders' convergence around their shared history of unknown ancestry makes abjection a central part of overcoming provincialism:

> *Jamaican*: . . . This West Indies talk is w'at a class o' doctor call symptomatic. It hold more than the eye can see one time, that's why me take to lookin' into hist'ry. An hist'ry tell me that dese same West Indian people is a sort of vomit you vomit up. Was a long time back England an' France an' Spain an' all the great nations make a raid on whoever live in them islands . . . all o' them, them vomit up what them din't want, an' the vomit settle there in the Caribbean Sea. It mix up with the vomit they make Africa vomit, an' the vomit them make India vomit, an' China an' nearly every race under the sun. An' just as vomit never get back in yuh stomach, these people, most o' them, never get back where them vomit from.
>
> (*Emigrants*, 66)

This passage reflects another jarring shift in Lamming's style, from narrative form to dramatic dialogue, in which he uses the typographic conventions of a script and Caribbean vernacular to approximate immediacy in the discussions aboard the ship. The particularity of West Indian English reveals the bodily marking of language in accent and syntax, just as the language of the body begins permeating the consciousness of individual islanders. They derive a fraught unity from identifying with the body's ejections. Characters hailing from disparate islands (and labeled simply as "Jamaican," "Grenadian," etc.) experience a rebirth as "West Indian" by collectively confronting their ancestral disinheritance and making sense of it in their own voices.

Prior to these discussions, the novel's narrator had described the Caribbean as a region variegated by linguistic differences and surviving under a casual ethos of "mutual misunderstanding" (*Emigrants*, 4). It is not until its protagonists move into the open water of the Atlantic that dialogue begins and vomit emerges as a guiding metaphor for the history that might invest such misunderstandings with the pull of affection rather than suspicion. A deliberately humiliating and formless image, vomit marks a turn away from the "peasant" rhetoric of groundedness that the Jamaican had earlier used to declare himself a "pure son o' de soil" (35). Instead, it turns toward the possibility of a regional collectivity organized by a newfound understanding of the limitations of certain kinds of local perception: the West Indies "hold more than the eye can see one time." Nationalism qua regionalism redirects perception from the knowable community of a single island to the partially unknowable community of the archipelago.

Lamming's fascination with the abject and ejected as a renovated basis for regional feeling in *The Emigrants* deviates from the call to arms usually associated with anticolonial nationalism. The novel's visceral metaphors introduce negativity, shame, and finally unrequited love into its expressions of imperial dissent. Yet these putatively weak positions also make room for new insights to emerge. In the wake of the group's cold reception in the motherland, Tornado, another of the emigrants, observes:

> "Seems to me," he said, "the people here see these things from their side. They know that England got colonies an' all that, an' they hear about the people in these far away places as though it wus all a story in a book, but they never seem to understan' that these people in these places got an affection for them that is greater than that of any allies in war-time. De sort o' feeling which we as children an' those o' us who never see the light, that feelin' we got is greater than any feelin' France could have for the English or the English for France. The name o' English rouse a remembrance in us that it couldn't have for any war-time ally."
>
> (*Emigrants*, 192)

Important arguments about Lamming's anticolonialism have identified Jean-Paul Sartre as its major influence.[48] These arguments tend to emphasize the misrecognitions and perpetual estrangement that shape encounters between black and white characters in the latter half of the novel. Yet a Sartrean vocabulary that presents relationships between the colonizer and the colonized as a form of existential antagonism misses the complex affective history of the emigrants' identification with "the name o' English." As the passage unfolds, Lamming uses Tornado's vernacular to draw subtle distinctions between the discrete political communities of England and France and the imperial affective community of Englishness that rouses the emigrants' remembrance. Tornado's words show that emigrants do not aspire to be English; they thought they already were. Colonial subjects' unrequited affection, Lamming suggests, distorts the development plots that characterize conventional immigrant fiction as well as the distinct borderlines of nation-state geography.

Lauren Berlant has argued that national citizenship cultivates a "politicized intimacy," which turns borders into sites of deep emotional conflict between those inside them and those outside them.[49] When the Caribbean migrants lay claim to England under the legal category of Commonwealth citizen, only to experience a border-crossing shot through with the retraction of Englishness into a national identity, they experience the full sensation of what it means to be nationless. In choosing to title his novel *The Emigrants*, as opposed to *The Immigrants*, Lamming figuratively suggests that his collective protagonists never arrive at their destination. Regardless of each emigrant's individual status, they exist as a group in a state of perpetual displacement brought on by the affective and legal disjunctions of a geopolitical regime best understood not simply as empire but as what Gary Wilder calls the "disjointed political form" of the imperial nation-state.[50] This designation reminds us of the double standard instantiated by England's nation-state borders and the putative borderlessness of Englishness. Whereas the emigrants see continuity and intimacy between colonial subjecthood and English national belonging, natives of England, "people here," see only strangers who should stay in the shadowy realms of elsewhere.

The emigrants' doubly deracinated status—as the residue of the Atlantic slave trade and as the illegitimate heirs of the British Empire—inaugurates West Indian nationalism in a moment of uncanny repetition between the slave ship and the emigrant ship, between blacks as commodities within liberalism's market economy and blacks as inter-national subjects attempting to cross over into full English citizenship, but finding themselves denied entry. The detainment of Lamming's emigrants recalls the dubious nationality of McKay's vagabonds, whose engagement with the corporeal and the visceral also arose from an encounter with the unfulfilled promises of imperial modernity.

Both novelists' strategic layering of their protagonists' nomadic presents upon their race's traumatic past evokes Houston Baker Jr.'s notion of critical memory, which he describes as a key faculty for black modernism. Baker injects critical memory with a nostalgia for ideas rather than places, thus extending Harris's and Mackey's recuperation of deracination. Specifically, Baker suggests that fruitful nostalgia lies not in the idealization of Africa as a lost home but in the promise of the Enlightenment vision of the public sphere as a "beautiful idea." Baker contends that the public sphere represents "a historically imagined 'better time' of reason." Although black peoples can never endorse the historical implementation of this idea, they too desire a share in the idea of citizenship it represents. Fully recognizing the ironies of such nostalgia, Baker suggests that a public sphere "expressively conceived as black" must be a "strangely distorting chiasmus: a separate and inverted opposite of white rationality in action."[51]

We see this chiasmus most powerfully in Lamming's portrayal of the Caribbean folk art of calypso aboard the emigrant ship. Lamming incorporates the calypso into *The Emigrants* to contest liberalism's conception of personhood and its contributions to the creation of black objecthood. Echoing McKay's strategy of portraying dance as an ecstatic mode of collectively confronting the proximity of blackness to "thingness," Lamming uses this folk form to explore those states of ecstasy and absorption deemed without critical faculty (irrational) by "white rationality." Rather than romanticize such states' otherness to reason, however, Lamming describes them through an inverted language of liberalism in which he transposes characteristics of the autonomous mind onto the ecstatic body:

> The calypso was only the occasion, the signal, perhaps merely the excuse for dancing; but the body was the dance itself. There was neither communication nor interpretation, the deliberate control of balance that makes for movement intended to attract the other's attention, call forth the other's sympathy and be measured by a sane and deliberate judgment. The other had been annihilated. There was only the body which was the dance itself, regulated, informed, nourished and dictated not only by its blood, but by some pervasive, measureless source of being that was its own logic of receptivity and transmission, a world that could be defined only through the presence of others, yet remained in its definition absolute, free, itself. The body was part of the source of its being and at the same time its being. It was within and outside itself simultaneously.
>
> (*Emigrants*, 94)

Lamming describes the dancing body as "ecstatically alone" (93). This condition returns black bodies to themselves but deviates from the logic of possessive individualism that defines the subject in liberal political theory. In this passage, the mind does not realize its being through governing the body; rather, the body appropriates to itself the capacities of consciousness. As both "the source of its being" and "being" itself, the body usurps the mind's function in an inversion of liberal rationality that provides a brief respite from the mental anguish of colonial double consciousness. Through the body's codes, Lamming also invokes and circumvents public-sphere activities most susceptible to contamination and misrecognition: communication, interpretation, sympathy, and judgment. Alone and "free, itself" in "the presence of others," the dancing body achieves an authenticity that is felt as the closing of a void; the body is "within and outside itself simultaneously."

The calypso is Lamming's "occasion" for turning the language of disembodied reason against itself. His description prefigures Baker's claim that theories of black being and belonging cannot derive from a straightforward resuscitation of liberal principles. It also constitutes a disidentification with "the name o' English" by providing a glimpse into an alternative logic of autonomy derived from an African diasporic cultural reservoir. Lamming's use of *occasion* activates its two definitions: first as an ephemeral event, and second as a reason or cause. The latter definition is important because it suggests that the calypso is more than a brief, transcendental respite from a bleak journey; it causes—that is, it makes possible—a new meditation on black identity and self-restoration.

Accordingly, as with McKay's use of jazz in *Banjo*, musicality in *The Emigrants* cannot be cordoned off from the narrative project of immanently confronting imperial modernity and shattering its upward-mobility plot. *The Emigrants* formalizes the experience of failed immigration (and failed citizenship claims) as a narrative filled with plotless suspension rather than carried forward by individual motivations or a clear line of causality. A microcosm of the novel's principled disassembling of causal order comes in the form of Azi's letter, a fragmented narrative within a fragmented narrative that, like the calypso, reflects a withdrawal from English authority.

Azi is an African student at Cambridge who befriends some of the Caribbean emigrants in London and serves as an intellectual conduit for their alienated condition. His letter, addressed to a white Englishman and intended as a resignation from Cambridge, argues for the "insignificance of events" in compelling social or psychological change: "The same errors are committed, the same consequences crush us. But nothing really *happens*. . . . If we need things to occur before we can change, it seems that what happens is wasted on us, or nothing ever really *happens*"

(*Emigrants*, 213). Stuckness, or stasis, for Azi, is an artifact of a certain relationship to history, whose event-based organization of time dooms individuals to reactiveness rather than anticipation, to following history's plots rather than questioning its premises. The letter's comments reflect on the novel's own privileging of anticipation over action, and its form, a series of disconnected passages without an identifiable beginning or end, suggests that suspending the ordering impulses of storytelling is key to changing the stories that England has told herself and those "who are called her subjects" (106). It is impossible to know, as the novel's inscrutable narrative voice tells us, whether the fragmentation of Azi's letter is the result of excerption or an attribute of its written form. Such opacity makes wholeness indecipherable from brokenness, the mutilation of form inseparable from form's reconstruction as something new.

Lamming quotes Azi's letter in "The Negro Writer and His World," an address he gave at the First International Congress of Black Writers and Artists, held in Paris in 1956.[52] Lamming began his speech by changing his topic. He had been invited to speak on "the Negro novel in English"; instead, he spoke about what it means to be a "Negro writer." He uses the letter to privilege epistemological dilemmas above the sociological problems that he argued black writers were expected to address with both directness and transparency. Lamming argued for a novel of ideas that would not allow legible protest to evade the conflicts over storytelling and subject formation that Azi's illegible letter foregrounds. Arguably even more grimoire than *Banjo*, *The Emigrants* is a narrative marked by arrhythmias and opacities that disrupt the habitual patterns of action and aspiration that both McKay and Lamming attributed to conventional plots and their reactive modes of protest. If there is a glimmer of hope in Lamming's bleak novel, it comes with the work's turn away from event-based history and toward a confrontation with time itself.

In *The Arcades Project*, Walter Benjamin outlines modern social types via their relationship to time: "Rather than pass the time, one must invite it in. To pass the time (to kill time, expel it): the gambler. Time spills from his every pore.—To store time as a battery stores energy: the flâneur. Finally, the third type: he who waits. He takes in time and renders it up in altered form—that of expectation."[53] Benjamin's unnamed type is embodied by Lamming's emigrants, whose perpetual displacement creates a condition of endless expectation: "We were all waiting for something to happen," the narrator announces at the start of the novel (*Emigrants*, 5).

On the third day of sailing, the wait continues and grows more elaborate: "The passengers, grouped or scattered here and there, were like men standing aimlessly at crossroads waiting for something to happen, hoping however that nothing would happen except the usual things: a pleasant voyage, a safe arrival" (25). Even the final page of the novel carries expectation with it: "Something was bound to happen" (282). The endless deferral of an event, resurgent in the novel's ending, signals to the reader the heaviness of a time that does not pass but only seems to grow more static as the narrative comes to a close.

Lamming's exploration of unquenchable anticipation would, at first, seem to expose waiting's inherent anxiety and absurdity. Simon Gikandi seminally characterizes Caribbean modernism as "writing in limbo."[54] The perpetual displacement of the emigrants fits that paradigm and then takes it a step further. Lamming is writing limbo into narrative by allowing time to accumulate in the accretion of calls for an event that never arrives, until one realizes that the event is expectation itself: time rendered up in its altered form. This is why Lamming articulates the emigrant experience as a "journey to an expectation."[55]

The richly enigmatic phrase captures more than the disjunction between the ideal and real England. In the antidevelopmental plot of the novel, collective expectation supplants individual maturation as a condition of civic preparedness. The emigrants do not need to become self-governing individuals to qualify for the living freedom of West Indian national belonging. Rather, they make the West Indies imaginable by becoming conscious of a new relationship to time: expectation of an expectation. Such an experience of time unforeclosed by action, event, or object, of course, fosters the negative emotions of anxiety and dread, but these emotions also bear a more genuine relationship to the future than what Bloch calls "filled emotions."

For Bloch, filled emotions, such as jealousy or greed, have clear objects of desire, the future achievement of which is imagined from the vantage point of an unchanging present. In other words, the achievement of a future goal does not account for the fact that the future is irreducible to the variables that structure desire in the present. Filled emotions block this insight by substituting "an unreal future, i.e. one in which nothing objectively new happens." This is the future to which Azi objects in his letter when he says "The same errors are committed, the same consequences crush us. But nothing really *happens*." What Bloch calls "expectant emotions," like anxiety and hope, do not suffer from the misperception of time's passage and thus "imply a real future; in fact that of the Not-Yet, of what has objectively not yet been there."[56]

I take this to mean that seemingly objectless emotions—emotions such as anxiety, which are generalized and diffuse and consequently not very amenable to plot, understood as intention and design—can motivate unforeseen ways of being and organizing the future. Plot's distension is important because it creates the formal conditions under which the reader, like the emigrants, can experience unbounded expectancy as, paradoxically, an unexpected kind of communal feeling. Together with Lamming's protagonists, we wait for something to happen. That something, the birth of national consciousness, happens at an unexpected moment—halfway through the novel, rather than as its culmination. Jumping the gun of plot time, the emigrants redraw the affective boundaries of their island communities and find the unintended object of their wait—the West Indies—within the temporal lag of their journey.

Waiting, understood as the expectation of expectation in the ship and as an unrelenting confrontation with time beyond it, is the condition under which Lamming's protagonists discover how to think and feel West Indian. This noncathartic state has gone unexamined in postcolonial theory because of its proximity to the imperial rhetoric of colonial immaturity and unpreparedness for self-rule, metaphorized as the waiting room of history. Yet, in offering a thoroughgoing contestation of liberal individualism's developmental plot, Lamming's experiments with narrative temporality in *The Emigrants* bypass the road to sovereignty outlined by Enlightenment principles. Its plotless aesthetics forges a self-authorizing path coincident with the experiences of those collectives denied entry into England's national culture. Waiting brings the emigrants a vernacular awareness of the contradictions of the imperial nation-state and enables them to encounter deracination as the engine of, rather than the enemy of, West Indian belonging.

Civitas Vaga and le Nouveau Roman Nègre

To conceive of what Levinson called "les nouveaux romans nègres" as an aesthetic category rather than a sociological curiosity is to understand how the purposeful negation of plot enables nomadic collectivism's survival and representation in the realm of language. By altering the body of the novel, McKay and Lamming ground collectivity not on the logic of bourgeois individualism or territorial nationalism but on an aestheticized populism that reframes that bedrock phrase of democracy, "We, the people," for supranational communities: the African diaspora for McKay and the West Indies Federation for Lamming. As Balibar writes, *civitas vaga*, or a "citizenship of the roads," is not a citizenship of the world but a "citizenship in the world."[57]

Balibar's definition of the world is compositionist as opposed to metaphysical. It encompasses the "complex system of spaces and movements that form the reality of what we call 'the world.'" *Civitas vaga*, in turn, strives to meet that available reality by proposing new sets of rights and practices in keeping with it. In a globalized world that is, more than ever, conditioned by the movement of people, Balibar endorses the right to circulate freely among countries as a fundamental human right, but one that has little hope of being enforceable because of the deep-seated territorialism lodged within European conceptions of the nation and the people. Returning to the late colonial era, and to novels of nomadic blackness that turned modernism toward new ends, helps us to identify social and narrative practices that denaturalize at least two couplings related to this philosophical problem: communal bonds with sedentariness, and bourgeois morality with good citizenship.

In McKay's case, vagabondage served as a conceit for rethinking the narrative of maturity or readiness that informed imperial enterprises in Europe, scientific socialism, and racial uplift projects in the United States. In adding dereliction to the dispositions of political critique, he had no particular future political community on the horizon, but he did, like Balibar, have actually existing political regimes as his target. By releasing the vagabond into the border-policing regimes of European nations, he reveals the disciplinary mechanisms at work in rendering entire groups not only dubious but grimoire: utterly illegible from the vantage point of the state. By turning that illegibility into a principle of narrative organization, a story without a plot, he trades individual assimilation for a structural transformation perhaps never to come.

For Lamming, an aestheticized populism was vital to articulating a more positive form of belonging beyond Europe, a Caribbean regionalism that would lay the affective ground for a West Indian nation. Emigration as historical activity and novel temporality allowed him to imagine the future West Indian citizenry as a people deracinated to the root. His creation of the emigrants alters the philosophical character of the citizen by making deracination the basis of their collective bond rather than the motivation for any one member's emergent individualism.

McKay and Lamming, though members of different generations, shared a desire to write about common people in an uncommon way. Their stories without plots give definition to liberalism's occlusions by rendering narrative time and space up in the altered form of les nouveaux romans nègres. These novels adapt modernist internationalism to those peoples, spaces, and movements that the world, as the sum of its various political structures, habitually excludes but is under ever-increasing pressure to accommodate.

4

ARCHIVAL LEGENDS

National Myth and Transnational Memory in the Works of Michael Ondaatje

He understood that America completes her West only on the coast of Asia.
—Charles Olson, *Call Me Ishmael*

Tectonic slips and brutal human violence provided random time-capsules of unhistorical lives.
—Michael Ondaatje, *Anil's Ghost*

Michael Ondaatje's oeuvre has always borne a fraught relationship to the historical novel, the genre to which his most well-known works lay claim. This is because it owes as much to plunges into the perceptual fields of memory as it does to historiographical grappling with collective narratives of the past. Ondaatje's early experimental writings—for example, *The Collected Works of Billy the Kid* (1970) and *Coming Through Slaughter* (1976)—retrace the lives of historical figures (William Bonney and the jazz musician Buddy Bolden), while his most widely read novels—*The English Patient* (1992) and *Anil's Ghost* (2000)—unfold amid the conflicts of World War II and the Sri Lankan civil war. Beyond their subject matter, Ondaatje's works reflect upon history as a mode of writing and a pattern of assembly. The books' trademark style depends on the aesthetics of the fragment, which eschews representations of history as either an impersonal social force or a recoverable totality. Perhaps the most concentrated symbol of Ondaatje's unorthodox historical vision comes from *The English Patient*: a copy of Herodotus's *The Histories*, which the protagonist, Almásy, transforms into a personal archive by superimposing passages from other works, ephemera, and handwritten notes of his own desert adventures over parts of Herodotus's text. Ondaatje uses the conceit of *The Histories*-turned-scrapbook to reverse the conventional order of archive and history, a maneuver that transforms a closed book into an open one.

The most influential theorists of the archive in the past fifty years have been Michel Foucault and Jacques Derrida, both of whom have described it as an architecture of control. Foucault's seminal definition established the archive as "first the law of what can be said. . . . [It] defines at the outset the system of [a statement's] *enunciability*" (emphasis in original).[1] Such singular enunciations are always to be disrupted in Derrida's philosophy, but he too begins his theoretical foray into the archive with an emphasis on authority. Embedded into *archive*'s etymology is the root *arkhe*, which denotes both commencement and commandment.[2] Indebted as we are to the work of Foucault and Derrida, we have grown accustomed to defining the archive as preceding and determining any possible claim to history—indeed, as conferring authority upon history. Whether in print, oral, or digital mediums, and despite any actual archive being the product of collection, organization, and transmission, the idea of the archive is synonymous with beginnings.[3] Ondaatje's novels affirm this connotative truth, but they also show us something else, which subjects it to pressure: historical narratives can generate new archives.

Almásy's individualized copy of *The Histories* encapsulates what is both exciting and distressing about Ondaatje's literary treatment of history. In transforming *The Histories* from a finished narrative into an expanding archive, Ondaatje suggests that history, like modernity, is an unfinishable project and, more importantly, an unstable genre—one that will bear the imprint of personal experience, desire, and apocrypha. When Almásy turns *The Histories* into a personal archive of his desert explorations, he reveals self-indulgence, not expertise—an indulgence that some critics have argued afflicts Ondaatje as well. A recurring charge against Ondaatje is that he takes on historical topics without a historicist's eye, expressing nostalgia for the past without adequate sensitivity to the dynamics of causality and continuity that link the past to the present.[4] Indeed, with his affection for depicting fleeting impressions and aestheticized respites in the midst of violent conflicts, Ondaatje would seem to revive those elements of modernist temperament that are most associated with an evasion of political conflict through escape into the private realm of consciousness.

I agree that Ondaatje walks a fine line between romanticizing and realistically portraying the past. However, I also propose that his work occasionally overindulges speculative, phenomenological, and aesthetic engagements with the past in order to activate nostalgia's ambiguously critical potential. Recalling the etymological roots of *nostalgia* in pain and homesickness, Ranjana Khanna emphasizes its connotation of wounding over its connotation of sentimentality, and suggests the former carries an "encrypted critical relation" to its object.[5] Interlacing pain and sweetness, nostalgia does not necessarily simplify the past, nor does it guarantee that its alteration in the mind's eye will act as a refuge from rather than a response to the demands of the present. Ondaatje's novels cultivate the symbolism of symbolic landscapes—like Almásy's "half-invented" desert, but also the American West of Billy the Kid and the sacred sites turned killing fields of Sri Lanka—as a way of exploring the interface between myth and history.[6] These discourses, which typically help to define the nation by creating a shared sense of the past, perform the opposite function in Ondaatje's work: they take sharing beyond the comfortable sentimental space of bounded tradition into the wider and more diffuse networks of global collectivity.

The transnationally shared pasts that Ondaatje's novels explore are made possible by what I call his archival method. Ondaatje develops an aesthetics and philosophy of the archive that magnify the instabilities of history, myth, and memory that Almásy's scrapbooking connotes at a metaphoric level. Where Almásy turns a historical text into an archival book, Ondaatje's archival novels also display strategies that give them an open-ended, unsynthesized, and shape-shifting quality. They use the archive as structure and style not so much to demystify the ideological structures of the nation or its icons but to immerse them in a proliferation of new materials, contexts, and technologies of meaning-making that break down the very boundaries that nationalist myths shore up.

In this sense, Ondaatje's novels certainly deviate from the realist function of the historical novel that Georg Lukács called "the awakening of national sensibility"; but perhaps more surprisingly, they also exceed the label of historiographic metafiction that has long been their designation.[7] Though this generic category of postmodernism has been crucial to explaining the self-consciousness of Ondaatje's novels about the narrative dimensions of history, it does not comparably address their aesthetic investment in the proliferation or materiality of artifacts. Nor does it speak to their interest in those not-always-textual traces of memory that remain invisible within the discourses of history and thus stand as chimeras because of their oblique relation to the real. In this respect, Ondaatje's novels present a version of the archive that is not entirely wedded to the historical and that can be affectively confounding—a version reminiscent of Foucault's reencounter with the archive in his late work "The Lives of Infamous Men."

If the Foucault of *The Archaeology of Knowledge* gives us a theory of the archive as a system that determines all forms of enunciation, the Foucault of "The Lives of Infamous Men" describes an actual archive whose materials evade enunciation. In the essay, Foucault recalls a set of prison records in the Bibliothèque Nationale that contains snatches of obscure lives whose only recognition came from their encounters with power. Foucault refers to these records as "strange poems," the intensity of which derives precisely from their brevity and archival contextualization as records to be saved.[8] Foucault aestheticizes the lives of his subjects not to deny or sanitize their historical existence but to capture their contact with the present. The essay becomes a meditation on how to represent obscure lives in a way that preserves the emotional force their meagerness has upon him and that remains true to the objective meagerness of available information. He arrives at the genre of the legend.

According to Foucault, legends (like chimeras) are defined by "a certain equivocation of the fictitious and the real." Though a legend often emerges from a surplus of stories that raise a historically real person to the level of myth, it may also derive from the opposite situation, in which the absence of information about a life effectively derealizes it, relegating it (as opposed to elevating it) to the status of myth. The archive thus becomes a space from which legends might emerge alongside histories, and it is in this respect that Ondaatje's archival method differentiates his work from the historical novel in its realist and metafictional modes. It is precisely because Ondaatje is as interested in mythography as he is in historiography that his works are able to dissect the stories that nations tell to define themselves not just as communities evolving over time but as communities that derive character, shape, and purpose from a particular understanding and performance of their origins. His archival method vivifies the reductions and remainders, which accompany the transformation of stored artifacts and fragments into stories with semantic power.[9]

In contending with the necessity for and limits of synthesis in the making of collective narratives, whether national or international, Ondaatje's archival method revives the epistemological quandaries that I have associated with Tagore's modernist methods of compilation and translation. Both writers see their work as intervening in the construction (and reconstruction) not just of national origin stories but also of stories of international relation and perception. By emphasizing the relationship between the transmission of content (across languages, media, and discursive register) and its solidification into meaningful and usable knowledge forms, Ondaatje shows that an archival sensibility that embraces rather than rejects chimeras is essential to engaging debates about national renovation and international justice.

The Collected Works of Billy the Kid and *Anil's Ghost* serve to exemplify Ondaatje's archival method as it develops around two very different kinds of chimeric national legends: the historical figure William Bonney who became the mythical antihero Billy the Kid, and the skeleton Sailor—an unidentified victim of state terror who comes to represent the "unhistorical lives" lost during Sri Lanka's civil war.[10] These legends—Billy the Kid in the conventional sense of an embellished identity, Sailor in the obscure sense of Foucault's infamous men—become flashpoints of collective definition in the novels as they reinscribe American and Sri Lankan national pasts within networks of transnational memory.

In *Collected Works*, Ondaatje transforms Billy from a national icon to a global one, working against the imperialist strains of frontier mythology and contemporary nativist strains of cultural property to present a mythology of the Wild West that arises from beyond an American discourse of national character. In turn, in *Anil's Ghost*, "Sailor," the skeletal remains of an unidentified victim, becomes the center of debates about how to read and rectify human rights abuses by the Sri Lankan state during the nation's civil war—whether by seeking justice in the legal-historical realm or by pursuing national reconstruction through the renovation of communal myths. The novel balances the struggles of the former path with the limitations of the latter, contextualizing the search for Sailor's identity within a larger meditation on the discourses of history, myth, and artistry that the novel's characters use to name him and to imagine national reconstruction in the wake of the war.

Taking both novels together, we observe Ondaatje elaborating collective pasts that move outward across multiple traditions rather than moving backwards within a single national tradition. At a formal level, his archival legends thus disturb the sense of national cohesion that realist versions of the historical novel helped to foster. At a historical and an ethical level, such disturbances pivotally adapt the genre to the contemporary cosmopolitical challenge of reframing national pasts—and by extension futures—through a wider matrix of cultural pathways and collective categories (for example, the ethnic, the religious, the transnational, or the abstract "human" of human rights).

Archiving Frontiers: *The Collected Works of Billy the Kid*

Ondaatje's rendition of the outlaw Bonney, aka Billy the Kid, tests national mythologies by taking the defining symbol of American (that is to say, U.S.) self-identity—the frontier—and subjecting it to transnational reinvention and critique. Ann Mandel described the Canadian reception of *Collected Works* as "praised by critics and readers and roundly condemned—to [Ondaatje's] delight—by federal MPs [members of parliament] for dealing with an *American* hero and outlaw" (her emphasis).[11] Ondaatje's afterword to the 2008 edition of *Collected Works* echoes Mandel's earlier assessment, but with respect to his reception in the United States: "I couldn't afford to go south [to the United States to write, in the 1960s] so it was an eventual delight when a review of the book [*Collected Works*] in a Texas newspaper a few years later complained that a Canadian had been allowed to edit the journals of Billy the Kid."[12] Ondaatje's pleasure is twofold: he appreciates that his work has been mistaken for Bonney's actual journals, blurring the line between primary source and secondary fiction; yet he seems even more satisfied with the way his work's archival mode, in suggesting editorship over authorship, defies notions of national propriety and thematic appropriateness on both sides of the Canada–United States border.[13]

In fact, the "Canadian" Ondaatje, who was born in Sri Lanka and moved to England at age nine, and then to Canada at nineteen (eight years before *Collected Works* was first published), uses the very American iconicity of Billy the Kid to counter nativism of the sort that permeated some of his book's reviews and, more significantly, to rewrite the frontier mythology that has become so crucial to narratives about American character. Character here is not just cultural but also a form of political unconscious that generates strong emotion around the delineating, claiming, and sharing of a tradition. As Ernest Gellner has argued, and the reactions of the members of Canadian parliament show, the strength and exploitation of those sentiments can turn desirable forms of national cohesion into dangerous and, in this case, petty nativism.[14]

The legend of Billy the Kid, of course, is inseparable from the cultural reproduction and political use of the American West as a symbolic landscape for the coalescence of national character. The frontier had begun to take on mythic status as early as 1893, with Frederick Jackson Turner's address "The Significance of the Frontier in American History." The frontier thesis, as is well known, shifted the foundation of U.S. identity away from the Atlantic world and toward the "Great West," where the conjuncture of "savagery and civilization" gave rise to peculiarly American qualities of individuality, ingenuity, and ruggedness.[15] Turner's thesis devalued European influence in favor of frontier transactions just as the actual frontier was closing down, making an imagined frontier central to his narrative of American history and laying the foundation for historical and popular perceptions of American identity as self-contained and exceptional.[16]

In *Collected Works*, Ondaatje reimagines frontier mythology not by debunking it, as many twentieth-century historians and novelists have done, but by using it to counter notions of American isolationism and exceptionalism that could be said to begin with the frontier thesis. He does this by mixing archival materials that have helped produce Billy the Kid as an American icon with Ondaatje's own poetry, prose, and photographs, which disperses construction of the "Wild West" beyond the United States. The form of *Collected Works* is thus remarkably resistant to classification as it weaves together elements of narrative, lyric, and scrapbook. It is told from both an omniscient perspective and Billy's own, taking us through the last year of Billy's life, from his initial skirmishes with the sheriff Pat Garrett to his arrest, escape, and eventual death at Garrett's hands. It also incorporates newspaper articles, interviews, excerpts from pulp novels, and popular historical accounts of Bonney's exploits, which remind us that "Billy" is a discursive creation. Ondaatje's assembly of these documentary and entertainment artifacts allows him to defamiliarize Billy's legend by experimenting with the very genres that have made him familiar to a global audience. As Lee Spinks has noted, "We think we know the story before we *read* the story," and I agree with Spinks that Ondaatje is referencing "our . . . imaginative investment in Billy's historical drama" when he creates an archive of Billy narratives.[17] In addition, however, *Collected Works* reflects upon the question of who that "our" is, particularly when it dissociates Billy from the distinctive Americanness that his legacy helped to produce.

Ondaatje uses several primary source texts in *Collected Works*, but the plot leading from Billy's first shoot-out with Garrett to his assassination is largely drawn from Walter Noble Burns's *The Saga of Billy the Kid* (1926). Burns's account is widely regarded as an embellished history that synthesized documentary materials with creative interpretations, including imaginatively staged conversations (or reenactments) among characters. As the generic label of "saga" promises, Burns's book is more accurately described as an exercise in mythography. The book was wildly successful, has never gone out of print since its publication, and is the guiding influence over popular impressions of the outlaw today.[18]

Ondaatje's choice of this best seller, more romance than history, as a primary source reinforces his investment in the West as a mythic space and perceptual category. His passages from Billy's point of view re-create the atmospheric conventions of the Western through a mix of exalted and graphic language. Billy's first words are "These are the killed," which becomes a dramatic refrain threading through his recitation of those he killed and those who were killed by his enemies, including Garrett. Billy's closing line in this lyric passage ("Blood a necklace on me all my life") establishes the mythology of the West, translating its violence into coarse beauty and the litany of the killed into a reflection of Billy's own metaphysical turmoil as he foresees his death ("and Pat Garrett/sliced off my head").[19] The conflicting tones of pathos and gore capture the West as it has been dramatized by writers like Burns, who transformed the skirmishes between outlaws and authorities in New Mexico and Texas into a potent cultural fantasy of antihero heroism.

Ondaatje's portrayal of Billy the Kid emphasizes Billy's awareness of his legacy within that national origin story, an awareness that oscillates between self-aggrandizement and self-dissection. By allowing Billy to reflect proleptically upon his future inscriptions within the numerous genres that fill *Collected Works*, Ondaatje disrupts the narrative's temporal unities precisely at moments in which his protagonist opens the spatial coordinates of American mythology beyond the United States. This formal strategy, which interrupts what Benedict Anderson so famously called the "meanwhile" of the realist novel's imagined community,[20] becomes a mechanism for reimagining frontier mythology as transnational movement:

> Not a story about me through their eyes then. Find the beginning, the slight silver key to unlock it, to dig it out. Here then is a maze to begin, be in.
>
> Two years ago Charlie Bowdre and I criss-crossed the Canadian border. Ten miles north of it ten miles south. Our horses stepped from country to country, across low rivers, through different colours of tree green. The two of us, our criss-cross like a whip in slow motion, the ridge of action rising and falling, getting narrower in radius till it ended and we drifted down to Mexico and old heat. That there is nothing of depth, of significant accuracy, of wealth in the image, I know. It is there for a beginning.
>
> (*Collected Works*, 17)

In this passage we witness Billy's refusal to abide by his placement within the American mythos by seemingly "whipping" over the United States in his oppositional search for self-definition. His particular evocation of "the beginning" is unusual for many reasons, not the least of which is that it is studded by pairs. These pairs eschew the certainty of a single point of origin, instead building a "maze" of visual and sonic echoes ("begin, be in"; "two years ago"; "two of us"; "ten miles north . . . ten miles south"; "criss-cross"; "rising and falling"). Ondaatje's insistent doubling, the symmetry of these phrases, generates a rare equanimity in Billy's voice as it refracts national unities of time and space through a continental criss-cross in which Canada and Mexico become explicit sites of "beginning" as well.

Ondaatje's deviation into an almost pastoral mode accompanies the expansion of American terrain from the national to the continental scale. In acknowledging this wider geography beneath the moniker "American," the passage dissociates Billy's self-consciousness from the history of consciousness that underlay frontier mythology's imperial forms. Instead, the vectored motion of westward expansion becomes more undulating beneath Billy and Charlie's meandering. Their criss-cross, their symmetry, and finally their narrowing radius bring together Canada and Mexico in a pattern of movement that seems to erase the distinctiveness of the United States altogether.

It is important that Billy betrays a certain lack of faith in his recollection ("That there is nothing of depth, of significant accuracy, of wealth in the image, I know"). This skepticism is part of how Ondaatje's transnational American scene changes the performance of beginnings.

Neither Billy nor Ondaatje aims to replace a national origin myth with a continental one as an absolute good; instead, the passage casts about for ways of remembering that disregard the impulse to singular belonging in the writing of both individual and collective selves. Although the character of Billy begins by disavowing the legend of Billy the Kid, *Collected Works* clearly manages to pluralize his origins through Billy's ever-growing archival afterlife—an afterlife that swerves beyond the expected sites and sources.

The text's opening page flaunts this point by introducing readers to a photographic outline with no picture within, followed by a passage excerpted from *Huffman, Frontier Photographer*, stating, "I send you a picture of Billy made from a Perry shutter as quick as it can be worked—Pyro and soda developer" (*Collected Works*, 1). Ondaatje plays here with mimetic representation, progressive temporality, and structures of address, denying us an image of Billy taken by his contemporary, L. A. Huffman (although other Huffman photographs are allowed to populate the book), suggesting that it is the partial blankness of the past that provides the occasion and the opportunity of the present to bring it to life. The empty photographic frame visually conveys a withholding of information that is also a statement about representation. The reality of Billy's existence as an icon is irreducible to a photographic portrait with its patina of the real, compression of historical distance, and illusions of rational-critical selfhood. Ondaatje uses its erasure to mediate between the highly localized Huffman gloss and the globalized future that the *Collected Works* will open through less direct and more diverse forms of mimesis.

As *Collected Works* proceeds, its amassed artifacts absorb Billy's character into the mythologies of the frontier. Interspersed interviews with Sally Chisum (daughter of John Chisum, a cattle baron and Billy's foe) and Billy's lover, Paulita Maxwell, depict him as a gentleman, always meticulously attired ("As far as dress was concerned/he always looked as if/he had just stepped out of a bandbox" [91]), while Billy's first-person passages capture the horrific violence he witnessed ("Jesus I never knew that did you/the nerves shot out/the liver running around there" [8]). The colloquy of these voices captures the classic antinomies of the frontier—the encounter between savagery and civility, to recall Turner's phrase—in the emergence of Billy as the archetypal outlaw. An excerpt from an actual pulp novel entitled *Billy the Kid and the Princess* and a fabricated interview with Billy in the *Texas Star* further bridge the production of his image to the modern-day culture industry, particularly when Billy anachronistically mentions a "Mr. Cassavetes" upon being asked how he will be remembered.[21]

The range of artifactual and invented excerpts that couple fairy tales with westerns captures the comic contradictions in Billy's legacy and culminates in a final photograph of Ondaatje himself as a young boy, in a garish cowboy costume (figure 4.1). The author's photo wryly recalls the empty photographic frame of the first page. Comparing these images suggests the extent to which Billy's legend has grown through the reproduction of his tale in the circulation of mass culture, but it also more immediately blurs the line between reception and production as the author, via a childhood photograph, takes his place within the narrative he has crafted.

By including a picture of himself within *Collected Works*, Ondaatje could be read as making a classically postmodern gesture of self-reference. If this is the case, then the nostalgic mood and grainy quality of the image remind us that postmodernism and modernism are never as distinct as stagist narratives of literary history imply. As a token of personal memory and self-implication in the fantasies of *Collected Works*, the author's photo is decidedly innocent. It is precisely this politically unfashionable longing that invites metafictional disruption back into a more concrete worldliness. In his afterword to the 2008 edition of *Collected Works*, Ondaatje reveals the location of the photograph as Sri Lanka, in the course of detailing his childhood love of westerns:

> I'd had an obsession with westerns since I was eight or nine—for even in Sri Lanka the myth of the American West had filtered down furtively among children in Colombo. I had a cowboy suit, with blatantly cheap-looking glass "jewels" on my cowboy belt as well as little leather holders for one's bullets, which always seemed to me to be a fey and fussy method of transporting bullets that would later be used to kill a mule or a woman or a sheriff. So, when our house in Boralesgamuwa was robbed, I was glad to see that the jewelled cowboy belt was also stolen, only to be returned by the police several months later.
>
> (113)

By remembering his past, Ondaatje's afterword ends up indirectly describing the picture in the main text, explicitly introducing a transnational context for frontier mythology in his recollections of the cowboy suit.

FIGURE 4.1 Michael Ondaatje as a child. Copyright © 1970 Michael Ondaatje. Reprinted by permission of Michael Ondaatje.

Such a context could only be guessed at in previous editions. Add this to the Canadian context of production that Ondaatje invokes later in the afterword, and we see that the 2008 edition of *Collected Works* solicits interpretations more attuned to medium specificity and circulation than the 1970 edition.

Arjun Appadurai has suggested that theorizing globalization provokes a renewed engagement with the idea of contextualization, defined not just as a practice of explanatory grounding but also as a generator of new kinds of production.[22] Appadurai considers context to be dynamic, whether an object is being assimilated or defamiliarized, particularly when supposedly distant or deterritorialized contexts (such as Sri Lanka as a site for cowboy culture) exert pressure on an object's definition. Although he is speaking of context from within the discipline of anthropology, Appadurai's insights are relevant to literary study and are conversant with methodologies in editorial theory and world literature that take variations of a text to be a valuable record of the work's interaction with the societies through which it has traveled. By refusing to draw sharp distinctions between text and paratext, figure and ground in *Collected Works*, we better understand the phenomenon of proliferation that is so central to the endurance of myth.

To be sure, Ondaatje's 2008 afterword contextualizes his work in explanatory ways that add to our background knowledge of *Collected Works*, but his archival method also allows for the afterword to be part of the work—to be read as another artifact in the collection, whose legend of Billy the Kid expands and alters to take on different implications in the latest edition. To read the afterword as blurring the line between context and artifact is, to borrow a phrase from Ann Laura Stoler, to read along the archival grain.[23] Such a reading traces the active process by which categories and facts change, and it shows that the contingency of epistemological apparatuses render Billy an always partially known, unfinished figure. The practices that bring him to light create both the glow and the haze surrounding him, intensifying his legend by heightening his inscrutability as more documents emerge.

The cover of the 2008 edition of *Collected Works* illustrates my claims by bringing new artifacts of Bonney's afterlife into the structure of his literary representation (see figure 4.2). In contrast to previous editions, which featured portraits of Billy on their covers (a choice that reduced the power of the blank photograph in the main text), the 2008 edition

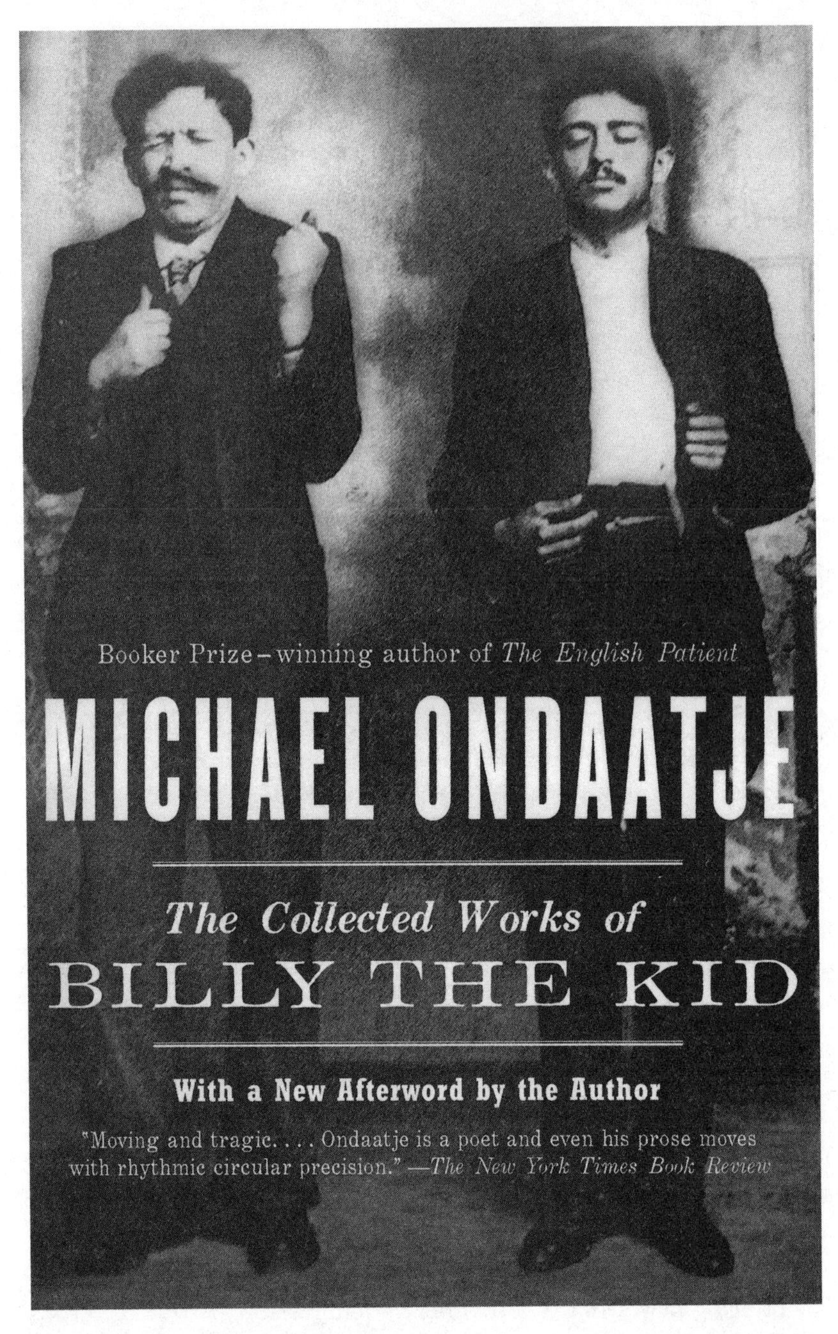

FIGURE 4.2 Front cover of Michael Ondaatje's *The Collected Works of Billy the Kid*, 2008 edition. Used by permission of Vintage Canada, a division of Penguin Random House Canada Limited.

features a photograph of two Mexican actors portraying Billy the Kid and Garrett.[24] This extra layer of mediation (a photograph of a cross-racial performance) beautifully encapsulates the relationship between artifice and artifact established throughout the rest of the work. In doing so, the cover also pulls from the archive another context (or "maze," to recall Ondaatje's image) from which Billy can "begin, be in." The form of *Collected Works* is accordingly kept open, leaving room for the possibility that more artifacts, more genres, and (with them) more contexts will and should be added to the legend of Billy.

Notably, Ondaatje's choices of proliferation—the Sri Lanka anecdote and the photograph of Mexican performers—vivifies a method that does not just dig deeper but also moves outward in an unlikely adaptation of the expansionist credo embedded within frontier mythology. What makes the 2008 *Collected Works* so interesting is the way in which its archival accumulations tie into a transnational theory of reception and production, multiplying the contexts of Billy's emergence in order to multiply the collectivities that frontier mythology serves. It follows that this edition of *Collected Works* offers something stronger than the claim that the American West "filtered down" into Colombo or, for that matter, across to Mexico, something contradictory to the imperial agency concentrated in Charles Olson's assertion that "America completes her West only on the coast of Asia."[25] Sri Lanka and Mexico range through the American West in the revised *Collected Works*, deranging Olson's frontier dream of completion and rearranging it as an open set to be occupied and extended by foreign nationals with their own ends. *Collected Works* thus counters notions of cultural property and propriety not by demystifying the frontier as a symbol of American identity and mythology but by redistributing it among agents of myth and memory beyond the United States.

Unhistorical Lives / Mythistorical Remains

If the archival form of *Collected Works* widens the geography of familiar, even iconic stories, changing them in the process, *Anil's Ghost* reanimates that form to tell stories of the "disappeared"—or, more precisely, to tell stories that capture the complexities of representing the disappeared when the written archive is painfully thin. The novel unfolds in Sri Lanka during the 1980s and 1990s, when the nation was riven by a Sinhalese majority government and a Tamil insurgency that was itself split between separatists fighting for a Tamil state and those fighting for better representation within the Sri Lankan state.[26]

The plot revolves around Anil Tissera, a Sri Lankan expatriate and forensic anthropologist working for an international human rights organization, likely affiliated with the United Nations. Her mission to investigate human rights abuses takes shape through her discovery of the skeleton she names Sailor. Anil finds Sailor in the "sacred historical site" of Bandarawela, a government-restricted zone, which leads her to conclude that the state has been using centuries-old ruins to camouflage its modern-day killings (*Anil's Ghost*, 52). With the help of partners on the ground—an archaeologist named Sarath Diyasena and a local artist by the name of Ananda—Anil sets out to identify Sailor as the victim of state-sponsored terror under the somewhat naive conviction that her findings will compel state accountability and ultimately secure justice for its victims. The novel's politics, however, quickly veer away from the global law-and-order scenario of Anil's imagination. Instead, *Anil's Ghost* develops into a narrative that questions the efficacy of its protagonist's ideals by diverting the main plot of historical recovery and justice-seeking through subplots that frame the contemporary Sri Lankan conflict within the distant pasts of Buddhist, Chinese, and other civilizations.

To summarize *Anil's Ghost* is to evoke a novel that could not seem more different from *Collected Works* in theme and setting. Where *Collected Works* reflects upon the legends that arise from a surplus of information and in the name of a powerful nation, *Anil's Ghost* concentrates on the crucial absence of information, on lives like Sailor's that were "disappeared" by the state and that come to represent national disintegration as opposed to national wholeness. Whereas Ondaatje distributes Billy across several transnational geographies to contest the time/space unities of Americanness, he uses Sailor to evaluate both globalist and localist responses to national fracture. The globalist sutures collective memory to the universal category of the human; the localist brings it back into an enclosed narrative of the nation. Neither response constitutes an adequate solution, leading the novel into a meditation on the work that memory does and the criteria of relevance that separate myth from history, and one group from another. These questions require Ondaatje to thematize the archival as well as to stylize it: the novel productively extends the definition of *archive* to include archaeological sites, Sailor's bones, and

Buddhist statues—each of which contextualizes the here and now of the civil war within several other histories and geographies of destructive memory loss.

Ondaatje's compilation of these disparate pasts and his paratactic way of arranging them became especially controversial with the release of this novel, as some critics claimed he took too much aesthetic license with the real lives lost during the turmoil. Tom LeClair wrote, "Ondaatje should distrust himself. Now I don't trust his collage method. It's a way to avoid banal 'old coin' cause and effect, the logic by which human rights are denied or defended."[27] LeClair's attribution of obfuscation to collage recalls the argument that Lukács made against modernist montage in 1938, when he argued that that the technique juxtaposed "heterogeneous, unrelated pieces of reality torn from their context."[28] What made montage (and modernism) so dangerous for Lukács was that, in claiming to represent the "chaos" of reality, it shrouded the relationship between the individual's experience of disintegration and the progressive integration of capitalism worldwide. Modernism's subjectivity obscured structural conditions and consequently perpetuated false consciousness by divorcing the experience of chaos from an analysis of the economic order.

Lukács's argument is obviously more generalizing than LeClair's, which addresses a particular historical conflict rather than the nature of "reality" as such. Still, the principle is the same. LeClair, too, believes that formal disjunction—for example, the dissolution of Ondaatje's "detective plot" into "rapid switching among characters, times, locales"—inhibits understanding of the conflict it portrays by substituting the experiences of some individuals for the root causes of the civil war. Collage's negative epistemological effects breed ethical violations for LeClair, who sees Ondaatje's mystifications as inadvertently exploiting the Sri Lankan dead rather than elegizing, honoring, or, most importantly, doing them justice.

LeClair's desire for a plot that solves rather than dissolves is warranted, but it misses the reality that Ondaatje is portraying and the historicist style of explanation that he is questioning. Ondaatje's archival method, of which collage is part but not all, expresses the conditions of incompleteness and unknowing that the war induced. In doing so, it uses Sailor as a Foucauldian "legend" to open up larger philosophical questions about the limits of historicism as responsible representation, particularly when conducted in the name of a human rights investigation that has no influence on national reconstruction. Like *Collected Works*, *Anil's Ghost* does not develop an archive that will set the historical record straight by supplying the "right" information; rather, it uses a variety of traces, documents, and artifacts to wed collective memory to a critical examination of Enlightenment rationalism's limits. Even if readers concede that cause-and-effect narratives are essential to assigning responsibility in historical conflicts, such narratives simplify the milieu that they describe and thus diminish responses that do not take the shape of a verdict.

The most powerful meditations on historicist logic and its rules of relevance come in the company of Sailor, as Ondaatje situates Anil's rigorously empirical task of forensic identification within a narrative of her more "tender" discoveries, which merit quoting at length:

> She loosened the swaddling plastic that covered Sailor. In her work Anil turned bodies into representatives of race and age and place, though for her the tenderest of all discoveries was the finding, some years earlier, of the tracks at Laetoli—almost-four-million-year-old footsteps of a pig, a hyena, a rhinoceros and a bird, this strange ensemble identified by a twentieth-century tracker. Four unrelated creatures that had walked hurriedly over a wet layer of volcanic ash. To get away from what? Historically more significant were other tracks in the vicinity, of a hominid assumed to be approximately five feet tall (one could tell by the pivoting heel impressions). But it was that quartet of animals walking from Laetoli four million years ago that she liked to think about.
>
> The most precisely recorded moments of history lay adjacent to the extreme actions of nature or civilization. She knew that. Pompeii. Laetoli. Hiroshima. Vesuvius (whose fumes had asphyxiated poor Pliny while he recorded its "tumultuous behaviour"). Tectonic slips and brutal human violence provided random time-capsules of unhistorical lives.
>
> (*Anil's Ghost*, 55)

There is a tendency in the critical literature on *Anil's Ghost* to define Anil as limited by her unflaggingly forensic gaze. Yet this rarely discussed passage illustrates a character that is not entirely in thrall to the norms of historical or scientific positivism. Anil is sentimentally attuned to what historical standards of significance leave out and to what they cannot answer—namely, how irregular collectives form in the midst of crisis and how the motivating circumstances of such relations ("To get away from what?") place the blind spots of forensic deduction into relief.

It is no mistake that animal prints fall outside the scope of historical significance. Their superfluity confirms the division of human and natural history, tacitly informing epistemic value, and thus lends insight into the development of the human as a category closed off from the animal.[29] It is the singular hominid, not the menagerie, that is supposed to matter to Anil, and yet, by pausing over the trivial "quartet of animals," she glimpses the dialectical emergence of the universal "human" in human rights. As Jacques Derrida has argued, the concept of "the animal" in philosophical discourse has enabled the concept of "the human" to emerge as a transcendent category precisely because it engenders a forgetting of actual animals. The plural *animals*, in Derrida's words, designate "all the livings things that man does not recognize as his fellows."[30]

The remains of a quartet of animals draw Anil away from her duties and into fellowship with the motley outside of "human being" as concept. Such remains also betoken Ondaatje's suspicion of the "human" as an abstract legal category, the neatness of which obscures the reality of individual lives as a condition of protecting them. Anil's fleeting recollection of the animals' prints conjures effects that are powerful for their brevity and inarticulateness—a set of fossil records that, like Foucault's strange poems of infamous men, bear silent witness to their own forgetting. Such witness would not be possible without Ondaatje's willingness to evoke the distracted and associative nature of Anil's thought. By indulging what Anil "liked to think about," as opposed to what she *should* think about, Ondaatje allows the personal memories of a wandering consciousness to mingle with scientific investigation and reorder the value of its findings.

Anil's affective response to ancient remains effectively casts doubt on her initial goal of removing Sailor from his swaddling plastic and placing him in a narrative as an identified figure. Anil's job demands that she turn "bodies into representatives of race and age and place," creating the legible evidence that public justice demands. Yet the movement of this passage sets the pursuit of such legibility next to a catalog of disasters that, in generating so much empirical detail, seem only to retreat from historical comprehension. The fieldwork and lab work of archaeology and forensics certainly function for Ondaatje as empirical sciences, but also, when allowed room, as interpretive arts that provide windows into phenomenological experience. Disciplines that treat the earth and bodies as archives, they preserve Anil's encounter with remains before rationalizing those remains into demographic data. Such preservation of experience gestures toward the contingency of historical knowledge and allows Ondaatje to insert hermeneutic reflection into his protagonist's positivist framework. Pompeii, Hiroshima, Vesuvius, and, specifically, Laetoli in Tanzania become nodes of a global disaster circuit that explains the conditions that produce the "most precisely recorded moments of history." If contextualizing Sailor within the landscape of transnational memory minimizes the here and now of his murder in Sri Lanka, it does so in an attempt to elucidate a larger range of possibility for deciphering the significance of "unhistorical lives" to national culture and international law. Bringing Sailor to demographic light, Ondaatje suggests, is insufficient for understanding how the zone of the unhistorical is delimited within those precisely recorded moments of "brutal human violence" and how it is sustained when human rights norms monopolize definitions of justice and remembrance.

Although Anil's memory of fieldwork makes it possible to enlarge and diversify the scales at which she (and we) might conceive a significant memory, her professional commitments to the human rights commission do not allow her to reevaluate the way official history is told:

> She remembered Clyde Snow, her teacher in Oklahoma, speaking about human rights work in Kurdistan: *One village can speak for many villages. One victim can speak for many victims.* She and Sarath both knew that in all the turbulent history of the island's recent civil wars, in all the token police investigations, not one murder charge had been made during the troubles. But this could be a clear case against the government.
>
> (*Anil's Ghost*, 178)

Anil cleaves closely to human rights principles, as articulated by Snow, when she claims that identifying Sailor not only will retrieve him from the "unhistorical dead" (note the revision in Anil's mind of "unhistorical lives") but also will perform an act of collective reclamation: "This representative of all those lost voices. To give him a name would name the rest" (56). *Anil's Ghost*, however, invites deep criticism of this metonymic ethos, questioning its real-world efficacy and the adequacy of restitution that it implies. The novel unravels Anil's mission by allowing it to succeed in its immediate ends—Anil does indeed identify Sailor's bones as the body of a "real" person, Ruwan Kumara—but then denies the identification any positive force when Anil meets a panel of Sri Lankan officials who refuse to ratify her findings.

Sailor's continued illegibility, even after Anil restores him to history as Kumara, illustrates what the novel calls, via Sarath, "the archaeological surround of a fact" (44). For Sarath, this surround refers immediately to the political climate of Sri Lanka, in which Anil's attempts to speak truth to power are not so much brave as futile, for the state will not recognize or act upon her findings in any way. As the source of such pragmatic reminders about the limits of truth in an authoritarian regime, Sarath often seems like the realist foil to Anil's misguided idealism. But the friction between them does not always leave Anil the loser. Rather, it prompts unpredictable position-taking around the function of time in the international politics of intervention.

We see the problem of temporality most vividly in Sarath's debates with Anil, when he describes excavating remnants from a fifth-century B.C. Chinese civilization and finding twenty female musicians killed in a ritual ceremony with their instruments (mainly bells) alongside them. These musicians were servants of an "ancient ruler" who, upon his death, wanted the women to accompany him into the next world (260). While Sarath recalls the beauty of those bells in the mythic language of ancientness, Anil sees another site of violence, and their conflictual interpretations lend insight into their respective senses of vocation:

> "Possibly it was those bells that made me an archaeologist."
> "Twenty murdered women."
> "It was another world with its own value system that came to the surface."
> "Love me, love my orchestra. You can take it with you! That kind of madness lies within the structure of all civilizations, not just in distant cultures."
>
> (261)

Sarath, a responsible historicist, can only see the deep past in terms of its externality to history and therefore uses myth to collapse cultural relativism with ethical relativism. He refuses to impose his norms on the past and consequently forgoes any kind of judgment beyond the aesthetic. Anil does not refuse ethical judgment, and she insinuates that Sarath's appreciation of the artifacts overlooks the patriarchy that made their presence possible. His attitude to the past facilitates certain occlusions in the present—for example, the failure to see how the power structures of an ancient civilization might be not only comparable to modern societies but indeed still operative within them.

Sarath's decision to separate his archaeological excavations and aesthetic judgments from his ethical and political judgment prevents him from seeing proximities between the temporally "distant cultures" that he idealizes and those contemporary forms of nation-state sovereignty that also perpetrate violence against their citizens. Where Sarath sees in ancient China a world separated by time's passage, Anil sees the bells in the vein of Benjamin's historical materialism: as relics of a civilization that are also signs of its barbarism. Ironically, the advocate of Eurocentric norms also imparts the postcolonial lesson. The question is whether she uses Sarath's memory of the dig to equate anachronistically the past with the present or uses it as a legitimation myth for human rights activities in general. If all societies carry the potential for violence against their members, then international organizations theoretically have a role to play in protecting the vulnerable.

That Anil and Sarath's debate turns on the fate of women may seem to have echoes of an imperial civilizing mission, but the fact that it is Anil, a former Sri Lankan citizen, making these claims suggests more than opportunism. There is no good position in the Sri Lankan conflict, and the story of the burial site highlights the problem of remembrance in the face of present concerns. Women or bells? Ondaatje gives us both, because gender violence, which remains at the center of human rights discourse in the present, cannot be relegated to the dustbin of history, even if 500 B.C. can.

Anil and Sarath's interpretive impasse broaches some of the most interesting conversations happening in world literature and postcolonial studies right now, particularly with regard to time scales that reactivate the distant past as part of a political present. Wai Chee Dimock, with her captivating *Through Other Continents* and its formulation of "deep time" for literary history, represents one powerful advocate for an enlarged scale of literary study, and the book has become a locus of debates around the uses, abuses, and conceptual challenges of doing literary history at a world scale. Dimock's concept of "deep time" does away with the calendar dates of American national history (e.g., 1776) and colonial history (e.g., 1620) as a basis for the foundation of American literature. In the place of a historically grounded period, she offers an open-ended scale enlargement that entangles the category of American literature in civilizational traditions, often non-Western, that are far older than the United States itself.[31]

Dimock's release of American literature from the nationally derived confines of period represents the conceptual audacity of transnational work and its cosmopolitan aspirations to resist American exceptionalism, but the approach has faced criticism from those who see the devil in the details. Djelal Kadir historicizes Dimock's refusal to historicize as an expression of U.S. imperial power, regardless of its good-faith attempts to counteract such power's encroachment into the realm of literary study.[32] Less-determinist appraisals have contemplated the purposes deep time might serve. Bruce Robbins asks what reactivating centuries of time might do our "planetary meta-narratives" and warns that scholars cannot assume the benefits of deep time without shouldering the hard work of historical analysis, the job of which is to meaningfully differentiate time so that progress and regress, violence and reparation can be measured and understood.[33]

Robbins's criticism of Dimock's concept begins with the presentation of her book's opening anecdote, which would seem to compare American soldiers invading Iraq to Mongols. Robbins's objection is not to the vilification of Americans but to the static use of the Mongols to signify barbarous action. I agree with Robbins that deep time makes it harder to historicize and easier to overlook comparisons that may perpetuate misconceptions and stereotypes. However, the comparison of Americans with Mongols, according to Dimock, is made by Iraqis, and the purpose of relating this is to emphasize American soldiers' astonishment at the conflation. This distinction opens up an element of deep time that frontally addresses what historicist criticism deemphasizes: the perceptions of historical actors.

Through Other Continents begins with a tragedy—the looting and burning of the archives of the Iraqi National Library and the Islamic Library. These institutions housed documents collected over millennia by Mesopotamian civilizations. Rather than blame the looters, however, Dimock placed the onus on the U.S.-led coalition army, for failing to observe "the international law of belligerent occupation," which demanded that they protect such sites of memory. Dimock invokes an event in recent history but narrates that event mythically. She does not detail the circumstances that made the destruction possible. Rather, she compresses those details to create a fable of American imperialism as barbarism—founded upon the disregard of knowledge and law.

The archives' destruction functions as a primal moment for Dimock's own project, crystallizing the need for deep time to explain how American and Iraqi perceptions of that destruction could be so intensely divided. Iraqis compared the American invasion to the Mongol invasion of 1258, which also resulted in the looting of archives, but Americans soldiers were dumbfounded by the comparison:

> Modern Iraqis see the actions of the United States as yet another installment of that long-running saga: "The modern Mongols, the new Mongols did that. The Americans did that." All of this made no sense to the marines. The year 1258 was long ago and far away. It is separate by 745 years from 2003. The United States has nothing to do with it.[34]

If Dimock is guilty of anything, it is of too confidently ventriloquizing Iraqi and American perspectives on the basis of a single quote (as Robbins himself notes), but she is not wrong to want to understand the collective sentiments out of which communication collapses. In identifying disparate concepts of time as the culprit behind intercultural misunderstanding, her aim is not to historicize the conflict but to show how ontologies of time structure the experience of history. Altering the ontology of time animating American literature, Dimock hopes to offer a conceptual rapprochement between the occupier's linear time of forgetting (or never knowing) and the occupied's recursive time of remembering.

The resonances between the deep time of world literature and anticolonial time become remarkably clear if we turn to an earlier essay by Robbins, which analyzed the uses of temporal scale not in terms of world literature but via the surprisingly overlapping agendas of human rights activists and humanists. Robbins perceptively argues that both wish to honor the victims of atrocity by making their suffering impervious to time's passing. This is what Anil does when she remembers "twenty murdered women" instead of beautiful bells, and this is what anticolonial writers and critics do when they resist historicism as ideologically colonial.

Robbins uses Leslie Marmon Silko's "oceanic" ontology of time to illustrate the anticolonial point of view, and I reproduce it here to show its resonance with Dimock's deep time:

> Time is an ocean, and so the fact that we're all sitting here right now is very dependent on what happened five hundred years ago; and you can't just say, "Aw, five hundred years ago, that's way in the past." No, that linearity, that emphasis of making time all strung out like a string, that's political, that's what colonialists do. . . . The colonialist always says, "Oh that was so long ago, we really can't address the things that've happened." . . . But [to] people who experience time as an ocean, what happened five hundred years ago is right here, just as much as what happened five minutes ago is right here. How can you say that five minutes ago is more important than five hundred years ago?[35]

Robbins argues against oceanic or deep time because of its potential for abuses in the wrong hands, such as those of the Serbians who rationalized present-day genocide in Kosovo on the basis of distant memories of Ottoman colonialism. Even in the right hands, Robbins posits, the deep time of remembered atrocity fetishizes remembrance as good-enough deed, while allowing the politics of selectivity intrinsic to public memory to persist unexamined or unarticulated: "No serious intellectual work could get done if there were not some assumptions about temporal scale, some standard deviation from moral absoluteness that helps us decide what or how or how much to remember and what or how or how much to forget. The present argument can be taken as first and foremost an invitation to make those assumptions explicit."[36]

Robbins calls for an airing of investments that acknowledges the imperfection of selectivity in the humanistic work of remembering and forgetting. What deep and oceanic time make explicit about their theorists' memory practices is that historical actors' *experiences* of time matter to the historical project of remembering the past, intervening in the present, and measuring the distinctions between past and present. Like Dimock, Silko centralizes experience in her temporal formulations and insists that people's everyday meaning-making processes be made visible and countable as part of history.

The virtue of these models of time, despite the very real dangers that Robbins and Kadir register, is the criticism that such models level against historicism's more scientific tendencies to dismiss human forms of perception as debased or illogical and thus to discount them as worthy objects of analysis. Diverse ontologies of time clarify history's embodiment in ways that historicism's rationalizing procedures do not. As historian Joseph Mali has argued, a people's "foundational myths" are "as real as the conditions and events in which they actually live." It is the conviction that historical events cannot be fully grasped without grasping the "ultimate narratives" of their participants that differentiates a modernist recognition of myth from a postmodernist relativizing of truth claims. Mali's claims are made on behalf of "mythistory," a revisionist discourse within modern historiography. Heir to Herodotus rather than to Thucydides, it seeks to rehabilitate the practices of "imagination, fabulation, and memorization" as integral parts of the historical record, and thus considers hermeneutic reflection as vital as positivist observation to expressing concrete reality.[37]

The intellectual work that I attribute to Dimock's deep time and Ondaatje's aesthetics is mythistorical. It commands a vast temporal scale because it is attempting to answer the question "What happened?" in Iraq and Sri Lanka in a way that retains the irrational elements that persist, and arguably are magnified, in times of atrocity. By addressing themselves to what historicism does not, Dimock and Ondaatje recognize the endurance of myth as the basis of communal histories, and they see their projects as intervening in the mythological shape of their subjects. Deep time proposes a new origin story for American literature, founded upon entanglement rather than exceptionalism.

Ondaatje's *Collected Works of Billy the Kid* prefigures that project and makes it explicitly mythistorical by taking up the national and global iconicity of Bonney as part of a transnationally circulating story of American identity. In *Anil's Ghost*, Ondaatje illuminates the processes by which present-day conflicts appropriate the past. In drawing on the ancient, he lends insight into strategies of legitimation: Anil's commitment to intervention based on the moral norms of human rights ("twenty murdered women") versus Sarath's commitment to grounding and perhaps suspending such norms on the basis of civilizational differences ("another world with its own value system"). China in 500 B.C., whether it normatively should be remembered in this context or not, is an unavoidable site of political force that reveals the foundations upon which historical actors lay their claims and defend their actions. The ancient is mobilized differently by competing epistemological projects, which in turn are shaped by distinct cultural attitudes. Ondaatje uses the Chinese ruin as a site of irreconcilable differences in how "we" remember and inhabit modernity. Its disputed significance conveys the messiness of the cosmopolitical force field: human rights activities are haunted by the legacy of Western imperialism, and postcolonial dissent to intervention is tainted by the propagandistic strategies of authoritarian, self-cannibalizing states.

The novel's scenarios of remembrance compel us to weigh Sarath's aestheticization of the deep past against Anil's politicization of it. Both sides are imperfect, and that is the point. They represent ethics as informed by the condensations of experience and education, the witnessing of history, and the compromises that come with it all. The structure of Anil and Sarath's dispute does nothing if not encourage oscillation between an investment in the particularities of cultural difference and a reluctance to allow cultural difference to neutralize the norm-making that enables ethical judgment and political action.

I think the novel courts this oscillation, especially in the passages that give it its archival form and multinational setting. On unnumbered pages, italicized, these passages interrupt the diegetic narrative, sometimes relating a past event unknown to Ondaatje's main characters and at other times taking the form of a found object, such as a letter or record, that a character (usually Anil) may have left behind or come across in the course of an investigation. The passages' visuality recalls the practices of collation and assembly that Ondaatje first used in *Collected Works*, and as in that text, the passages serve to enlarge the geography into which the main plot of establishing Sailor's identity dissolves. To read these italicized passages together is to draw the Sri Lankan civil war into a transhistorical and transnational network of memory loss.

Ondaatje draws comparisons between the Sri Lankan killing fields and a raided Buddhist temple in China's Shanxi province, where Japanese archaeologists had excised twenty-four Bodhisattva sculptures, the broken pieces of which sit in various museums in the West: "This was the place of a complete crime. Heads separated from bodies. Hands broken off" (*Anil's Ghost*, 12). Ondaatje includes a "found letter" from Anil to a

Hollywood film director—an artifact of her life in Texas with her girlfriend, Leaf, who is suffering from Alzheimer's in the novel's present: "We are forensic scientists and have been arguing about where on his body Mr. Marvin was shot" (258). Still another passage takes the form of a partial record of Sri Lanka's disappeared:

> Kumara Wijetunga, 17. 6th November 1989. At about 11:30 p.m. from his house.
>
> Prabath Kumara, 16. 17th November 1989. At 3:20 a.m. from the home of a friend.
>
> Kumara Arachchi, 16. 17th November 1989. At about midnight from his house.

The passage goes on to provide seven more names and then the following lines: "The colour of a shirt. The sarong's pattern. The hour of disappearance" (41).

Sourced from Amnesty International reports, the passage purports to be a segment of the printed archive that Anil reads before discovering Sailor's "archive of bones."[38] At one level, these names, combined with the other extradiegetic passages in the novel, suggest Benjaminian shards—pasts that defy assimilation into the narrative of continuity that Anil equates with returning Sailor to history (her ideal of justice) and that Sarath considers unattainable under conditions on the ground in Sri Lanka. At another level, these passages recall the comparative gestures made by Anil—in her debate with Sarath and in her examination of Sailor, through the prism of Laetoli, Vesuvius, and Hiroshima—those multiple sites of preservation that precede Sri Lanka's and that highlight the destruction that motivates and humbles historical projects.

Ondaatje's artifactual images (the Chinese temple, the Hollywood letter, and the record of the Sri Lankan missing) represent several incompatible orders of loss that the novel nonetheless asks us to consider together. Here, transnational memory leaves readers more helpless than partisan. We are faced not with choosing between Anil's or Sarath's worldviews but with observing the moment before views coalesce into an ordered world. This is how Ondaatje evokes the sensation of being in the archive, in both of Foucault's senses of the term. His formal organization acknowledges the mystery and disorientation of being among material stored but not storied; at the same time, it understands this moment as the fundamental ground of knowledge itself.

Despite his characters' inclinations, Ondaatje's archival method places Sailor within a network of locations from which no consistent narrative can be drawn without sacrifice or, to use Robbins's word, selectivity. It thus makes the full disclosures that the characters cannot. Anil's faith in universal truths (whether in the form of empirical facts or moral norms) and Sarath's commitment to relative ones (in the form of historical contexts and situated values) lead them to tether Sailor's fate to recognizable collectivities—the legal community of the human for Anil, and the failed nation-state for Sarath. Archival form, however, makes that tethering difficult because it articulates the unarticulated premises and analytic modes behind ethico-political convictions. By linking together discrepant geographies of loss and allowing all sorts of remains—shards, bones, letters, and records—to retain their fragmented form, Ondaatje evokes, indeed enunciates, the moment prior to enunciation even as his characters must necessarily attempt to overcome that moment to produce politically meaningful narratives.

Anil's Ghost, then, despite its protagonist's mission, slows Sailor's return to the historical dead and pauses over its uses. He, like the quartet of animals, captures the imagination only as a spectral memory, and this raises the unnerving possibility that the Sri Lankan killing fields should not simply be politically diagnosed but should be kept preserved, as a "time-capsule of unhistorical lives." The time capsule metaphor itself reveals why the novel is so frustrating to those who demand a historicist analysis of the Sri Lankan civil war rather than an aesthetics of its material remains. The time capsule, as a mode of preservation, conjures the human, all too human aspects of preservation: objects of selection that align personal importance with sociological significance; direct attempts to control how one's present will appear to future recipients; an attempt to freeze time in a box and bury it.[39]

These attitudes toward time all threaten to disqualify the contents of a time capsule as objects of historical knowledge because of their notional and idiosyncratic qualities. Yet it is the implicit normativity of what constitutes good, usable material that Ondaatje tests by valuing the intimacy between time capsules and popular remembrance, between the archaeology of knowledge and archival form. He responds to the Sri Lankan civil war—an event that seems to be nothing if not internal to the nation—by asserting that a larger and less uniform geography might be necessary to understand, if not the specific course of the nation's violence, then its citizens' exposure to violence, which cannot be remembered, harnessed, integrated, or, most importantly, redressed by a linear historical narrative that delegitimizes alternative temporal structures. He sacrifices causality and demystification within the national context in favor of correlation and comparison across transnational and transhistorical fields in order to hold *Anil's Ghost* accountable to those people whose stories are erased by the facticity needed to achieve international legal recognition. This is why, when we finally learn Sailor's "real" identity—that is, when Anil succeeds in turning the skeleton into Ruwan Kumara, a "representative of race and age and place"—the information is treated untriumphantly and is quickly laid aside. The novel continues to refer to Kumara as Sailor even after Anil has made the skeleton a member of the "historical dead," and it continues to turn Sri Lanka's communal future away from broken state apparatuses and toward technologies of myth-making that will address national fissures by appealing to older and wider kinds of collectivity.

The novel channels this commitment to myth into an ending that may be nostalgic for the ancientness of the ancient, but it uses that nostalgia critically to engage the possibility of national reconstruction and reconciliation. The final pages of *Anil's Ghost* feature Ananda restoring a vandalized and shattered statue of the Buddha in yet another sacred site that, though supposedly "neutral" and "innocent," had become a killing field during the war (*Anil's Ghost*, 300). Throughout the novel, Ananda's artistic skills foil Anil's scientific ones; his first task—to construct a model of Sailor's face for identification purposes—foreshadows his final task of restoring the Buddha. Ananda's rendering of Sailor, we learn earlier in the novel, does not resemble any one person but is rather a projection of his grief at having lost his wife in the war: "He [Sarath] would already know as she [Anil] did that no one would recognize the face. It was not a reconstruction of Sailor's face they were looking at" (188).

Ananda's first sculpture, then, reinforces Sailor's symbolic function within the novel as the icon of national fracture and collective trauma, a symbolism that his last sculpture, the Buddha, will attempt to both exorcise and memorialize: "The [Buddha's] eyes, like his [Ananda's] at this moment, would always look north. As would the great scarred face half a mile away, which he had helped knit together from damaged stone, a statue that was no longer a god, that no longer had its graceful line but only the pure sad glance Ananda had found" (306). This passage embeds the national fissures of Sri Lanka in the Buddha's gaze north, a muted reference to the largely Hindu Tamil separatist region where fighting had begun. The cracked face of the statue ("no longer a god") keeps alive the deformation of religious values under the majority Buddhist Sinhalese government.

The critical appeal of the reconstructed statue lies in the way it changes the object of nostalgia from the nation itself to the nation's now complex position within the transnational and even transhistorical net that Buddhism casts throughout the novel: in the stolen bodhisattvas from Shanxi and in the sacred sites within Sri Lanka, themselves older than the nation. The archival passages of *Anil's Ghost* and Sailor's archive of bones resolve inside the scarred totality of the sculpture. Buddhism's association with the persecution of Hindu Tamils makes it undeniably problematic as the novel's concluding symbol of national reconciliation, yet the conditions of the statue's restoration are hopeful. It is only by disaffiliating the Buddha from the Sinhalese state by having a victim of that state repair it, and by tying it to a supranational geography, that Ondaatje can make a claim for its unifying power taking precedence over its ethnocentric deployment and corruption.

The difficulties of such a utopian vision are clear: Ondaatje arguably re-silences Sailor (this time mythically, not historically) by replacing the skeleton with the Buddha as the novel's final image of social recovery. Yet it is worth considering Sailor's muteness as a reminder of present actors' limits in the face of the past's otherness. Whether they are historians, scientists, writers, or visual artists, the most Ondaatje and his protagonists can do is mediate how the past resonates with the present, and that mediation entails bringing different degrees of the past (recent versus ancient) and different kinds of remembering (mythical versus historical) into meaningful convergence. The sacred statue's implication in historical violence shows its susceptibility to resignification, but such resignifying is also what holds out the possibility of Buddhism's rehabilitation within Sri Lanka. By showing how enduring myths can also change, Ondaatje's archival legends help readers to appreciate the coherence that myth provides but to question any notion of ossification in myth's persistence through cultural memory.

The structure of *Anil's Ghost* works against such ossification when we consider that it has not one but several endings. In the first ending, Anil leaves Sri Lanka, contemplating her own place in the Western media's narcissistic narratives of heroism: "American movies, English books—remember how they all end? . . . The American or the Englishman gets on a plane and leaves. That's it. The camera leaves with him" (*Anil's Ghost*, 285). Another ending takes the form of an encounter between Sarath's brother, Gamini, and Sarath's corpse, after Sarath has been tortured and murdered for aiding Anil. The third and penultimate ending features a public riot in Sri Lanka in which the president is assassinated—perhaps the result of Anil's report, although the novel does not specify this. To read the novel as displaying, perhaps even archiving, several endings rather than settling for one recalls *The Collected Works of Billy the Kid*, in which the sense of an ending was precisely unending. Each artifact in that work promised to extend and disable Billy's concrete definition by generating continual reinterpretations, and every ending in *Anil's Ghost* extends Sailor's reverberations over those who would form an interpretive community around him.[40]

Billy and Sailor thus take shape through the projections of their many authors and artifactual remains. Indeed, their importance to Ondaatje's transnational dissection and renovation of national mythologies depends precisely on their remaining legends, as opposed to becoming the real (in the positivist sense) William Bonney and Ruwan Kumara. The archive as a formal paradigm enables Ondaatje to experiment with both the proliferation of cultural artifacts in the American context and the dearth of information in the Sri Lankan one. Moreover, it enables him to use the polarities of these cases to stage a larger examination of collective memory's capacity to shift and multiply the scales of imagined community: national, international, human. Where one would expect specific national identities to be shored up by a return to recognizable icons (the American outlaw of *Collected Works* and the Sri Lankan Buddha that replaces Sailor at the end of *Anil's Ghost*), Ondaatje's archival legends change the collectivity to be renewed and the apertures by which the national and the international become plausible attachments. They divert national symbols through transnational geographies not only to multiply the number of groups that may lay claim to them but also to blur the boundaries among those groups.

This strategy of reinscription is an important one for cultivating coalitional thinking about collective memory, an invitation that Michael

Rothberg has already extended through his concept of "multidirectional memory." Rothberg cogently argues that memory, particularly public memory, is too often perceived in terms of competition for scarce resources. To jar that entrenched understanding, he conceives a model based on the "interplay of disparate acts of remembrance," in which one group's memories might help lend meaning and value to another's.[41] By defamiliarizing figures of nostalgia for one group and showing their interception by another, Ondaatje begins the slow and multidirectional process of separating collective pasts from isolationist paradigms of community and from the myths of origin, lineage, and belonging that they sustain.

L. P. Hartley famously wrote, "The past is a foreign country: they do things differently there."[42] Ondaatje's archival legends revive this striking metaphor of the strangeness of personal memory and transpose it to the domain of the political and the transnational, literalizing it in the process. *Collected Works* and *Anil's Ghost* show what national pasts might look like when formulated through foreign countries; they reinterpret the boundaries of cultural memory and discover that the past moves at differential rates. Over to some and ongoing to others, the past is essential to collective self-definition. Ondaatje's literary works grapple with its phenomenological density and preserve those subaltern modes of retrospection that might otherwise go unseen and unfelt in materialist histories of conflict.[43] His modernist project retains internationalism's critical edge without sacrificing or simplifying its sentimental ends.

5

ROOT CANALS

Zadie Smith's Scales of Injustice

> The fact is if we followed the history of every little country in this world—in its dramatic as well as its quiet times—we would have no space left in which to live our own lives or to apply ourselves to our necessary tasks, never mind indulge in occasional pleasures, like swimming. Surely there is something to be said for drawing a circle around our attention and remaining within that circle. But how large should this circle be?
> —Zadie Smith, "The Embassy of Cambodia"

> These banks are too big to fail. They're too big to manage. They're too big to regulate. They're too complex to understand and they're too risky to exist.
> —Phil Angelides, chairman of the U.S. Financial Crisis Inquiry Commission

A literary study of internationalism is particularly well suited to parsing the facts and values of "integration," one of the most prevalent bywords for describing the social, economic, and cultural effects of globalization today. Of course, the fact/value split is never neutral, a point reinforced by juxtaposing two dictionary definitions of *integrate*. The *Oxford English Dictionary*'s first definition is "To render entire or complete; to make up, compose, constitute (a whole)," whereas in *Merriam-Webster*, one definition is "to make (something) a part of another larger thing."[1] The *Oxford* definition, with its softer phrasing, imbues integration with the traditional values of aesthetic form. "Completion" and "wholeness" suggest a desirable unity, whereas *Merriam-Webster*'s "make part" intimates the coercion and oppression that both Marxian and biopolitical approaches have, in their differing ways, aligned with life under large systems.

Global capitalism is the largest of those large systems, and if my epigraph from Phil Angelides is to be believed, the most damagingly integrated because the most damagingly concentrated. Banks "too big to fail . . . too big to manage . . . too big to regulate . . . too complex to understand . . . too risky to exist" were bailed out, as the story goes, in order to save the entire financial system from collapse. According to such reasoning, to use the language of the Occupy movement, the 1 percent's demise means the 99 percent's demise as well. That this is a story of injustice goes without saying. That the injustice stems from hypocrisy regarding dependence and distribution deserves more examination.

I begin this chapter with Angelides's reference to the banks not because "too big to fail" is a powerful excuse for preserving in the short term a way of life that is unsustainable in the long term. That much we know. I begin with the banks because, in becoming targets of rightful anger, they also become metonyms, parts substituting for wholes, that, in this case, leave the most complicated parts of a whole story untold. As meetings of the World Social Forum and, more popularly, Occupy demonstrations in hundreds of cities around the world have shown, assigning blame to certain actors, such as investment banks, only puts an institutional face on a systemic crisis that includes the relaxation of environmental protection standards, the weakening of labor unions, increasing student debt, and increasing wealth inequality.

Economist Branko Milanović has identified the last of these factors, wealth inequality, as the root cause of the global financial crisis, and he argues that it should occasion a debate about the scale at which conversations about inequality operate. Economists usually measure inequality on a national scale because it is the nation-state that distributes access to benefits and entitlement programs to offset that inequality. However, as "the world becomes more integrated," Milanović argues, global inequality, or wealth disparity between the poorest and the richest people in the world, becomes a more salient category—one that explains events that become paranoid media spectacles in developed countries, such as the rise of piracy in the Indian Ocean, the spread of a flu epidemic that originated in Mexico, and unabated migration to the European Union and the United States.[2]

Milanović's study of global inequality invites us to think about how world-systemic problems of poverty make themselves known, and how they continue to be obscured through the metonymic shorthand of nationality in phrases like "Somali pirates" or "the Mexican flu." The project of international solidarity, so thrillingly displayed in the spread of popular uprisings, bears with it an obligation to reveal the perniciousness of such shorthand and to contend with how global inequality fissures "the 99 percent." According to Milanović's numbers, 20 percent of the world's population enjoys 83 percent of the total world income. While we in wealthy countries can and should protest that global form of income inequality, we also cannot ignore the fact that many of those who belong to the 99 percent, intellectually and emotionally, might also belong to the 20 percent, economically.

This contradiction demands attention because membership in advantaged communities cannot just be shrugged off and because keeping visible the wealth disparities across the Global North and Global South insinuates necessary scale-reflection into conversations about critiquing and resisting capitalism as a global phenomenon. "Too big to fail" should have multiple referents—the banking institutions, to be sure, but also the larger networks of uneven development and wealth distribution of which these institutions are only one node. Confronting relative privilege is not about implying, exposing, or judging contradictions in financial status and political conviction as evidence of hypocrisy. Rather, it is the discomfiting but essential position from which to think about how national and global scales of inequality fit together.

Zadie Smith's fictions are particularly keen on exploring conflicts and continuities of scale alongside communities' conflicts and continuities of interest. *White Teeth*, for example, turns a multicultural, national story of England into an international story of the British Empire by turning a painful dental procedure, the root canal, into a metaphor for deciphering the causalities of migration in all their personal and historical complexity. Chapters entitled "The Root Canals of Alfred Archibald Jones and Samad Miah Iqbal," "The Root Canals of Mangal Pande," and "The Root Canals of Hortense Bowden" inject recursion into the novel's largely progressive plot, suggesting that readers who want to understand English community circa the 1970s to the 1990s (the primary setting of the novel) will need to know something about the Eastern Europe of 1945, the India of 1857, and the Jamaica of 1900, respectively. The claim fits well with the epigraph to *White Teeth*, "The past is prologue," and with the larger insistence of multicultural British fiction that, in the stuttering words of Salman Rushdie's Whiskey Sissodia, "The trouble with the Engenglish is that their history happened overseas so they dodo don't know what it means."[3]

But the narrative structure of Smith's root canals also sits in uneasy relation to the clarifications of framing that "the past is prologue" implies. "Root Canal" chapters pop up to break the time–space unities of the novel, and they interrupt, confuse, and diffuse exposition as a matter of performing it. Dubbed "dizzying in a good way" by Caryl Phillips, "hysterical" in a bad way by James Wood, Smith's narrative strategies in her first novel establish her ongoing interest in the ambivalence of causality: wanting to know the determinative forces and individual choices that explain the present, and fearing that knowing more will not guarantee understanding more or acting any more rightly.[4]

In her 2008 essay "Two Paths for the Novel," Smith furnished readers with a much-debated argument about the "future of the Anglophone novel." The path of lyrical realism, represented by Joseph O'Neill's *Netherland*, would, however anxiously, evince a belief in the "transcendent importance of form" and in the liberal self, characterized by an "essential fullness and continuity." The alternative path of the avant-garde, represented by Tom McCarthy's *Remainder*, would less anxiously reject philosophical idealism in favor of the poststructuralist critique of totalities. Such a novel would embrace the matter that resists form, with form understood here, in McCarthy's words (quoted by Smith), as the attempt to "ingest all of reality into a system of thought, to eat it up, to penetrate and possess it."[5]

Smith gives the edge to McCarthy for bringing readers to the limits of individual consciousness and for inspiring an awareness of conceptual failure amid the sheer materiality of language. In doing so, she also stakes out the legacy of modernism that anticipates McCarthy's principles—"the negations of Beckett. The paradoxical concrete abstractions of Kafka. The scatological thingy-ness of Joyce at his most antic." These strategies are examples of what Smith calls "overwhelming narration." They convey an off-kilter extremity ("There's too much here, too much to process, just too much") that is also an epistemological position ("a narration defined by absence, by partial knowledge, for we can only know it by the marks it has left").

Whatever we think of Smith's sketches of realism and the avant-garde, her appraisal of McCarthy's residual modernism reveals something about her own.[6] Smith's formal and conceptual preoccupations are with the excess that signals human finitude ("partial knowledge") and with the acts of sense-making that arise from those overwhelmed states of being in which a self comes into both consciousness and collapse in the face of unsolvable dilemmas. They draw her oeuvre together, and, because not inherently limited to global capitalism, become remarkably rich roads into the critique of its inequalities and occlusions while also functioning as sharp engagements with the epistemologies of totality used to describe it. Unlike McCarthy, who aligns himself with a more orthodox poststructuralism, Smith imagines totality as a chimera to be preserved and uses the analytical resources of literary form to imagine what an immanent wholeness, a wholeness without transcendence of the structures or obscurities of modernity, might look like.

As Martin Jay's magisterial study of "totality" established, the term is a contested one within the history of Western Marxism, and it embeds understandings of holism not limited to Marxism.[7] Generally speaking, totality can refer to the possibility and necessity of complete understanding (a legacy of Enlightenment thought that comes to equate knowledge with mastery and individual self-possession). It can also refer to an underlying reality of which the surface is a symptom (a legacy of Marxism, which comes to privilege systemic causes over individual actions or inactions). Alternatively, it can denote the antimodern organicism of cultures as intact expressions of a people (à la Herder) or refuges from an alienating industrialization (à la Raymond Williams). I use "totality" and "holism" in this chapter to reflect on the interplay between systemic critique and self-critique in Smith's work. This results in an examination of how her fiction intersects with the thought of Marxian advocates of world-systemic totality, such as Fredric Jameson and Immanuel Wallerstein, as well as how it retains progressive cosmopolitan critique's focus on the individual's ethical and epistemological dilemmas in the face of a globalizing world of increasing inequality.

Smith's root canals, as metaphor and narrative form, portray the global whole as relational, composed in the Saidian terms of overlapping territories and intertwined histories.[8] As metaphor, they capture the overwhelming project of discerning causality over long distances. As narrative form, they embrace techniques of digression and extraneousness as paradoxically essential sources of literary organization and political reflection. Yet Smith's root canals as media forms—chapters in a book—also promote the generalization, division, and abstraction of stories into bounded units as necessary tools of meaning-making.

Nicholas Dames has argued that the literary history of the chapter—that plain and perennially overlooked element of the novel form, and of book form more broadly—discloses a whole host of concerns about the art of understanding. On one hand, chapters function as "miniature narratives that observe Aristotle's 'unities' of time, place, and action, and that can be extracted from the stream of life as a whole." On the other, that extractable holism raises the specter of compromised understanding: "A comprehension of smaller parts rather than coherent wholes might, Locke worried, be a lesser comprehension."[9] Although Dames attributes a fear of partial knowledge to Locke, the attribution is equally applicable, in the context of my argument, to Marxian methodologies that warn against reification, and to Smith herself, who realizes the always present danger of obscuring the whole story while trying to tell it. Smith makes the anxieties of partial knowledge a principle concern of her writing, and her interest in root canals in *White Teeth*, as both metaphors for long-distance causalities and instances of distinctly bounded chapters, augers her later fiction's formal experiments with size, scale, and division-drawing.

Smith's interest in the "partness" of wholes and the wholeness of parts manifests most strongly through her persistent return to northwest London—the site of her most recent novel, *NW*, and a variety of essays and short fiction. Like Joyce in the early twentieth century, Smith, in the early twenty-first, returns to her home city as part of a proleptic, if not preemptive, act of memorialization. Whereas Joyce contended from afar with the destruction of Dublin in the wake of the 1916 Easter Rising, Smith fears the succumbing of northwest London to the privatizing forces of gentrification—forces whose "slow violence" might inhibit the comparison with a spectacular uprising and yet are just as—if not more—erosive of the social fabric.[10] Both writers conceive of their respective homes as marginal and provincial, but where Joyce reckoned all of Dublin as both hospitable and insular, Smith divides London into parts—parts that at times need to be understood as wholes in order to achieve a comprehension that might be described as fuller rather than lesser. Joyce drew our attention to the disparities between the Irish colonial city, British metropole, and European continent; Smith multiplies the cores and peripheries within London and without. She traces London's internal geography of power as a way of reflecting upon what it means to inhabit a global city, a center of finance capital and culture that is also internally riven by its status.[11]

Smith's northwest London fictions apportion to themselves the problem of deciphering wholeness and causality as they range from economically materialist accounts to more local and individual stories. Smith seeks out conflicts of scale because she understands framing as integral to understandings of wholeness. Her fictions work through international realities that look like contradictions from the point of view of national culture alone. For example, they show that dearly held local histories might be the province of recent arrivals to a country, and that class distinctions are often far more inimical to the goals of self-described democratic societies than the conflicts caused by ethnic pluralism. Still, her fictions do not always privilege the global scale as the superior ground of comprehension. Smith's use of formal strategies to evoke the partiality of knowledge—its framing and its incompleteness—constructs the challenge of rendering the whole as the overwhelming challenge of seeing at multiple scales.

Smith's root canals may be dizzying, but they are also demotic, illustrative of the everyday realities of interconnection that are masked by commonplace understandings of collectivity, such as the one offered in the first epigraph of this chapter. Although the speaker deems it eminently reasonable to draw "a circle around our attention," the final interrogative ("But how large should this circle be?") hints at the need for a messier geometry of collective affiliation.[12] I use the word *demotic* with respect to Smith's root canals for another reason as well: as a cognate of *democracy*, it connects styles of ordinary speech, such as clichés, slang, idioms, and adages, to styles of being a demos—that is, a people—civically as opposed to ethnically defined.

Smith's prose has been celebrated for making multiculturalism seem demotic; her writing reflects and complements England's status as a "mongrel nation" comprising people from multiple ethnic backgrounds.[13] Yet, given multiculturalism's emphasis on ethnicity and nationhood, civic and economic orientations toward democracy have gone comparatively unexamined in her work. James Procter, drawing on Stuart Hall, rightly notes, "As difference gets incorporated, reworked, and pieced out according to the logic of late global capitalism, it is worth asking whether (ethnic) difference is still capable of making a difference."[14] By pursuing a more refined understanding of how ethnic and civic culture overlap, Smith's northwest London fictions bring an analysis of class along with an analysis of scale to the fore in modernist internationalism.

Measure for Measure

From Greco-Roman to modern times, scales have symbolized the abstract concept of justice in the West. Scale iconography implies that justice is quantifiable and inheres in processes in which impersonality guarantees their impartiality. This, of course, is a specifically liberal ideal of justice, and its blindness to the embodiment of people has been subjected to thoroughgoing critique. Yet the scales of justice, as a phrase if not an iconic image, might be interpreted in another way. Instead of imagining scales as the measuring tools of vested authority, we might think of scales as the tools for measuring the vestments of such authority. This is what Nancy Fraser does when she characterizes the contemporary moment as one in which the scale of justice is beyond consensus. Proliferating standards of measuring justice, from the traditional (for example, the distribution of divisible goods) to the more recent (for example, the recognition of group specificity, or the demand for new political arenas beyond the nation-state), produce doubt as to whether there is one proper scale of justice and, indeed, point to the multiplicity of scales under which justice might be conceived.[15]

Smith's fictions share Fraser's concern with balancing multiple scales of justice, and this is nowhere better illustrated than in her 2013 short story "The Embassy of Cambodia." Originally published in the *New Yorker*, the eleven-page story imagines obstacles to justice within liberal democracies that have defined constituencies and across global circuits that do not. Writing in a genre defined by its scale, Smith explores the challenges of scaling that were metaphorized and formalized by the root canal chapters in *White Teeth*. These challenges include balancing the disruption of boundaries with the necessity of drawing boundaries, properly arraying parts and wholes, and deciphering causality across multiple geographies. For Smith, the short story's renowned containment becomes an opportunity to visualize the strategies of enclosure and continuity that draw awareness to the inorganic production of wholeness and constituency—in stories and in communities.

"Embassy" explores the relationship between formal wholes and social wholes at the level of structural organization, plot, and narrative voice. The story unfolds in numbered sections of varying length and according to the following format: 0–1, 0–2, 0–3 . . . One reviewer used the term "chapters" in scare quotes, a choice that highlights their oddity through the mixing up of scales: the partitioning vocabulary of long-form fiction strangely applies to short-form fiction.[16] Like chapters, Smith's sections are of varying length, but they are measured by paragraphs instead of pages. Some are several paragraphs long, others one paragraph only, and even if one peeks at the end, the numbers evoke an infinite set within a finite story. This paradox reveals something perhaps so obvious it has gone unnoticed: the short story is a literary form in which the whole is not supposed to have visible parts. Generally read in one sitting, the short story is the preeminent narrative example of a unified and organic whole. Yet Smith insists on partitioning it and displaying its mechanical "pieceness." By creating so many divisions where none are expected, Smith introduces questions of judgment where they were not previously legible—between sections of the story but also between characters and places represented in the story.

The divided whole is a fitting conceit, given Smith's focus on varieties of social order, from the microcollectivity of the household to the macrocollectivities of nations and continents. The protagonist of "Embassy" is Fatou, a domestic servant from the Ivory Coast who is living with an upper-middle-class South Asian family, the Derawals, in Willesden, a section of northwest London. Fatou works for room and board, and her employers hold her passport. She has no monetary income. Several times in the story, she compares her situation to that reported in a "discarded" newspaper article about a "Sudanese 'slave'" living in London and wonders if she too is a slave. (She concludes that she is not, but the question hangs in the air.) Smith does not explain how Fatou arrived in London, but we know "her father, not a kidnapper" oversaw her migration from the Ivory Coast to Ghana, where they worked together at a hotel, and then paid for her single passage from Libya to Italy ("Embassy," section 0–7).

Smith's incomplete sketch of Fatou's journey from the Ivory Coast to Willesden traces a migration route that, since 1999, has brought more than two hundred thousand people to the Italian island of Lampedusa, if not to London. Mattathias Schwartz calls Lampedusa a "zone of global limbo, where developed nations decide who is most deserving of a new life on the other side of the wall."[17] The wall here is an allusion to the larger discourse surrounding European Union migration policies, which has won the continent the title of "Fortress Europe."[18] The moniker forms a linguistic riposte to the European Commission's European Neighbourhood Policy, the stated goal of which was to create "a zone of prosperity and friendly neighborhood" among member and nonmember states, but which also demanded that nonmembers ramp up their own border security against migrants deemed undesirable within Europe.[19]

Smith does not allow the details of such policies into "Embassy," but she raises the specter of their absence with a narrative voice that declares "we" don't really want the details anyway. To return once more to the first epigraph of this chapter:

> The fact is if we followed the history of every little country in this world—in its dramatic as well as its quiet times—we would have no space left in which to live our own lives or to apply ourselves to our necessary tasks, never mind indulge in occasional pleasures, like swimming. Surely there is something to be said for drawing a circle around our attention and remaining within that circle. But how large should this circle be?
>
> ("Embassy," section 0–9)

The speaker here is not Fatou. It introduces itself in the story's second paragraph as "we, the people of Willesden." The phrasing evokes not just a collectivity but also a demos, which worries for Fatou without making any gesture of inclusion or self-implication in her fate. The choral narration, however, with its repetition of "we" and "our," slowly draws a circle around the reader as the narrator aligns provinciality with common sense and equates the avoidance of world news with the impossibility of following "the history of every little country in this world." The narrator's normative claims naturalize insularity by harnessing scale and number, implying that an impossibly large and single field of attention would be required to care about many little countries. Smith uses the "we" to expose the link between a rhetoric of limited resources (here, of attention) and an ethos of communitarianism, which conceives of belonging as singular and finite rather than multiple and ongoing. That is, the size of the group is more important than multiplying the number and kinds of groups to which one can belong—for example, to Willesden and the European Union.[20]

The brevity of the short story form would seem to support the narrator's point of view, but "Embassy" uses the discreteness of numbers against the discreteness of countries. The ability of a short story to absorb the sectioning capacity of long forms suggests that expanding attention is possible but requires changing one's principle of scale rather than measuring more units with it. In "Embassy," Smith calls for multiple measures of distance, and she reveals the absurdities of proximity that are overlooked by sharply separating Willesden from "far-off" countries. After all, the Sudanese slave to whom Fatou compares herself lives in London, yet her plight makes no greater claim to the Derawals' attention (or the narrator's) than if she had lived in Khartoum. The localism of solidarity here has as much to do with socioeconomic and racial measures of closeness as it does with physical and national measures of distance.

Smith makes this point in various ways throughout "Embassy," which turns Willesden's streets into a symbolic landscape of access points, walls, and guarded entryways that recall the neighborhood–fortress dyad of the new Europe. The titular Embassy of Cambodia stands, as a sign of Willesden's gentrification, on the side of the street with "private residences . . . [featuring] Corinthian pillars," thought to be owned by "wealthy Arabs" ("Embassy," section 0–1). It is surrounded by an eight-foot wall, which blocks the narrator's view of everything but conspicuously non-Cambodian people coming and going, and a shuttlecock rising above the wall from a game of badminton.[21] A kind of objective correlative for prestige (in the form of a walled-off governmental institution) and marginality (directed at a poor country known to the narrator only for the genocide of its people), the embassy casts the shadow of state relations and official hospitality over the lackluster hospitality meted out to ordinary people without means.

Next door to the embassy is a health center, also private, where Fatou goes to swim. In another nod to the inequities of hospitality (more welcoming to the rich than to the poor and to singles than to groups), she gains entry by pilfering her employers' many unused guest passes. But security tightens when she attempts to bring her own guest, a Nigerian friend, Andrew, to the pool, using two guest passes simultaneously. Smith allows setting to blur the line between elected and enforced forms of partial vision, embedding not just Fatou but also the "we" narrator in a multicultural social hierarchy that it initially seemed to survey from an Archimedean point. Sometimes the voice of "we" is omniscient, capable of entering Fatou's consciousness through free indirect discourse and recalling memories of her hotel work in Ghana. Other times, it is limited, never able to see over the wall of the embassy. Inconsistency in the narrator's access seems part of the story's point, and it gives way to a series of destabilizing revelations. In sections 0–3 and 0–6, "we" slips into "I." In section 0–13, "I" reveals that it is one of the "distressed souls" in a "dingy retirement home." By withholding some details of her narrator's embodied identity (for example, race and gender) and yielding others (for example, approximate age and class), Smith uses multiculturalism's lessons to bring its less emphasized categories into view.

In doing so, however, she does not affirm by rote the principle that disembodied universality masks its own particularity and exclusivity. She lets the destabilization of narrative voice, through a technique known as metalepsis, bring the totalizing category of representation itself up for scrutiny:

> Of the Old and New People of Willesden I speak; I have been chosen to speak for them, though they did not choose me and must wonder what gives me the right. I could say, "Because I was born at the crossroads of Willesden, Kilburn, and Queen's Park!" But the reply would be swift and damning: "Oh, don't be foolish, many people were born right there; it doesn't mean anything at all. We are not one people and no one can speak for us. It's all a lot of nonsense. We see you standing on the balcony, overlooking the Embassy of Cambodia, in your dressing gown, staring into the chestnut trees, looking gormless. The real reason you speak in this way is because you can't think of anything better to do."
>
> ("Embassy," section 0–13)

In Gerard Genette's definition of the term from *Narrative Discourse*, metalepsis transgresses the boundaries between "two worlds, the world *in* which one tells, the world *of* which one tells" (emphasis mine).[22] Each world is a level, and to cross between them, as Smith's narrator does by being seen standing on the balcony, is to cross "the threshold of embedding" that the narrative had established.[23] This crossing over puts the coherence of distinct narrative worlds into crisis in order to cast doubt on the coherence of social worlds. The "we" splits into an antagonistic "you" and a "gormless" "I" that undercuts the authority of the narrator while reasserting the question, posed earlier in the story, about how best to shape and weigh attention. *Gormless* derives from the English dialect word *gaumless*, meaning without "heed" or "attention." By using this rare vernacular word in an otherwise standard English work, Smith suggests that jumping from "I" to "we," even in the most local communities ("we, the people of

Willesden") is always an act of abstraction, a creation of a deracinated totality where there was none, and thus is an act of collective representation that is no less troubling or inescapable when the relevant whole is local than if the relevant whole were national or global.

Metalepsis thus opens up the possibility of feeling international solidarity by denaturalizing solidarities that conceive of local connections as more real than those at larger scales. Smith's narrator appropriates the language of representative democracy only to flummox it: "I have been chosen to speak for them, though they did not choose me and must wonder what gives me the right." The narrative voice contemplates its status as a teller of Willesden tales, and rejects the rationale that being born in a place gives one special purchase on the stories of that place.[24]

This is not to say that Smith denies the existence or value of local knowledge, but she does contest the legitimacy that nativity confers, especially when so many others were born in that place, too, and would be equally qualified to narrate, according to such limited criteria. It bears mentioning that this anxiety is also the anxiety of leftist intellectuals whose willingness to see the social whole often goes hand in hand with delimiting groups that do not ratify them as their speakers. Such anxiety over representation thus belongs not only to Smith's narrator but also to Smith herself, who has of late earned the moniker "the bard of Willesden Green."[25]

When the narrator in "Embassy" speaks on behalf of "the people of Willesden" while reflecting on what constrains and taints representation, one cannot help but see the relationship forming between authorial identity and a democratic aesthetics that reflects upon Smith herself as a writer and intellectual. In order to broach the always thorny political question of who gets to speak and why, Smith does not pontificate so much as demote her bardic substitute to the status of a nosy neighbor. The air of gossip the story takes on contributes to its political analysis and to Smith's self-construction, via the narrator, as someone not fully authorized to tell her tale.

Priscilla Wald's study of authorship and democratic nationhood differentiates between official stories of nation-building, drawn from the law, political speeches, and literary organizations, and unofficial stories of national analysis, drawn from writers whose style oscillates between "conformity and incomprehensibility."[26] Such stylistic oscillation conveys the ambivalence of belonging to a national community and the consequences of pushing the boundaries of a "we" beyond instant recognizability. Smith's style in "Embassy" is not idiomatically difficult, but it relies on metalepsis and partitioning to align discovery with misunderstandings that can be seen only in retrospect. Transgressing narrative levels reveals our previous understandings about the coherence of Willesden's community to be not just misplaced assumptions but, to recall Dames's phrase, lesser comprehensions. Creating an awareness of degrees of understanding, Smith makes reflection on the processes of measurement an active part of reading her short story. Pausing over the distinctions between the world of the narrator and the world of the narrated reveals the gap between the constituted whole "we, the people of Willesden" and the ever-changing dynamics of actually existing groups, as signified by the "Old and New People of Willesden." This alteration to the ritual language of democratic culture suggests that ongoing processes of migration should revise enduring notions of constituency, and thus it agitates the narrator's circle of attention but does not explode it.

"Embassy" ends with two more twists that exploit narrative levels: one that readers and Fatou share, and one for readers alone. In the final section of the story, Fatou is fired without explanation. The narrator assures us that she is not fired for taking guest passes, and we identify, however briefly, with the precariousness of a domestic worker's position. Fatou leaves the Derawal house and waits for Andrew on the street outside the Embassy of Cambodia, where readers, aligned with the choral narrator, return to the privileged position of watching her:

> Many of us walked past her that afternoon, or spotted her as we rode the bus, or through the windscreens of our cars, or from our balconies. Naturally, we wondered what this girl was doing, sitting on damp pavement in the middle of the day. We worried for her. We tend to assume the worst, here in Willesden. We watched her watching the shuttlecock. Pock, smash. Pock, smash. As if one player could imagine only a violent conclusion and the other only a hopeful return.
>
> ("Embassy," section 0–21)

The ending compresses the major motifs Smith has used throughout the story: the casually generalizing narrative voice that draws conclusions out of speculations; the repetition of "pock, smash" to punctuate Fatou's routine (now broken); and metalepsis around "we," though it is smoother here because the reader is more prepared for it. It is also smoother because the "we" absorbs competing perspectives and allows them to converge on a single point, Fatou, who is the object of their shared curiosity and concern. Yet, any potential power the cohering demos of Willesden may gain from their common sympathy is undermined by the mise en abyme syntax, "we watched her watching the shuttlecock," which signals to readers that we, one level above the narrator, are yet another collectivity watching from a greater height.

The conclusion of "Embassy," with its implication of the reader, also reveals the final punchline: the story does not just contain passages about badminton; it is contained by its rules. Twenty-one points are necessary to win a match, and we have witnessed a crushing defeat in section 0–21. Surely, it is tempting to see Fatou as the metaphorical loser in this match, but traversing narrative levels from the diegetic to the extradiegetic and finally to the arrangement of numbered sections confirms the literal: she is not even a player. Neither, really, is the demos "we, the people of Willesden," however divided or united, for they do not see their own embedding within the game that structures their fate. Dramatic irony pervades the ending as only the reader sees the game, and the most powerful players, those whose policies decide people's fates, remain out of sight.

Smith's creative and varied use of division in the short story, in the form of metalepsis and segmentation, contributes to internationalist thought by multiplying the scales at which attention should be conceived and collectivities should be abstracted, but it stops short of granting literature more agency than it has to change conditions of global inequality. Indeed, the short story's ending encapsulates a recurring concern about literary realms of representation that Smith first explicitly pondered in the essay "This Is How It Feels to Me," written just after 9/11 in response to an essay by James Wood calling for a return to interiority in the contemporary novel. She writes: "Does anyone want to know the networks behind those seeming simplicities, the paths that lead from September 11 back to Saudi Arabia and Palestine, and then back to Israel, back further to the second world war, back once more to the first? Does anyone care what writers think about that? Does it help?"[27]

Pondering the root canals, "the networks behind those seeming simplicities" of terrible events, is exactly what the narrator of "Embassy" finds too unwieldy. It is also what the residents of Willesden cannot do as they focus their attention on Fatou's individual's plight without noticing the structural injustices, represented by the badminton game, in which they, too, are embedded. The scale of division in "Embassy"—a short story told in twenty-one parts—suggests that the whole story may inhere within the sum of its parts but that it will also conjure irresolvable remainders. For example, the end of the story/game is the beginning of a crucial gap between the knowledge of the story's readers and that of its residents. Dramatic irony is what makes "Embassy" disturbing, generative, and poignant in its engagement with democratic language and principles. The story forces us to ask how such principles can survive in a securitized era when citizenries do not understand how little they know, or how little they want to know. This is a question to which I will return in my closing reading of *White Teeth*.

Takin' Liberties

"The Embassy of Cambodia" suggests that changing the scales at which we conceive democracy and justice requires measuring measurement. This "meta-measurement" involves not only considering how multicultural, political, and geographic variables interact in determining spheres of collective attention but also acknowledging the limits of measurement when standards of justice become either incommensurable with each other or overwhelmed by the injustices they aim to rectify. *NW* and "The North West London Blues," both published in 2012, the year before "Embassy," tackle these aporias of measurement as well, and add to them the history of class struggle and literary canon formation in England.

Smith reaches back into the deep past for her epigraph to *NW*: "When Adam delved and Eve span, / Who was then the gentleman?"[28] What looks like an evocation of religious etiology against the historical development of social hierarchy is actually an allusion to a defining event in English history. Smith quotes from a sermon given by the Lollard priest John Ball during the Peasants' Revolt of June 1381. This rebellion marks the first time the lower classes (artisans, laborers, and serfs) marched on London (and elsewhere across England) to protest increased taxation that would disproportionately affect commoners over lords, the policies of serfdom, and various other practices that concentrated wealth among the church and gentry. Ball's teachings reinforced the connection between the Fall and class hierarchy and advocated the replacement of private property with common ownership.

In the last days of the revolt, Ball was hanged, drawn, and quartered. He remains a central figure in radical histories of England and has been imagined as a distant ancestor to participants of the Occupy movements (ongoing since 2011) and London's Democracy Village (2010).[29] Ball plays such a role in Lindsey German and John Rees's *A People's History of London*, in which they argue that "the London of the twenty-first century is reproducing the conditions that gave rise to radical and socialist ideas in the past." German and Rees point to higher levels of wealth inequality within London compared to the rest of England, the shortage of affordable housing, and the proliferation of jobs that pay less than the London Living Wage as among the factors that have given rise to increased political activism and social unrest.[30]

"The North West London Blues" contributes to such a people's history via a Raymond Williams–style evocation of residual ways of life and their ebbing resistance to the encroachments of capital. The essay considers gentrification and privatization through the particularly painful closing of the Willesden Green Library Centre to make way for "private luxury flats."[31] Smith presents the loss of the library center as not just the loss of a public resource but also the forsaking of "a different kind of social reality" in which values beyond the fiscal and wealth accumulation might be perpetuated. That previous reality of the commons, operant under duress in the present, was granted limited room to flourish through the English welfare state. It is an institution to which Smith credits, well, her entire life:

> Some people owe everything they have to the bank accounts of their parents. I owe the state. Put simply, the state educated me, fixed my leg when it was broken, and gave me a grant that enabled me to go to university. It fixed my teeth (a bit) and found housing for my veteran father in his dotage. . . . To steal another writer's title: England made me.

Smith's gratitude to a welfarist England is not without its complications. Despite her anger at England's role in dismantling its social safety net and contributing to "new, shared global reality in which states deregulate to privatize gain and reregulate to nationalize loss," her fondness for the welfare state may rankle more radical critics of neoliberalism who have regarded welfare as more collusive with capitalism than critical of it. Her appreciation also does not grapple with the persistence of imperial norms within the development and discourse of welfare policy in the 1950s and 1960s.[32] Still, Smith's defense of the welfare state is worth entertaining because it lends insight into *NW*'s less sanguine reflections on upward mobility and into her situation as a self-declared English writer whose work has pushed postcolonialism beyond the borders of its usual self-recognition.[33]

In an essay that defends the common space of the library as a form of patriotic Englishness, Smith undercuts the measures of literary culture by which her own work has achieved its place within the canon of British fiction. Smith's reputation as a writer of multiculturalism regularly places her in a genealogy that begins with the Windrush generation and continues with the likes of Salman Rushdie, Caryl Phillips, Hanif Kureishi, and Andrea Levy, among others.[34] Yet her "theft" and recontextualization of Graham Greene's title *England Made Me* suggests that the path of black British literary history, with its guiding categories of race and ethnicity, is only half the story. If migrants remade England into an international zone, their interactions with the institutions of the welfare state also brought them into the complicated, because not always *inhospitable*, fold of English national culture. Whereas Greene coined "England made me" as an indictment of a culture in the midst of imperial decline, Smith reuses it sincerely and fully embraces her indebtedness to a nation that she now too perceives as in decline.

Of course, Smith's nostalgia is for neither empire nor cultural homogeneity, which is why it is both odd and potent that "The North West London Blues" repurposes the more xenophobic tropes of national decline—the disappearance of cherished institutions and the unrecognizability of one's environment—to make a case against the invasion of capital rather than of immigrants. By claiming her domestic entanglements with England, Smith is able to protest its complicity in the "new global reality" of neoliberal deregulation. As *neo-* implies, contemporary globalization embeds a renewal of earlier forms of imperial liberalism, which Smith tends to forget in "North West London Blues," even as she remembers them elsewhere in her fiction. Yet her claims to English nativity put an interesting spin on postcolonial critique by interjecting attenuated strangeness (though strangeness, nonetheless) and the middle-distance view of history back into its narratives of domination.

Postcolonial critics, like modernist writers, have generally espoused tactics of defamiliarization and unsettlement. Paul Gilroy, for example, argues that bringing colonial history back into the narrative of England's self-making is valuable not simply as ideological demystification but also as a form of estrangement that induces critical distance from the norms and values of one's perceived native culture.[35] Smith modifies this strategy of estrangement by adopting the viewpoint of a visiting expatriate rather than an alien or migrant. Her neighborhood has changed, as has her class status, and the jarring disjunction is more historical than geographic—Willesden now versus Willesden then. Smith's reacquaintance with place is a reacquaintance with the effect of government policy on her own success, and her reference points in the near past are what make the threat of permanent austerity under David Cameron's conservative regime so hard to stomach.

Smith's willingness to claim her Englishness but to redirect tropes of Englishness—the rural countryside, the bounded village—to a London neighborhood distinguished by its postal zoning, state-sponsored institutions (from the library to council housing), and racial diversity supersedes the canonical dividing lines between devolution-oriented English writing (as represented by Greene, Kingsley Amis, and Philip Larkin) and anti-assimilationist black British writing. By scrambling these subdivisions, Smith's work makes a sense of English place compatible with a sense of other places, the *elsewhere* so important to a postcolonial history of the present. It also creates affection for those institutions that help make domesticity compatible with internationalism, at least in some residents' experiences. As Smith writes of the library, "We find it pleasant to remember that we have as much right to a local history as anyone, even if many of us arrived here only recently and from every corner of the globe."

NW is Smith's foray into cultivating that nimble localism, which can bring a 1381 epigraph by John Ball into alignment with the vast world-systemic distances and ideological battles that pervade a "two-mile square of city" (*NW*, 6). Smith uses northwest London not for its allegorical continuity with the wider nation or world but for its disproportional relation to divisions of space conceived at those larger scales. The modest size and "peripherally core" location of the region disturb, for example, a world-systemic vocabulary of global spatial distinctions, but without receding into a bucolic organicism. NW is a postal code abbreviation, after all—a state-created abstraction. By insisting on a scale largely unnoticed or insignificant beyond London and making it vital to dissecting the dismantling of social democracy, Smith marks out the neighborhoods of *NW* as danger zones—endangered by the encroachments of privatization and dangerous to the ideology of austerity touted by conservative politicians.

Smith's novel follows four main characters, Leah, Felix, Natalie (born Keisha), and Nathan, each of whom grew up on the Caldwell Estate (public housing) and find themselves adrift in lives of varying economic security but unvarying personal dissatisfaction. All are restless individuals with fraught relationships to individualism and upward mobility as liberalism's prevailing mechanism of success. Building on Bruce Robbins's literary history of the welfare state, Amanda Claybaugh favorably reviewed *NW* for tapping into the contemporary demise of social democracy's collective ethos and the complacency that has greeted its loss. Yet the novel fails, in her estimation, to find an antidote to that complacency: "[Smith] wants to restore a vision of the political beyond the personal, but [is] hard-pressed to find one."[36]

Claybaugh does not begrudge Smith's failure to articulate "a politics adequate to our present neoliberal moment," perhaps because Claybaugh does not hold a wide-ranging oppositional critique of neoliberalism to be the ultimate measure of a novel's success. Neither do I. But the language of Claybaugh's review also suggests that she thinks an adequate politics is unachieved because its scope would have to be as comprehensive as neoliberalism itself. A consistent "vision" to match a definable "neoliberal moment"—such is the diction of literary and cultural critique, which, whether intended or not, creates totalities out a host of complex economic processes and political decisions and then demands totality from oppositional stances to them.

I give *NW* more credit than Claybaugh does as a novel of neoliberal critique, because it takes the comprehensive and the totalizing as objects of analysis rather than analytical givens. It attends to the ways in which the processes designated by neoliberalism are not as coherent as our critical language implies, even if they are aptly described as systematic. As Christoph Hermann has written, in his extensive analysis of neoliberal policies:

> We do not want to leave the impression that neoliberalism is a well-developed and coherent political strategy. Many of the policies are in fact contradictory and pragmatic responses to the shortcomings

> and antinomies of neoliberal assumptions as formulated in the Washington Consensus. . . . While neoliberalism is an international agenda, the implementation of neoliberal policies is, nevertheless, dependent on local struggles and compromises."[37]

Emphasizing a perspective that shuttles between the "international agenda" and "the local struggles and compromises" seems valuable because it recognizes sites of potential resistance to the agenda without overstating them and, with regard to critical parlance, invites reflection on the implications of phrases such as "the age of neoliberalism" or "the era of global capitalism."[38] Such declarations of period serve as rhetorical limit points against which scholars occasion and conceptualize critique. While these limit points are necessary for situating our work and performing analyses of power, they also are homogenizing abstractions that, in creating an undifferentiated horizon, aggrandize the formations they designate.

The unusual scales of Smith's writing are intent on interrogating and deflating the language of aggrandizement and codification, as is evident in her wry invocation of academic language as it filters into the everyday life of the educated classes:

> "I never know what's reasonable," said Imran. "Ten percent? Fifteen? Twenty?" Global consciousness. Local consciousness. Consciousness. And lo they saw their nakedness and were not ashamed. "You're fooling yourself," said Frank. "You can't get anything on the park for less than a million." The mistake was to think that money precisely signified—or was equivalent to—a particular arrangement of bricks and mortar. The money was not for these poky terraced houses with their short back gardens. The money was for the distance the house put between you and Caldwell. "That skirt," said Natalie Blake, pointing to a picture in the supplement, "but in red."
>
> (*NW*, 299–300).

This passage, like the rest of Smith's novel, pulls off the difficult task of satirizing and sympathizing at once. Set at a restaurant during brunch, the proprieties of tipping, the pipe dreams of real estate, and the distinctions of taste provide scattershot examples of the economic standing of the upper middle class, while the sardonic interjections of the narrator capture the enduring inequalities and desperately preserved distances embedded in such standing. The distance from Caldwell—the council estate "full of people from the colonies and the Russiany lot" (86)—is, for Natalie in particular, the distance from her previously unassimilated, more racially marked self, Keisha, and from the collective "mongrel" congregations whose presence in England constitutes an abject multiculturalism. The narrator's idiom, versed in technical terms and biblical allusion, registers the contradictory impulses of pride and self-loathing that define upward mobility as not just assimilation into an empowered class but also complicity with the precariousness that class hierarchy creates—whether it is immediately perceptible, as in the image of a waiter dependent on tips, or as structurally removed as the global economic inequalities that bring migrants to England from the former colonies and "Russiany" countries. Dismissive of academic haughtiness, but absolutely fluent in it (like the characters at brunch), Smith's narrator shows the enlightened vocabulary of "consciousness" to be a glib form of comprehension. Indeed, its glibness is integral to the elite's partial vision—the epiphenomenon of a psychological and geopolitical insulation that is more clarifying than it should be.

A discomfiting partiality of vision, then, is what defines Smith's portrayal of privilege in *NW*—discomfiting to the narrator and to Natalie, who cannot always decide whether she wishes to forget or remember her humble origins. Partiality, here, carries the double meaning of preference and incompleteness and recalls Fredric Jameson's influential argument that even if postmodern subjects could cognitively map themselves in relation to the impossibly complex totality of "society's structures as a whole," it is not clear that they would want to violate "the intimate space" of their "privacy" or "extended body."[39] If "Global consciousness. Local consciousness. Consciousness" had the force the words implied, perhaps they would not be so easy to list off. Whether Smith is directly familiar with Jameson's argument or not, *NW* shows an awareness of postmodernism's lessons—the waning of affect and the depoliticization of the subject—but renders them up to a renewed form of interrogation. Concepts integral to liberalism and phenomenology, such as privacy and the extended body, respectively, become topics that the novel addresses in relationship to large systems.

Take the opening section of the novel—a two-page chapter that features an unnamed woman (we later learn she is Leah) relaxing. I quote at length to capture the flavor of Smith's prose and because the layering of detail through short, simple sentences, some only one word long, combats excerption. Smith insists on the *slow* accretion of detail and, like a poet, deploys line arrangement on the page as part of the novel's form:

> The fat sun stalls by the phone masts. Anti-climb paint turns sulphurous on school gates and lampposts. In Willesden people go barefoot, the streets turn European, there is a mania for eating outside. She keeps to the shade. Redheaded. On the radio: I am the sole author of the dictionary that defines me. A good line—write it out on the back of a magazine. In a hammock, in the garden of a basement flat. Fenced in, on all sides.
>
> Four gardens along, in the estate, a grim girl on the third floor screams Anglo-Saxon at nobody. Juliet balcony, projecting for miles. It ain't like that. Nah it ain't like that. Don't you start. Fag in hand. Fleshy, lobster-red.
>
> I am the sole
>
> I am the sole author
>
> Pencil leaves no mark on magazine pages.
>
> (*NW*, 3)

This section goes on as the redhead turns the catchy radio phrase over in her mind and gives up trying to write it down. The act of writing, coupled with external distractions, unfinishes the finished phrase:

> I am the
>
> the sole
>
> Ash drifts down into the garden below, then comes the butt, then the box. Louder than the birds and the train and the traffic. Sole sign of sanity: a tiny device tucked in the ear. I told im stop takin liberties. Where's my cheque? And she's in my face chattin breeze. Fuckin liberty.
>
> I am the sole. The sole. The sole
>
> She unfurls her fist, lets the pencil roll. Takes her liberty. Nothing else to listen to but this bloody girl. At least with eyes closed there is something else to see. Viscous black specks. Darting water boatmen, zig-zagging. ZigZag. Red-river? Molten lake in hell? The hammock tips.
>
> (4)

There is much to observe in these passages, and I will start with what is most germane to Smith's skewering of liberal psychology in the production of Englishness: the absence of privacy in the breakdown of the *hortus conclusus*, or "enclosed garden." This symbolic space of refuge has long entwined definitions of Englishness (the quintessential English garden) with the values of liberalism (private property facilitates the privacy of the soul). Smith's opening suggests that this idyll of the liberal-national community is under attack from all sides—the seeming madwoman on the estate whose class status calls up the collectivist racial origins of Englishness ("screaming Anglo-Saxon at nobody") and the newfound "European" character of Willesden streets, which calls up the foreign influences of the city. Yet the dual assaults of welfare and cosmopolitanism turn out to be red herrings for the real problem, which is, of course, the liberal individualism of Englishness itself, encapsulated in the "good line" turned mangled mantra: "I am the sole author of the dictionary that defines me." Smith elevates liberal individualism only to bring it crashing down to earth as Leah's extended body fails her. The pencil cannot write on the magazine's glossy pages; the hammock sends her tumbling out. If partial vision suggests a preference for incomplete knowledge about one's place in the world's hierarchies, a preference that Smith also explored in "The Embassy of Cambodia" and "This Is How It Feels to Me," the opening of *NW* insists that the choice not to know is an increasingly unsustainable one.

Smith's avowed interest in "the networks behind those seeming simplicities" brings her novels into overt engagement with the limits and possibilities of individual consciousness as a mediator of what Jameson has called "the geopolitical unconscious."[40] Smith may reject individualism as an index of English values, as in the passage above, but her approach to structural determination does not preclude the quandaries of self-determination. Rather than replacing "I" with dehumanizing systems as the "sole authors" of the "dictionary that defines me," she insists on posing the question, however compromised, of what it means to take one's liberty, and whether it is ever possible to do so without "takin liberties" from someone else. Facing this question, like Leah's hammock (which we later discover is "communal and so not her hammock" [*NW*, 21]), tips the balance of what readers might like to think of as earned privilege and what they must see as unearned. It also pits the grubbiness of demotic language against the idealism of liberal democracy.

Of course, there is quite a bit about the opening of *NW* to keep the reader off balance. Leah's stream of consciousness ("Viscous black specks. Darting water boatmen, zig-zagging. ZigZag. Red-river? Molten lake in hell?") offers a pun on free thought: that the bedrock of a liberal-democratic society might be more unorganized, speculative, and impressionistic than principled, exalted, and enduring. Leah is precisely not a visionary, but her wandering mind allows Smith to open up the gap between seeing and knowing, between immediately observed phenomena ("viscous black specks"; "zig-zagging") and the acts of impulsive imagination that render disparate abstract forms into the particular things ("water boatmen"; "Red-river?") that might better lend themselves to narrative meaning.

Against the perspectival command that having "a vision" or fully elaborated global/local consciousness implies, Smith turns to traditionally modernist formal strategies to evoke semiconscious states in which complicity and criticism, like immersive experience and reflective understanding, dwell together. She suggests that we are never as in control of our identities as sole authorship implies, and that the role of writing is not to perform or thwart definition absolutely but to engage it as a conceptual and material process in which meaning-making is both elusive and irresistible. Parataxis, recursion, and syntactic decomposition become useful for her because they display the delays, decisions, successes, and failures that go into cognition, and they call up the microacts of measurement and classification that suffuse ordinary thought. Smith's homage is to Joyce, especially, here. As a writer who mixed impressionism and naturalism, Joyce expanded the protocols of definition to include perspectivalism alongside objectivity—seemingly antagonistic styles of accounting that implicate self in system and system in self.

If Smith uses the impressionism of sensory perception and decontextualized detail (what I have called stream of consciousness) against the ossification of conceptual abstractions like self-possession, she also uses it to suggest that seeing objectively entails seeing one's own failures of perception alongside an external reality. The fourth section of *NW*, entitled "Crossing," features Natalie's desperate night journey back to Caldwell and her childhood haunts in the wake of her husband's discovery of her marital infidelities. "Crossing" is subdivided into chapters that keep track of her itinerary through NW with cartographic precision.[41] For example, "Willesden Lane to Kilburn High Road," (*NW*, 360) is followed by "Shoot

Up Hill to Fortune Green" (371), yet the naturalist itinerary culminates atop Hornsey Lane Bridge in a cognitive map that layers Natalie's impressions and symbolic desires upon the physical distances of London:

> The view was cross-hatched. St Paul's in one box. The Gherkin in another. Half a tree. Half a car. Cupolas, spires. Squares, rectangles, half-moons, stars. It was impossible to get any sense of the whole. From up here the bus lane was a red gash through the city. The tower blocks [Caldwell] were the only things that made any sense, separated from each other, yet communicating. From this distance they had a logic, stone posts driven into an ancient field, waiting for something to be laid on top of them, a statue, perhaps, or a platform.
>
> (384)

This passage moves from parataxis to hypotaxis and situates Natalie's disordered and fragmented sight within the ordered sense of her failure to see, an indication of her forming a reflective impression.[42] Whereas parataxis erodes distinctions between words, phrases, and sentences, creating syntactic units that fail to comply with grammatical standards of wholeness or completion, hypotaxis supplies a framework into which Smith can situate Natalie's confusion and differentiate between two ideas of the whole: the whole as objectively real (the fractured totality of London) and the whole as a projection of scale ("From this distance they [the towers] had a logic"). Certainly, Caldwell's "logic" might be chalked up to Natalie's agitation and rebellion against her bourgeois lifestyle, but it can also be understood as the finally acknowledged "platform" supporting her upward mobility.

It is no accident that Smith's twist on the panorama includes a wrought-iron fence, which we are told earlier in the passage was erected by the state to block suicidal jumpers.[43] Infrastructure (the bridge and the barrier) both enables and impedes views, locking Natalie into a scene "cross-hatched" by motifs of autonomy and dependence. Read symbolically, this passage offers a mythic portrait of social democracy's compromises, a suturing of liberalism and socialism with the necessary trade-offs to both. Read literally, it creates a link between perceptible realities and the scale that creates them. The disrupted panorama, as a literary device, does not essentialize parts and wholes. Rather, it fractures at the scale of city while totalizing at the scale of the estate, dramatizing the discontinuities rather than the metonymies of scale. Caldwell, as part, cannot be substituted for the whole of London here. It is its own totality.

Natalie's panorama, like Leah's stream of consciousness, slows down the sense-making process to show the aggregation of objects into scenes and the disaggregation of scenes into objects. Producing coherence and incoherence rather than simply capturing them, the disrupted panorama provides a vehicle through which to reflect upon the contingency of collective units (the city versus the estate) as well as upon our own roles in constructing the totalities that we observe. Natalie's impeded view conveys the finitude of perception ("It was impossible to get any sense of the whole") and the infinitude of what lies beyond perception in, as Jameson puts it, the "unlived, abstract conceptions of the geographic totality."[44]

Where Smith and Jameson differ is in their definitions of totality. For Jameson, as stated in *The Geopolitical Aesthetic*, there is only one proper object of totality: the unrepresentable whole of the world-system. For Smith, totalities are the by-products of scale, the cognitive tool by which individuals measure and comprehend units as meaningful wholes. The advantage of paying attention to these units, which mediate between human finitude and systemic infinitude, is a thicker description of the real—its presence is crafted once it is found and its absence is illuminated if the crafting successfully overwhelms ("There's too much here, too much to process, just too much").[45]

Smith's rendering of Natalie's simultaneous comprehension and incomprehension is reminiscent of a statement from T. J. G. Locher, from which Wallerstein took inspiration in his early formulation of the world-system as his decisive unit of analysis: "One should not confuse totality with completeness. The whole is more than the assembled parts, but it is surely also less."[46] The whole as an agent of both fuller and lesser comprehension is what Smith ponders throughout her northwest London fictions, but with decidedly more anxiety than Locher or Wallerstein. Unlike Wallerstein, who in his first major articulation of the term, deemed the world-system the "correct unit of analysis" because it was the only unit that actually constituted a system, Smith is concerned with reopening the debate over what counts as a proper unit of analysis or agent of causality. This is because Smith is interested in the people caught up in systems and the nontrivial effect that a sense of place can have on our understanding of systems. She makes her own scales to bring northwest

London into view and to create a view from it that defamiliarizes London as global financial capital by disaggregating its icons ("St Paul's in one box. The Gherkin in another.") and reaggregating Caldwell, the relic of the welfare state.

Smith's granular account of northwest London offers an alternative to systems theory for thinking about long-distance distributions of power. She affirms the effect of systems on individual lives but is wary of the singular logic that systems thinking can produce, as in Wallerstein's designation of the world-system as the primary and proper unit of analysis, to which other units are subordinated. Smith's work addresses at least one gap between the totality of the world-system and the completeness of a world-systems account of global inequality by zeroing in on spaces of contradiction. The internal periphery that *NW* presents does not subordinate the local or national scales to the global but instead shows their "hit-and-miss convergences," those sites of overlap and misunderstanding that are, at best, understudied and, at worst, canceled out or abstracted away by the urge to systematize them.[47]

One such site shows the uncomfortable intersection of national and global inequality, which is addressed in *NW* through the juxtaposition of three black men. The first is Nathan Bogle, a "born and bred" Londoner working as a pimp. The second, Rodney, is the studious son of Caribbean immigrants, who, like his one-time girlfriend Natalie, makes it to college but does not assimilate into its social rituals. He falls short of becoming a lawyer and opens a dry cleaning business instead. The third, Michel, an African-Algerian immigrant, is Leah's husband and came to England after experiencing a lack of opportunity in France. Like Fatou from "The Embassy of Cambodia," Michel has crossed the international division of labor; unlike her, he is fully enthralled to liberal individualism. This is a logic that he codes English, not French, and he deems it an escape from the constraints of group identity: "In France, you're African, you're Algerian, who wants to know? There's no opportunity, you can't move! Here, you can move" (*NW*, 32).

Michel and Nathan, like Leah and Natalie, are particularly important foils in *NW*, with Nathan, the native Londoner, voicing a sentiment about England that is opposite of Michel's: "There's no way to live in this country when you're grown. Not at all. They don't want you, your own people don't want you, no one wants you" (376). Simplistic alone, Michel's and Nathan's divergent appraisals of England are complex together because they call up the friction between competing scales and operations—Michel's national comparisons and Nathan's temporal reflections—that cannot be absorbed into a single frame of reference without attenuating the conflict most in need of addressing. Michel's short-term experiences across several countries highlight the opportunities in England that Nathan's "born and bred" nativity prevents him from seeing. In turn, Nathan's nativity points out the latent hostility of the immigrant Michel's "English dream," which, as Toni Morrison argued in the U.S. context, is built on the backs of those who have experienced generations of discrimination within the migrant's host country.[48] Both the national and the transnational offer partial visions, but it is their parallax, their multiple perspectives on England from different angles, that tells a more complete and necessarily more complex story. This story does not sanctify the disempowered or create a competition among oppressions, but it shows that no one scale should unquestionably trump another when talking about injustice.

Every character in *NW*, even those lowest on the class ladder, occupies a position that could be described as exploited or beneficiary, depending on whether a national or an international scale is privileged. Read back into a systems-oriented logic, this finding could be seen as obscuring the totality, but I would prefer to see it as making systemic accounts of the distribution of power more complete. *NW* brings the parallax of scale into view not to discredit the role of structural determination in people's and nations' lives (quite the opposite, given its opening passage) but to make the messiness of its workings and the consequent conflicts of perspective easier to see.

Bruce Robbins has addressed some of these conflicts by broaching the incompatibilities between support for the national welfare state and regard for matters of global inequality. Welfare's resolutely national scale makes it difficult to imagine extending entitlements or redistribution schemes beyond the nation-state, and the history of empire casts a pall over the financing of welfare institutions in developed nations.[49] Even so, that very pall is a reminder that politics happens in impure spaces and that moving forward through scalar impasses is often more awkward than elegant. Robbins offers one way through the impasse of the international division of labor by treating seriously what deterministic thinking rarely does: individual people and chance.

Building on the work of Gayatri Spivak and Bernard Williams, Robbins makes a case for transnational upward mobility through moral luck, which denotes a factoring in of conditions beyond one's control in the making of decisions that will determine the kind of person one will become. Moral luck heightens the recognition of chance and accidents of birth, which give certain people head starts over others, and thus injects fortune (in both senses of the word) into narratives of deservedness, especially among those who have succeeded. It thus introduces a more uniform acceptance of luck's role in life's outcomes, which valuably mediates the opposing views that Smith captures in a conversation between the struggling Nathan ("Bad luck follows me") and the successful Natalie ("I don't believe in luck") (*NW*, 375).

For Spivak, the difference between fortune as monetary privilege and fortune as luck is negligible, and accepting it reinforces one's complicity with an unequal world. For Robbins, the difference is not negligible. He does not accept moral luck outright but embraces "being unable to say a simple 'no.' "[50] It is the equivocation between guilt and luck that turns the compromised condition of complicity, defined by birth or assimilation into a privileged nation, into an occasion for dwelling on the uses of success's moral ambiguities. If the only way to accept comparative advantage is equivocally, then luck's morality inheres not just in its unpredictable role in shaping a future self but also in its revelation of the myriad ways in which advantage is conferred beyond the quantifiable. Moral luck thus debunks individualist autonomy in a different way than does structural determination. It interjects uncertainty into narratives of success and failure and, by giving presence to the unknown, intimates that we will never know the full extent of our dependencies.

In *NW*, luck and guilt rub together, creating the moral friction out of which more social democratic energies might emerge:

> "I just don't understand why I have this life," she [Leah] said, quietly.
>
> "What?"
>
> "You, me, all of us. Why that girl and not us. Why that poor bastard on Albert Road. It doesn't make sense to me."
>
> Natalie frowned and folded her arms across her body. She had expected a more difficult question.

> "Because we worked harder," she said . . . "We were smarter and we knew we didn't want to end up begging on other people's doorsteps."
>
> (*NW*, 400)

Leah here is bothered by outcomes—why her own and Natalie's lives are relatively comfortable while others' are more precarious—"that girl" is Shar, who is a local sex worker with a drug problem, and "that poor bastard" is Felix, who was murdered earlier in the day, possibly by Nathan (Smith leaves it ambiguous). If, for Natalie, the equation for success is simple, for Leah, there are more variables at play than work, intelligence, and desire. Asking why them and not us is not a gesture toward the randomness of the universe. It is an insinuation of moral luck into everyday lives that allows Smith to point out, in a language that supplements but is irreducible to sociological and systemic critique, the many ways in which we are not the sole authors of the dictionaries that define us. Whereas sociological approaches tend to emphasize comparative advantages and opportunity differentials as the source of racialized class hierarchies, moral luck considers how deindividuating forces such as timing, sudden inspiration, or fortunate accident play a role in upward mobility. The chanciness of upward mobility, which Leah sees and Natalie "works hard" to ignore, appends the qualitative unpredictability of any one individual's success or failure to the quantitative predictability of success based on group metrics. Acknowledging luck leaves Leah self-divided about the justness of outcomes, and it is one way in which Smith unbundles the individual from individualism.

Retaining, but also disabling, the individual matters, if we want to change the patterns of affiliation that persist under the name of democracy. If a more cynical definition of the democratic would point to the illusions of equality and fairness that underpin actually existing hierarchies, Robbins and, it seems, Smith's recuperation of luck activates both more uncertain and more prismatic forms of consciousness in which an uncontrollable referencing of other peoples and scenes levels hierarchies of attention and care. The dependencies to which moral luck awaken Leah also turn her attention to peoples and places that seem outside her sphere of control. Leah fails to help Shar, and never had the opportunity to help Felix, yet these two characters still count—through agitated, if not quite uncontrollable, referencing—as part of her sphere of attention precisely because of their resistance to being recast under the safely contained identities of the "needy" or "disposable." Being more inclusive, as a condition of what Sianne Ngai calls "obstructed agency" rather than beneficent control, is what distinguishes Smith's democratic impulse from the traditional underpinnings of liberalism.[51] It helps us see through the liberal rhetoric of autonomy and self-reliance into the reality of upward mobility as facilitated by various forms of dependence on and complicity with societal structures that exclude radical social transformation.

In this case, the suspension of individual agency among "risen" individuals offers a way of understanding and maneuvering beyond what Wallerstein calls the twentieth-century consolidation of a worldwide liberal "geoculture." Grounded in Woodrow Wilson's principle of self-determination for nations, which theoretically attributed formal sovereignty to every state, and Franklin Delano Roosevelt's principles of economic development, which promised a limited redistribution of wealth to developing countries in the form of aid, liberal geoculture masked the continued economic subordination of developing countries by endorsing the political autonomy that came with decolonization.[52] Such a system is commonly understood as neocolonialism, but it can also be phrased idiomatically, if a little crudely, as wealthy nations pulling the ladder of success up behind them. As Doron Ben-Atar has argued, the United States' industrial growth went hand in hand with its smuggling of European inventions and technologies into its factories. Economic development and piracy complemented one another, yet the United States has been a leading enforcer of strict intellectual property regimes that disavow its own history and retard contemporary developing countries' attempts to "steal" in their turn.[53]

By occluding the historical relationship between dependence and innovation in developed nations and stymying it for developing ones, liberal geoculture fosters a global economic climate in which foreign aid produces perpetual debt, and non-Western innovation is greeted as a threat to democracy itself. Yet there is a distinction between democracy as an ideology of Euro-American geocultural hegemony and democracy as a radical leveling of unjust hierarchies through the redistribution of attention, opportunity, and material wealth. Such redistribution responds to the "visitations" (note here that "Visitation" is the title of the opening and closing sections of *NW*) of the unexpected and unwanted, and in raising questions about deservedness, bears witness to the historical double standards that have inhibited global justice.

With Natalie and Leah, Smith takes us to that edge of liberal individualism in which the apparent achievement of self-sufficiency tips over into self-destruction and paralysis. It is these characters' amorphous dissatisfactions that counteract the insulations of selfhood and militate against its equation with freedom. If we transpose Smith's insight about liberalism's principles of individuality onto liberalism's principles of nationhood, we see that the self-determination of nations, like the sole authorship of individuals, is a tantalizingly simple but misguided substitute for the transnational causalities (i.e., root canals) that explain uneven development.

The Full Story

I take *White Teeth* to be Smith's earliest attempt to assume the formidable task of comprehension signified by the root canal. Bringing her later insights into global and local inequality to bear, I return to that first novel to reflect on its pursuit of wholeness and accountability in a world of secrets and misinformation. Smith brings these issues to the fore of the novel in the section entitled "Irie 1990, 1907," which begins with the following epigraph drawn from Nabokov's *Lolita*: "In this wrought-iron world of criss-cross cause and effect, could it be that the hidden throb I stole from them did not affect *their* future?" (Nabokov's italics).[54] The epigraph, coming as it does from the infamous Humbert Humbert, might signal an evasion of responsibility for his rape of Lolita, one of his "nymphets," but in the context of the novel, it is in fact the opposite. Humbert is actually contemplating whether he bears outsize responsibility for the fates of the children about whom he fantasizes but with whom he never interacts.

Smith adapts Humbert's speculations about "criss-cross cause and effect," which he suggests spawn "great and terrible wonder," to address those scenarios in which pinpointing causality is difficult if not impossible.[55] Puzzles of cause and effect are numerous in *White Teeth*, and, like a wrought-iron fence, the novel's "root canal" chapters swirl through the main narrative, going backwards in time and outward in space to discern causality:

> Apropos: it's all very well, this instruction of Alsana's to look at the thing close up; to look at it dead straight between the eyes; an unflinching and honest inspection that would go beyond the heart of the matter to its marrow, beyond the marrow to the root—but the question is how far back do you want? How far will *do*? The old American question: what do you want—*blood*? Most probably more than blood is required: whispered asides; lost conversations; medals and photographs; lists and certificates, yellowing paper bearing the faint imprint of brown dates. Back, back, *back*.
>
> (*White Teeth*, 71; Smith's italics)

Smith's sentences are long and full. They mix statements with questions, repetitions of emphasis (looking "close up" and "dead straight") with repetitions that turn in unexpected directions (the question of "how far back" dovetails with the "old American question"). Finally, they contain lists that equalize the intangible and the tangible in a gesture toward naming the irretrievable totality of history.

Yet Smith's interest in the disorder of the past should not be mistaken for resignation in the face of causality's long distances. If the narrative structure of "The Embassy of Cambodia" suggests that global networks of power have become too shadowy and immense to be fully deciphered by Smith's characters, in *White Teeth* her characters make every effort to locate themselves in history and to figure out "a whole bunch of other stuff that Makes Shit Happen" (*White Teeth*, 4). In pursuing causality, the novel addresses itself to history, but also to philosophy, religion, demography, and genetic engineering.

The novel's ambition, briefly alluded to at the start of this chapter, was famously and negatively nominalized as "hysterical realism" by James Wood. What is less often remembered about that moniker is that Wood defines hysteria in terms of scale disjunction. He attributes hysteria to novels with sociological ambitions that diminish feeling and cast the genre's essential humanism into doubt. Wood objects to the unconvincing air of the "big" novel's "profusion" and "relatedness," which he argues breeds incredulity in the reader and makes paranoia an intrinsic feature of the subgenre. Going big, for Wood, renders the contemporary novel a pale caricature of the nineteenth-century novel and evades larger "awkward" questions about the limits of "novelistic storytelling."[56] Novels may have the capacity for large-scale representation, but they cannot transcend the individual and still be effective novels. The "inhuman stories," which Wood attributes to the big novels of Smith, Rushdie, David Foster Wallace, and Don DeLillo, are not aesthetic paradoxes but generic oxymorons.

Wood makes a conservative argument against the stretching of the novel's form, from portraying the lives of individuals as bearers of beauty and truth (what Smith termed "lyrical realism," in "Two Paths for the Novel") to portraying forces that determine or explain individual lives, with or without their conscious awareness. Smith, on the other hand, transvalues inhuman stories for bringing readers to the limits of individual consciousness and for inspiring an awareness of lack amid the sheer materiality of language. Her big novels, in making size visible and palpable—so much so that Wood receives it as a grotesque deformity—compel reflection on the epistemological frameworks and humanistic values that regard them as failures.

In losing Wood's esteem, the scalar abnormalities of *White Teeth* draw attention to his criteria for judgment. In particular, they literalize the metaphors of a classically satisfying aesthetic experience—fullness and plenitude—and by doing so, they call attention to satiety as a form of complacency. Smith detangles a meaningful whole from a digestible whole and uses the "too much" of overwhelming narration as a formal obstacle to the reductions of abstraction and synthesis that, read more positively, would be understood as the transcendent achievements of form. Smith is suspicious of such a totality because it forecloses other points of view and disavows the processes that go into making the whole meaningful. But that does not mean she is unsympathetic to the human, all too human desire for answers and, thus, for finished form.

Irie, for example, is "sick of never getting the whole truth" from her parents and rues a "history you never entirely uncovered, [a] rumor you never unravelled" (*White Teeth*, 314). What Irie must contend with, though, is that getting the whole truth *pace* Wood might be intellectually and emotionally disabling. As Samad tells Archie, "Full stories are as rare as honesty, precious as diamonds. If you're lucky enough to uncover one, a full story will sit on your brain like lead" (210). Samad makes a distinction between full stories and stories that fulfill. The latter satisfy, in part, because they meet the existing conventions of novelistic possibility; the former weigh down and stymie both pleasure and thought with the unprocessed matter of "impossibly particular information."

Smith sets the plentiful particularities of information—the useless, random, redundant, or overblown detail—against a range of epistemological devices that streamline information and derive universal laws from it. A family tree (281), a timeline (204–205), and a mathematical equation (203) stud the pages of *White Teeth*, reflecting the novel's obsession with the way knowledge is presented and the uses to which it is put. A case in point is Norman Tebbit's infamous cricket test, which Smith reproduces: "Which side do they cheer for? . . . Are you still looking back to where you came from or where you are?" (103). Although the test, used to deduce an immigrant's loyalty, is obviously facile, its glibness is part of its charm. It is easily learned and easily administered—just one piece of information yields conclusions as stark and immediate as they are simplistic and specious.

Devised in 1990 and resurfacing after the 2005 London bombings, in which the culprits were British-born children of immigrants, the cricket test reflects the continuities between assimilationist models of immigration and isolationist models of national culture that disavow responsibility for knowing about other countries or about the intranational ethnic communities that are lumped together as Asian or black. Tebbit is not interested in causality—the economic and political conditions that bring immigrants to England or the domestic conditions that sustain inequality, discrimination, and separatism within the nation. He is interested in classification and the categorical nature of loyalty.

The fullness of *White Teeth* is an aesthetic riposte to the meagerness of the cricket test's data and methodology. Smith's commitment to "impossibly particular information" contests the speciousness of prizing bits of information while ignoring many other bits. It affirms an interest in causality that drives one to demand more information and further explanation, even if the full story delays gratification. Smith's earliest novel thus advances an answer to the question I posed earlier: How can democratic principles survive the counterintuitive effects of an information age in which citizenries are likely to misapprehend how little they know or how little they want to know? Perhaps this is accomplished, in part, by writers devising forms that create desires rather than catering to them.

There will, of course, be many other parts as well: reconsidering the scale of democracy in ways that take into account participatory assemblies and direct democracy as a response to the criticism of representative democracy, implicit in "The Embassy of Cambodia," and preserving public spaces that allow people to gather freely and that expand opportunity in sociological but also intellectual and emotional ways. This, crucially, is what Smith loves not just about the Willesden Greene library center but also about the independent bookshop housed in its complex: "It is run by Helen. Helen is an essential local person. I would characterize her essentialness in the following way: 'Giving the people what they didn't know they wanted' " ("North West London Blues").

For Smith, the complexities of causality are manifold, and they cannot be grasped without opening ourselves up to what we do not know we want. This is often an austere position, but it can also be a warm one. The "whole truth" is well worth pursuing precisely because it defies testable proportions, which is to say, what we already know, and thus stages a clearing ground along with the clutter. Displaying the power to generalize, but also suspending impulses to abstract, synthesize, and formulate, Smith's narrative strategies give readers an understanding of why we must seek out the whole story. They also incline us toward recognizing the partial nature of various kinds of wholeness. Her fiction differentiates between comprehensibility and comprehensiveness and shows us the way to making the full story the fulfilling one.

EPILOGUE

MIGRITUDE—THE RE-MEDIATED WORK OF ART AND ART'S MEDIATING WORK

> Have you ever set out to search for a missing half?
> The piece that isn't shapely, elegant, simple. The half
> that's ugly, heavy, abrasive. Awkward to the hand. Gritty
> on the tongue.
> —Shailja Patel, *Migritude*

Zadie Smith published "The Embassy of Cambodia" in 2013, in the midst of a surge of migration to Europe, particularly among African and Syrian refugees trying to escape violent conflicts and civil wars in their home nations. The years 2014 and 2015 saw a surge within that surge as Europe's migration "problem" morphed into the "global migrant crisis," as it is portrayed by the metropolitan news media. The United Nations High Commissioner for Refugees found that the number of people forcibly displaced at the end of 2014 had reached 59.5 million, up from 51.2 million in 2013 and the highest number on record.[1]

Although such numbers may be unprecedented, it is worth contextualizing them. The mass displacements of 2014 recall the aftermath of World War II, the only other time in recorded history that global displacement exceeded 50 million people. In the wake of that war, national leaders agreed upon the need for stronger international frameworks of cooperation, as evidenced by the founding of the United Nations (1945) and the issuance of the Universal Declaration of Human Rights (1948)—imperfect but necessary attempts to protect peoples unprotected by nation-states. In the wake of 2014, the efficacy of such international frameworks is more than ever in question as small wars proliferate across developing nations such as Afghanistan, Iraq, Somalia, Sudan, Syria, Yemen, and others. UN High Commissioner for Refugees António Guterres laments, "It is terrifying that on the one hand there is more and more impunity for those starting conflicts, and on the other there is seeming utter inability of the international community to work together to stop wars and build and preserve peace."[2] Nowhere is the pressing need for internationalism better embodied than in the matter of forced displacement brought on by, if not world war, a world of wars.

If, as political philosopher Thomas Nail has declared, "the twenty-first century is the century of the migrant," then how do we square unparalleled levels of displacement with the retrenchment of national borders and the resurgence of xenophobic politics across Europe, North America, South Africa, and other nations confronted with the resettlement of migrant peoples?[3] The answer is more complicated than an administrative rhetoric of scarce resources, high unemployment, or a lack of infrastructure would suggest. Indeed, the treatment of mass displacement as a "global migrant crisis" speaks less to the plight of the migrant than to the plight of states, which perceive themselves to be under assault. Their alarm is symptomatic of some of the most intractable elements within ideologically national models of belonging—elements that prize autarky over exchange and that link the reproduction of communal identity to racial and territorial continuity.

This book has been about how a revitalized concept of modernist internationalism can contest such isolationist aspects of national cultures and even take narratives of communal cohesion beyond identitarian claims. The tradition examined here shows how place-based models of belonging have begotten circulation-based models of expulsion, such that bounded territories become the unspoken foundations of obligation and fellowship. Modernist internationalism, reconfigured in historically specific and beyond-European terms, helps us to understand why mass displacement is perceived as an assault on states. Its analyses of global inequality and securitized borders offer vital insight into the ongoing resistance to internationalism, and its cultivation of transnational memories and supranational solidarities opens up pathways for overcoming such resistance.

The specters of criminality and fugitivity hang over nomadic collectives—whether vagabonds, emigrants, or refugees—because states moralize transience as part of their border-policing regimes. Such regimes are historical as well as territorial. The most vulnerable migrants, those most vilified and most denied political membership, often embody the unwanted memories and unacknowledged histories of host and transit nations. This has certainly been the case in the European Union and the United States, both of which have been reluctant to acknowledge the persistence of imperial legacies and the fallout of free trade as sources of forced migration to their borders.

Drawing borders around historical memory may seem abstract, but the consequences of such memory policing are palpable in the increasingly vehement calls for fences and walls to protect "rightful" citizens from "illegal" migrants, who are stigmatized on the basis of race and religion. In her study of walls, Wendy Brown observes that such physical structures form psychic defenses against a globalized modernity: "Walls cleave the reality of global interdependence and global disorder with stage set productions of intact nationhood, autonomy and self-sufficiency."[4] Yet, as the theatricality of "stage set productions" implies, such psychic defense is itself awash in angst because it rests upon exaggerated displays of state power and unenforceable definitions of national identity and domestic territory. Brown's study reveals walls to be the Potemkin villages of contemporary states under globalization—concrete-and-metal manifestations of populist paranoia and sovereign power in crisis. Built to impose and intimidate, walls inadvertently convey the state's distress; they are chilling twenty-first-century examples of what Rabindranath Tagore described as the despotic desire for "hard, clear-cut, perfect form."

From Tagore onward, the writers converging in this study have rethought the boundaries of the work of art in order to challenge despotic and autarkic theories of national community. In particular, they have revisited the principles and practices of the literary form that we call modernist to imagine more interdependent models of nationhood and to reflect upon as well as diversify styles of political belonging and internationalist expression. Approaching the work of art not as the transcendence of resistant material but as the mediation of it, they generate a modernist internationalism in tune with its various medium dependencies—with the translations that make it available to multiple audiences (Tagore); with the processes of collation, printing, and reprinting that necessarily destabilize notions of formal unity (Michael Ondaatje); and with the sheer force of language, which overwhelms attempts to shape it into an emblem of national culture or global transparency (James Joyce and Zadie Smith). Modernist internationalism's deliberate chimeras of form are a riposte to the fortress state's despotic forms of "intact nationhood." They take apart, with language, those walls and fences that are intended to detain racialized migrant bodies and to secure borders that always, somehow or another, end up being crossed.

Some might ask what such a dismantling is worth. What can language, especially literary language, really do in the face of such solid objects and the rising tide of displacement? Literary form is precisely the mechanism by which writers have tried to answer that question. They have used form to explore the limits and possibilities of the artwork and of art's work with respect to political agency. In wryly contemplating the value of literary experimentation as a kind of sociopolitical intervention (recall Joyce's "genial illusion" and McKay's jovial self-definition as an internationalist who is also a politically "bad nationalist"), modernists have refined literature's capacity to reveal the world by reflecting on its capacity to change it. Beyond this, they have advanced new techniques within the realm of form to address the abstract causalities and long-distance accountabilities of a globalizing modernity as matters of figuration and feeling.

By teasing out the semiotic dimensions of the solid world and the cosmopolitical dimensions of various types of chimeric longing, modernist internationalism beyond Europe does not just invite readers to imagine communities differently—outside the paradigm of bounded, discrete, and singular entities. It also asks us to contend with the increasing unknowability of communities as collective membership, political agency, and social obligation grow more diffuse and deterritorialized. Most importantly, it confronts us with the partiality of knowledge, making legible in literary form the epistemological illegibility, confusion, and opacity that arise when writers, readers, and works cross lines of power.

The works that populate the present book have tested the limits of cosmopolitical knowledge in various ways—by bringing major and minor languages into contact, by directing attention to small islands and (for metropolitan readers) faraway wars, and by broaching large-scale economic processes in local ways. Their writers have questioned the adequacy of literary form for such tasks and, by working within its constraints, have widened its repertoire. Their innovations have come from wrestling with rather than aggrandizing the agency of literature.[5] But formal experiments also serve as absolutely necessary exercises in hubris, inasmuch as each writer comes to question rather than accept those lines of political compromise that separate legitimate desires from illegitimate ones, achievable goals from unachievable chimeras.

This account of modernist internationalism brings me to a work that explicitly thematizes the mediated nature of its agency in the world and uses its self-reflexivity to theorize forced migration not simply as a tragic sociological condition or troubling demographic pattern but as the will to survive. Shailja Patel's *Migritude* premiered as "a 90-minute theatre show complete with set, choreography, dance, soundscape, and visuals" in Berkeley, California, in 2006.[6] It tells the story of Patel's origins in displacement as a Kenyan of Indian descent and her subsequent migrations to Britain and the United States. Patel unfolds her tale by unfolding and displaying a series of saris from her trousseau—a gift from her mother for a marriage that Shailja knows will never take place. Patel recontextualizes the saris (symbols of her mother's unfulfilled wishes, as well as costumes of straight femininity) and uses them as tapestries that trace out the legacies of imperialism. Her family's story of expulsion from Uganda under Idi Amin's dictatorship and their resettlement in Kenya crosses with a larger indictment of the ills of empire and postcolonial nationhood, especially as they have been enacted on the bodies of women. Patel performed *Migritude* in Austria, Italy, Zanzibar, and elsewhere, including Nairobi, where it was the closing event at the World Social Forum in 2007. She subsequently re-mediated the show into an experimentally written book, and it is specifically the print version of *Migritude* that I offer as this study's closing chimera of form.

Turning a show into a book is a paradoxical sort of task because it involves creating something new that is also a tribute to an antecedent and, for many readers, missed occasion. By constantly alluding to a highly orchestrated event, the print version makes us privy to the prior life of the object in our hands, but in such a way as to make us aware of the distances and proximities being negotiated in the move from stage to page. The print *Migritude* is thus a self-reflexive work of art but not a self-contained one. It suggests that migration stories must be told in migrating ways. They must convey differential degrees of access (some parts of a re-mediated story will be well preserved while others will be transformed or lost), and they must make participants think about where they arrive in the history of a work's production and reception.

Migritude foregrounds the life cycles of a work of art and proceeds by dividing the reader's subjectivity. On one hand, we are made to feel like migrants ourselves—groping our way through a story that has already begun and whose premises are never going to be completely available to us. On the other, we are made to feel our own sedentariness as the work migrates to us through a subsequent media form. Given that no one—not even the author herself, as we shall see—has access to the whole history of this re-mediated work of art, *Migritude* comes to incarnate the ideas of partial knowledge and medium dependency, which philosophically underpin modernist internationalism beyond Europe. Because the work's print iteration emerges out of the conjuncture of theatrical performance and textual form, it also lends some external purchase on the specificities of the literary mode that has preoccupied *Chimeras of Form*.

Migritude accentuates the idea that its own survival is predicated on its ability to theorize its changing mediums and audiences. This technological and aesthetic lesson is also an epistemological one, in that the work provincializes the choice of reading (as opposed to viewing or embodying) as the preeminent way of coming into knowledge about such a viscerally painful experience as forced migration or expulsion. Moreover, it is a political lesson, in that the work's re-mediation from show to book inflects its author's anxieties about crossing the borders between protest and art, stage and page. As a self-identified artist and activist, Patel's challenge is to address empirical histories of forced migration sensitively, without turning migrant bodies into sterile statistics or spectacles of a state crisis that is extensively covered in the news media but only cursorily felt through it.[7]

Patel's rearticulation of mass displacement turns away from journalistic discourse by exploring what Carrie Noland calls, in the context of Negritude poetry, "the constructive process of subjectivation in writing." Noland's emphasis on the Negritude poets' implication in "modernist print culture" revises the dominant reception of these poets as political because their poems were expressive of empirical selves and representative of an oppressed people's collective experience. By emphasizing the mediation and modulation of print in the making of a subjectivity, Noland argues that the political dimension of Negritude poetry is never reducible to empirical expressivity, nor is it irradiated by an extreme aestheticism. The political quality of art lies in its negotiation of aesthetic play within historical parameters of responsibility—parameters that the work of art is not just subject to but is also, itself, capable of setting.[8]

Patel's *Migritude*, like the Negritude poetry with which it resonates, faces the problem of subjectivation in print and of giving voice to collective pain through a medium that disembodies voice, especially when it is compared with theater. Patel approaches this problem by hybridizing print—that is, she grafts principles of performance theory onto her practices of literary form and book design. The print version of *Migritude* comprises four main parts that are relentlessly recursive and occasionally tangential. Part I ("Migritude") presents the text of the play itself, under sixteen chapter headings. Part II ("The Shadow Book") rehearses the play again by repeating the chapter headings of part I. However, instead of Patel's stage monologues, we get her interior monologue and reminiscence about how she and her collaborators put the play together. Collaborators here include people with both strong and weak ties to the production: those who officially worked on the play, such as Patel's director, Kim Cook; those who informed Patel's memories in the play, such as her mother or people she dated; and those who viewed the play, such as a bookshop owner in Italy. Part III ("The Making and Other Poems") features poems, several of which had appeared in earlier drafts of *Migritude* but had been cut from the stage script.

Part IV ("The Journey") presents an unusual timeline that mixes the political history pertinent to *Migritude*'s empirical scope with the self-reflexive history of its theatrical performance and print re-mediation. The timeline draws on deep time and implies that the production of *Migritude* began in the sixth century B.C. (when one of its visual motifs, "boteh / ambi / paisley," was first recorded, in Central Asia) and ends with its 2010 print publication by Kaya Press in New York (*Migritude*, 129–133). Then, however, two subsequent interviews with Patel in this section stretch the work's life further. The first, conducted by Emanuele Monegato, is based not on the play (which Monegato never saw) but on a translated version of *Migritude*, which he first encountered in an Italian/English edition. The second interview is by Vanita Reddy, who attended the first performance of *Migritude* in Berkeley but presumably did not read the Italian/English edition of it.

The organization of materials in part IV extends the idea of collaboration in part II, wherein many participate in the "journey" of the work by entering into it at different points in its life, from conception to performance to translation. Those who enter into its life also crucially extend that life, making the model for the production of *Migritude* more evolutionary than stationary. Indeed, the allusion to the sixth century B.C., the deep time of human history, suggests that *Migritude* itself extends the life of ancient arts, like paisley design, which become re-mediated motifs displayed on Patel's stage saris and, later, on her book pages.

Patel's evolutionary approach to re-mediation seems less indebted to a technologically determined media theory than to one of the major principles of performance theory, that "performance is an executed copy of an original that does not exist, except as a retrospective understanding or prescient expectation, an implicit compact between the performer and the spectator, but one subject to renegotiation in a heartbeat."[9] Joseph Roach's quote emphasizes iteration and revision as key aspects of performance. Through them, an auratic version of the "original" work is replaced by a temporalized one in which "an original" becomes the product of cumulative and collaborative knowledge ("a retrospective understanding") or acts as the placeholder for anticipating that form of knowledge ("a prescient expectation"). Either way, *Migritude* transposes the iteration and revision of multimedia theatrical performance to multigeneric print in order to bring the evolutionary ambit of performance into its specifically literary forms of migritude.

I have taken the time to delineate the contents of the book because they bespeak the printed work's capacity to orchestrate text and paratext, to mix up genres of poetic performance with those of information storage and documentary retrieval. Even if read in silence and isolation, *Migritude* is a textual object that conveys the ritual tied up in public performance. It uses each generic iteration to widen its circle of actual and potential collaborators, to include readers of the book in multiple languages as well as spectators of the play in multiple locales.

Migritude, in other words, makes a point of its internationalism by making a point of its re-mediation from performance to print. Re-mediation is also the method by which the printed book dramatizes the thorniness inherent to subjectivation, particularly when an individual self becomes entangled with the voicing of an oppressive collective fate. The word *migritude* is a portmanteau of *migrant* and *attitude*, but *migrit-* is also a homophone of "my grit," a reference to the resistant material of migrant life, which becomes the artist's possession to transform and yet is also beyond her capacity to shape utterly. The neologism *migritude* further sparks the polysemy of *attitude* as a concept that blurs the boundaries between individual and collective, mental disposition and embodied gesture, historicized perspective and aesthetic category.

By mobilizing these many aspects of attitude, Patel generates the communal voice of migritude while also voicing her struggle with her own aesthetic agency and the political agency of art. This approach necessarily veers between the Scylla of self-indulgence and the Charybdis of unreflectively speaking on behalf of others. Take, for example, sections of Patel's timeline that compress her work history with world history:

> 2003: Kenyan survivors of rape by British soldiers begin legal action against Britain's Ministry of Defense. I am laid off from my job—become a full-time artist . . .
>
> 2009: Mau Mau veteran survivors and Kenya Human Rights Commission file suit in the British High Court for reparations from the British government for torture. Lieto Colle edition of *Migritude* is shortlisted for the Camaiore International Poetry Prize.
>
> (*Migritude*, 132–133)

In these sections, Patel affords stories of legal redress and reparation the same weight as stories of personal setbacks, decision-making, and professional success. Such a tactic is motivated by the staid conviction that "we cannot know ourselves or our nations—or meet the truth of our present moment—until we look at how we got there" (128). Yet it is the method of convergence, in which self-witness and self-gratification enmesh with projects of collective witness and transitional justice, that gives the print *Migritude* a controversial edge that is distinct from the theatrical version. The self-reflexivity associated with tracking the work's life and the artist's autobiography leads to dilemmas of representation and proportion. How does one balance an interest in the aesthetic and the personal with a commitment to the historical and the collective? Pondering this question, as we shall see, allows Patel to address head-on the relationship between poetic invention and political change.

"The Making," the titular poem of part III (the section containing poems cut from the stage version), claims the immediacy of disclosure. It is about taking a leap forward over "everything I didn't know, all the skills and resources I didn't have, the gut terror of not knowing what I was doing" (100). The lyric "I" here confesses Patel's inner turmoil at the very moment of deciding to make *Migritude*, yet it also, by virtue of being written, modifies and improvises upon that personal confession to take on the tumultuous leaps of migration as a policed public activity. The poem's most compelling stanzas render the mediation of the migrant plight impossible without the artist's risk and fortitude; in turn, the referent for such risk and fortitude quickly exceeds the artist:

> Make it from rage / every smug idiotic face you've
> ever wanted to smash / into the carnage of war every
> encounter / that's left your throat choked / with what
> you dared not say excavate / the words that hid in your
> churning stomach through visa controls / words you
> swallowed down / until over the border they are / still
> where they knew / you would return for them
>
> (124)

This stanza, at first, seems born out of Patel's own experience of migrating from the Global South to the Global North. In using apostrophe to address herself, however, she expands and elevates the referent "you" beyond herself. It begins to name and encompass members of a wider migrant collective who not only have shared similar experiences of rage, silencing, and impotence in the face of border control but also have found themselves performing obedience in ways that put their words at odds with their feelings. By performing on stage, Patel would reclaim her body from imposed regulations through motion, gesture, and costume. By performing on the page, she uses lineation and punctuation to evoke a body choking and churning—a body that, precisely because it is disembodied by print, becomes less yoked to Patel herself.

This pained and disoriented body, the migrant body, is not exteriorized, as in journalistic or photographic accounts, but is interiorized through the breakdown of poetic lines. The line is often described as the basic unit of poetry—a segment that, like the chapter in prose, indicates internal wholeness even if it is only part of a larger work. Patel slashes that wholeness typographically in ways that sometimes set off meaningful syntactic phrases and other times interrupt them so as to inject opacity into transparent language. For example, in the line "you dared not say excavate / the words that hid in your," *excavate* is slashed or amputated from the phrasal body in which it makes the most semantic sense. Lineally, Patel performs the "carnage of war" by bringing meaningful syntactic units into collision and creating the debris of dangling or misplaced words. In another poetic line from this stanza ("swallowed down / until over the border they are / still") the slash marks combined with enjambment suggest a brief respite from turmoil as the churning stomach goes "still," once over the border. In the pause created by that respite, the speaker returns to the scene of violence and retrieves her words ("where they knew / you would return for them").

For a work obsessed with motion in both topic and form, stillness stands out. It connotes a sense of refuge drawn from within the migrant body rather than from without. In that sense, the stillness within migritude expresses a core power and consistency internal to displaced people (migrants or refugees) for whom places like Europe and the United States represent not beacons of hope but gambles for survival. Counterintuitively, the abstractions of print abet Patel's efforts to express migritude viscerally and collectively. Using the affordances of print to write poetry that sticks in the throat, she recovers the innards of migrant bodies and reimagines the unspoken language of border crossing in a specifically literary medium. It is from within the province of the literary that Patel crafts a migrant voice and reconnects with art's political potential:

> Make it knowing that art / is not political change / make
> it a prayer / for real political change / a homage to your
> heroes a libation / to your gods
>
> (124)

As if to suggest the limits of art's power, poetic language grows plainer here. Patel reminds readers that she knows the difference between art and "real political change." Art is not regime change, reparation, transitional justice, or asylum—a variety of real-world causes that appear in *Migritude* and to which an activist might pledge herself. In not being those things, Patel seems to suggest, "it"—the aesthetic production that is *Migritude*—must throw its lot in with putatively unreal, devotional acts like prayer, homage, and libation.

Patel rightly acknowledges the limitations of her stage and page performances as interventions into the empirical conflicts that they figure. However, her shuttling from history to theology, empiricism to spirituality, too quickly cedes the specificity of art's agency by metaphorically conflating it with religiosity, ethereality, and subordination. In Patel's positive definition of art as "a prayer for real political change," "real" is the test by which art's worldly agency fails. The real separates Patel's activism from her artistry, which veers toward the otherworldly. But is the implication that art's work must consign itself to the realm of the unreal accurate?

Migritude would suggest otherwise. By contemplating its own interventions as an actor in the world and maker of audiences/collaborators, the "performance book" ends up lending a sharper understanding of art's activity in the world. The re-mediated work negotiates between the empirical description of migration situations (including its own) and the unempirical sentiments that compose a migrant attitude, between external reference to history and current events and internal reference to structure, style, and its own processes of production and reception. The constant oscillation between the documentation of historical events and a printed performance that, through generic organization, figuration, and lineal patterns, reshapes the perception of history and collective resilience is what determines the making of the poem. *Making*—a gerund that derives noun from verb, an object from an action—signals the particular craft and graft of *Migritude* as a work that crosses the desire for empirical political change with the unempirical but nonetheless perception-altering figurations of literary form. This work of art's embodied self-reflexivity, its attention to itself as a vehicle of and for mediation, becomes an unexpected resource for critically examining the "real" of politics and for undoing the presuppositions of immediacy and transparency that underlie it.

If it is the ultimate chimera of form to imagine that art's work may effect political change, then, as the writers gathered in this study have shown over and over again, that is a chimera worth pausing over. Rather than overstate or discredit art's political agency, these writers have grappled with it to better understand when to build and when to question the bridge between the indirect action of literary form and the direct action of protest. Art's work, as they have modeled it, has been to develop medium-specific strategies for engaging and analyzing internationalism as an actually existing and often internally riven discourse. Those strategies, as each chapter here has argued in its own way, have channeled and reshaped the incompatibilities of internationalist discourse to render more articulate the possibilities for political transformation latent within them.

Such aesthetic projects alone cannot solve problems of policy, but they exert agency by being propaedeutic. That is, they offer readers preliminary instruction in discerning the power dynamics, social struggles, and intellectual impasses of modernity as a globalizing force. They show us how state and cultural violence are implicit in established ways of thinking about collective membership as bounded and territorialized, and they devise new metaphors, images, words, and categories for rethinking belonging and political obligation with feeling and force. Propaedeutics exist to prime the faculties for more advanced study; they do not circumscribe judgment but cultivate its exercise. Their value is shot through with utopian impulses, to be sure, but it is not the concept of utopia that best articulates the methods or stakes of modernist internationalism beyond Europe.

I have turned to and fleshed out the comparatively undernourished concept of the chimera to offer a model of illegitimate longing in place of utopia's grandly empowered visions. The chimera's conjunction of possibility with impossibility, triviality with intensity, and fantasy with self-deception is most appropriate to theorizing a modernism of colonized and minoritized writers who found themselves unable to follow the party lines of liberal or socialist, nationalist or antinationalist internationalisms. As these writers wove their political frustrations and desires into aesthetic form, they found a suppleness in literature that is missing from more propositional kinds of discourse. They used that suppleness to address the blind spots created by clear ideological oppositions and to stimulate new categories of relation among contradictory views. The internal conflicts that led them astray from organized politics led them to social scenes of impracticality, failed aspiration, and ambiguous agency. Mining these chimeric sites for critical insight, they arrived at unpredictable configurations of anticolonial and global imagination.

The conceptual power of their chimeras differs markedly from the conceptual power of utopia as defined by Fredric Jameson and Theodor Adorno. Jameson identifies the power and paradox of utopia as rooted in its "constitutive secessionism, a withdrawal or 'de-linking' from the empirical and historical world." For Adorno, such secessionism guarantees utopia's autonomy from the existing world, as does its heroic refusal to be tamed by the representational resources available to that world.[10] The defiance of form is the source of utopia's prestige and its radicalism. Chimeras, on the contrary, exist in form; they yoke imagination to empiricism, aesthetic innovation to historical exigency. They are weaker, less absolute figures of hope but also more attached ones. Chimeras of form carry the taint rather than the glamour of impossibility because they remain immanent to modernity, attentive to its domains of discounted experience, and embroiled in disputes with its most authoritative ways of knowing.

NOTES

Introduction: Chimeras of Form

1. Judith Butler, "What Is Critique? An Essay on Foucault's Virtue (2001)," in *The Judith Butler Reader*, ed. Sara Salih with Judith Butler (Malden, MA: Wiley-Blackwell, 2004), 307.

2. Bruce Robbins, *Feeling Global: Internationalism in Distress* (New York: New York University Press, 1999), 7; and Kwame Anthony Appiah, *Cosmopolitanism: Ethics in a World of Strangers* (New York: Norton, 2006), xv.

3. Salman Rushdie, *The Satanic Verses* (New York: Random House, 1988), 382.

4. Jon Hegglund argues that mapmaking represents one way in which communal feeling becomes geographic; that is, it becomes less entwined with local experiences and immediate encounters and more engaged with abstract matters of distance and totality in the imagining of communities beyond one's visible surroundings. See Hegglund, *World Views: Metageographies of Modernist Fiction* (Oxford: Oxford University Press, 2012), 7–8. Baal's attempts to map thus evoke the tension between the knowable and the unknowable as the artist attempts to gain control over not only a wider and more chaotic expanse but also a new concept of country.

5. Jed Esty, *Unseasonable Youth: Modernism, Colonialism, and the Fiction of Development* (Oxford: Oxford University Press, 2012), 202.

6. Raymond Williams, *The Country and the City* (Oxford: Oxford University Press, 1973), 165–166.

7. Pheng Cheah, "Introduction Part II: The Cosmopolitical Today," in *Cosmopolitics: Thinking and Feeling Beyond the Nation*, ed. Pheng Cheah and Bruce Robbins (Minneapolis: University of Minnesota Press, 1998), 31, 38.

8. Caroline Levine, *Forms: Whole, Rhythm, Hierarchy, Network* (Princeton, NJ: Princeton University Press, 2015), 17.

9. Fredric Jameson, "Future City," *New Left Review* 21 (May–June 2003): 76.

10. See Martha Nussbaum, "Patriotism and Cosmopolitanism," in *For Love of Country?*, ed. Joshua Cohen (Boston: Beacon Press, 1996), 2–20; and U.S. Social Forum, "Declaration of the Social Movements Assembly—World Social Forum 29 March 2013, Tunisia," Facebook post, March 31, 2013, https://www.facebook.com/ussocialforum/posts/10151324541686472.

11. Sianne Ngai, *Ugly Feelings* (Cambridge, MA: Harvard University Press, 2005), 22.

12. For three of the most influential examples, see Ernest Gellner, *Nations and Nationalism* (Ithaca, NY: Cornell University Press, 1983); Benedict Anderson, *Imagined Communities: Reflections on the Origins and Spread of Nationalism* (London: Verso, 1983); and Eric Hobsbawm, *Nations and Nationalism Since 1780* (Cambridge: Cambridge University Press, 1992).

13. Brian C. Schmidt, *The Political Discourse of Anarchy: A Disciplinary History of International Relations* (Albany: State University of New York Press, 1998).

14. Edward Hallett Carr, *The Twenty Years' Crisis, 1919–1939* (1939; repr., New York: Perennial, 2001), 8, 13.

15. Carr, *Twenty Years' Crisis*, 238.

16. Samuel Moyn, "The Political Origins of Global Justice" (Cyril Foster Lecture in International Relations, University of Oxford, November 2013), 4. Transcript courtesy of the author.

17. United Nations General Assembly, "Declaration on the Establishment of a New International Economic Order," May 1, 1974, http://www.un-documents.net/s6r3201.htm. For a fuller history of the formation of the New International Economic Order and its history within the Non-Aligned Movement, see Vijay Prashad, *The Darker Nations: A People's History of the Third World* (New York: The New Press, 2007); and Gilbert Rist, *The History of Development*, 3rd ed. (London: Zed Books, 2008), 140–171.

18. Moyn, "Political Origins," 10–22.

19. Lawrence Rainey, ed., *Modernism: An Anthology* (Oxford: Blackwell, 2005), xxii.

20. Graham Hough, *Image and Experience: Studies in a Literary Revolution* (London: Duckworth, 1960), 4–5.

21. Hugh Kenner, "The Making of the Modernist Canon," *Chicago Review* 34, no. 2 (Spring 1984): 49–61.

22. Susan Stanford Friedman, "Definitional Excursions: The Meanings of Modern/Modernity/Modernism," *Modernism/Modernity* 8, no. 3 (September 2001): 508.

23. Jahan Ramazani, *A Transnational Poetics* (Chicago: University of Chicago Press, 2009), xii.

24. For an overview of such studies, see Douglas Mao and Rebecca Walkowitz, "The New Modernist Studies," *PMLA* 123, no. 3 (2008): 737–748.

25. Laura Doyle and Laura Winkiel, eds., *Geomodernisms: Race, Modernism, Modernity* (Bloomington: Indiana University Press, 2005), 3–4.

26. Pamela Caughie, *Disciplining Modernism* (New York: Palgrave Macmillan, 2009), 9.

27. Mark Wollaeger, introduction to *The Oxford Handbook of Global Modernisms*, ed. Mark Wollaeger with Matt Eatough (New York: Oxford University Press, 2012), 5. In addition to the edited collections mentioned here, a range of monographs have redefined modernism as transnational. Jessica Berman argues that "reading modernism transnationally" will draw attention to the social and political contexts of modernist exchange over the more entrenched pathways of formal influence. Christopher GoGwilt finds grounding for transnational comparison by treating the literary passage philologically, meaning as "a dislocation or tropological displacement of material culture." Matthew Hart has distinguished transnationalism from international modernism by arguing that transnational approaches capture the "situational" nature of culture. See Berman, *Modernist Commitments: Ethics, Politics, and Transnational Modernism* (New York: Columbia University Press, 2012), 9; GoGwilt, *The Passage of Literature: Genealogies of Modernism in Conrad, Rhys, and Pramoedya* (Oxford: Oxford University Press, 2010), 219; and Hart, *Nations of Nothing but Poetry: Modernism, Transnationalism, and Synthetic Vernacular Writing* (Oxford: Oxford University Press, 2010), 17–18.

28. Paul Saint-Amour, *Tense Future: Modernism, Total War, Encyclopedic Form* (Oxford: Oxford University Press, 2015), 37–43.

29. See, for example, Dilip Gaonkar, ed., *Alternative Modernities* (Durham, NC: Duke University Press, 2001); and Satya Mohanty, ed., *Colonialism, Modernity, and Literature: A View from India* (New York: Palgrave Macmillan, 2011).

30. I borrow the phrase from Nergis Ertürk, who has warned against deploying a global modernist gaze that merely confirms European modernism's self-image. See Ertürk, "Modernism Disfigured: Turkish Literature and the Other West," in *The Oxford Handbook of Global Modernisms*, ed. Mark Wollaeger with Matt Eatough (New York: Oxford University Press, 2012), 530.

31. For examples of singular modernity proponents, see Fredric Jameson, *A Singular Modernity: Essay on the Ontology of the Present* (London: Verso, 2002); and James Ferguson, "Decomposing Modernity," in *Global Shadows: Africa in the Neoliberal World Order* (Durham, NC: Duke University Press, 2006), 176–193.

32. Gary Wilder, *Freedom Time: Negritude, Decolonization, and the Future of the World* (Durham, NC: Duke University Press, 2015), 10–11.

33. "Communism of the idea" is from Susan Buck-Morss, "The Gift of the Past," *Small Axe* 14, no. 3 (November 2010): 183.

34. Here my efforts build on the interventions of Simon Gikandi, Alejandro Mejías-López, and Eric Hayot. Gikandi points to how various institutions of modernism (criticism, commentary, museum culture) have anxiously grappled with the place of non-European cultures, particularly African ones, in the making of modernist art and literature. Such institutions have historically acknowledged the role of foreign cultural practices while denying them the authority of "influence." Gikandi shows how disavowing cross-cultural encounter as the condition of

possibility for modernism became foundational to the Eurocentric "ideology of modernism." Mejías-López's study of Latin American *modernismo*, a movement begun by Rubén Darío in Nicaragua, is also a salutary reminder of the gap between modernism as a multilingually lived assemblage of historical–aesthetic movements and modernism as a literary–historical institution. Mejías-López cites a critical tradition of scholarship on *modernismo* that, against the movement's own self-definition, suggested that its writers "lived a mirage" of modernity. Such a consensus consequently devalued the purchase of Latin American *modernismo* within the origin story of modernism, further insulating the latter term from its non-European contexts. Hayot, building on René Girard's concept of mimetic desire, advocates for giving imitation and desire for the Other pride of place in new theories of modernism. He reminds readers that Ezra Pound's famous dictum "make it new," a phrase that has become a metonym of modernist ideology itself, was in fact adapted from an entry in Morrison's dictionary of Chinese, which attributed the phrase to an inscription on a Shang dynasty basin. Such studies show that modernism's particular Europeanness is the product of an institutional history that, if uncontested, would actually continue to perpetuate a colonial epistemology. See Gikandi, "Picasso, Africa, and the Schemata of Difference," *Modernism/Modernity* 10, no. 3 (2003): 475; Mejías-López, *The Inverted Conquest: The Myth of Modernity and the Transatlantic Onset of Modernism* (Nashville, TN: Vanderbilt University Press, 2009), 17; and Hayot, "Chinese Modernism, Mimetic Desire, and European Time," in *The Oxford Handbook of Global Modernisms*, ed. Mark Wollaeger with Matt Eatough (New York: Oxford University Press, 2012), 161.

35. Outside the disciplinary domain of international relations, Manu Goswami provides a valuable guide to the convergence of anticolonial intellectual history and interwar internationalisms. See Goswami, "Imaginary Futures and Colonial Internationalisms," *American Historical Review* 117, no. 5 (December 2012): 1461–1485.

36. On the ramifications of standard time, see Peter Galison, *Einstein's Clocks, Poincaré's Maps: Empires of Time* (New York: Norton, 2003); and Adam Barrows, *The Cosmic Time of Empire: Modern Britain and World Literature* (Berkeley: University of California Press, 2010). For a history of the passport, see John Torpey, *The Invention of the Passport: Surveillance, Citizenship, and the State* (Cambridge: Cambridge University Press, 1999).

37. Rebecca Walkowitz's model of critical cosmopolitanism has influenced my understanding of modernism as a category that can be used to identify specific intellectual projects rather than simply describing the biographical, historical, or social conditions under which those projects are pursued. See Walkowitz, *Cosmopolitan Style: Modernism Beyond the Nation* (New York: Columbia University Press, 2006), 7. Modernist internationalism diverges from critical cosmopolitan-

ism, however, in the role that difference (colonial, national, racial, or linguistic) plays in its formulations. While Walkowitz shows how cosmopolitanism blurs such differences within Britain, I focus on the way such differences circulate across global lines of power.

38. See, for example, Tsitsi Jaji, *Africa in Stereo: Modernism, Music, and Pan-African Solidarity* (Oxford: Oxford University Press, 2014).

39. David James and Urmila Seshagiri propose a return to a more strictly periodized modernism, in part as a tool for historicizing contemporary literature and in part to preserve the distinctive formal energies of early twentieth-century art. See James and Seshagiri, "Metamodernism: Narratives of Continuity and Revolution" *PMLA* 129, no. 1 (2014): 87–100.

40. In thinking outside of teleological approaches, Srinivas Aravamudan has argued that the early Enlightenment model of *translatio* provides an alternative to the "nationalist straitjackets" that come to circumscribe and confer meaning on particular literary works. *Translatio* targets acts of literary transmission and cultural borrowing, which reveal the "hybrid genealogies" of seemingly homogenous literary categories. Aravamudan poses *translatio* as a corrective to the inevitable exclusiveness of teleological literary histories that tend to narrow narratives of causality rather than broaden them. Such narrowing produces certain effects; for example, the rise of the English novel, "'spontaneously generated' from native soil rather than in dialogue with the East." See Aravamudan, "East–West Fiction as World Literature: The Hayy Problem Reconfigured," *Eighteenth-Century Studies* 47, no. 2 (2014): 209, 216.

41. Mark Granovetter, "The Strength of Weak Ties," *American Journal of Sociology* 78, no. 6 (1973): 1360.

42. Bruce Robbins, "Introduction Part 1: Actually Existing Cosmopolitanism," in *Cosmopolitics: Thinking and Feeling Beyond the Nation*, ed. Pheng Cheah and Bruce Robbins (Minneapolis: University of Minnesota Press, 1998), 3.

43. Jürgen Habermas, "Modernity: An Unfinished Project," in *Habermas and the Unfinished Project of Modernity*, ed. Maurizio Passerin d'Entrèves and Seyla Benhabib (Cambridge, MA: MIT Press, 1997), 38–58.

44. The hybrid feeling of pessoptimism was coined in Emile Habiby, *The Secret Life of Saeed: The Pessoptimist*, trans. S. K. Jayyusi and T. Le Gassick (1974; repr., Northampton, MA: Interlink, 2003).

45. M. H. Abrams, *The Mirror and the Lamp: Romantic Theory and the Critical Tradition* (Oxford: Oxford University Press, 1953), 161, 167.

46. David Hume, "Of Simplicity and Refinement in Writing" (1742), in *Essays Moral, Political, and Literary* (Indianapolis, IN: Liberty Classics, 1987), 196–197.

47. Rabindranath Tagore, *Nationalism* (New York: Macmillan, 1917), 15.

48. Claude McKay, *A Long Way from Home* (1937; repr., New Brunswick, NJ: Rutgers University Press, 2007), 230–231.

49. Stefan Collini, "What Is Intellectual History?," *History Today* 35, no. 10 (October 1985), http://www.historytoday.com/stefan-collini/what-intellectual-history.

50. Such criticisms are iterated in the discourse recounted in Collini, "What Is Intellectual History?" as well as in more recent collections on new directions in the field. See, for example, Darrin M. MacMahon and Samuel Moyn, eds., *Rethinking Modern European Intellectual History* (Oxford: Oxford University Press, 2014); Mia E. Bay et al., eds., *Toward an Intellectual History of Black Women* (Chapel Hill: University of North Carolina Press, 2015); and Samuel Moyn and Andrew Sartori, eds., *Global Intellectual History* (New York: Columbia University Press, 2015).

51. Raymond Williams, *Writing in Society* (London: Verso, 1983), 231.

52. Étienne Balibar, "The Nation Form: History and Ideology," in *Race, Nation, Class: Ambiguous Identities*, ed. Étienne Balibar and Immanuel Wallerstein (London: Verso, 1991), 94–95.

53. Pheng Cheah, *Spectral Nationality: Passages of Freedom from Kant to Postcolonial Literatures of Liberation* (New York: Columbia University Press, 2003), 32–33.

54. Ibid., 12.

55. Ibid., 388–391.

56. Ibid., 9.

57. Bruno Latour, *Reassembling the Social: An Introduction to Actor–Network Theory* (Oxford: Oxford University Press, 2005).

58. Geoffrey Galt Harpham, *On the Grotesque: Strategies of Contradiction in Art and Literature* (Princeton, NJ: Princeton University Press, 1982), 21–22.

59. Here, I join Vilashini Cooppan in arguing against stagist and progressivist notions of history in which globalism is portrayed as superseding nationalism rather than developing alongside it. I also build on the insights of John Marx, who has noted the relevance of early twentieth-century debates about empire to ongoing criticisms of and engagements with international governance under the rubric of globalization. See Cooppan, *Worlds Within: National Narratives and Global Connections in Postcolonial Writing* (Stanford, CA: Stanford University Press, 2009); and Marx, *Geopolitics and the Anglophone Novel, 1890–2011* (Cambridge: Cambridge University Press, 2012).

60. My thanks to Leela Gandhi for helping me clarify this point in my argument.

61. Anna Tsing, for instance, has argued against "assumptions of global newness" in the field of anthropology. See Tsing, "The Global Situation," *Cultural Anthropology* 15, no. 3 (2000): 333. Such assumptions grant unprecedented social effects to contemporary forms of globalization without adequately considering their prehistories.

62. Ann Cvetkovich associates the term "public feelings" with a "more expansive definition of political life," a definition in which "political identities are implicit within structures of feeling, sensibilities, everyday forms of cultural expression and affiliation that may not take the form of recognizable organizations or institutions." See Cvetkovich, "Public Feelings," *South Atlantic Quarterly* 106, no. 3 (Summer 2007): 462.

63. Zadie Smith, *White Teeth* (New York: Vintage International, 2000), 282 and 448.

64. The use of "minorly" here is meant to invoke the "minor" in Gilles Deleuze and Félix Guattari, *Kafka: Toward a Minor Literature*, trans. Dana Polan (Minneapolis: University of Minnesota Press, 1986). There, the minor designates a style of writing that deterritorializes or forms an internal other to the major language in which it appears. English has, of course, become the preeminent major language of globalization.

65. Boris Groys, *The Total Art of Stalinism: Avant-Garde, Aesthetic Dictatorship, and Beyond*, trans. Charles Rougle (1992; repr., London: Verso, 2011), 3, 36, 78.

66. Rabindranath Tagore, *The Home and the World*, trans. Surendranath Tagore (1919; repr., London: Penguin Books, 2005), 197.

1. Autotranslations: Rabindranath Tagore's Internationalism in Circulation

1. During the summer of 1930, Rabindranath Tagore also staged dialogues with French writer Romain Rolland and physicist Albert Einstein, the latter of whom served as a member of the League of Nations International Committee on Intellectual Cooperation. Although Tagore registered doubts about the power of the League of Nations to facilitate peace among states, his participation in committee activities and the pacifist movement remained steady, from his signing of Rolland's manifesto for intellectual autonomy, "La déclaration pour l'indépendance de l'esprit" (1919), to the publication of his correspondence with Gilbert Murray under the title *East, West* (1935) in the International Committee's Open Letter series.

2. Rabindranath Tagore and H. G. Wells, "Tagore and Wells," in *A Tagore Reader*, ed. Amiya Chakravarty (New York: Macmillan, 1961), 107.

3. In a letter to Macmillan, dated November 5, 1918, Tagore claimed collaborative authorship and approval of the novel in ways he would refuse to do for the translated novels published in its wake: "My nephew Surendranath has translated the latest novel of mine which I think you will find acceptable. A large part of it I have done myself and it has been carefully revised." See Rabindranath Tagore, *The Home and the World*, trans. Surendranath Tagore (1919; repr., London: Penguin Books, 2005), viii. All subsequent citations refer to this edition.

4. See, for example, Nabaneeta Sen, "The 'Foreign Reincarnation' of Rabindranath Tagore," *Journal of Asian Studies* 25, no. 2 (February 1966): 275–286; and Mahasweta Sengupta, "Translation, Colonialism, and Poetics: Rabindranath Tagore in Two Worlds," in *Translation, History, and Culture*, ed. Susan Bassnett and André Lefevre (London: Pinter, 1990), 56–64.

5. Rebecca Beasley, "Modernism's Translations," in *The Oxford Handbook of Global Modernisms*, ed. Mark Wollaeger with Matt Eatough (New York: Oxford University Press, 2012), 567. See also Stephen G. Yao, *Translation and the Languages of Modernism* (New York: Palgrave Macmillan, 2002).

6. Here my work builds on methodologies from world literature as theorized by David Damrosch, who argues that circulation and translation transform what is often construed as a singular literary work into a literary network comprising various editions and translations. Such a network calls for a reexamination of the relationship between originality and derivation—the aesthetics of a work and its material transformations through media and languages. Damrosch, *What Is World Literature?* (Princeton, NJ: Princeton University Press, 2003).

7. Important works by literary scholars that respond to Tagore's resurgence within nonliterary discourses of cosmopolitanism include Bruce Robbins, *Feeling Global: Internationalism in Distress* (New York: New York University Press, 1999); and Rebecca Walkowitz, "Cosmopolitan Ethics," in *The Turn to Ethics*, ed. Marjorie Garber, Beatrice Hanssen, and Rebecca L. Walkowitz (New York: Routledge, 2000), 221–230.

8. See Martha Nussbaum, "Patriotism and Cosmopolitanism," in *For Love of Country?*, ed. Joshua Cohen (Boston: Beacon Press, 1996), 2–20; Isaiah Berlin, *The Sense of Reality: Studies in Ideas and Their History* (New York: Farrar, Straus and Giroux, 1997); Ranajit Guha, *Dominance Without Hegemony: History and Power in Colonial India* (Cambridge, MA: Harvard University Press, 1998), 108–110; Dipesh Chakrabarty, *Provincializing Europe: Postcolonial Thought and Historical Difference* (Princeton, NJ: Princeton University Press, 2000), 149–180; Ashis Nandy, *The Illegitimacy of Nationalism: Rabindranath Tagore and the Politics of the Self* (Delhi: Oxford India, 1994); and Amartya Sen, "Tagore and His India," *New York Review of Books*, June 26, 1997, http://www.nybooks.com/articles/archives/1997/jun/26/tagore-and-his-india.

9. The excerpt from the *Athenaeum* review is available in first editions of Rabindranath Tagore, *Nationalism* (New York: Macmillan, 1917). All subsequent citations refer to this edition. The *Nation* review is reprinted in Kalyan Kundy, Sakti Bhattacharya, and Kalyan Sircar, eds., *Imagining Tagore: Rabindranath and the British Press (1912–1941)* (Delhi: Shishu Sahitya Samsad, 2000), 321–322.

10. Jeremy Braddock, *Collecting as Modernist Practice* (Baltimore: Johns Hopkins University Press, 2012), 6.

11. Rebecca Walkowitz, "For Translation: Virginia Woolf, J. M. Coetzee, and Transnational Comparison," in *The Legacies of Modernism*, ed. David James (Cambridge: Cambridge University Press, 2012), 257.

12. Krishna Kripalani, *Rabindranath Tagore: A Biography* (New Delhi: UBS Publishers Distributors, 2008), 292.

13. Rabindranath Tagore, "The Protest of a Seer," *Times Literary Supplement*, September 13, 1917. Reprinted in *Imagining Tagore: Rabindranath and the British Press (1912–1941)*, ed. Kalyan Kundy, Sakti Bhattacharya, and Kalyan Sircar (Delhi: Shishu Sahitya Samsad, 2000), 290.

14. Gauri Viswanathan, "Synthetic Vision: Internationalism and the Poetics of Decolonization," in *Nation, Language, and the Ethics of Translation*, ed. Sandra Bermann and Michael Wood (Princeton, NJ: Princeton University Press, 2005), 327.

15. Samuel Kinser, *Rabelais' Carnival: Text, Context, Metatext* (Berkeley: University of California Press, 1990), 17.

16. Indeed, the name Tagore itself is an Anglicization of Thakur, which means "Lord"—an allusion to social hierarchy that would be unintelligible to general English readers.

17. Mary Louise Pratt, "Arts of the Contact Zone," *Profession* (1991): 34.

18. My thinking about the relationship between cultural autarky and national autonomy is informed by Gary Wilder's work on democratic federalism and multinational statism. See Wilder, *Freedom Time: Negritude, Decolonization, and the Future of the World* (Durham, NC: Duke University Press, 2015).

19. Partha Chatterjee, *Nationalist Thought and the Colonial World: A Derivative Discourse* (London: Zed Books, 1986), 11.

20. Partha Chatterjee, *The Nation and its Fragments* (Princeton, NJ: Princeton University Press, 1993), 6.

21. Rey Chow, "The Old/New Question of Comparison in Literary Studies: A Post-European Perspective," *ELH* 71, no. 2 (2004): 289–311.

22. Ibid., 301.

23. H. D. Harootunian, "Ghostly Comparisons: Anderson's Telescope," *Diacritics* 29, no. 4 (1999), 145.

24. It is worth pointing out the problems that oral performance poses for world literature. Tagore's re-mediation of lectures into print discounts "their lives as oral texts," an oversight that Caroline Levine has argued routinely afflicts scholarship in world literature. Even if oral versions of the entries in *Nationalism* are lost to the ephemerality of performance, registering their contribution to the anthology's transnational network activates useful questions about which modalities of circulation count in current formulations of world literature. Levine, "The Great Unwritten: World Literature and the Effacement of Orality," *MLQ* 74, no. 2 (2013): 219.

25. *Jatiprem* can be rendered as *jati-prem*, or "nation-love." *Jati* has a very complex philological history in Bengali. Like *nation*'s ties to *natal*, *jati*'s etymological meaning is "to be born." In the nineteenth and early twentieth centuries, when Tagore was writing, *jati* could designate a race, tribe, or caste—any group that might fall under the category of an ethnos. See Swarupa Gupta, "*Samaj*, *Jati*, and *Desh*: Reflections on Nationhood in Late Colonial Bengal," *Studies in History* 23, no. 2 (2007): 177–203.

26. Pradip Kumar Datta, "The Interlocking Worlds of the Anglo-Boer War in South Africa and India," in *South Africa and India: Shaping the Global South*, ed. Isabel Hofmeyr and Michelle Williams (Johannesburg: Wits University Press, 2011), 59.

27. Quoted in Sisir Kumar Das, ed., *The English Writings of Rabindranath Tagore*, vol. 1 (New Delhi: Sahitya Akademi, 1994), 629.

28. David Porter, "The Crisis of Comparison and the World Literature Debates," *Profession* (2011): 253.

29. See Ezra Pound, "Rabindranath Tagore," *Fortnightly Review* 93, no. 555 (March 1913): 571–579. For more on this, see Aarthi Vadde, "Putting Foreignness to the Test: Rabindranath Tagore's Babu English," *Comparative Literature* 65, no. 1 (2013): 15–25.

30. The history of title changes to *Ghare Baire* is interesting to note. The first English translation, which appeared in the Calcutta-based journal *The Modern Review* in 1918–1919, was called *At Home and Outside*. The international English translation was retitled *The Home and the World*.

31. Manu Goswami, *Producing India: From Colonial Economy to National Space* (Chicago: University of Chicago Press, 2004), 15.

32. Hannah Arendt, *The Origins of Totalitarianism* (London: Harcourt, 1948), 230.

33. Goswami, *Producing India*, 10, 242–277.

34. Ibid., 181–182.

35. For a comprehensive account of Bankim Chandra Chatterjee's significance to the development of the novel in India, see Priya Joshi, *In Another Country: Colonialism, Culture, and the English Novel in India* (New York: Columbia University Press, 2002), especially 141–171.

36. In the 2005 Penguin Classics edition, William Radice authored a supplementary note section, whereas the 2001 Macmillan India edition offers a more complicated updating of the Tagores' translation. The main text contains added paragraphs of "fresh translation," without cutting or otherwise disturbing the original translation. The book also contains a substantial appendix by Sri Sukhendu Ray, which offers supplementary notes and alternative translations of the original translation. The purpose of this endeavor seems to have been to restore

nuances of meaning that had been lost in the initial translation, without denying readers the authorial imprint of Tagore over the 1919 translation.

37. Tagore, *Home and the World*, 17.

38. James Clifford, *The Predicament of Culture* (Cambridge, MA: Harvard University Press, 1988), 94.

39. Georg Lukács, "Tagore's Gandhi Novel," review of *The Home and the World*, by Rabindranath Tagore, *Marxist Internet Archive*, accessed November 3, 2014, http://www.marxists.org/archive/lukacs/works/1922/tagore.htm.

40. E. M. Forster, "*The Home and the World*," in *Abinger Harvest* (London: Harcourt, 1936), 330–331.

41. Anne McClintock, *Imperial Leather: Race, Gender, and Sexuality in the Colonial Contest* (London: Routledge, 1995), 34 and 209.

42. It seems fitting also that the "hideous confusion" of foreign and domestic commodity continues down from imperial history into our own contemporary moment. Pears soap is now "Made in India," and the Indian producer owns all rights to the brand.

43. Hannah Arendt, "The Crisis in Culture: Its Social and Political Significance," in *Between Past and Future* (New York: Viking Press, 1968), 220.

44. Ibid., 219.

45. Nussbaum, "Patriotism and Cosmopolitanism."

46. Robbins, *Feeling Global*, 161–162.

47. Maulana Mohamed Ali, *Selected Writings and Speeches*, ed. Afzal Iqbal (Lahore: Ashraf Press, 1944), 77.

48. Rabindranath Tagore, "A Vision of India's History," in *A Tagore Reader*, 196.

2. Alternating Asymmetry: International Solidarity and Self-Deception in James Joyce's *Dubliners* and "Cyclops"

1. Arthur Power's 1970 essay entitled "James Joyce—The Internationalist" represents a good example of the type of scholarship on Joyce that aligned national belonging with provincialism. Power's essay leaves the reader with the impression that Joyce's internationalism derived from a dismissive rejection of Ireland rather than an attempt to situate it within the Continental framework of Europe. See Power, "James Joyce—The Internationalist," in *A Bash in the Tunnel: James Joyce by the Irish*, ed. John Ryan (Brighton: Clifton Books, 1970), 181–188. Andrew Gibson, writing on the history of Joyce criticism, argues that for decades the "Poundian" tradition, which accentuated Joyce's Europeanness, won out over the "Wellsian" tradition, which emphasized Joyce's entanglements with Ireland. Gibson, *Joyce's*

Revenge: History, Politics, and Aesthetics in "Ulysses" (Oxford: Oxford University Press, 2002), 1–3. My account in this chapter joins recent attempts by R. Brandon Kershner, Tekla Mecsnóber, and Gayle Rogers to think past the opposition between Europeanness (as international standard) and Irishness (as national culture) in order to consider the intersection of Irish nationalism with continental politics. See R. Brandon Kershner, "Introduction: Joycean Unions," in *Joycean Unions: Post-Millennial Essays from East to West*, European Joyce Studies 22, ed. R. Brandon Kershner and Tekla Mecsnóber (Amsterdam: Rodopi, 2013), 5–15; and Gayle Rogers, *Modernism and the New Spain: Britain, Cosmopolitan Europe, and Literary History* (Oxford: Oxford University Press, 2014), 63–95.

2. Marjorie Howes and Derek Attridge point out the limited usefulness of the critical practice of contrasting Joyce's "tolerant cosmopolitan modernism with the narrow Irish nationalism he rejected." Such moralizing oppositions forgo an analysis of the interdependence of modernism and nationalism and consequently hew toward incorrectly confirming modernism's remoteness from issues of collective identity and international analysis. Howes and Attridge, introduction to *Semicolonial Joyce*, ed. Derek Attridge and Marjorie Howes (Cambridge: Cambridge University Press, 2000), 11.

3. Declan Kiberd, *Inventing Ireland* (Cambridge, MA: Harvard University Press, 1995), 151.

4. My account of Joyce's aesthetics as more of a counterweight to revivalism than an outright rejection of it builds on Pericles Lewis's argument that Joyce internalized some of the assumptions that animated the cultural revival and the Gaelic League, even if he disagreed with their methods and solutions for advancing the race via a reclamation of lost origins. See Lewis, *Modernism, Nationalism, and the Novel* (Cambridge: Cambridge University Press, 2000), 38.

5. Lauren Berlant, *Cruel Optimism* (Durham, NC: Duke University Press, 2011), 2.

6. Mikhail Bakhtin, *Rabelais and His World*, trans. Hélène Iswolsky (Bloomington: University of Indiana Press, 1965), 21–22.

7. James Joyce, "The Day of the Rabblement," in *The Critical Writings*, ed. Ellsworth Mason and Richard Ellmann (New York: Viking, 1959), 70.

8. Joseph Valente, "James Joyce and the Cosmopolitan Sublime," in *Joyce and the Subject of History*, ed. Mark A. Wollaeger, Victor Luftig, and Robert Spoo (Ann Arbor: University of Michigan Press, 1996), 61.

9. Emer Nolan, *James Joyce and Nationalism* (London: Routledge, 1995), 130.

10. I borrow the language of "effective motives" and "avowed intentions" from Robert Pippin, *Hollywood Westerns and American Myth: The Importance of Howard Hawks and John Ford for Political Philosophy* (New Haven, CT: Yale University Press, 2010), 134. My understanding of self-deception in this chapter also has been informed by Pippin, *Nietzsche, Psychology, and First Philosophy* (Chicago: Univer-

sity of Chicago Press, 2010), especially 85–104. Pippin's work on self-deception has ranged from individual forms, in which subjects develop complex and puzzling ways of hiding their desires from themselves, to collective forms, in which, Pippin argues, modern states (especially liberal ones) come to rely upon origin stories that deny their foundational violence.

11. Robert Spoo, *James Joyce and the Language of History: Dedalus' Nightmare* (Oxford: Oxford University Press, 1994), 123.

12. Joyce observed the speech at the Law Students' Debating Society, in 1901, and, while living in Trieste, also purchased Taylor's pamphlet entitled "The Language of the Outlaw." See Neil R. Davison, *James Joyce, "Ulysses," and the Construction of Jewish Identity: Culture, Biography, and the "Jew" in Modernist Europe* (Cambridge: Cambridge University Press, 1998), 80.

13. James Joyce, *Ulysses*, ed. Hans Walter Gabler (1922; corrected text, New York: Vintage Books, 1986), 116–118. All subsequent citations refer to this edition.

14. Thomas Kabdebó, *A Study in Parallels* (Dublin: Four Courts Press, 2001).

15. Arthur Griffith's influence and Hungary's long-standing place within Irish anticolonialism helps to explain why Hungary continued to stand out at the turn of the twentieth century despite the rising tide of what Andrew Gibson calls "'emergent nation' internationalism." Gibson's examination of Irish periodicals such as the *Workers' Republic* and the *United Irishman* shows a rise in Irish affiliation with other small nations: "[Anticolonial] struggles grouped together the Davids—Ireland, Hungary, Norway, Finland, Poland, Serbia, to which some added Cuba, Haiti, the Philippines, and more—against the Goliaths dominating them." Gibson, *The Strong Spirit: History, Politics, and Aesthetics in the Writings of James Joyce, 1898–1915* (Oxford: Oxford University Press, 2013), 18–19.

16. Arthur Griffith, *The Resurrection of Hungary: A Parallel for Ireland* (1904; 3rd ed., Dublin: Whelan and Son, 1918), 70–71.

17. Diana Fuss, *Identification Papers* (New York: Routledge, 1995), 2.

18. Kiberd, *Inventing Ireland*, 151.

19. James Joyce, *Stephen Hero*, ed. Theodore Spencer with John J. Slocum and Herbert Cahoon (New York: New Directions, 1944), 62.

20. Richard Ellmann, *James Joyce*, rev. ed. (Oxford: Oxford University Press, 1982), 164–165. It should be noted that Ellmann does not use "Irish" to connote Joyce's national belonging, as critics in Irish or postcolonial studies have sometimes done. Instead, he uses it to connote the colonial environment about which Joyce wrote, and he tends to produce an image of Joyce that aligns the colonial with the provincial.

21. James Joyce, *Dubliners* (1914; repr., New York: Quality Paperback Book Club, 1996), 49. All subsequent citations refer to this edition.

22. Vincent J. Cheng, *Joyce, Race, and Empire* (Cambridge: Cambridge University Press, 1995), 106.

23. "Wealthy and cosmopolitan crowd" is from Cheng, *Joyce, Race, and Empire*, 107. Seamus Deane suggests that friendship is the ruse by which Jimmy, like his father, sacrifices nationalism to a vague humanism. See Deane, "Dead Ends: Joyce's Finest Moments," in *Semicolonial Joyce*, ed. Derek Attridge and Marjorie Howes (Cambridge: Cambridge University Press, 2000), 23.

24. My distinction between comparisons that establish equivalence and those that establish similitude is indebted to Natalie Melas's postcolonial theory of comparison. See Melas, *All the Difference in the World: Postcoloniality and the Ends of Comparison* (Stanford, CA: Stanford University Press, 2006).

25. In the critical history of "After the Race," some have viewed Jimmy as the target of a purposeful con. Robert M. Adams speculates that Routh and Ségouin planned the card game to fleece Jimmy of his money. Adams, "A Study in Weakness and Humiliation," in *James Joyce's Dubliners: A Critical Handbook*, ed. James R. Baker and Thomas F. Staley (Belmont, CA: Wadsworth, 1969), 103. This possibility also has been raised in Cheng, *Joyce, Race, and Empire*, 108; and Deane, "Dead Ends," 23.

26. See Andrew Goldstone, *Fictions of Autonomy: Modernism from Wilde to de Man* (Oxford: Oxford University Press, 2013), 25. The Wilde quote is from *An Ideal Husband*.

27. Joyce, of course, was not immune to using such vocabulary himself in his nonfiction, calling the Irish "the most belated race in Europe" in "The Day of the Rabblement" (Mason and Ellmann, *Critical Writings*, 70). His fiction, however, affords an opportunity to think beyond the polemical propositions and conflicting characterizations of Ireland threaded throughout his letters and essays. Enda Duffy treats "After the Race" as primarily a "tale of class resentments" rather than colonial comparisons, but in both our readings speed is the motif through which Joyce unfolds various forms of social antagonism and envy. Duffy, *The Speed Handbook: Velocity, Pleasure, Modernism* (Durham, NC: Duke University Press, 2009), 127–128.

28. James Joyce to Grant Richards, May 20, 1906, in Richard Ellmann, ed., *Selected Letters of James Joyce* (London: Faber and Faber, 1975), 88.

29. Walter Benjamin, "The Author as Producer," *New Left Review* I/62 (July–August 1970): 96.

30. James Joyce, *A Portrait of the Artist as a Young Man* (1916; repr., New York: Penguin, 1993), 220.

31. David Kurnick, *Empty Houses: Theatrical Failure and the Novel* (Princeton, NJ: Princeton University Press, 2011), 153–154.

32. Ernst Bloch, *Literary Essays*, trans. Andrew Joron and others (Stanford, CA: Stanford University Press, 1998). Hope, for Bloch, must be "unconditionally disappointable" (341) in order for it to presage radical political transformation—that is, the kind of transformation that transcends preexisting structures of change.

33. Deane, "Dead Ends," 36.

34. Saikat Majumdar, *Prose of the World: Modernism and the Banality of Empire* (New York: Columbia University Press, 2013), 46–47.

35. Ellmann, *Selected Letters*, 89–90.

36. David Lloyd, "'Counterparts,' Dubliners, and Temperance Nationalism," in *Semicolonial Joyce*, ed. Derek Attridge and Marjorie Howes (Cambridge: Cambridge University Press, 2000), 145–147.

37. Joyce, *Dubliners*, 41, 48. Luke Gibbons reads Maria's repetition of the stanza as the transformation of "enabling rituals into their immobilizing opposites," but he tends to associate that paralysis more with pathology and tragedy than with the kindling of resistance through bodily refusal. Gibbons, "'Have You No Homes to Go To?' James Joyce and the Politics of Paralysis," in *Semicolonial Joyce*, ed. Derek Attridge and Marjorie Howes (Cambridge: Cambridge University Press, 2000), 162.

38. Joyce, *Portrait*, 276. Here my reading of Joyce's uncreated racial conscience is informed by but is not quite the same as Pericles Lewis's theological interpretation of the meaning of uncreated conscience. Lewis defines "uncreated" not as something "brand new" created ex nihilo (out of nothing) but as a reenactment and reshaping of "the eternal substance that precedes and conditions all his [Stephen's] personal experiences." That substance is precisely his race, which is not meant to be overcome like so much resistant material but to be the impetus for the modernist harmonizing of "individual consciousness and the external reality it confronts." See Lewis, *Modernism*, 2, 4. In my understanding of Joyce's uncreated conscience with respect to *Dubliners*, "uncreated" does not refer transcendentally to an Irish race enduring in and beyond history but rather to a set of seemingly inert gestures that persist as the waste material of an increasingly politicized and self-conscious project of racial nationalism.

39. Joyce, *Ulysses*, 14, 78, 158.

40. Ellmann, *Selected Letters*, 271.

41. Robert E. Spoo and Enda Duffy have argued that *Ulysses*, though set in 1904, registers events concurrent with its composition, such as the Easter Rising and the Great War. See Spoo, "'Nestor' and the Nightmare: The Presence of the Great War in *Ulysses*," *Twentieth Century Literature* 32, no. 2 (1986): 137–154; Duffy, *The Subaltern Ulysses* (Minneapolis: University of Minnesota Press, 1994); and Duffy, "Disappearing Dublin: Ulysses, Postcoloniality, and the Politics of Space," in *Semicolonial Joyce*, ed. Derek Attridge and Marjorie Howes (Cambridge: Cambridge University Press, 2000), 37–58. Although I am not suggesting that we allow the future of the novel's composition to trump the timeframe in which the narrative is set, I believe, like Paul Saint-Amour, that "the forward-looking elements of *Ulysses*" need to be recovered to arrive at historically situated arguments that match the complex temporalities of the novel. See Saint-Amour, *Tense*

Future: Modernism, Total War, Encyclopedic Form (Oxford: Oxford University Press, 2015), 227.

42. Gibson, *Joyce's Revenge*, 122.

43. Joyce, *Ulysses*, 276.

44. Karen Lawrence, *The Odyssey of Style* (Princeton, NJ: Princeton University Press, 1981), 103.

45. It also contradicts Joyce's compositional methods. Michael Groden's examination of the drafts of "Cyclops" shows that, contrary to what readers might expect, Joyce wrote the parodies first, then developed the barroom setting, and finally created the first-person narrative voice. Groden, " 'Cyclops' in Progress, 1919," *James Joyce Quarterly* 12, no. 1–2 (Fall 1974–Winter 1975): 134.

46. Enda Duffy (*Subaltern Ulysses*, 110–111) has identified an implicitly liberal and unwittingly anti-Irish bias in the critical history of *Ulysses*, evidenced by tendencies to attack the citizen's aggressive language while leaving Bloom's platitudinous claims unexamined. For an account of the respectability politics behind what David Lloyd calls "temperance nationalism," see Lloyd," 'Counterparts,' Dubliners, and Temperance Nationalism," 141.

47. Duffy, *Subaltern Ulysses*, 112.

48. David Kazanjian, *The Colonizing Trick: National Culture and Imperial Citizenship in Early America* (Minneapolis: University of Minnesota Press, 2003), 137.

49. Don Gifford, *"Ulysses" Annotated: Notes for James Joyce's "Ulysses"* (Berkeley: University of California Press, 1988), 358.

50. George Bernard Shaw to Sylvia Beach, October 10, 1921, in Richard Ellmann, ed., *Letters of James Joyce*, vol. 3 (New York: Viking Press, 1966), 50. My thanks to Paul Saint-Amour for pointing me to this letter.

51. Margot Norris, *Virgin and Veteran Readings of "Ulysses"* (New York: Palgrave Macmillan, 2011), 202.

3. Stories Without Plots: The Nomadic Collectivism of Claude McKay and George Lamming

1. "Nicolae Gheorghe," *Economist*, August 17, 2013, http://www.economist.com/news/obituary/21583590-nicolae-gheorghe-campaigner-rights-roma-died-august-8th-aged-66-nicolae.

2. European Parliament, "Resolution on Discrimination Against the Roma," September 25, 1995, http://eur-lex.europa.eu/LexUriServ/LexUriServ.do?uri=CELEX:51995IP0974:EN:HTML.

3. Étienne Balibar, "Toward a Diasporic Citizen? From Internationalism to Cosmopolitics," in *The Creolization of Theory*, ed. Françoise Lionnet and Shu-Mei Shih (Durham, NC: Duke University Press, 2011), 207.

4. Joseph Slaughter, *Human Rights Inc.: The World Novel, Narrative Form, and International Law* (New York: Fordham University Press, 2007), 106.

5. Nancy Armstrong, *How Novels Think* (New York: Columbia University Press, 2005), 28, 35.

6. See Paul Gilroy, *The Black Atlantic: Modernity and Double Consciousness* (Cambridge, MA: Harvard University Press, 1993), 7; and Carole Boyce Davies, *Black Women, Writing, and Identity: Migrations of the Subject* (London: Routledge, 1994), 12.

7. Brent Edwards, *The Practice of Diaspora* (Cambridge, MA: Harvard University Press, 2003), 13–14.

8. A recent special issue of *Modernism/Modernity* entitled "The Harlem Renaissance and the New Modernist Studies" encourages and exemplifies such bridging work by undertaking the project of rethinking the institutionally separated but historically related categories of modernism and the Harlem Renaissance. Adam McKible and Suzanne W. Churchill, the editors of the issue, seek to redress the "critical practices that occlude and obscure the connections between the field(s) of study" while also remaining wary of conflating the fields. See McKible and Churchill, "Introduction: In Conversation: The Harlem Renaissance and the New Modernist Studies," *Modernism/Modernity* 20, no. 3 (2013): 429. Previous studies that have argued for reading black writers not only as adjacent to modernism but also as modernist themselves include Jennifer Wilks, *Race, Gender, and Comparative Black Modernism: Suzanne Lacascade, Marita Bonner, Suzanne Césaire, Dorothy West* (Baton Rouge: Louisiana State University Press, 2008); Miriam Thaggert, *Images of Black Modernism: Visual and Verbal Strategies of the Harlem Renaissance* (Amherst: University of Massachusetts Press, 2010); and James Smethurst, *The African American Roots of Modernism: From Reconstruction to the Harlem Renaissance* (Chapel Hill: University of North Carolina Press, 2011).

9. An important exception to this claim is the work of Kate A. Baldwin, who traces the "transnational genealogies of black internationalism" beyond the African diaspora to Russia and later the Soviet Union. Baldwin's focus on Russia leads her to examine the interracial solidarities underpinning black internationalism, which leads her work to deviate from what she calls "standard accounts of a black transnationalism" descended from Gilroy's paradigm of the Black Atlantic. Baldwin, *Beyond the Color Line and the Iron Curtain* (Durham, NC: Duke University Press, 2002), 4, 85.

10. Claude McKay's disinterest in returning to the Caribbean partially explains why he is read primarily as a Harlem Renaissance writer, whereas Lamming's dedication to theorizing the West Indian novel has traditionally placed his oeuvre within the West Indian national tradition. See Sandra Pouchet Paquet, *The Novels of George Lamming* (London: Heinemann, 1982). However, recent

works on both figures have established the difficulty of assigning them to just one national tradition. For a reading of McKay that emphasizes his diasporic Caribbean origins, see Louis Chude-Sokei, *The Last "Darky": Bert Williams, Black-on-Black Minstrelsy, and the African Diaspora* (Durham, NC: Duke University Press, 2006), 207–248. For studies that have recast Lamming as an immigrant writer in the British tradition, see John Clement Ball, *Postcolonial Fiction and the Transnational Metropolis* (Toronto: University of Toronto Press, 2004), 101–175; and J. Dillon Brown, *Migrant Modernism: Postwar London and the West Indian Novel* (Charlottesville: University of Virginia Press, 2013).

11. George Lamming, "Interview with George Lamming," in *Kas-Kas: Interviews with Three Caribbean Writers in Texas*, ed. Ian Munro and Reinhard Sander (Austin, TX: African and Afro-American Research Institute, 1972), 16.

12. See Heather Love, *Feeling Backward: Loss and the Politics of Queer History* (Cambridge, MA: Harvard University Press, 2007); and Immanuel Kant, "An Answer to the Question: 'What Is Enlightenment?'," in *Kant: Political Writings*, 2nd ed., ed. Hans Reiss, trans. H. B. Nisbet (Cambridge: Cambridge University Press, 1991), 54–60.

13. Claude McKay, *Banjo: A Story Without a Plot* (New York: Harper, 1929), 137. All subsequent citations refer to this edition.

14. Claude McKay, *Home to Harlem* (1928; repr., Boston: Northeastern University Press, 1987), 227–228.

15. Michael North, *The Dialect of Modernism* (Oxford: Oxford University Press, 1994), 113.

16. Ibid., 123.

17. W. E. B. Du Bois, "Two Novels: Nella Larsen, *Quicksand*, and Claude McKay, *Home to Harlem*," *Crisis* 35 (1928): 202.

18. Claude McKay to James Weldon Johnson, April 30, 1928, in Wayne F. Cooper, *Claude McKay: Rebel Sojourner in the Harlem Renaissance* (Baton Rouge: Louisiana State University Press, 1987), 247.

19. Shane Vogel, *The Scene of Harlem Cabaret: Race, Sexuality, Performance* (Chicago: University of Chicago Press, 2009), 133.

20. See Wayne F. Cooper, ed., *The Passion of Claude McKay: Selected Poetry and Prose, 1912–1948* (New York: Schocken Books, 1973), 138.

21. See Smethurst, *African American Roots*, 208; Dewey Jones, "Dirt," *Chicago Defender* (July 27, 1929): 12; and André Levinson, "De Harlem à la cannebière," *Les Nouvelles Littéraires* (September 14, 1929): 7.

22. Levinson, "De Harlem à la cannebière."

23. Charles Baudelaire, *Ouevres complètes*, tome 1 (Paris: Gallimard, 1975), 71.

24. Peter Brooks, *Reading for the Plot: Design and Intention in Narrative* (Cambridge, MA: Harvard University Press, 1992), 7.

25. Ibid., 12.

26. Levinson, "De Harlem à la cannebière."

27. Cooper, *Claude McKay: Rebel Sojourner*, 254. Cooper's reading of *Banjo* tends to be shaped by his attribution of a nostalgic primitivism to McKay himself. When Jake in *Home to Harlem* and Banjo in *Banjo* are referred to as picaros, it is on the basis of such precivilized qualities as natural instinct and elemental will, rather than a studied response to the adverse conditions of an inhospitable social order.

28. W. E. B. Du Bois, "Review of Claude McKay's *Banjo* and Nella Larsen's *Passing*," *Crisis* 36 (July 1929): 234.

29. William J. Maxwell, "Global Poetics and State-Sponsored Transnationalism," *American Literary History* 18, no. 2 (2006): 360.

30. See Cooper, *Claude McKay: Rebel Sojourner*, 190.

31. Joel Nickels has written persuasively about how McKay's suspicion of authoritarian central planning led him to explore anarchist philosophies of political organization in *Banjo* and in his nonfiction. Nickels, "Claude McKay and Dissident Internationalism," *Cultural Critique* 87 (Spring 2014): 10–11.

32. Leela Gandhi, *Affective Communities: Anticolonial Thought, Fin-de-Siècle Radicalism, and the Politics of Friendship* (Durham, NC: Duke University Press, 2006), 59.

33. Ibid., 179.

34. Edwards, *Practice of Diaspora*, 210, 220–221.

35. My thanks to Marina Magloire for her felicitously titled graduate seminar paper "The Metaphysics of Partying in Three Modernist Novels."

36. Sianne Ngai, *Ugly Feelings* (Cambridge, MA: Harvard University Press, 2005), 100.

37. For a discussion of Bataille's theories in relationship to his frequenting of jazz clubs, see Brent Edwards, "The Ethnics of Surrealism," *Transition* 78 (1998): 115. Edwards (*Practice of Diaspora*, 223) also notes how Bataille's and McKay's similar accounts of primitivism reconfigure the usual divisions of modernist classification in which black literature would be separated from European theory.

38. George Bataille, *Visions of Excess*, trans. Allen Stoekl (Minneapolis: University of Minnesota Press, 1985), 102.

39. Amy Hollywood, *Sensible Ecstasy: Mysticism, Sexual Difference, and the Demands of History* (Chicago: University of Chicago, Press, 2002), 85.

40. Ernst Bloch, "Something's Missing: A Discussion Between Ernst Bloch and Theodor Adorno on the Contradictions of Utopian Longing (1964)," in Ernst Bloch, *The Utopian Function of Art and Literature: Selected Essays*, trans. Jack Zipes and Frank Mecklenberg (Cambridge, MA: MIT Press, 1988), 1–18.

41. The queer-theoretical dimensions of male friendship in *Banjo* are thoroughly explored by Michelle Ann Stephens, who finds that McKay's novel

anticipates contemporary queer theory's challenge to the values embedded in the heterosexual marriage contract and the heteronormative nation-state. See Stephens, *Black Empire: The Masculine Global Imaginary of Caribbean Intellectuals in the United States, 1914–1962* (Durham, NC: Duke University Press, 2005), 167–204.

42. Seyla Benhabib, *The Rights of Others: Aliens, Residents, and Citizens* (Cambridge: Cambridge University Press, 2004).

43. George Lamming, introduction to *In the Castle of My Skin* (Ann Arbor: University of Michigan Press, 2001), xxxvi–xxxvii.

44. George Lamming, *The Pleasures of Exile* (Ann Arbor: University of Michigan Press, 1992), 45.

45. George Lamming, *The Emigrants* (1954; repr., Ann Arbor: University of Michigan Press, 1994), 25. All subsequent citations refer to this edition.

46. Wilson Harris, "History, Fable, and Myth in the Caribbean and Guianas" (1970), repr., *Caribbean Quarterly* 54, no. 1–2 (March–June 2008): 22.

47. Nathaniel Mackey, *Discrepant Engagements: Dissonance, Cross-Culturality, and Experimental Writing* (Cambridge: Cambridge University Press, 1993), 170.

48. See Janet Butler, "The Existentialism of George Lamming," *Caribbean Review* 11, no. 4 (1982): 15, 38–39; and Mary Lou Emery, *Modernism, the Visual, and Caribbean Literature* (Cambridge: Cambridge University Press, 2007).

49. Lauren Berlant, "Citizenship," in *Keywords for American Cultural Studies*, ed. Bruce Burgett and Glenn Hendler (New York: New York University Press, 2007), 37.

50. Gary Wilder, *The French Imperial Nation-State: Negritude and Colonial Humanism Between the Two World Wars* (Chicago: University of Chicago Press, 2005), 7. Though Wilder's research focuses on the constitutive contradictions of French republicanism, in which colonial racism is an operation of rather than a failure of imperial univeralism, his argument becomes particularly resonant with the changes to English imperial policy that came into effect with the British Nationality Act of 1948. The act instituted the category of "Citizen of the United Kingdom and Colonies." By creating the possibility for Commonwealth citizenship and loosening border regulations for colonial subjects traveling to England, the law held out the affective promise of blurring the line between Englishness and Britishness, although that line was firmly patrolled in a variety of ways upon the arrival of racialized subjects in England.

51. Houston A. Baker Jr., "Critical Memory and the Black Public Sphere," in *The Black Public Sphere: A Public Culture Book*, ed. Black Public Sphere Collective (Chicago: University of Chicago Press, 1995), 12–14.

52. George Lamming, "The Negro Writer and His World," in *The George Lamming Reader: The Aesthetics of Decolonisation*, ed. Anthony Bogues (Kingston: Ian Randle Publishers, 2011), 3.

53. Walter Benjamin, *The Arcades Project*, ed. Rolf Tiedemann, trans. Howard Eiland and Kevin McLaughlin (Cambridge, MA: Harvard University Press, 1999), 107. For drawing my attention to this quote, I am grateful to Theodore Martin, "The Long Wait: Timely Secrets of the Contemporary Detective Novel," *Novel: A Forum on Fiction* 45, no. 2 (2012): 165.

54. See Simon Gikandi, *Writing in Limbo: Modernism and Caribbean Literature* (Ithaca, NY: Cornell University Press, 1992), 12–16.

55. See Lamming, *Pleasures of Exile*, 211–229.

56. See Ernst Bloch, *The Principle of Hope*, vol. 1, trans. Neville Plaice, Stephen Plaice, and Paul Knight (Cambridge, MA: MIT Press, 1995), 74–75.

57. Balibar, "Toward a Diasporic Citizen?," 224.

4. Archival Legends: National Myth and Transnational Memory in the Works of Michael Ondaatje

1. Michel Foucault, *The Archaeology of Knowledge*, trans. A. M. Sheridan Smith (New York: Pantheon, 1972), 129.

2. Jacques Derrida, *Archive Fever: A Freudian Impression*, trans. Eric Prenowitz (Chicago: University of Chicago Press, 1996), 1–5.

3. Irving Velody argues that the archive sets the conditions of possibility for humanistic and sociological research. Historian Carolyn Steedman sees interest in the archive as symptomatic of a modern disposition toward wanting "to know and to have the past." Digital humanist Matthew Kirschenbaum retains the emphasis on beginnings with respect to digital archives when he argues that "the conceit of a 'primary record' can no longer be assumed to be coterminous with that of a 'physical object.' Electronic texts, files, feeds, and transmissions of all sorts are also now, indisputably, primary records." See Velody, "The Archive and the Human Sciences: Notes Towards a Theory of the Archive," *History of the Human Sciences* 11, no. 4 (November 1998): 1; Steedman, *Dust: The Archive and Cultural History* (Manchester: Manchester University Press, 2001), 75; and Kirschenbaum, "The .txtual Condition: Digital Humanities, Born-Digital Archives, and the Future Literary," *DHQ* 7, no. 1 (2013), http://www.digitalhumanities.org/dhq/vol/7/1/000151/000151.html.

4. See, for example, Tom LeClair, "The Sri Lankan Patients," *The Nation*, June 19, 2000: 31–33; Qadri Ismael, "A Flippant Gesture Toward Sri Lanka: A Review of Michael Ondaatje's *Anil's Ghost*," *Pravada* 6, no. 9 (2000): 24–29, which argues that, in broaching an ongoing historical conflict, *Anil's Ghost* should have been more straightforwardly factual and even equitable in its presentation of Sinhalese and Tamil characters; and Arun Mukherjee, *Oppositional Aesthetics: Readings from a Hyphenated Space* (Toronto: TSAR, 1994). For readings that defend the novel

from such criticisms through engagement with religion, see Marlene Goldman, "Representations of Buddhism in Ondaatje's *Anil's Ghost*," in *Comparative Cultural Studies and Michael Ondaatje's Writings*, ed. Steven Tötösy de Zepetnek (West Lafayette, IN: Purdue University Press, 2005), 27–37; and John McClure, *Partial Faiths: Postsecular Fiction in the Age of Pynchon and Morrison* (Athens: University of Georgia Press, 2007). For a cosmopolitan stance, see Katherine Stanton, *Cosmopolitan Fictions: Ethics, Politics, and Global Change in the Works of Kazuo Ishiguro, Michael Ondaatje, Jamaica Kincaid, and J. M. Coetzee* (New York: Routledge, 2009).

5. Ranjana Khanna, "Frames, Contexts, Community, Justice," *Diacritics* 33, no. 2 (Summer 2003): 18.

6. Michael Ondaatje, *The English Patient* (New York: Vintage International, 1992), 150. Bruce Robbins presents an important recuperative reading of *The English Patient* that notes that the novel acknowledges Almásy's historical erasures in a way that the character does not, evidenced partly by the novel's allusion to the "half-invented world of the desert" that Almásy inhabits. Robbins, *Feeling Global: Internationalism in Distress* (New York: New York University Press, 1999), 166.

7. Georg Lukács, *The Historical Novel*, trans. Hannah Mitchell and Stanley Mitchell (Boston: Beacon, 1962), 25. For the coining of the phrase "historiographic metafiction," see Linda Hutcheon, *A Poetics of Postmodernism: History, Theory, Fiction* (Oxford: Routledge, 1988), 105–124. Approaches to Ondaatje's fiction through the generic lens of historiographic metafiction include Hutcheon, *The Canadian Postmodern: A Study of Contemporary Canadian Fiction* (Oxford: Oxford University Press, 1988); W. M. Verhoeven, "Naming the Present/Naming the Past: Historiographic Metafiction in Findley and Ondaatje," in *Shades of Empire in Colonial and Post-Colonial Literatures*, ed. C. C. Barfoot and Theo D'haen (Amsterdam: Rodopi, 1993), 283–299; Lee Spinks, *Michael Ondaatje* (Manchester: Manchester University Press, 2009); Ursula Kluwick, "The Personal and the Public: Michael Ondaatje's Historiographic Metafiction and the Question of Political Engagement," in *A Sea for Encounters: Essays Towards a Postcolonial Commonwealth*, ed. Stella Borg Barthet (Amsterdam: Rodopi; 2009), 273–286; and Christopher McVey, "Reclaiming the Body of the Past: Michael Ondaatje and the Body of History," *Journal of Modern Literature* 37, no. 2 (2014): 141–160.

8. Michel Foucault, "The Lives of Infamous Men," in *Michel Foucault: Power, Truth, Strategy*, ed. Meaghan Morris and Paul Patton (Sydney: Feral, 1979), 76, 80.

9. Ondaatje's use of literary form thus anticipates the experiential or phenomenological turn within more recent theories of the archive as they have unfolded within postcolonial and African diasporic studies. Antoinette Burton, for example, challenges the objectivity of the archive by examining how scholars' bodily particularities inflect their encounters with and experiences of archives. Ann Laura Stoler moves away from a theory of the archive that assumes omniscience

and total control, and this in turn shapes her departure from equally strong theories of state power. She argues that the archive exemplifies the anxieties and confusions of colonial governance wherein affective knowledge, perception and misperception, played a decisive role in shaping political rationality. Brent Edwards draws on Roland Barthes's *Camera Lucida*, Arlette Farge's *Le goût de l'archive*, and the late Foucault to address the sensation of the archive as that which exceeds historical intelligibility. Edwards places renewed emphasis on the effect of archival material on a particular viewer, and he values the muteness of artifacts over their capacity to make history readily available. See Burton, ed., *Facts, Fictions, and the Writing of History* (Durham, NC: Duke University Press, 2005); Stoler, *Along the Archival Grain: Epistemic Anxieties and Colonial Common Sense* (Princeton, NJ: Princeton University Press, 2009); and Edwards, "The Taste of the Archive," *Callaloo* 35, no. 4 (Fall 2012): 944–972.

10. Michael Ondaatje, *Anil's Ghost* (New York: Vintage International, 2000), 55. All subsequent citations refer to this edition. The war did not come to an official end until 2004, after the novel was published.

11. Ann Mandel, "Michael Ondaatje," *Dictionary of Literary Biography: Canadian Writers Since 1960—Second Series*, ed. W. H. New (Detroit: Gale Research, 1987), 276.

12. Michael Ondaatje, *The Collected Works of Billy the Kid* (New York: Vintage International, 2008), 115. All subsequent citations refer to this expanded edition, though the 1970 and other editions are also discussed. The 2008 edition contains important changes from previous editions, including a new afterword by Ondaatje and a new cover that makes explicit the work's transnational politics. My decision to privilege this edition of *Collected Works* draws on Ondaatje's involvement in extending it, and on the theories of the "fluid text," by John Bryant, and of "transmission," by Andrew Piper. Both have established the importance of publication history, revision, and reprinting to the interpretation of a work as both text and object. See Bryant, *The Fluid Text: A Theory of Revision and Editing for Book and Screen* (Ann Arbor: University of Michigan Press, 2002); and Piper, *Dreaming in Books: The Making of the Bibliographic Imagination in the Romantic Age* (Chicago: University of Chicago Press, 2009). My thanks to Fiona Somerset for the Bryant reference.

13. For clarity, I use the name Bonney when referring to the historical figure, but Billy or Billy the Kid when referring to Ondaatje's character.

14. Ernest Gellner, *Nations and Nationalism* (Ithaca, NY: Cornell University Press, 1983).

15. Frederick Jackson Turner, "The Significance of the Frontier in American History," in *Rereading Frederick Jackson Turner: "The Significance of the Frontier in American History" and Other Essays*, ed. John Mack Faragher (New Haven, CT: Yale University Press, 1999), 32.

16. Thomas Bender makes a revisionist claim for Turner, asserting that Turner was not as "trapped in his rhetoric" of American self-containment as those he influenced. He invokes an earlier essay entitled "The Significance of History," in which Turner writes of European history as refusing "the bounds of a nation," to draw a historical precedent for transnational awareness among American historians. Bender, "Historians, the Nation, and the Plenitude of Narratives," in *Rethinking American History in a Global Age*, ed. Thomas Bender (Berkeley: University of California Press, 2002), 1–21.

17. Spinks, *Michael Ondaatje*, 50.

18. Richard W. Etulain, introduction to *The Saga of Billy the Kid*, by Walter Noble Burns (Albuquerque: University of New Mexico Press, 1999), ix–xviii.

19. Ondaatje, *Collected Works*, 2.

20. Benedict Anderson, *Imagined Communities: Reflections on the Origins and Spread of Nationalism* (London: Verso, 1983), 25.

21. Ondaatje, *Collected Works*, 88. Paul Newman actually played Billy in *The Left Handed Gun* (1958), the film to which Ondaatje is possibly referring. John Cassavetes played a violent young gunman in the western *Saddle the Wind*, also released in 1958.

22. Arjun Appadurai, *Modernity at Large: Cultural Dimensions of Globalization* (Minneapolis: University of Minnesota Press, 1996), 184.

23. Stoler (*Along the Archival Grain*) uses this phrase in reference to the Dutch colonial archives, whose organization, she argues, reflects not the absolute control of an imperial government but the anxieties attendant to maintaining its power.

24. The 2008 cover photograph, taken in 1930, is from the archive of Romualdo García, an early pioneer of Mexican photography in the nineteenth century and a contemporary of Bonney and Huffman. Previous editions of *Collected Works* that featured historical photographs of Bonney include the 1997 edition released by Anansi Press (the original publishers, in 1970); the Vintage 1996 edition; and the 2004 Bloomsbury edition. The 1974 Norton edition features the title of the work, with no photographs, and the first Anansi edition features an image of a man on a horse, though the man is not Bonney.

25. Charles Olson, *Call Me Ishmael* (Baltimore: Johns Hopkins University Press, 1997), 117.

26. I take these ethnic distinctions with a grain of salt. Far from being reified entities, Tamil and Sinhalese are internally heterogeneous groups whose linguistic and religious differences do not map neatly along ethnic lines. As E. Valentine Daniel and Manav Ratti argue, to pretend that they do is to perpetuate a simplified narrative of the conflict. See Daniel, *Charred Lullabies: Chapters in an Anthropography of Violence* (Princeton, NJ: Princeton University Press, 1996); and Ratti, "Michael Ondaatje's *Anil's Ghost* and the Aestheticization of Human Rights," *ARIEL: A Review of International English Literature* 35, no. 1–2 (2004): 121–139.

27. LeClair, "The Sri Lankan Patients," 32–33. Spinks (*Michael Ondaatje*, 230), though more favorably disposed to the novel, also criticizes formal elements of Ondaatje's work that "deny the specificity" of the Sri Lankan civil war.

28. Georg Lukács, "Realism in the Balance," in *The Norton Anthology of Theory and Criticism*, ed. V. B. Leitch et al. (New York: Norton, 2001), 1045.

29. The severance of human from natural history has become a fecund site of analysis for postcolonial studies and environmental criticism, particularly in the wake of Dipesh Chakrabarty, "The Climate of History: Four Theses," *Critical Inquiry* 35, no. 3 (2009): 197–222. However, in an unpublished manuscript, Priscilla Wald introduces into these fields a wrinkle that comes straight out of the history of human rights. Wald traces how Julian Huxley borrowed concepts from natural history to arrive at his definition of the human, which he instituted as the founding director of the United Nations Educational, Scientific and Cultural Organization (UNESCO). Huxley used theories of evolution and the concept of species to unite humans through their biological sameness and to discredit racial essentialism. Of course, such a species-centered definition of the human does not alter claims to human transcendence; it reinforces them. This is why other species, understood as part of nature, can serve to delimit the human as a definitional category in Anil's investigation.

30. Jacques Derrida, *The Animal That Therefore I Am*, ed. Marie-Louise Mallet, trans. David Wills (New York: Fordham University Press, 2008), 34.

31. Wai Chee Dimock, *Through Other Continents: American Literature Across Deep Time* (Princeton, NJ: Princeton University Press, 2006).

32. Djelal Kadir, review of *Through Other Continents: American Literature Across Deep Time*, by Wai Chee Dimock, *Comparative Literature Studies* 45, no. 3 (2008): 370–372.

33. Bruce Robbins, "The Uses of World Literature," in *The Routledge Companion to World Literature*, ed. Theo D'haen, David Damrosch, and Djelal Kadir (London: Routledge, 2012), 389. Robbins has since begun developing a vocabulary for such measurement, in "Prolegomena for a Cosmopolitanism in Deep Time," *Interventions* 18, no. 2 (2016): 172–186. Another major engagement with Dimock's deep time is Mark McGurl's, which welcomes the reflection on periodization and scale that deep time enables despite drawing less-optimistic conclusions for its perceptual effects. See McGurl, "The Posthuman Comedy," *Critical Inquiry* 38, no. 3 (2012): 533–553.

34. Dimock, *Through Other Continents*, 2.

35. Leslie Marmon Silko, quoted in Bruce Robbins, "Temporizing: Time and Politics in the Humanities and Human Rights," *boundary 2* 32, no. 1 (2005): 194.

36. Robbins, "Temporizing," 198.

37. Joseph Mali, *Mythistory: The Making of a Modern Historiography* (Chicago: University of Chicago Press, 2003), 9, 23, 27.

38. I borrow the phrase "archive of bones" from Antoinette Burton, who uses it to place *Anil's Ghost* at the center of debates about postcolonial historiography and the relative merits of positivist history (as represented by forensic science in the novel) compared with other Western and non-Western modes of articulating historical truths. Burton, "Archive of Bones: Anil's Ghost and the Ends of History," *Journal of Commonwealth Literature* 38, no. 1 (2008): 39–56.

39. William E. Jarvis, *Time Capsules: A Cultural History* (Jefferson, NC: McFarland: 2003), especially 50–82.

40. This point is related to Joseph Slaughter's argument that the reason Anil's mission fails is that there is no "democratic public sphere" in Sri Lanka to form an interpretive community around Sailor and give his life legibility within the national context. Slaughter, *Human Rights, Inc.: The World Novel, Narrative Form, and International Law* (New York: Fordham University Press, 2007), 190. Where I differ from Slaughter is in claiming that Anil's team illustrates a dysfunctional kind of interpretive community in which each member's adoption of a different interpretive tactic only intensifies Sailor's symbolic function within the novel.

41. Michael Rothberg, *Multidirectional Memory: Remembering the Holocaust in the Age of Decolonization* (Stanford, CA: Stanford University Press, 2009), 309.

42. L. P. Hartley, *The Go-Between* (1953; repr., New York: New York Review of Books, 2002), 1.

43. See Dipesh Chakrabarty, particularly the chapter "Minority Histories, Subaltern Pasts," for a trenchant meditation on "relationships to the past" that remain intractable to historical methods of investigation and thus indescribable within their prevailing disciplinary conventions. Chakrabarty, *Provincializing Europe: Postcolonial Thought and Historical Difference* (Princeton, NJ: Princeton University Press, 2000), 101.

5. Root Canals: Zadie Smith's Scales of Injustice

1. *Oxford English Dictionary Online*, s.v. "integrate," accessed August 4, 2014, http://dictionary.oed.com; and *Merriam-Webster* (online), s.v. "integrate," accessed August 4, 2014, http://www.merriam-webster.com/dictionary/integrate.

2. Branko Milanović, "Global Income Inequality by the Numbers: In History and Now—An Overview" (Policy Research Working Paper 6259, World Bank, Washington, DC, November 2012): 2; and Milanović, *The Haves and Have-Nots: A Brief and Idiosyncratic History of Global Inequality* (New York: Basic Books, 2011), 160–161.

3. Zadie Smith, *White Teeth* (New York: Vintage International, 2000); and Salman Rushdie, *The Satanic Verses* (New York: Random House, 1988), 351.

4. Caryl Phillips, "Mixed and Matched," review of *White Teeth*, by Zadie Smith, *Guardian*, January 9, 2000, http://www.theguardian.com/books/2000/jan/09/fiction.zadiesmith; and James Wood, "Human, All Too Inhuman: The Smallness of the 'Big' Novel," *New Republic* 24 (July 2000), 41–45.

5. Zadie Smith, "Two Paths for the Novel," *New York Review of Books*, November 20, 2008, http://www.nybooks.com/articles/archives/2008/nov/20/two-paths-for-the-novel/.

6. Christopher Holmes offers a clarifying account of the limitations of such oppositions by tracing them through Smith's and James Wood's essays on the state of the contemporary novel. Holmes, "The Novel's Third Way: Zadie Smith's Hysterical Realism," in *Reading Zadie Smith: The First Decade and Beyond*, ed. Philip Tew (London: Bloomsbury Academic, 2013), 141–155.

7. Martin Jay, *Marxism and Totality: The Adventures of a Concept from Lukács to Habermas* (Berkeley: University of California Press, 1984), especially 21–81.

8. I am paraphrasing Edward Said, *Culture and Imperialism* (New York: Vintage, 1994).

9. Nicholas Dames, "Trollope's Chapters," *Literature Compass* 7, no. 9 (2010): 856–857.

10. Rob Nixon, *Slow Violence and the Environmentalism of the Poor* (Cambridge, MA: Harvard University Press, 2011). Paul Saint-Amour argues that Joyce's claims of "exhaustive documentation" in *Ulysses*, usually at the center of debates about his naturalism, also need to be understood within the historical context of Easter 1916, which made the destruction of Dublin seem like "a real possibility." Paul Saint-Amour, "Over Assemblage: *Ulysses* and the *Boîte-en-Valise* from Above," *European Joyce Studies* 15 (October 2003): 54.

11. For sociological and geographic approaches to the global city, see Saskia Sassen, *The Global City: New York, London, Tokyo*, 2nd ed. (Princeton, NJ: Princeton University Press, 2001); and Doreen Massey, *World City* (Cambridge: Polity Press, 2007).

12. Zadie Smith, "The Embassy of Cambodia," *New Yorker*, February 11 and 18, 2013, section 0–9.

13. For an account of the novel and its reception in relationship to multiculturalism, see Dominic Head, "Zadie Smith's *White Teeth*: Multiculturalism for the Millennium," in *Contemporary British Fiction*, ed. Richard J. Lane, Rod Mengham, and Philip Tew (Cambridge: Polity Press, 2003), 106–119.

14. James Procter, "New Ethnicities, the Novel, and the Burdens of Representation," in *A Concise Companion to Contemporary British Fiction*, ed. James F. English (Malden, MA: Blackwell, 2006), 113. In the context of Turkish-German literature, B. Venkat Mani writes of the importance of attending to how ethnos and demos overlap in order to avoid fetishizing multicultural difference and inclusivity. The goal, instead, is to produce a more complex account of negotiated belonging

between "the native and the naturalized, the inherited and the inhabited, the fated and the willed." Mani, *Cosmopolitical Claims: Turkish-German Literatures from Nadolny to Pamuk* (Iowa City: University of Iowa Press, 2007), 11.

15. Nancy Fraser, *Scales of Justice: Reimagining Political Space in a Globalizing World* (New York: Columbia University Press, 2009), 3.

16. Louise Doughty, review of *The Embassy of Cambodia*, by Zadie Smith, *Guardian*, November 4, 2013, http://www.theguardian.com/books/2013/nov/04/embassy-of-cambodia-zadie-smith-review.

17. Mattathias Schwartz, "The Anchor," *New Yorker*, April 21, 2014, 79.

18. The 2006 Schengen Borders Code is a particularly important policy in establishing the "fortress." It relaxed borders among European Union nations while tightening borders around Europe, particularly for African and Asian nationals.

19. Commission of the European Communities, "Wider Europe—Neighbourhood: A New Framework for Relations with our Eastern and Southern Neighbours" (Brussels: Commission of the European Communities, March 11, 2003): 4. http://www.enpi-info.eu/library/content/communication-commission-wider-europe%E2%80%94-neighbourhood-new-framework-relations-our-eastern-and.

20. The irony of Smith's story is that it presages the United Kingdom's decision to withdraw from the European Union. The "Brexit" vote is the latest and most powerful example of the backlash against internationalism. Its implications are yet to be seen.

21. The visitors, until the very end of the story, are white, which is why the narrator regards them as not Cambodian.

22. Gerard Genette, *Narrative Discourse: An Essay in Method*, trans. Jane Lewin (Ithaca, NY: Cornell University Press, 1983), 236.

23. Gerard Genette, *Narrative Discourse Revisited*, trans. Jane Lewin (Ithaca, NY: Cornell University Press, 1988), 88.

24. I use "it" because it is gender neutral.

25. Lauren Elkin, review of *NW*, by Zadie Smith, *Daily Beast*, September 2, 2012, http://www.thedailybeast.com/articles/2012/09/02/nw-by-zadie-smith-review.html.

26. Priscilla Wald, *Constituting Americans: Cultural Anxiety and Narrative Form* (Durham, NC: Duke University Press, 1995), 3.

27. Zadie Smith, "This Is How It Feels to Me," *Guardian*, October 13, 2001, http://www.theguardian.com/books/2001/oct/13/fiction.afghanistan.

28. Zadie Smith, *NW* (New York: Penguin, 2012). All subsequent citations refer to this edition.

29. Democracy Village started as a temporary settlement in Parliament Square to protest Britain's invasion of Afghanistan. It mushroomed to encompass a variety of leftist issues, including land and labor reform and antiglobalization protests.

30. Lindsey German and John Rees, *A People's History of London* (London: Verso, 2012), 11–12.

31. Zadie Smith, "The North West London Blues," *New York Review of Books*, June 2, 2012, http://www.nybooks.com/blogs/nyrblog/2012/jun/02/north-west-london-blues/.

32. Jordanna Bailkin tracks the relationship between decolonization and the welfare state, and her findings show how welfarism continued to be implicated in imperial and hegemonic practices—hence the afterlife, rather than the end, of empire. Bailkin, *The Afterlife of Empire* (Berkeley: University of California Press, 2012).

33. Michael Szalay cogently argues, "Little is gained and much is lost when we let a scorn for liberalism occlude the often nuanced and conflicted work performed by political abstractions." Szalay, *New Deal Modernism: American Literature and the Invention of the Welfare State* (Durham, NC: Duke University Press, 2000), 22. I think Smith's defense of the welfare state reflects the nuances and conflicts of her politics, which should be explored rather than smoothed over. She credits the welfare state with her personal success, but in her fiction she also seems to be aware of and reckoning with both the fallout and the dismantling of that imperfect system.

34. I have tried to loosen up this classification pattern by noting that Smith also displays affinities with writers of locality and class, such as Thomas Hardy and David Peace. See Aarthi Vadde, "Narratives of Migration, Immigration, and Interconnection," in *The Cambridge Companion to British Fiction after 1945*, ed. David James (Cambridge: Cambridge University Press, 2015), 61–78.

35. Paul Gilroy, *Postcolonial Melancholia* (New York: Columbia University Press, 2005), 67–68.

36. Amanda Claybaugh, "Coming of Age on the Council Estate," *Public Books*, February 14, 2013, http://www.publicbooks.org/fiction/coming-of-age-on-the-council-estate.

37. Christoph Hermann, "Neoliberalism in the European Union," *Studies in Political Economy* 79 (2007): 67. "Washington Consensus" is itself a much-disputed term. It was coined by John Williamson in 1989 to refer to a ten-point policy platform governing trade between the developed and developing world. Policy points that laid the foundation for what we understand as neoliberalism include deregulation, liberalization of trade, market-determined interest rates, privatization of state enterprises, and marginal tax rates. One less-pernicious policy point included the shifting of public spending from subsidies to primary education, health care, and infrastructure investment. In the 1990s and 2000s, the institutions of the Washington Consensus, mainly the International Monetary Fund and the World Bank, came under attack by antiglobalization activists, and the term came to encompass a larger set of neoliberal practices, beyond Williamson's initial delineation.

38. Timothy Mitchell has also raised concerns about the misimpressions to which critical representations of social processes can contribute. In particular, he has raised the issue of what I would call overcoherence—that is, attributing to forces such as capitalism, the economy, and technology an "internal rationality, an element of sameness, or an inherent power" that they do not have. Such critical language unwittingly buys into and substantiates the illusions of coherence that proponents of market-based or large, top-down systems claim for them. Timothy Mitchell, *Rule of Experts: Egypt, Technopolitics, Modernity* (Berkeley: University of California Press, 2002), 14.

39. Fredric Jameson, *Postmodernism, or, the Cultural Logic of Late Capitalism* (Durham, NC: Duke University Press, 1990), 51, 315.

40. Fredric Jameson, *The Geopolitical Aesthetic: Cinema and Space in the World System* (Bloomington, Indiana University Press, 1992), 3.

41. It is well known that Joyce boasted that if Dublin were destroyed it could be reconstructed from *Ulysses*. Richard Ellmann, "The Limits of Joyce's Naturalism," *Sewanee Review* 63, no. 4 (1955): 567. Smith's novel at times evokes a similar precision. Smith reproduces a Google Maps route between two places, juxtaposed with a deeply sensory account of what it feels like to walk a London street. Wendy Knepper, writing on the "spatially oriented aesthetic" of *NW*, argues that such juxtapositions illustrate the interactive and immersive sides of the novel. The endeavor to create new kinds of immersion is the basis for what Knepper calls Smith's "late modernist techniques." Knepper, "Revisionary Modernism and Postmillennial Experimentation in Zadie Smith's *NW*," in *Reading Zadie Smith: The First Decade and Beyond*, ed. Philip Tew (London: Bloomsbury Academic, 2013), 116. I would add that the interactive dimension of *NW* continues in the digital publicity for the novel, which featured "naturalist" YouTube videos that overlaid readings from the text onto the London streets and buildings they reference.

42. Jesse Matz has theorized modernist impressions as playing a mediating role between sensations and ideas and, in doing so, blurring the oppositions between them. I have this definition in mind in my own argument. Matz, *Literary Impressionism and Modernist Aesthetics* (Cambridge: Cambridge University Press, 2001).

43. Tanya Agathocleous has discussed the history of the panorama's ideological significance, ranging from Victorians' attempts to gain purchase on the "chaos" of urban space and the mystery of global wholeness to its more contemporary associations with the totalizing and ordering gaze of European imperialism. Agathocleous, *Urban Realism and the Cosmopolitan Imagination* (Cambridge: Cambridge University Press, 2011), especially 69–114.

44. Jameson, *Postmodernism*, 52.

45. Smith, "Two Paths for the Novel."

46. Immanuel Wallerstein, *The Modern World-System I: Capitalist Agriculture and the Origins of the European World-Economy in the Sixteenth Century* (New York: Academic Press, 1974), 7–8.

47. I borrow the quoted phrase from Anna Tsing, "The Global Situation," *Cultural Anthropology* 15, no. 3 (2000): 333.

48. Toni Morrison, "On the Backs of Blacks," in "The New Face of America," special issue, *Time* 142, no. 21 (November 18, 1993): 57.

49. Bruce Robbins, *Upward Mobility and the Common Good: Toward a Literary History of the Welfare State* (Princeton, NJ: Princeton University Press, 2007), 233.

50. Ibid., 240.

51. Sianne Ngai, *Ugly Feelings* (Cambridge, MA: Harvard University Press, 2005), 14.

52. Immanuel Wallerstein, *After Liberalism* (New York: The New Press, 1995), 102–103. The existence of foreign aid may seem like an exception to the claim that welfare is resolutely national. However, the politics of foreign aid, which is given voluntarily, is not equivalent to the politics of welfare's domestic entitlements, which are regarded as a state's obligation to its citizens.

53. Doron Ben-Atar, *Trade Secrets: Intellectual Piracy and the Origins of American Industrial Power* (New Haven, CT: Yale University Press, 2004), xv–xviii.

54. Quoted in Smith, *White Teeth*, 219. All subsequent citations refer to this edition.

55. Vladimir Nabokov, *The Annotated Lolita*, ed. Alfred Appel Jr. (New York: Vintage, 1991), 21.

56. Wood, "Human, All Too Inhuman," 42.

Epilogue: *Migritude*—The Re-Mediated Work of Art and Art's Mediating Work

1. United Nations High Commissioner for Refugees, "World at War," *UNHCR Global Trends: Forced Displacement in 2014*, June 18, 2015, http://unhcr.org/556725e69.html, 5. The United Nations High Commissioner for Refugees has been tracking refugee populations since its creation, in 1951.

2. United Nations High Commissioner for Refugees, "Worldwide Displacement Hits All-Time High as War and Persecution Increase," June 18, 2015, http://www.unhcr.org/558193896.html.

3. Thomas Nail, *The Figure of the Migrant* (Stanford, CA: Stanford University Press, 2015), 1.

4. Wendy Brown, *Walled States, Waning Sovereignty* (Brooklyn, NY: Zone Books, 2010), 98.

5. I owe the phrase "aggrandizing agency" to Amanda Anderson, "The Temptations of Aggrandized Agency: Feminist Histories and the Horizon of Modernity," *Victorian Studies* 43, no. 1 (Autumn 2000): 43–65.

6. Shailja Patel, *Migritude* (New York: Kaya Press, 2010), 2. All subsequent citations refer to this edition.

7. The most powerful example of the migrant body as journalistic spectacle, emerging from contemporary coverage of refugees, is the image of Alan Kurdi, the three-year-old Syrian boy who drowned while trying to reach Europe. Recirculating and "memeifying" his image has renewed debate about the ethics of distributing such images of the dead. Kurdi's image elicits a powerful emotional response and plays an important role in humanizing refugees. Its power, however, reinforces a victim narrative that emphasizes the need for Western compassion over the need to explore the interiority or capability of refugees.

8. Carrie Noland, *Voices of Negritude in Modernist Print: Aesthetic Subjectivity, Diaspora, and the Lyric Regime* (New York: Columbia University Press, 2015), 3, 6, 199.

9. Joseph R. Roach, "Performance Studies," in *Critical Theory and Performance*, ed. Janelle G. Reinelt and Joseph R. Roach (Ann Arbor: University of Michigan Press, 2007), 457.

10. Fredric Jameson, *Archaeologies of the Future: The Desire Called Utopia and Other Science Fictions* (London: Verso, 2005), 23. Adorno's understanding of utopia derives from his reading of Hegel. In his dialogue with Ernst Bloch, Adorno affirms "the prohibition of casting a picture of utopia actually for the sake of utopia, and that has a deep connection to the commandment, 'Thou shalt not make a graven image!'" Bloch, "Something's Missing: A Discussion Between Ernst Bloch and Theodor Adorno on the Contradictions of Utopian Longing (1964)," in Ernst Bloch, *The Utopian Function of Art and Literature: Selected Essays*, trans. Jack Zipes and Frank Mecklenberg (Cambridge, MA: MIT Press, 1988), 11. The representation of utopia in any form not only degrades its value but also threatens its very integrity as a concept of utter transformation. This is not to say that genres of utopian writing do not exist, of course. However, as Jameson points out, such genres are ironically at odds with utopia as a concept.

BIBLIOGRAPHY

Abrams, M. H. *The Mirror and the Lamp: Romantic Theory and the Critical Tradition*. Oxford: Oxford University Press, 1953.

Adams, Robert M. "A Study in Weakness and Humiliation." In *James Joyce's Dubliners: A Critical Handbook*, edited by James R. Baker and Thomas F. Staley, 101–104. Belmont, CA: Wadsworth, 1969.

Agathocleous, Tanya. *Urban Realism and the Cosmopolitan Imagination*. Cambridge: Cambridge University Press, 2011.

Ali, Maulana Mohamed. *Selected Writings and Speeches*, edited by Afzal Iqbal. Lahore: Ashraf Press, 1944.

Anderson, Amanda. "The Temptations of Aggrandized Agency: Feminist Histories and the Horizon of Modernity." *Victorian Studies* 43, no. 1 (Autumn 2000): 43–65.

Anderson, Benedict. *Imagined Communities: Reflections on the Origins and Spread of Nationalism*. London: Verso, 1983.

Appadurai, Arjun. *Modernity at Large: Cultural Dimensions of Globalization*. Minneapolis: University of Minnesota Press, 1996.

Appiah, Kwame Anthony. *Cosmopolitanism: Ethics in a World of Strangers*. New York: Norton, 2006.

Aravamudan, Srinivas. "East–West Fiction as World Literature: The Hayy Problem Reconfigured." *Eighteenth-Century Studies* 47, no. 2 (2014): 195–231.

Arendt, Hannah. "The Crisis in Culture: Its Social and Political Significance." In *Between Past and Future*, 194–222. New York: Viking Press, 1968.

——. *The Origins of Totalitarianism*. London: Harcourt, 1948.

Armstrong, Nancy. *How Novels Think*. New York: Columbia University Press, 2005.

Bailkin, Jordanna. *The Afterlife of Empire*. Berkeley: University of California Press, 2012.

Baker, Houston A., Jr. "Critical Memory and the Black Public Sphere." In *The Black Public Sphere: A Public Culture Book*, edited by Black Public Sphere Collective. Chicago: University of Chicago Press, 1995.

Bakhtin, Mikhail. *Rabelais and His World*. Translated by Hélène Iswolsky. Bloomington: University of Indiana Press, 1965.

Baldwin, Kate A. *Beyond the Color Line and the Iron Curtain*. Durham, NC: Duke University Press, 2002.

Balibar, Étienne. "The Nation Form: History and Ideology." In *Race, Nation, Class: Ambiguous Identities*, edited by Étienne Balibar and Immanuel Wallerstein, 86–106. London: Verso, 1991.

——. "Toward a Diasporic Citizen? From Internationalism to Cosmopolitics." In *The Creolization of Theory*, edited by Françoise Lionnet and Shu-Mei Shih, 207–225. Durham, NC: Duke University Press, 2011.

Ball, John Clement. *Postcolonial Fiction and the Transnational Metropolis*. Toronto: University of Toronto Press, 2004.

Bataille, George. *Visions of Excess*. Translated by Allen Stoekl. Minneapolis: University of Minnesota Press, 1985.

Baudelaire, Charles. *Oeuvres completes*. Tome 1. Paris: Gallimard, 1975.

Bay, Mia E., Farah J. Griffin, Martha S. Jones, and Barbara D. Savage, eds. *Toward an Intellectual History of Black Women*. Chapel Hill: University of North Carolina Press, 2015.

Beasley, Rebecca. "Modernism's Translations." In *The Oxford Handbook of Global Modernisms*, edited by Mark Wollaeger with Matt Eatough. New York: Oxford University Press, 2012.

Ben-Atar, Doron. *Trade Secrets: Intellectual Piracy and the Origins of American Industrial Power*. New Haven, CT: Yale University Press, 2004.

Bender, Thomas. "Historians, the Nation, and the Plenitude of Narratives." In *Rethinking American History in a Global Age*, edited by Thomas Bender, 1–21. Berkeley: University of California Press, 2002.

Benhabib, Seyla. *The Rights of Others: Aliens, Residents, and Citizens*. Cambridge: Cambridge University Press, 2004.

Benjamin, Walter. *The Arcades Project*. Edited by Rolf Tiedemann. Translated by Howard Eiland and Kevin McLaughlin. Cambridge, MA: Harvard University Press, 1999.

——. "The Author as Producer." *New Left Review* I/62 (July–August 1970): 83–96.

Berlant, Lauren. "Citizenship." In *Keywords for American Cultural Studies*, edited by Bruce Burgett and Glenn Hendler, 37–42. New York: New York University Press, 2007.

——. *Cruel Optimism*. Durham, NC: Duke University Press, 2011.

Berlin, Isaiah. *The Sense of Reality: Studies in Ideas and Their History*. New York: Farrar, Straus and Giroux, 1997.

Berman, Jessica. *Modernist Commitments: Ethics, Politics, and Transnational Modernism*. New York: Columbia University Press, 2012.

Bloch, Ernst. *Literary Essays*, translated by Andrew Joron and others. Stanford, CA: Stanford University Press, 1998.

——. *The Principle of Hope*. Vol. 1. Translated by Neville Plaice, Stephen Plaice, and Paul Knight. Cambridge, MA: MIT Press, 1995.

——. "Something's Missing: A Discussion Between Ernst Bloch and Theodor Adorno on the Contradictions of Utopian Longing (1964)." In *The Utopian Function of Art and Literature: Selected Essays*, translated by Jack Zipes and Frank Mecklenberg, 1–18. Cambridge, MA: MIT Press, 1988.

Braddock, Jeremy. *Collecting as Modernist Practice*. Baltimore: Johns Hopkins University Press, 2012.

Brooks, Peter. *Reading for the Plot: Design and Intention in Narrative*. Cambridge, MA: Harvard University Press, 1992.

Brown, J. Dillon. *Migrant Modernism: Postwar London and the West Indian Novel*. Charlottesville: University of Virginia Press, 2013.

Brown, Wendy. *Walled States, Waning Sovereignty*. Brooklyn, NY: Zone Books, 2010.

Bryant, John. *The Fluid Text: A Theory of Revision and Editing for Book and Screen*. Ann Arbor: University of Michigan Press, 2002.

Buck-Morss, Susan. "The Gift of the Past." *Small Axe* 14, no. 3 (November 2010): 173–185.

Burton, Antoinette. "Archive of Bones: Anil's Ghost and the Ends of History." *Journal of Commonwealth Literature* 38, no. 1 (2008): 39–56.

——, ed. *Facts, Fictions, and the Writing of History*. Durham, NC: Duke University Press, 2005.

Butler, Janet. "The Existentialism of George Lamming." *Caribbean Review* 11, no. 4 (1982).

Butler, Judith. "What Is Critique? An Essay on Foucault's Virtue (2001)." In *The Judith Butler Reader*, edited by Sara Salih with Judith Butler, 302–322. Malden, MA: Wiley-Blackwell, 2004.

Carr, Edward Hallett. *The Twenty Years' Crisis, 1919–1939*. 1939. Reprint, New York: Perennial, 2001.

Caughie, Pamela. *Disciplining Modernism*. New York: Palgrave Macmillan, 2009.

Chakrabarty, Dipesh. "The Climate of History: Four Theses." *Critical Inquiry* 35, no. 3 (2009): 197–222.

——. *Provincializing Europe: Postcolonial Thought and Historical Difference*. Princeton, NJ: Princeton University Press, 2000.

Chatterjee, Partha. *The Nation and its Fragments*. Princeton, NJ: Princeton University Press, 1993.

——. *Nationalist Thought and the Colonial World: A Derivative Discourse*. London: Zed Books, 1986.

Cheah, Pheng. "Introduction Part II: The Cosmopolitical Today." In *Cosmopolitics: Thinking and Feeling Beyond the Nation*, edited by Pheng Cheah and Bruce Robbins, 20–41. Minneapolis: University of Minnesota Press, 1998.

——. *Spectral Nationality: Passages of Freedom from Kant to Postcolonial Literatures of Liberation*. New York: Columbia University Press, 2003.

Cheng, Vincent J. *Joyce, Race, and Empire*. Cambridge: Cambridge University Press, 1995.

Chow, Rey. "The Old/New Question of Comparison in Literary Studies: A Post-European Perspective." *ELH* 71, no. 2 (2004): 289–311.

Chude-Sokei, Louis. *The Last "Darky": Bert Williams, Black-on-Black Minstrelsy, and the African Diaspora*. Durham, NC: Duke University Press, 2006.

Claybaugh, Amanda. "Coming of Age on the Council Estate." *Public Books*. February 14, 2013. http://www.publicbooks.org/fiction/coming-of-age-on-the-council-estate.

Clifford, James. *The Predicament of Culture*. Cambridge, MA: Harvard University Press, 1988.

Collini, Stefan. "What Is Intellectual History?" *History Today* 35, no. 10 (October 1985): 46–54.

Conrad, Joseph. Author's note (1920) in *The Secret Agent: A Simple Tale*. 1907. Reprint, New York: Penguin Classics, 2007.

Cooper, Wayne F. *Claude McKay: Rebel Sojourner in the Harlem Renaissance*. Baton Rouge: Louisiana State University Press, 1987.

——, ed. *The Passion of Claude McKay: Selected Poetry and Prose, 1912–1948*. New York: Schocken Books, 1973.

Cooppan, Vilashini. *Worlds Within: National Narratives and Global Connections in Postcolonial Writing*. Stanford, CA: Stanford University Press, 2009.

Cvetkovich, Ann. "Public Feelings." *South Atlantic Quarterly* 106, no. 3 (Summer 2007): 459–468.

Dames, Nicholas. "Trollope's Chapters." *Literature Compass* 7, no. 9 (2010): 855–860.

Damrosch, David. *What Is World Literature?* Princeton, NJ: Princeton University Press, 2003.

Daniel, E. Valentine. *Charred Lullabies: Chapters in an Anthropography of Violence*. Princeton, NJ: Princeton University Press, 1996.

Das, Sisir Kumar, ed. *The English Writings of Rabindranath Tagore*. Vol. 1. New Delhi: Sahitya Akademi, 1994.

Datta, Pradip Kumar. "The Interlocking Worlds of the Anglo-Boer War in South Africa and India." In *South Africa and India: Shaping the Global South*, edited by Isabel Hofmeyr and Michelle Williams, 56–81. Johannesburg: Wits University Press, 2011.

Davies, Carole Boyce. *Black Women, Writing, and Identity: Migrations of the Subject*. London: Routledge, 1994.

Davison, Neil R. *James Joyce, "Ulysses," and the Construction of Jewish Identity: Culture, Biography, and the "Jew" in Modernist Europe*. Cambridge: Cambridge University Press, 1998.

Deane, Seamus. "Dead Ends: Joyce's Finest Moments." In *Semicolonial Joyce*, edited by Derek Attridge and Marjorie Howes, 21–36. Cambridge: Cambridge University Press, 2000.

Deleuze, Gilles, and Félix Guattari. *Kafka: Toward a Minor Literature*. Translated by Dana Polan. Minneapolis: University of Minnesota Press, 1986.

Derrida, Jacques. *The Animal That Therefore I Am*. Edited by Marie-Louise Mallet. Translated by David Wills. New York: Fordham University Press, 2008.

——. *Archive Fever: A Freudian Impression*. Translated by Eric Prenowitz. Chicago: University of Chicago Press, 1996.

Dimock, Wai Chee. *Through Other Continents: American Literature Across Deep Time*. Princeton, NJ: Princeton University Press, 2006.

Doughty, Louise. Review of *The Embassy of Cambodia*, by Zadie Smith. *Guardian*. November 4, 2013. http://www.theguardian.com/books/2013/nov/04/embassy-of-cambodia-zadie-smith-review.

Doyle, Laura, and Laura Winkiel, eds. *Geomodernisms: Race, Modernism, Modernity*. Bloomington: Indiana University Press, 2005.

Du Bois, W. E. B. "Review of Claude McKay's *Banjo* and Nella Larsen's *Passing*." *Crisis* 36 (July 1929): 234.

——. "Two Novels: Nella Larsen, *Quicksand*, and Claude McKay, *Home to Harlem*." *Crisis* 35 (1928): 202.

Duffy, Enda. "Disappearing Dublin: Ulysses, Postcoloniality, and the Politics of Space." In *Semicolonial Joyce*, edited by Derek Attridge and Marjorie Howes, 37–58. Cambridge: Cambridge University Press, 2000.

——. *The Speed Handbook: Velocity, Pleasure, Modernism*. Durham, NC: Duke University Press, 2009.

——. *The Subaltern Ulysses*. Minneapolis: University of Minnesota Press, 1994.

Edwards, Brent. "The Ethnics of Surrealism." *Transition* 78 (1998): 115.

——. *The Practice of Diaspora*. Cambridge, MA: Harvard University Press, 2003.

——. "The Taste of the Archive." *Callaloo* 35, no. 4 (Fall 2012): 944–972.

Elkin, Lauren. Review of *NW*, by Zadie Smith. *Daily Beast*. September 2, 2012. http://www.thedailybeast.com/articles/2012/09/02/nw-by-zadie-smith-review.html.

Ellmann, Richard. *James Joyce*. Rev. ed. Oxford: Oxford University Press, 1982.

——. *Letters of James Joyce*. Vol. 3. New York: Viking Press, 1966.

——. "The Limits of Joyce's Naturalism." *Sewanee Review* 63, no. 4 (1955).

——, ed. *Selected Letters of James Joyce*. London: Faber and Faber, 1975.

Emery, Mary Lou. *Modernism, the Visual, and Caribbean Literature*. Cambridge: Cambridge University Press, 2007.

Ertürk, Nergis. "Modernism Disfigured: Turkish Literature and the Other West." In *The Oxford Handbook of Global Modernisms*, edited by Mark Wollaeger with Matt Eatough, 529–550. New York: Oxford University Press, 2012.

Esty, Jed. *Unseasonable Youth: Modernism, Colonialism, and the Fiction of Development*. Oxford: Oxford University Press, 2012.

Etulain, Richard W. Introduction to *The Saga of Billy the Kid*, by Walter Noble Burns. Albuquerque: University of New Mexico Press, 1999.

Ferguson, James. *Global Shadows: Africa in the Neoliberal World Order*. Durham, NC: Duke University Press, 2006.

Forster, E. M. "*The Home and the World*." In *Abinger Harvest*, 330–332. London: Harcourt, 1936.

Foucault, Michel. *The Archaeology of Knowledge*. Translated by A. M. Sheridan Smith. New York: Pantheon, 1972.

——. "The Lives of Infamous Men." In *Michel Foucault: Power, Truth, Strategy*, edited by Meaghan Morris and Paul Patton, 76–91. Sydney: Feral, 1979.

Fraser, Nancy. *Scales of Justice: Reimagining Political Space in a Globalizing World*. New York: Columbia University Press, 2009.

Friedman, Susan Stanford. "Definitional Excursions: The Meanings of Modern/Modernity/Modernism." *Modernism/Modernity* 8, no. 3 (September 2001): 493–513.

Fuss, Diana. *Identification Papers*.New York: Routledge, 1995.

Galison, Peter. *Einstein's Clocks, Poincaré's Maps: Empires of Time*. New York: Norton, 2003.

Gandhi, Leela. *Affective Communities: Anticolonial Thought, Fin-de-Siècle Radicalism, and the Politics of Friendship*. Durham, NC: Duke University Press, 2006.

Gaonkar, Dilip, ed. *Alternative Modernities*. Durham, NC: Duke University Press, 2001.

Gellner, Ernest. *Nations and Nationalism*. Ithaca, NY: Cornell University Press, 1983.

Genette, Gerard. *Narrative Discourse: An Essay in Method*. Translated by Jane Lewin. Ithaca, NY: Cornell University Press, 1983.

——. *Narrative Discourse Revisited*. Translated by Jane Lewin. Ithaca, NY: Cornell University Press, 1988.

German, Lindsey, and John Rees. *A People's History of London*. London: Verso, 2012.

Gibbons, Luke. "'Have You No Homes to Go To?' James Joyce and the Politics of Paralysis." In *Semicolonial Joyce*, edited by Derek Attridge and Marjorie Howes, 150–171. Cambridge: Cambridge University Press, 2000.

Gibson, Andrew. *Joyce's Revenge: History, Politics, and Aesthetics in "Ulysses."* Oxford: Oxford University Press, 2002.

——. *The Strong Spirit: History, Politics, and Aesthetics in the Writings of James Joyce, 1898–1915*. Oxford: Oxford University Press, 2013.

Gifford, Don. *"Ulysses" Annotated: Notes for James Joyce's "Ulysses."* Berkeley: University of California Press, 1988.

Gikandi, Simon. "Picasso, Africa, and the Schemata of Difference." *Modernism/Modernity* 10, no. 3 (2003): 455–480.

——. *Writing in Limbo: Modernism and Caribbean Literature*. Ithaca, NY: Cornell University Press, 1992.

Gilroy, Paul. *The Black Atlantic: Modernity and Double Consciousness*. Cambridge, MA: Harvard University Press, 1993.

——. *Postcolonial Melancholia*. New York: Columbia University Press, 2005.

GoGwilt, Christopher. *The Passage of Literature: Genealogies of Modernism in Conrad, Rhys, and Pramoedya*. Oxford: Oxford University Press, 2010.

Goldman, Marlene. "Representations of Buddhism in Ondaatje's *Anil's Ghost*." In *Comparative Cultural Studies and Michael Ondaatje's Writings*, edited by Steven Tötösy de Zepetnek, 27–37. West Lafayette, IN: Purdue University Press, 2005.

Goldstone, Andrew. *Fictions of Autonomy: Modernism from Wilde to de Man*. Oxford: Oxford University Press, 2013.

Goswami, Manu. "Imaginary Futures and Colonial Internationalisms." *American Historical Review* 117, no. 5 (December 2012): 1461–1485.

——. *Producing India: From Colonial Economy to National Space*. Chicago: University of Chicago Press, 2004.

Granovetter, Mark. "The Strength of Weak Ties." *American Journal of Sociology* 78, no. 6 (1973): 1360–1380.

Griffith, Arthur. *The Resurrection of Hungary: A Parallel for Ireland*. 1904. 3rd ed. Dublin: Whelan and Son, 1918.

Groden, Michael. "'Cyclops' in Progress, 1919." *James Joyce Quarterly* 12, no. 1–2 (Fall 1974–Winter 1975): 119–165.

Groys, Boris. *The Total Art of Stalinism: Avant-Garde, Aesthetic Dictatorship, and Beyond*. Translated by Charles Rougle. 1992. Reprint, London: Verso, 2011.

Guha, Ranajit. *Dominance Without Hegemony: History and Power in Colonial India*. Cambridge, MA: Harvard University Press, 1998.

Gupta, Swarupa. "*Samaj*, *Jati*, and *Desh*: Reflections on Nationhood in Late Colonial Bengal." *Studies in History* 23, no. 2 (2007): 177–203.

Habermas, Jürgen. "Modernity: An Unfinished Project." In *Habermas and the Unfinished Project of Modernity*, edited by Maurizio Passerin d'Entrèves and Seyla Benhabib, 38–59. Cambridge, MA: MIT Press, 1997.

Habiby, Emile. *The Secret Life of Saeed: The Pessoptimist*. Translated by S. K. Jayyusi and T. Le Gassick. 1974. Reprint, Northampton, MA: Interlink, 2003.

Harootunian, H. D. "Ghostly Comparisons: Anderson's Telescope." *Diacritics* 29, no. 4 (1999): 135–149.

Harpham, Geoffrey Galt. *On the Grotesque: Strategies of Contradiction in Art and Literature*. Princeton, NJ: Princeton University Press, 1982.

Harris, Wilson. "History, Fable, and Myth in the Caribbean and Guianas." 1970. Reprint, *Caribbean Quarterly* 54, no. 1–2 (March–June 2008): 5–38.

Hart, Matthew. *Nations of Nothing but Poetry: Modernism, Transnationalism, and Synthetic Vernacular Writing*. Oxford: Oxford University Press, 2010.

Hartley, L. P. *The Go-Between*. 1953. Reprint, New York: New York Review of Books, 2002.

Hayot, Eric. "Chinese Modernism, Mimetic Desire, and European Time." In *The Oxford Handbook of Global Modernisms*, edited by Mark Wollaeger with Matt Eatough, 149–172. New York: Oxford University Press, 2012.

Head, Dominic. "Zadie Smith's *White Teeth*: Multiculturalism for the Millennium." In *Contemporary British Fiction*, edited by Richard J. Lane, Rod Mengham, and Philip Tew, 106–119. Cambridge: Polity Press, 2003.

Hegglund, Jon. *World Views: Metageographies of Modernist Fiction*. Oxford: Oxford University Press, 2012.

Hermann, Christoph. "Neoliberalism in the European Union." *Studies in Political Economy* 79 (2007): 61–89.

Hobsbawm, Eric. *Nations and Nationalism Since 1780*. Cambridge: Cambridge University Press, 1992.

Hollywood, Amy. *Sensible Ecstasy: Mysticism, Sexual Difference, and the Demands of History*. Chicago: University of Chicago Press, 2002.

Holmes, Christopher. "The Novel's Third Way: Zadie Smith's Hysterical Realism." In *Reading Zadie Smith: The First Decade and Beyond*, edited by Philip Tew, 141–154. London: Bloomsbury Academic, 2013.

Hough, Graham. *Image and Experience: Studies in a Literary Revolution*. London: Duckworth, 1960.

Howes, Marjorie, and Derek Attridge, eds. Introduction to *Semicolonial Joyce*, edited by Derek Attridge and Marjorie Howes, 1–20. Cambridge: Cambridge University Press, 2000.

Hume, David. "Of Simplicity and Refinement in Writing." 1742. In *Essays Moral, Political, and Literary*, 196–202. Indianapolis, IN: Liberty Classics, 1987.

Hutcheon, Linda. *The Canadian Postmodern: A Study of Contemporary Canadian Fiction*. Oxford: Oxford University Press, 1988.

——. *A Poetics of Postmodernism: History, Theory, Fiction*. Oxford: Routledge, 1988.

Ismael, Qadri. "A Flippant Gesture Toward Sri Lanka: A Review of Michael Ondaatje's *Anil's Ghost*." *Pravada* 6, no. 9 (2000): 24–29.

Jaji, Tsitsi. *Africa in Stereo: Modernism, Music, and Pan-African Solidarity*. Oxford, Oxford University Press, 2014.

James, David, and Urmila Seshagiri. "Metamodernism: Narratives of Continuity and Revolution." *PMLA* 129, no. 1 (2014): 87–100.

Jameson, Fredric. *Archaeologies of the Future: The Desire Called Utopia and Other Science Fictions*. London: Verso, 2005.

——. "Future City." *New Left Review* 21 (May–June 2003): 65–79.

——. *The Geopolitical Aesthetic: Cinema and Space in the World System*. Bloomington: Indiana University Press, 1992.
——. *Postmodernism, or, the Cultural Logic of Late Capitalism*. Durham, NC: Duke University Press, 1991.
——. *A Singular Modernity: Essay on the Ontology of the Present*. London: Verso, 2002.
Jarvis, William E. *Time Capsules: A Cultural History*. Jefferson, NC: McFarland, 2003.
Jay, Martin. *Marxism and Totality: The Adventures of a Concept from Lukács to Habermas*. Berkeley: University of California Press, 1984.
Jones, Dewey. "Dirt." *Chicago Defender* (July 27, 1929), 12.
Joshi, Priya. *In Another Country: Colonialism, Culture, and the English Novel in India*. New York: Columbia University Press, 2002.
Joyce, James. "The Day of the Rabblement." In *The Critical Writings*, edited by Ellsworth Mason and Richard Ellmann, 68–72. New York: Viking, 1959.
——. *Dubliners*. 1914. Reprint, New York: Quality Paperback Book Club, 1996.
——. *A Portrait of the Artist as a Young Man*. 1916. Reprint, New York: Penguin, 1993.
——. *Stephen Hero*. Edited by Theodore Spencer with John J. Slocum and Herbert Cahoon. New York: New Directions, 1944.
——. *Ulysses*. 1922. Corrected text edited by Hans Walter Gabler. New York: Vintage Books, 1986.
Kabdebó, Thomas. *A Study in Parallels*. Dublin: Four Courts Press, 2001.
Kadir, Djelal. Review of *Through Other Continents: American Literature Across Deep Time*, by Wai Chee Dimock. *Comparative Literature Studies* 45, no. 3 (2008): 370–372.
Kant, Immanuel. "An Answer to the Question: 'What Is Enlightenment?'" In *Kant: Political Writings*, edited by Hans Reiss, translated by H. B. Nisbet, 54–60. 2nd ed. Cambridge: Cambridge University Press, 1991.
Kazanjian, David. *The Colonizing Trick: National Culture and Imperial Citizenship in Early America*. Minneapolis: University of Minnesota Press, 2003.
Kenner, Hugh. "The Making of the Modernist Canon." *Chicago Review* 34, no. 2 (Spring 1984): 49–61.
Kershner, R. Brandon. "Introduction: Joycean Unions," in *Joycean Unions: Post-Millennial Essays from East to West*, edited by R. Brandon Kershner and Tekla Mecsnóber, 5–15. European Joyce Studies 22. Amsterdam: Rodopi, 2013.
Khanna, Ranjana. "Frames, Contexts, Community, Justice." *Diacritics* 33, no. 2 (Summer 2003): 11–41.
Kiberd, Declan. *Inventing Ireland*. Cambridge, MA: Harvard University Press, 1995.
Kinser, Samuel. *Rabelais' Carnival: Text, Context, Metatext*. Berkeley: University of California Press, 1990.

Kirschenbaum, Matthew. "The .txtual Condition: Digital Humanities, Born-Digital Archives, and the Future Literary." *DHQ* 7, no. 1 (2013). http://www.digitalhumanities.org/dhq/vol/7/1/000151/000151.html.

Kluwick, Ursula. "The Personal and the Public: Michael Ondaatje's Historiographic Metafiction and the Question of Political Engagement." In *A Sea for Encounters: Essays Towards a Postcolonial Commonwealth*, edited by Stella Borg Barthet, 273–286. Amsterdam: Rodopi, 2009.

Knepper, Wendy. "Revisionary Modernism and Postmillennial Experimentation in Zadie Smith's *NW*." In *Reading Zadie Smith: The First Decade and Beyond*, edited by Philip Tew, 111–126. London: Bloomsbury Academic, 2013.

Kripalani, Krishna. *Rabindranath Tagore: A Biography*. New Delhi: UBS Publishers Distributors, 2008.

Kundy, Kalyan, Sakti Bhattacharya, and Kalyan Sircar, eds. *Imagining Tagore: Rabindranath and the British Press (1912–1941)*. Delhi: Shishu Sahitya Samsad, 2000.

Kurnick, David. *Empty Houses: Theatrical Failure and the Novel*. Princeton, NJ: Princeton University Press, 2011.

Lamming, George. *The Emigrants*. 1954. Reprint, Ann Arbor: University of Michigan Press, 1994.

——. "Interview with George Lamming." In *Kas-kas: Interviews with Three Caribbean Writers in Texas*, edited by Ian Munro and Reinhard Sander. Austin, TX: African and Afro-American Research Institute, 1972.

——. *In the Castle of My Skin*. Ann Arbor: University of Michigan Press, 2001.

——. "The Negro Writer and His World." In *The George Lamming Reader: The Aesthetics of Decolonisation*, edited by Anthony Bogues. Kingston: Ian Randle Publishers, 2011.

——. *The Pleasures of Exile*. 1960. Ann Arbor: University of Michigan Press, 1992.

Latour, Bruno. *Reassembling the Social: An Introduction to Actor–Network Theory*. Oxford: Oxford University Press, 2005.

Lawrence, Karen. *The Odyssey of Style*. Princeton, NJ: Princeton University Press, 1981.

LeClair, Tom. "The Sri Lankan Patients." *The Nation*, June 19, 2000. http://www.thenation.com/article/sri-lankan-patients#.

Levine, Caroline. *Forms: Whole, Rhythm, Hierarchy, Network*. Princeton, NJ: Princeton University Press, 2015.

——. "The Great Unwritten: World Literature and the Effacement of Orality." *MLQ* 74, no. 2 (2013): 217–237.

Levinson, André. "De Harlem à la cannebière." *Les Nouvelles Littéraires* (September 14, 1929): 7.

Lewis, Pericles. *Modernism, Nationalism, and the Novel.* Cambridge: Cambridge University Press, 2000.

Lloyd, David. "'Counterparts,' Dubliners, and Temperance Nationalism." In *Semicolonial Joyce*, edited by Derek Attridge and Marjorie Howes, 128–149. Cambridge: Cambridge University Press, 2000.

Love, Heather. *Feeling Backward: Loss and the Politics of Queer History.* Cambridge, MA: Harvard University Press, 2007.

Lukács, Georg. *The Historical Novel.* Translated by Hannah Mitchell and Stanley Mitchell. Boston: Beacon, 1962.

——. "Realism in the Balance." In *The Norton Anthology of Theory and Criticism*, edited by V. B. Leitch et al. New York: Norton, 2001.

——. "Tagore's Gandhi Novel." Review of *The Home and the World*, by Rabindranath Tagore. *Marxist Internet Archive.* Accessed November 3, 2014. http://www.marxists.org/archive/lukacs/works/1922/tagore.htm.

Mackey, Nathaniel. *Discrepant Engagements: Dissonance, Cross-Culturality, and Experimental Writing.* Cambridge: Cambridge University Press, 1993.

MacMahon, Darrin M., and Samuel Moyn, eds. *Rethinking Modern European Intellectual History.* Oxford: Oxford University Press, 2014.

Majumdar, Saikat. *Prose of the World: Modernism and the Banality of Empire.* New York: Columbia University Press, 2013.

Mali, Joseph. *Mythistory: The Making of a Modern Historiography.* Chicago: University of Chicago Press, 2003.

Mandel, Ann. "Michael Ondaatje." In *Dictionary of Literary Biography: Canadian Writers Since 1960—Second Series*, edited by W. H. New. Detroit: Gale Research, 1987.

Mani, B. Venkat. *Cosmopolitical Claims: Turkish–German Literatures from Nadolny to Pamuk.* Iowa City: University of Iowa Press, 2007.

Mao, Douglas, and Rebecca Walkowitz. "The New Modernist Studies." *PMLA* 123, no. 3 (2008): 737–748.

Martin, Theodore. "The Long Wait: Timely Secrets of the Contemporary Detective Novel." *Novel: A Forum on Fiction* 45, no. 2 (2012): 165–183.

Marx, John. *Geopolitics and the Anglophone Novel, 1890–2011.* Cambridge: Cambridge University Press, 2012.

Massey, Doreen. *World City.* Cambridge: Polity Press, 2007.

Matz, Jesse. *Literary Impressionism and Modernist Aesthetics.* Cambridge: Cambridge University Press, 2001.

Maxwell, William J. "Global Poetics and State-Sponsored Transnationalism." *American Literary History* 18, no. 2 (2006): 360–364.

McClintock, Anne. *Imperial Leather: Race, Gender, and Sexuality in the Colonial Contest.* London: Routledge, 1995.

McClure, John. *Partial Faiths: Postsecular Fiction in the Age of Pynchon and Morrison*. Athens: University of Georgia Press, 2007.

McGurl, Mark. "The Posthuman Comedy." *Critical Inquiry* 38, no. 3 (2012): 533–553.

McKay, Claude. *Banjo: A Story Without a Plot*. New York: Harper, 1929.

——. *Home to Harlem*. 1928. Reprint, Boston: Northeastern University Press, 1987.

——. *A Long Way from Home*. 1937. Reprint, New Brunswick, NJ: Rutgers University Press, 2007.

McKible, Adam, and Suzanne W. Churchill. "Introduction: In Conversation—The Harlem Renaissance and the New Modernist Studies." *Modernism/Modernity* 20, no. 3 (2013): 427–431.

McVey, Christopher. "Reclaiming the Body of the Past: Michael Ondaatje and the Body of History." *Journal of Modern Literature* 37, no. 2 (2014): 141–160.

Mejías-López, Alejandro. *The Inverted Conquest: The Myth of Modernity and the Transatlantic Onset of Modernism*. Nashville, TN: Vanderbilt University Press, 2009.

Melas, Natalie. *All the Difference in the World: Postcoloniality and the Ends of Comparison*. Stanford, CA: Stanford University Press, 2006.

Milanović, Branko. "Global Income Inequality by the Numbers: In History and Now—An Overview." Policy Research Working Paper 6259. Washington, D.C.: World Bank, 2012 (November). http://www-wds.worldbank.org/external/default/WDSContentServer/IW3P/IB/2012/11/06/000158349_20121106085546/Rendered/PDF/wps6259.pdf.

——. *The Haves and Have-Nots: A Brief and Idiosyncratic History of Global Inequality*. New York: Basic Books, 2011.

Mitchell, Timothy. *Rule of Experts: Egypt, Technopolitics, Modernity*. Berkeley: University of California Press, 2002.

Mohanty, Satya, ed., *Colonialism, Modernity, and Literature: A View from India*. New York: Palgrave Macmillan, 2011.

Morrison, Toni. "On the Backs of Blacks." In "The New Face of America," special issue, *Time* 142, no. 21 (November 18, 1993), 57.

Moyn, Samuel. "The Political Origins of Global Justice." Cyril Foster Lecture in International Relations presented at the University of Oxford, November 2013.

Moyn, Samuel, and Andrew Sartori, eds. *Global Intellectual History*. New York: Columbia University Press, 2015.

Mukherjee, Arun. *Oppositional Aesthetics: Readings from a Hyphenated Space*. Toronto: TSAR, 1994.

Nabokov, Vladimir. *The Annotated Lolita*. Edited by Alfred Appel Jr. New York: Vintage, 1991.

Nail, Thomas. *The Figure of the Migrant*. Stanford, CA: Stanford University Press, 2015.

Nandy, Ashis. *The Illegitimacy of Nationalism: Rabindranath Tagore and the Politics of the Self*. Delhi: Oxford India, 1994.

Ngai, Sianne. *Ugly Feelings*. Cambridge, MA: Harvard University Press, 2005.

Nickels, Joel. "Claude McKay and Dissident Internationalism." *Cultural Critique* 87 (Spring 2014): 1–37.

Nixon, Rob. *Slow Violence and the Environmentalism of the Poor*. Cambridge, MA: Harvard University Press, 2011.

Nolan, Emer. *James Joyce and Nationalism*. London: Routledge, 1995.

Noland, Carrie. *Voices of Negritude in Modernist Print: Aesthetic Subjectivity, Diaspora, and the Lyric Regime*. New York: Columbia University Press, 2015.

Norris, Margot. *Virgin and Veteran Readings of "Ulysses."* New York: Palgrave Macmillan, 2011.

North, Michael. *The Dialect of Modernism*. Oxford: Oxford University Press, 1994.

Nussbaum, Martha. "Patriotism and Cosmopolitanism." In *For Love of Country?*, edited by Joshua Cohen, 2–20. Boston: Beacon Press, 1996.

Olson, Charles. *Call Me Ishmael*. Baltimore: Johns Hopkins University Press, 1997.

Ondaatje, Michael. *Anil's Ghost*. New York: Vintage International, 2000.

——. *The Collected Works of Billy the Kid*. New York: Vintage International, 2008.

——. *The English Patient*. New York: Vintage International, 1992.

Paquet, Sandra Pouchet. *The Novels of George Lamming*. London: Heinemann, 1982.

Patel, Shailja. *Migritude*. New York: Kaya Press, 2010.

Phillips, Caryl. "Mixed and Matched." Review of *White Teeth*, by Zadie Smith. *Guardian*. January 9, 2000. http://www.theguardian.com/books/2000/jan/09/fiction.zadiesmith.

Piper, Andrew. *Dreaming in Books: The Making of the Bibliographic Imagination in the Romantic Age*. Chicago: University of Chicago Press, 2009.

Pippin, Robert. *Hollywood Westerns and American Myth: The Importance of Howard Hawks and John Ford for Political Philosophy*. New Haven, CT: Yale University Press, 2010.

——. *Nietzsche, Psychology, and First Philosophy*. Chicago: University of Chicago Press, 2010.

Porter, David. "The Crisis of Comparison and the World Literature Debates." *Profession* (2011): 244–258.

Pound, Ezra. "Rabindranath Tagore." *Fortnightly Review* 93, no. 555 (March 1913): 571–579.

Power, Arthur. "James Joyce—The Internationalist." In *A Bash in the Tunnel: James Joyce by the Irish*, edited by John Ryan, 181–188. Brighton: Clifton Books, 1970.

Prashad, Vijay. *The Darker Nations: A People's History of the Third World*. New York: The New Press, 2007.

Pratt, Mary Louise. "Arts of the Contact Zone." *Profession* (1991): 33–40.

Procter, James. "New Ethnicities, the Novel, and the Burdens of Representation." In *A Concise Companion to Contemporary British Fiction*, edited by James F. English, 101–120. Malden, MA: Blackwell, 2006.

Rainey, Lawrence, ed. *Modernism: An Anthology*. Oxford: Blackwell, 2005.

Ramazani, Jahan. *A Transnational Poetics*. Chicago: University of Chicago Press, 2009.

Ratti, Manav. "Michael Ondaatje's *Anil's Ghost* and the Aestheticization of Human Rights." *ARIEL: A Review of International English Literature* 35, no. 1–2 (2004): 121–139.

Rist, Gilbert. *The History of Development*. 3rd ed. London: Zed Books, 2008.

Roach, Joseph R. "Performance Studies." In *Critical Theory and Performance*, edited by Janelle G. Reinelt and Joseph R. Roach, 457–461. Ann Arbor: University of Michigan Press, 2007.

Robbins, Bruce. *Feeling Global: Internationalism in Distress*. New York: New York University Press, 1999.

——. "Introduction Part 1: Actually Existing Cosmopolitanism." In *Cosmopolitics: Thinking and Feeling Beyond the Nation*, edited by Pheng Cheah and Bruce Robbins, 1–19. Minneapolis: University of Minnesota Press, 1998.

——. "Prolegomena for a Cosmopolitanism in Deep Time." *Interventions* 18, no. 2 (2016): 172–186.

——. "Temporizing: Time and Politics in the Humanities and Human Rights." *boundary 2* 32, no. 1 (2005): 191–208.

——. *Upward Mobility and the Common Good: Toward a Literary History of the Welfare State*. Princeton, NJ: Princeton University Press, 2007.

——. "The Uses of World Literature." In *The Routledge Companion to World Literature*, edited by Theo D'haen, David Damrosch, and Djelal Kadir, 383–392. London: Routledge, 2012.

Rogers, Gayle. *Modernism and the New Spain: Britain, Cosmopolitan Europe, and Literary History*. Oxford: Oxford University Press, 2014.

Rothberg, Michael. *Multidirectional Memory: Remembering the Holocaust in the Age of Decolonization*. Stanford, CA: Stanford University Press, 2009.

Rushdie, Salman. *The Satanic Verses*. New York: Random House, 1988.

Said, Edward. *Culture and Imperialism*. New York: Vintage, 1994.

Saint-Amour, Paul. "Over Assemblage: *Ulysses* and the *Boîte-en-Valise* from Above." *European Joyce Studies* 15 (October 2003): 21–58.

——. *Tense Future: Modernism, Total War, Encyclopedic Form*. Oxford: Oxford University Press, 2015.

Sassen, Saskia. *The Global City: New York, London, Tokyo*. 2nd ed. Princeton, NJ: Princeton University Press, 2001.

Schmidt, Brian C. *The Political Discourse of Anarchy: A Disciplinary History of International Relations*. Albany: State University of New York Press, 1998.

Schwartz, Mattathias. "The Anchor." *New Yorker*. April 21, 2014.

Sen, Amartya. "Tagore and His India." *New York Review of Books*. June 26, 1997. http://www.nybooks.com/articles/archives/1997/jun/26/tagore-and-his-india/?pagination=false.

Sen, Nabaneeta. "The 'Foreign Reincarnation' of Rabindranath Tagore." *Journal of Asian Studies* 25, no. 2 (February 1966): 275–286.

Sengupta, Mahasweta. "Translation, Colonialism, and Poetics: Rabindranath Tagore in Two Worlds." In *Translation, History, and Culture*, edited by Susan Bassnett and André Lefevre, 56–64. London: Pinter, 1990.

Slaughter, Joseph. *Human Rights, Inc.: The World Novel, Narrative Form, and International Law*. New York: Fordham University Press, 2007.

Smethurst, James. *The African American Roots of Modernism: From Reconstruction to the Harlem Renaissance*. Chapel Hill: University of North Carolina Press, 2011.

Smith, Zadie. "The Embassy of Cambodia." *New Yorker*. February 11 and 18, 2013.

——. "The North West London Blues." *New York Review of Books*. June 2, 2012. http://www.nybooks.com/blogs/nyrblog/2012/jun/02/north-west-london-blues/.

——. *NW*. New York: Penguin, 2012.

——. "This Is How It Feels to Me." *Guardian*. October 13, 2001. http://www.theguardian.com/books/2001/oct/13/fiction.afghanistan.

——. "Two Paths for the Novel." *New York Review of Books*. November 20, 2008. http://www.nybooks.com/articles/archives/2008/nov/20/two-paths-for-the-novel/.

——. *White Teeth*. New York: Vintage International, 2000.

Spinks, Lee. *Michael Ondaatje*. Manchester: Manchester University Press, 2009.

Spoo, Robert. *James Joyce and the Language of History: Dedalus' Nightmare*. Oxford: Oxford University Press, 1994.

——. "'Nestor' and the Nightmare: The Presence of the Great War in *Ulysses*." *Twentieth Century Literature* 32, no. 2 (1986): 137–154.

Stanton, Katherine. *Cosmopolitan Fictions: Ethics, Politics, and Global Change in the Works of Kazuo Ishiguro, Michael Ondaatje, Jamaica Kincaid, and J. M. Coetzee*. New York: Routledge, 2009.

Steedman, Carolyn. *Dust: The Archive and Cultural History*. Manchester: Manchester University Press, 2001.

Stephens, Michelle Ann. *Black Empire: The Masculine Global Imaginary of Caribbean Intellectuals in the United States, 1914–1962*. Durham, NC: Duke University Press, 2005.

Stoler, Ann Laura. *Along the Archival Grain: Epistemic Anxieties and Colonial Common Sense*. Princeton, NJ: Princeton University Press, 2009.

Szalay, Michael. *New Deal Modernism: American Literature and the Invention of the Welfare State*. Durham, NC: Duke University Press, 2000.

Tagore, Rabindranath. *Ghare Baire*. 1916. Reprint, Calcutta: Bharati-Bhabana, 1936.

——. *The Home and the World*. Translated by Surendranath Tagore. 1919. Reprint, London: Penguin Books, 2005.

——. *Naibedya*. 1901. Reprint, Santiniketan, India: Visva-Bharati Prakashan, 1962.

——. *Nationalism*. New York: Macmillan, 1917.

——. "The Protest of a Seer." *Times Literary Supplement*, September 13, 1917.

——. "A Vision of India's History." In *A Tagore Reader*, edited by Amiya Chakravarty, 182–196. New York: Macmillan, 1961.

Tagore, Rabindranath, and H. G. Wells. "Tagore and Wells." In *A Tagore Reader*, edited by Amiya Chakravarty, 106–109. New York: Macmillan, 1961.

Thaggert, Miriam. *Images of Black Modernism: Visual and Verbal Strategies of the Harlem Renaissance*. Amherst: University of Massachusetts Press, 2010.

Torpey, John. *The Invention of the Passport: Surveillance, Citizenship, and the State*. Cambridge: Cambridge University Press, 1999.

Tsing, Anna. "The Global Situation." *Cultural Anthropology* 15, no. 3 (2000): 327–360.

Turner, Frederick Jackson. "The Significance of the Frontier in American History." In *Rereading Frederick Jackson Turner: "The Significance of the Frontier in American History" and Other Essays*, edited by John Mack Faragher, 31–60. New Haven, CT: Yale University Press, 1999.

Vadde, Aarthi. "Narratives of Migration, Immigration, and Interconnection." In *The Cambridge Companion to British Fiction After 1945*, edited by David James, 61–78. Cambridge: Cambridge University Press, 2015.

——. "Putting Foreignness to the Test: Rabindranath Tagore's Babu English." *Comparative Literature* 65, no. 1 (2013): 15–25.

Valente, Joseph. "James Joyce and the Cosmopolitan Sublime." In *Joyce and the Subject of History*, edited by Mark A. Wollaeger, Victor Luftig, and Robert Spoo, 59–82. Ann Arbor: University of Michigan Press, 1996.

Velody, Irving. "The Archive and the Human Sciences: Notes Towards a Theory of the Archive." *History of the Human Sciences* 11, no. 4 (November 1998): 1–16.

Verhoeven, W. M. "Naming the Present/Naming the Past: Historiographic Metafiction in Findley and Ondaatje." In *Shades of Empire in Colonial and Post-Colonial Literatures*, edited by C. C. Barfoot and Theo D'haen, 283–299. Amsterdam: Rodopi, 1993.

Viswanathan, Gauri. "Synthetic Vision: Internationalism and the Poetics of Decolonization." In *Nation, Language, and the Ethics of Translation*, edited by Sandra Bermann and Michael Wood, 326–345. Princeton, NJ: Princeton University Press, 2005.

Vogel, Shane. *The Scene of Harlem Cabaret: Race, Sexuality, Performance*. Chicago: University of Chicago Press, 2009.

Wald, Priscilla. *Constituting Americans: Cultural Anxiety and Narrative Form*. Durham, NC: Duke University Press, 1995.

Walkowitz, Rebecca. "Cosmopolitan Ethics." In *The Turn to Ethics*, edited by Marjorie Garber, Beatrice Hanssen, and Rebecca L. Walkowitz, 221–230. New York: Routledge, 2000.

——. *Cosmopolitan Style: Modernism Beyond the Nation*. New York: Columbia University Press, 2006.

——. "For Translation: Virginia Woolf, J. M. Coetzee, and Transnational Comparison." In *The Legacies of Modernism*, edited by David James, 243–263. Cambridge: Cambridge University Press, 2012.

Wallerstein, Immanuel. *After Liberalism*. New York: The New Press, 1995.

——. *The Modern World-System I: Capitalist Agriculture and the Origins of the European World-Economy in the Sixteenth Century*. New York: Academic Press, 1974.

Wilder, Gary. *Freedom Time: Negritude, Decolonization, and the Future of the World*. Durham, NC: Duke University Press, 2015.

——. *The French Imperial Nation-State: Negritude and Colonial Humanism Between the Two World Wars*. Chicago: University of Chicago Press, 2005.

Wilks, Jennifer. *Race, Gender, and Comparative Black Modernism: Suzanne Lacascade, Marita Bonner, Suzanne Césaire, Dorothy West*. Baton Rouge: Louisiana State University Press, 2008.

Williams, Raymond. *The Country and the City*. Oxford: Oxford University Press, 1973.

——. *Writing in Society*. London: Verso, 1983.

Wollaeger, Mark. Introduction to *The Oxford Handbook of Global Modernisms*, edited by Mark Wollaeger with Matt Eatough, 3–24. New York: Oxford University Press, 2012.

Wood, James. "Human, All Too Inhuman: The Smallness of the 'Big' Novel." *New Republic* 24 (July 2000): 41–45.

Yao, Stephen G. *Translation and the Languages of Modernism*. New York: Palgrave Macmillan, 2002.

INDEX

Abrams, M. H., 22
access, "The Embassy of Cambodia" and, 192–193
Adams, Robert M., 246n25
Adorno, Theodor, 133, 231, 264n10
aesthetic individualism, Joyce and, 31
aestheticist literature, servants in, 87
aesthetic judgment, ethnic distinction as artifacts of, 70
aesthetic representation, social upheaval and limits of, 1–2
African diaspora, 111, 119, 249n9
"After the Race" (Joyce), 83–90, 94
Agathocleous, Tanya, 262n42
agency, mediated nature of, 222–223
Ali, Maulana Mohamed, 70–71
alternating asymmetry, Joyce and, 31, 75–76, 96, 97–98
American invasion of Iraq, 171–172
Amis, Kingsley, 200
Amnesty International, 176
Anandamath (Chatterjee), 61
Anderson, Benedict, 156
Angelides, Phil, 182–183
Anil's Ghost (Ondaatje), 32–33, 149, 163–181; archival materials used in, 164–166, 176; archival method and, 153, 176–177; context for, 163–164; destruction of Bodhisattva sculptures and, 175–176; endings in, 180; gender violence and, 170; globalist and localist response to national fracturing, 164; historical standards of significance and, 166–167; human rights principles and, 168–169; memory and, 164, 167, 168; myth and ethical relativism in, 169–170; mythistorical and, 174–175; nostalgia in, 179; reconstruction of fractured Buddha and, 178–180; significance of remains, 166–168; temporality in, 169, 170; time capsule metaphor in, 177–178; use of collage in, 165
animals, historical significance of remains, 166–167
anthology: battle between method and content and, 46; nationalism and, 42, 43; *Nationalism* and, 42–43
anticolonialism, Joyce and, 93–94
anticolonial nationalism, 48
anticolonial theory of internationalism, 13–14
anticolonial time, deep time and, 172–174
Appadurai, Arjun, 161
Appiah, Kwame Anthony, 3–4
apposition, 100–103
appropriation, nationalism and, 50–51
Apter, Emily, 54
Arab Spring, 80
"Araby" (Joyce), 92, 94
Aravamudan, Srinivas, 237n40
Arcades Project, The (Benjamin), 144–145
archaeological surround of a fact, 169

Archaeology of Knowledge, The (Foucault), 152
archival legends, Ondaatje's use of, 32–33
archival method, Ondaatje's, 151–153, 176–177, 180. See also *Anil's Ghost* (Ondaatje); *Collected Works of Billy the Kid, The* (Ondaatje)
archives: collective memory and, 180; digital, 253n3; legends and, 152; looting and burning of Iraqi National Library, 171–172; theory of, 150, 152, 254–255n9
Arendt, Hannah, 60, 69, 70
Aristotle, 187
Armstrong, Nancy, 110
assimilation, selectivity of, 50–51
Athenaeum (journal), 42
Attridge, Derek, 244n2
autarchy, 47
autarky: cultural, 23, 48, 241n18; Tagore and, 31, 47–48, 72–73
"Author as Producer, The" (Benjamin), 90
authorship, democratic nationhood and, 194–195
autonomy: rethinking, 19; Russian avant-garde ideology of, 35–36; in Swadeshi movement, 66
autotranslation, 7–8; chimeras of form and Tagore and, 73; compiling *Nationalism* and, 42–58; of *The Home and the World*, 58–68; interplay of illegibility and translatability in, 23; of "The Sunset of the Century," 53–58; Tagore and, 23, 30–31, 39, 40–41, 73. *See also* Tagore, Rabindranath
avowed intentions, 78, 244n10

Bailkin, Jordanna, 261n31
Baker, Houston, Jr., 141–142
Bakhtin, Mikhail, 77
Baldwin, Kate A., 249n9
Balibar, Étienne, 27, 32, 109, 111, 147–148
Ball, John, 197–198, 200
Banjo: A Story Without a Plot (McKay), 20, 25, 32, 116; grimoire form of, 132–133; international nomadism and, 129; jazz and, 127–129, 130–132; "Jelly Roll," 127–129, 131; negative structural grammar in, 119–120; plotlessness of, 133; rejection of racial consciousness in, 118; reviews of, 118–119; role of music in, 125–129, 130–132; vagabondage and, 120–123, 125, 133–134; youthfulness and, 121–122
banks, too big to fail, 182–183
Barthes, Roland, 255n9
Bataille, George, 129–130, 131, 251n37
Baudelaire, Charles, 119
Beach, Sylvia, 103–104
Beasley, Rebecca, 40
Beckett, Samuel, 185
Beitz, Charles, 13
Ben-Atar, Doron, 213
Bender, Thomas, 256n16
Bengali origins of "The Sunset of the Century," 53–54
Bengali poems, translation of, 73
Benhabib, Seyla, 32, 133
Benjamin, Walter, 31, 90, 144, 170
Berlant, Lauren, 76–77, 141
Berlin, Isaiah, 41
Berman, Jessica, 235n27
Bibliothèque Nationale, 152
bildungsroman, 110, 113, 114, 121
Billy the Kid, 32–33, 149, 180. See also *Collected Works of Billy the Kid, The* (Ondaatje)
Billy the Kid and the Princess (pulp novel), 158

Black Atlantic, 111, 249n9
black collectivity, limitation of nation-centered paradigms for, 111
black consciousness, ecstasy and, 130–131
black internationalism, 111–112, 122, 125–126, 132, 249n9
black mortality, commerce and, 128–129
black objectification/stereotypes, McKay and, 126–129
black writers, as modernists, 249n8
Bloch, Ernst, 91, 133, 145–146, 246n32, 264n10
Bodhisattva sculptures, destruction of, 175–176
Boer War, Tagore poems in response to, 54
Bolden, Buddy, 149
Bonney, William. *See* Billy the Kid
borders: migrants and, 220, 221; nation-state, 60, 141
boundaries, balancing disruption of, 189
boundaries of art, autarkic theories of national community and, 221
Braddock, Jeremy, 42
British Nationality Act (1948), 252n50
Brooks, Peter, 119–120
Brown, Wendy, 221
Bryant, John, 255n12
Buck-Morss, Susan, 18
Buddha, reconstruction of fractured, in *Anil's Ghost*, 178–180
Buddhist temple, raided, 175–176
Burns, Walter Noble, 156
Burton, Antoinette, 254n9, 258n38
Butler, Judith, 2

calypso, in *The Emigrants*, 142
Camera Lucida (Barthes), 255n9
Cameron, David, 200
capitalism: integration and global, 182–183; vagabondage and, 122–123
Carpenter, Edward, 124
Carr, E. H., 10–11, 12, 25
Cassavetes, John, 159, 256n21
caste system, Indian, 51–52
Caughie, Pamela, 16
causality, Smith and, 185, 186, 188, 208–209, 214–215, 217–218
Celtic nationalism, 84
Chakrabarty, Dipesh, 17, 41, 257n29, 258n43
Chakravarty, Ajit Kumar, 55
Chalfen, Marcus, 34–35
chapters: history of, 187; Smith and, 187, 189–190
Chatterjee, Bankim Chandra, 61, 242n35
Chatterjee, Partha, 48
Cheah, Pheng, 6, 27–29
Chicago Defender (newspaper), 118
chimeras: biotechnological connotation of, 29; defined, 9; diagnostic function of, 10; Joyce and, 78–79, 89, 90–91, 92–94; Smith and totality as, 185–186; utopia vs., 231
chimeras of form, 7; defined, 9; delimiting range of possible and, 1–2, 3–4; as figures of modernist internationalism, 8–9; *Migritude* and, 223–230; modernist grotesque and, 21–29; modernist internationalism and, 12; modernity and, 231; as riposte to nationhood, 221
China, raided Buddhist temple, 175–176
Chisum, John, 158
Chisum, Sally, 158
Chow, Rey, 52
Churchill, Suzanne W., 249n8

citizenship: *The Emigrants* and, 134, 135; territoriality and, 110–111; transnational, 109–110
civitas vaga, 109, 111, 146–148
"Clay" (Joyce), 93, 94
Claybaugh, Amanda, 201
Clifford, James, 63
cohesive power of weak ties, 20
collaboration: *Migritude* and, 225; Tagore and, 39, 62, 239n3
collage, 19; Ondaatje's use of, 32, 165
Collected Works of Billy the Kid, The (Ondaatje), 32–33, 149, 154–163; archival materials used in, 155, 156, 157–158, 161–163; archival method in, 153; contextualization of, 161; cover of, 161–163; ending of, 180; mythistorical and, 174; 2008 edition, 154, 161–163, 255n12
collective memory, archives and, 180–181
collectivism, Lamming and narrative, 135–136
collectivity: archival form and, 177; based on shared taste, 69; metaphors for, 29; root canal metaphor and, 188; social arrangements of, 7
Collini, Stefan, 25
colonial, aligned with provincial, 245n20
colonial culture, internationalism and, 64–68
colonialism: Hungarian parallel and, 80–81; Joyce and, 76, 78–79; Joyce and anticolonialism, 93–94
Coming Through Slaughter (Ondaatje), 149
commerce, black mortality and, 128–129
communal forms, 7
communal organicism, 27
"Communal Patriot, The" (Ali), 70–71
communal patriotism, 71–72
comparison: postcolonial theory of, 246n24; post-European perspective on, 52–53
compilation, anthology and method of, 46, 47
Comrade (newspaper), 70
Conrad, Joseph, 40
conscience, Joyce and uncreated racial, 247n38
Constab Ballads (McKay), 116
contact zones, in *Nationalism*, 45
contextualization, 161
Cook, Kim, 225
Cooppan, Vilashini, 238n59
corporation novel, 26
cosmopolitanism, 3–4; critical, 236–237n37; internationalism and, 9–10
cosmopolitical, shifting force field of, 6
Countess Cathleen, The (Yeats), 84
Country and the City, The (Williams), 26
Crescent Moon, The (Tagore), 42
cricket test, 217
critical cosmopolitanism, 236–237n37
critical memory, black modernism and, 142
cruel optimism, 76–77
cultural autarky, 23, 48, 241n18
cultural internationalism, 11
Cvetkovich, Ann, 239n62
"Cyclops" (Joyce), 31–32, 95–105, 106

Dames, Nicholas, 187, 195
Damrosch, David, 240n6
Daniel, E. Valentine, 256n26
Darío, Rubén, 236n34

Davies, Carole Boyce, 111
Davis, Thomas, 80
Deane, Seamus, 91, 246n23
décalage, 111
decolonization, welfare state and, 261n31
deep time, 170–174, 257n33
"Definitional Excursions: The Meanings of Modern/Modernity/Modernism" (Friedman), 15
Deleuze, Gilles, 239n64
DeLillo, Don, 216
Deliverer, The (Gregory), 79
democracy, liberal geoculture and, 213–214
Democracy Village, 198, 260n28
demos: ethnos and, 259–260n14; Smith and, 188, 191, 196
deprovincializing modernism, 14–21
deracination: Lamming and, 135, 138–139, 141–142, 148; McKay and, 114, 116, 122, 134; Roma and, 109
Derrida, Jacques, 28, 150, 167
despotism, Tagore and, 36
Detroit Journal, on *Nationalism*, 43–44
digital archives, 253n3
Dimock, Wai Chee, 170–172, 173, 174
Disciplining Modernism (Caughie), 16
discrimination, intranational, 51–52
Doheny, Michael, 80
domesticity, in *The Home and the World*, 66–68
Doyle, Laura, 16
Dubliners (Joyce), 31, 83, 84, 88–94; alternating asymmetry in, 85; chimera in, 89; epiphanies in, 91–94; indictment of provinciality and colonial paralysis in, 88
Du Bois, W. E. B., 19; review of *Banjo*, 122; review of *Home to Harlem*, 116–117, 118
Duffy, Enda, 100, 246n27, 247n41, 248n45

East, Tagore and persistence of, 49, 50–51
Easter Rising (1916), 80, 187, 247n41, 259n10
Eastman, Max, 124
economic inequality, 3. *See also* inequality
economic insulation, Swadeshi nationalism and, 61, 66–68
Economist (periodical), 108
ecstasy: Lamming and, 142–143; McKay and, 130–132
Edwards, Brent, 111, 125–126, 255n9
effective motives, 78, 244n10
Eglinton, John, 94
Einstein, Albert, 239n1
Eliot, T. S., 14, 40
Ellmann, Richard, 84, 245n20
"Embassy of Cambodia, The" (Smith), 20, 205, 218, 219; access theme in, 192–193; authorial identity and democratic aesthetics and, 194; badminton rules and, 196; balancing multiple scales in, 189–197; ending of, 195–196, 197; measurement in, 192, 195, 197; relationship between formal and social wholes and, 189–190; segmentation in, 189–190, 191–192, 195, 196; use of metalepsis in, 193–194
Emigrants, The (Lamming), 20, 32; anticolonialism in, 140; Azi's letter, 143; calypso in, 142–143; citizenship and, 134, 135; dissolution of "I" in, 138; dramatic dialogue in, 139–140; mutilation of form in, 136–137; narrative temporality in, 145–147; overcoming provincialism in, 139; use of vernacular in, 139–141

emigration, Lamming and, 112
emotions: expectant, 146; filled, 145–146
Engels, Friedrich, 124
England Made Me (Greene), 199
English authority, withdrawal from in *The Emigrants*, 143–144
Englishness: Britishness and, 252n50; *The Emigrants* and, 140–141; *NW* and, 203–205; Smith and, 199, 200, 203–205
English Patient, The (Ondaatje), 149, 150, 254n6
epiphanies, in *Dubliners*, 91–94
Epiphanies (Joyce), 91
Ertürk, Nergis, 235n30
Essay on Genius (Gerard), 22
Esty, Jed, 5, 121
ethical relativism, myth and, 169–170
ethnic distinctions, aesthetic judgment and, 70
ethnic stereotypes, Tagore and, 66
ethnos, demos and, 259–260n14
"Eumaeus" (Joyce), 105
Europe: migration to, 219–220; modernism and, 14–20
European Neighbourhood Policy, 190–191
European reception of *The Home and the World*, 63–64
European Union, 109; migration policies, 190–191, 260n18; response to migrants, 220–221
"Eveline" (Joyce), 83, 84, 90, 92–93, 94
expatriation, modernism and, 121
expectant emotions, 146

Farge, Arlette, 255n9
Faulkner, William, 15
Feeling Global (Robbins), 3
fiction, provincial, 26
filled emotions, 145–146
First International Congress of Black Writers and Artists, 144
fluid text, 255n12
forced migration: *Migritude* and, 223–230; nation-states and, 220–221
force fields, cosmopolitical and shifting, 6
foreign aid, 213, 263n51
formalism, defense of, 6–7
form and formlessness, prose and, 116
form fields, 6–7
Forster, E. M., 63–64
"Fortress Europe," 190–191, 260n18
Foucault, Michel, 150, 152, 255n9
foundational myths, 174
Fraser, Nancy, 189
Fréine, Seán de, 75
Friedman, Susan Stanford, 15
frontier, Ondaatje's reinvention of myth of American, 154–155, 156–158, 163
Fuss, Diana, 81
FutureMouse, 34–35
futurism, tropes of, 113

Gaelic League, 75, 79, 82, 244n4
Gandhi, Leela, 124
Gandhi, Mohandas, 63
García, Romualdo, 256n24
Gardener, The (Tagore), 42
Garrett, Pat, 155, 156, 163
Gellner, Ernest, 154–155
Genette, Gerard, 193
gentrification, "The North West London Blues" and, 198–200
geoculture, liberal, 213–214
Geomodernisms (Doyle and Winkiel), 16
Geopolitical Aesthetic, The (Jameson), 208
geopolitical unconscious, 205
Gerard, Alexander, 22
German, Lindsey, 198

Ghare Baire, 59, 62, 242n30. See also *Home and the World, The* (Tagore)
Gheorghe, Nicolae, 32, 108
Gibbons, Luke, 247n37
Gibson, Andrew, 95, 243–244n1, 245n15
gigantism, 96–97
Gikandi, Simon, 145, 235–236n34
Gilbert schema, 96
Gilroy, Paul, 111, 200, 249n9
Girard, René, 236n34
Gitanjali (Tagore), 39, 42, 55
global capitalism, integration and, 182–183
global city, 187, 259n11
global inequality: international solidarity and, 183–184; national inequality and, 209–211
globalization: intellectual history of, 2; social effects of contemporary, 238n61; wealth inequality and, 183–184
global justice, 2–3; cosmopolitan theories of, 13; international relations and, 10; *NW* and, 210; reshaping reader consciousness and, 12
global migrant crisis, 33–34, 219–220
GoGwilt, Christopher, 235n27
Goldstone, Andrew, 87
Goswami, Manu, 60, 236n35
Granovetter, Mark, 20
Greene, Graham, 199, 200
Gregory, Lady, 79
Griffith, Arthur, 80–83, 84, 95–96, 245n15
grimoire: *Banjo* and, 119, 123, 129, 132–133; Lamming and, 136–137
Groden, Michael, 248n45
grotesque: Bakhtin on, 77; Harpham on, 30; *Home to Harlem* and, 117; Joyce and, 76–77, 93, 96; modernist, 21–29
Groys, Boris, 35
Guattari, Félix, 239n64
Guha, Ranajit, 41
guilt, luck and, 211–212
Guterres, António, 219–220
gypsies, 108–109

Habermas, Jürgen, 21
Habiby, Emile, 237n44
"Hades" (Joyce), 94
Hall, Stuart, 188
Handbook of Global Modernisms (Wollaeger), 17
Hardy, Thomas, 261n33
Harlem Renaissance, McKay and, 20, 32, 112, 249n10
"Harlem Renaissance and the New Modernist Studies, The," 249n8
Harlem Shadows (McKay), 116
Harootunian, H. D., 53
Harpham, Geoffrey Galt, 30
Harris, Wilson, 138–139
Hart, Matthew, 235n27
Hartley, L. P., 181
Hayot, Eric, 235–236n34
Hegel, Georg Wilhelm Friedrich, 264n10
Hegglund, Jon, 233n4
Herder, Johann, 186
Hermann, Christoph, 201–202
Herodotus, 149, 174
Hindu nationalism, 41, 48, 60–62, 65–68, 70–72
Hindu Tamils, 164, 179, 256n26
historical actors, memory and experience of time and, 173–174
historical materialism, 170
historical novel, Ondaatje and, 149, 151, 152
Histories, The (Herodotus), 149, 150
historiographic metafiction, 151, 254n7

history: archive and, 150; interface with myth, 151; Ondaatje's theory of, 150–151; stagist and progressivist, 238n59
Hobbes, Thomas, 10
holism, 186, 187
Hollywood, Amy, 131
Holmes, Christopher, 259n6
Home and the World, The (Tagore), 36, 39; aesthetic preference and ethnic stereotype in, 65–66; as "babu" novel, 63–64; circulation of goods across borders and, 59–60; colonial culture and, 64–68; domesticity and, 66–68; double plot of, 69–70; footnotes in, 62–63; Pears soap symbolism in, 66–68; reception of in Europe, 63–64; recombinatory strategies in, 40; Swadeshi nationalism and, 60–62, 65–68; taste and, 64–66, 69–72; translating, 58–68
Home to Harlem (McKay), 114–118, 133
hope, Bloch and, 246n32
Hough, Graham, 14, 15
Howes, Marjorie, 244n2
Huffman, Frontier Photographer (Huffman), 158
Huffman, L. A., 158
human, definition of, 167, 257n29
humanists, temporal scale and, 172–174
human rights activists, temporal scale and, 172–174
human rights interventionism, 3
human rights law/principles, 109–110; *Anil's Ghost* and, 168–169; Universal Declaration of Human Rights, 109, 219
Hume, David, 22–23
Hungarian parallel, 80–83, 245n15; "After the Race" and, 85–89; Joyce and, 83–89, 95–96; race and, 81–82
Hutcheon, Linda, 254n7
Huxley, Julian, 257n29
Hyndman, Henry, 124–125
hypotaxis, 207
hysterical realism, *White Teeth* and, 215–216

Ibsen, Henrik, 84
"I Dream that I Dwelt" (Joyce), 93
Indian nationalism, 41, 48, 60–62, 65–68, 70–72
individual: individualism and, 212, 214; plot and, 110
individualism: individual and, 212, 214; international, 109; Smith and, 205, 212, 214
inequality: economic, 3; global, 183–184, 209–211
innovation, dependence and, 213
integration: defined, 182; global capitalism and, 182–183
intellectual history, 25
international individualism, 109
internationalism, 9–14; anticolonial and liberal theories of, 13–14; archival legends and, 33; black, 111–112, 122, 125–126, 132, 249n9; chimera as symbol for, 9; colonial culture and, 64–68; of McKay, 24–25; political imagination of, 8–9; real-world politics and, 3, 4; tensions between national interests and cosmopolitan identifications and, 75; vagabond, 125; Wells-Tagore debate on effect of, 37–38
International Monetary Fund, 261n37
international relations, realist view of, 10–11
international solidarity, 3, 19; global inequality and, 183–184; Ireland and,

75; Joyce and, 84, 88–89, 99–105; metalepsis and, 193–194
In the Castle of My *Skin* (Lamming), 135
intranational discrimination, 51–52
Iraqi National Library, looting and burning of, 171–172
Irish–French alliance, 86–87
Irish Homestead (newspaper), 83, 84
Irish–Jewish parallel, 79–80, 102–103, 104–106
Irish Literary Revival, 75, 84
Irish Literary Theatre, 78
Irish literature: Hungarian parallel and, 80–83; Moses–Parnell typology and, 79
Irish nationalism, 84; continental politics and, 74, 80, 244n1, 245n15; Joyce and, 244n2
Irish revivalism, 31, 244n4; cultural insularity of, 75; Joyce's criticism of, 82–84, 99–100
Irish seoinini, 82
Irish solidarity, Joyce and, 74–75
isolationism, autarky and, 47
"Ithaca" (Joyce), 105–106
Ivory Coast, migration from, 190

Jamaican dialect, McKay and, 116
James, David, 237n39
"James Joyce—The Internationalist" (Power), 243n1
Jameson, Fredric: on failure of socialist internationalism, 9; geopolitical unconscious and, 205; totality and, 186, 203, 208; on utopia, 231, 264n10
jatiprem, 54, 242n25
Jay, Martin, 186
jazz: in *Banjo*, 127–129, 130–132; Bataille on, 129–130, 131
Jewish–Irish parallel, 79–80, 102–103, 104–106
Jones, Dewey, 118
Joyce, James, 8, 20, 31–32, 185; "After the Race," 83–89; alternating asymmetry and, 75–76; apposition and, 100–103; chimeras and, 78–79, 90–91, 92–94; criticism of Irish revivalism, 82–84; gigantism and, 96–97; grotesque and, 93, 96; Hungarian parallel and, 83–89, 95–96; Irish liberation and, 89–90; Irish solidarity and, 74–75; memorialization and, 187; moral history and, 90, 91–92; national parallelism and, 79–94; *A Portrait of the Artist as a Young Man*, 90, 94, 114, 121; psychology of colonial subject and, 78–79; pushing boundaries of literary form, 76; on role of artist, 77–78; self-deception and, 84, 89, 90; Smith and, 206; *Stephen Hero*, 83, 84, 87, 92, 95. See also *Dubliners* (Joyce); *Ulysses* (Joyce)
judgment, standards of, 4–5
justice: global, 10, 12, 13, 210; scales and, 189
"Justice and International Relations" (Beitz), 13

Kabdebó, Thomas, 80
Kadir, Djelal, 171, 174
Kafka, Franz, 185
Kant, Immanuel, 69, 70
Kaya Press, 225
Kazanjian, David, 100–101
Kenner, Hugh, 15
Kershner, R. Brandon, 244n1
Khanna, Ranjana, 151
Kiberd, Declan, 75, 82
Kinser, Samuel, 44
Kirschenbaum, Matthew, 253n3
Knepper, Wendy, 262n40

knowable communities, 5–6
knowledge/knowing: chimeras of form and limits of, 2; scale of, 26; Smith and partiality of, 188
künstlerroman, 114
Kurdi, Alan, 264n7
Kureishi, Hanif, 199
Kurnick, David, 91

Lamming, George, 8, 20, 32; aestheticized populism and, 147, 148; anticolonialism and, 140–141; classification of, 249–250n10; deracination and, 135, 138–139, 141–142, 148; grimoire aesthetics and, 137; narrative collectivism and, 135–136; on peasant writing, 136–137; plotless novels of, 111–113; as postcolonial writer, 112; Sartre and, 140–141; use of plotlessness, 134–135. See also *Emigrants, The* (Lamming)
Lampedusa, 190
"Language of the Outlaw, The" (Joyce), 245n12
Larkin, Philip, 200
Latour, Bruno, 29
Lawrence, Karen, 96
League of Nations, 11; International Committee on Intellectual Cooperation, 10, 239n1
LeClair, Tom, 165
legend, Foucault on, 152. See also *Collected Works of Billy the Kid, The* (Ondaatje)
Lenin, Vladimir, 124
Levin, Harry, 14, 15
Levine, Caroline, 6–7, 241n24
Levinson, André, 118–119, 120–121, 129, 147
Levy, Andrea, 199
Lewis, Pericles, 244n4, 247n38
liberal geoculture, 213–214
liberation, national organicism and, 27–28
Linati schema, 96, 106
literary form: sociopolitical intervention and, 222; as stabilizing force, 5
literary network, circulation and translation and, 240n6
"A Little Cloud" (Joyce), 90, 94
"Lives of Infamous Men, The" (Foucault), 152
Lloyd, David, 92, 248n45
localism, Smith and, 200–201
Locher, T. J. G., 208
Locke, John, 187
Lolita (Nabokov), 214
London, Smith and northwest, 187–188; "The North West London Blues," 197–200, 218. *See also* "Embassy of Cambodia, The" (Smith); *NW* (Smith); *White Teeth* (Smith)
London Living Wage, 198
Love, Heather, 113
luck, guilt and, 211–212
Lukács, Georg, 63, 64, 151, 165
lyrical realism, 216

Mackey, Nathaniel, 138–139
Macmillan (publisher), 62, 239n3
Majumdar, Saikat, 91
Mali, Joseph, 174
Mandel, Ann, 154
Mani, B. Venkat, 259–260n14
Mann, Thomas, 14
Mao, Douglas, 15
mapping a country, 1–2, 4–5, 233n4
Marx, John, 238n59
Marxism, totality and, 186
mass displacement, 219–220
mature thought, in internationalism, 11

Matz, Jesse, 262n41
Maxwell, William J., 123
McCarthy, Tom, 185, 186
McClintock, Anne, 67
McGurl, Mark, 257n33
McKay, Claude, 8, 20, 32; black objectification/stereotypes and, 126–129; classification of, 249–250n10; deracination and, 114, 116, 122, 134; embellishment, disorientation, surveillance and, 24–25; exploration of black community in novels, 117; Harlem Renaissance and, 20, 32, 112, 249n10; *Home to Harlem*, 114–118; musical ecstasy and, 127–129, 130–132; plotless novels of, 111–113; socialism and, 117, 124–125; vagabondage and, 120–124, 125, 133, 147–148. See also *Banjo: A Story Without a Plot* (McKay)
McKible, Adam, 249n8
measurement, in "The Embassy of Cambodia," 192, 195, 197
Mecsnóber, Tekla, 244n1
Mejías-López, Alejandro, 235–236n34
Melas, Natalie, 246n24
memorialization, Smith and, 187
memory: in *Anil's Ghost*, 164, 167, 168; archives and collective, 180; black modernism and critical, 142; collective, 180–181; experience of time and, 173–174; multidirectional, 181; Ondaatje and, 149, 151
Merriam-Webster, 182
metalepsis, 193–194, 195–196
method, in anthology, 46, 47
Middle Passage, 138–139
migrant body, 228–229, 264n7
migration: to Europe, 219–220; European Union policies on, 190–191, 260n18. *See also* forced migration
migratory subjectivity, 111
Migritude (Patel), 34; as re-mediated work of art, 223–230
Milanovic, Branko, 183, 184
mimesis, 158
mimetic desire, 236n34
minor, 239n64
Mirror and the Lamb, The (Abrams), 22
mise en abyme structure, in *Nationalism*, 52
Mitchel, John, 80
Mitchell, Timothy, 262n37
modernism, 16–17; chimeric model of literary form and, 7; cross-cultural encounter and, 235n34; deprovincializing, 14–21; modernity and, 6; non-European literatures and, 17; transnational, 235n27; tropes, 113
Modernism: An Anthology (Rainey), 14
Modernism/Modernity (journal), 249n8
modernismo, 236n34
Modernist grotesque, 21–29
modernist internationalism: chimeras of form and, 12; critical cosmopolitanism vs., 236–237n37; forced displacement and, 220–221; Joyce and, 31; knowable and, 6; mediated nature of agency and, 222–223; neoclassicist vision of, 14–15; reformulation of, 2–3; unknowability of communities and, 222
modernity, 16–17; central contradiction of, 5; globalizing processes of, 19; modernism and, 6
modernization of literature, decline of knowable and, 5–6
Monegato, Emanuele, 225
Mongol invasion of Iraq, 172
montage, 165
moral history, Joyce and, 90, 91–92

moral luck, 211–213
Morrison, Toni, 210
Moses–Parnell comparison, 79
Moten, Fred, 100
"Mourn—and then Onward!" (Yeats), 79
Moyn, Samuel, 13
multiculturalism: the novel and, 259n13; Smith and, 188, 192–193, 199
multidirectional memory, 181
music: in *Banjo*, 125–129, 130–132; in *The Emigrants*, 142–143; Wells and Tagore on, 39
Muslims, Indian nationalism and, 64–66, 70–72
mutilation of form in *The Emigrants*, 137–139
mythistorical, 174–175
mythography, 156
myths: *Anil's Ghost* and, 169–170; foundational, 174; interface with history, 151; legend and, 152. See also *Collected Works of Billy the Kid, The* (Ondaatje)

Nabokov, Vladimir, 214
Nagel, Thomas, 2, 9, 10–11, 13
Naibedya (Tagore), 53–54
Nail, Thomas, 220
Nandy, Ashis, 41
Narrative Discourse (Genette), 193
national autarky, state sovereignty and, 8
national autonomy, cultural autarky and, 241n18
national community, autarkic theories of, 221
nationalism, 10; anthology and, 42, 43; anticolonial, 48; autarkic, 31, 47–48, 72–73; Celtic, 84; Irish, 84, 244n1, 244n2, 245n15; romantic theories of, 27–28; selection and, 49–51; Swadeshi, 41, 48, 60–62, 65–68, 70–72; temperance, 248n45; transnational processes of selection and, 49–50; via regionalism, 139–140; Westernization and, 48–49; West Indian, 141–142, 145, 146
Nationalism (Tagore), 39; as anthology, 42–43, 46; assimilation vs. appropriation and, 50–51; autotranslation of, 23; comparison in, 52–53; compiling, 42–58; connection between nationalism and Westernization in, 48–49; main text, 44–45, 50; "Nationalism in India," 46, 51–52; "Nationalism in Japan," 45–46, 49, 50–51; "Nationalism in the West," 45; opening preface, 45–46, 47; oral performance and, 241n24; paratexts, 44–45, 47, 53; on power dynamics of cultural contact, 43–44; prefaces, 50, 52–53; recombinatory strategies in, 40; remainders of, 53; second preface, 45, 46–47, 53; "The Sunset of the Century," 42, 46, 53–58; title page, 44
national organicism, 27–29
national parallelism, 75; "After the Race" and, 84–89; Irish–Jewish parallel, 79–80, 102–103, 104–106; *Ulysses* and, 98–107. *See also* Hungarian parallel; Joyce, James
nationhood, authorship and democratic, 194–195
Nation (periodical), 42
nation-state: borders of, 60, 141; Cheah on, 27–29; forced displacement and, 220–221; universalistic within and particularistic without, 60
nativism, *The Collected Works of Billy the Kid* and, 154
Negritude poets, 224

Negroes in America (McKay), 124
"Negro Writer and His World, The" (Lamming), 144
"Negro Writer to His Critics, A" (McKay), 118
neoclassicist vision of modernist internationalism, 14–15
neoliberalism, 261n36; Smith's critique of, 199, 201–202
Netherland (O'Neill), 185
New Criticism, 16
New International Economic Order (NIEO), 13
new modernist studies, 15
New Statesman (journal), 44
New Yorker (magazine), 189
New York Herald-Tribune (newspaper), 118
Ngai, Sianne, 10, 128, 213
Nickels, Joel, 251n31
Nolan, Emer, 78
Noland, Carrie, 224
nomadic collectivism, 112, 146–147. *See also* Lamming, George; McKay, Claude
nomadism, Roma and, 108–109
Norris, Margot, 105
North, Michael, 116
"North West London Blues, The" (Smith), 197–200, 218
nostalgia: in *Anil's Ghost*, 179, 181; Ondaatje and, 150–151; Smith and, 199
nostalgic primitivism, 251n27
Nouvelles Littéraires (periodical), 119
Novalis, 27
novel: corporation, 26; multiculturalism and, 259n13; plotless, 111–113; regional, 26–27; *rentier*, 26; Smith on future of Anglophone, 185; university, 26
Nussbaum, Martha, 9, 41, 70
NW (Smith), 187, 197–198; disrupted panorama in, 207–208; distributions of power, 209; Englishness and, 203–205; individualism and individual in, 212, 214; interactive dimension of, 206–207, 262n40; intersection of national and global inequality, 209–210; localism and, 200–201; moral luck and, 211–213; partiality of vision in, 203, 205; portrayal of privilege in, 202–203; review of, 201; self-determination and, 205–206; use of stream of consciousness in, 206–207, 208; welfare state and, 199

O'Brien, William Smith, 80
obstructed agency, 213
Occupy movement, 183, 198
oceanic ontology of time, 173–174
"Of Simplicity and Refinement in Writing" (Hume), 22–23
Olson, Charles, 163
Ondaatje, Michael, 20, 32–33, 107; archival method of, 151–153, 176–177, 180; historical novel and, 149, 151, 152; history as unfinishable project and, 150–151; interface of myth and history and, 151; mythistorical and, 174–175; photo of as young boy, 159, 160; reframing national pasts, 153–154; reinscription and, 180–181; Tagore and, 152–153. See also *Anil's Ghost* (Ondaatje); *Collected Works of Billy the Kid, The* (Ondaatje)
O'Neill, Joseph, 185
optimism, cruel, 76–77
oral performance, world literature and, 53, 241n24
organicism: ideologies of, 27; national, 27–29

overcoherence, 262n37
Oxford English Dictionary, 47, 182

Paine, Thomas, 124
panorama: ideological significance of, 262n42; in *NW*, 207–208
parallax, 97
parataxis, 206, 207
paratexts, *Nationalism*'s, 44–45, 47, 53
Parnell, Charles Stewart, 79
partiality of vision, in *NW*, 203, 205, 210
participant analyst, reader as, 63
Patel, Shailja, 34, 223–230
Peace, David, 261n33
Pears soap, 66–68, 243n42
Peasants' Revolt (1381), 197–198
peasant writing, Lamming on, 136–137
People's History of London, A (Rees), 198
performance theory, 226
perspectivism, 19
pessoptimism, 21, 237n44
Phillips, Caryl, 185, 199
Piper, Andrew, 255n12
Pippin, Robert, 244–245n10
plot: bildungsroman and, 110; individuality and, 110; power of, 119–120
plotlessness, 25, 32. *See also* Lamming, George; McKay, Claude
plotless novels, 111–113. See also *Banjo: A Story Without a Plot* (McKay); *Emigrants, The* (Lamming)
poetic invention, political change and, 227–231
political change, poetic invention and, 227–231
political collectivism, Joyce and, 31
political life, defined, 239n62
Political Theory and International Relations (Beitz), 13
populism: aetheticized, 147, 148; deracination and, 135
Porter, David, 58
Portrait of the Artist as a Young Man, A (Joyce), 90, 94, 114, 121
postcolonial critique, 199–200
Pound, Ezra, 14, 39, 40, 59, 236n34
Power, Arthur, 243n1
power, distributions of, 209
Practice of Diaspora, The (Edwards), 111
Pratt, Mary Louise, 45
prefaces, in *Nationalism*, 45–47, 50, 52–53
primitivism, nostalgic, 251n27
Procter, James, 188
proliferation, frontier mythology and, 161, 163
propaedeutics, 231
prose, form and formlessness and, 116
Proust, Marcel, 14
provincial, colonial aligned with, 245n20
provincial fiction, 26
provincialism, national belonging and, 243n1
Provincializing Europe (Chakrabarty), 17
pseudotranslation, 54
public feelings, 239n62
public performance, printed work of, 223–230
puns, theory of, 138

Quidditas, epiphanies and, 92, 93

Rabelais, François, 77
race: "After the Race" and, 87–89; socialism and, 124; *Ulysses* and, 95, 96
racial consciousness, McKay and, 117–119, 125

racial stereotypes: Hungarian–Irish parallel and, 81–82; McKay and, 126–129
Radice, William, 242n36
Rainey, Lawrence, 14
Ramazani, Jahan, 15
Ratti, Manav, 256n26
Rawls, John, 13
Ray, Sri Suhendu, 242n36
reader consciousness, reshaping borders of, 12
realism: combined with utopianism, 12; hysterical, 215–216; lyrical, 216
recursion, 206
Reddy, Vanita, 225
"Red Hanrahan" (Yeats), 84
Rees, John, 198
reflections, Tagore's translations as, 55–56, 59
regional novel, 26–27
Reid, Vic, 136
reinscription, 180–181
Remainder (McCarthy), 185
re-mediated work of art (*Migritude*), 223–230
rentier novel, 26
Resurrection of Hungary, The: A Parallel for Ireland (Griffith), 80–81, 82–83, 84, 95–96
revision, 19
Richards, Grant, 89, 92
rights: of others, 133–134; of transnational people, 109–110. *See also under* human rights
Roach, Joseph, 226
Robbins, Bruce: attachment at a distance and, 20; deep time and, 171, 172–174, 257n33; on *The English Patient*, 254n6; on global inequality and welfare state, 210–211; on *The Home and the World*, 70; on internationalism, 3; literary history of the welfare state and, 201
Rogers, Gayle, 244n1
Rolland, Romain, 239n1
Roma, 108–109
Roosevelt, Franklin Delano, 213
root canal metaphor, Smith and, 33, 184–185, 186–187, 188, 214–215
Rothberg, Michael, 180–181
Rushdie, Salman, 1–2, 4–5, 8, 184, 199, 216
Russell, George William, 94
Russian avant-garde ideology of autonomy, 35–36

Saga of Billy the Kid, The (Burns), 156
Saint-Amour, Paul, 17, 247–248n41, 259n10
Sartre, Jean-Paul, 140–141
Satanic Verses, The (Rushdie), 1–2
scale, Smith and, 189–197, 200–201, 207–208, 209
scale iconography, 189
Schengen Borders Code, 260n18
Schlegel, Friedrich, 27
Schleiermacher, Friedrich, 27
Schwartz, Mattathias, 190
scientific socialism, 124–125
"Scylla and Charybdis" (Joyce), 94
segmentation, in "The Embassy of Cambodia," 189–190, 191–192, 195, 196
selection, nationalism and, 49–51
self-deception, Joyce and, 84, 89, 90
self-definition, collective, 181
self-determination, Smith and, 205–206
self-recognition, Hungarian parallel and, 81
self-reference, in *The Collected Works of Billy the Kid*, 159, 160
Selvon, Sam, 136

Sen, Amartya, 41
Seshagiri, Urmila, 237n39
Shaw, George Bernard, on *Ulysses*, 103–104
short story: as literary form, 190; Smith and, 191–192
"Significance of History, The" (Turner), 256n16
"Significance of the Frontier in American History, The" (Turner), 155
Silko, Leslie Marmon, 173–174
Sinhalese, 256n26
Sinn Féin, 75, 80, 95
"Sisters, The" (Joyce), 83, 84
Slaughter, Joseph, 110, 258n40
Smethurst, James, 118
Smith, Zadie, 2, 8, 20, 107; causality and, 208–209, 214–215, 217–218; Englishness and, 199, 200; FutureMouse and, 34–35; individualism and individual and, 205, 212, 214; memorialization and, 187; multiculturalism and, 188, 192–193, 199; neoliberal critique and, 199, 201–202; northwest London and, 187–188; "The North West London Blues," 197–200; root canal metaphor and, 33, 184–185, 186–187, 188, 214–215; scale and, 189–197, 200–201, 207–208, 209; stream of consciousness and, 206–207, 208; totality and, 185–186, 208; use of metalepsis, 193–194, 195–196; welfare state and, 198–199, 261n32. *See also* "Embassy of Cambodia, The" (Smith); *NW* (Smith); *White Teeth* (Smith)
social arrangements of collectivities, 7
social exposure, 91
socialism: McKay and, 117; utopian vs. scientific, 124–125
socialists, internationalism and, 9–10
social upheaval, limits of aesthetic representation and, 1–2
solidarity: Irish, 74–75; localism of, 192; McKay and race as grounds for, 118. *See also* international solidarity
Songs of Jamaica (McKay), 116
Souls of Black Folk, The (Du Bois), 19
spectrality, 28
Spinks, Lee, 155
spiritual truancy, McKay and, 116–117
Spivak, Gayatri, 211
Spoo, Robert E., 79, 247n41
Spring in New Hampshire (McKay), 116
Spring of Nations, 80
Sri Lankan civil war. See *Anil's Ghost* (Ondaatje)
Stalinism, autonomy and, 35–36
state sovereignty, national autarky and, 8
state-sponsored transnationalism, 123
Steedman, Carolyn, 253n3
Stephen Hero (Joyce), 83, 84, 87, 92, 95
Stephens, Michelle Ann, 251–252n41
Stoler, Ann Laura, 161, 254–255n9, 256n23
stream of consciousness, Smith and, 206–207, 208
subjectivation: *Migritude* and, 224–225; Negritude poets and, 224
"Sunset of the Century, The" (Tagore), 42, 46; Bengali origins of, 53–54. See also *Nationalism* (Tagore)
Swadeshi nationalism, 41, 48, 60–62, 65–68, 70–72
symbolic landscape, symbolism of, 151
syntactic decomposition, 206
Szalay, Michael, 261n32

Tagore, Rabindranath, 2, 8, 20, 221; antinationalism of, 41; autarkic

nationalism and, 31, 47–48, 72–73; authorial and collective identity of, 44–45; autotranslation and, 23, 30–31, 39, 40–41, 73; Bengali writings of, 58–59; collaborative translation and, 39, 62, 239n3; combining poems, 54–55; compiling *Nationalism*, 42–58; damaged reputation of, 39–40; debate with Wells, 10, 37–38; defining national collectivity, 57; on effect of internationalism, 37–38; on musical notation systems, 39; Ondaatje's archival method and, 152–153; reconsideration of, 41; Rolland and Einstein and, 239n1; Swadeshi nationalism and, 41, 48, 60–62, 65–68, 70–72; taste and, 69–72; translating *The Home and the World*, 58–68; translation of Bengali poems, 73; translations as reflections and, 55–56, 59; treatment of Bengali works as repositories of materials, 40–41; utopian internationalism and, 31; *Visva-Bharati* and, 61, 72–73. See also *Home and the World, The* (Tagore); *Nationalism* (Tagore)
Tagore, Surendranath, 39, 62, 239n3
Tamils, 164, 179, 256n26
taste: collectivity based on shared, 69–70; ethnic stereotype and, 63–64; production of identity and, 64–66; Tagore and, 69–72
Taylor, John F., 79, 245n12
Tebbit, Norman, 217
techne, 28–29
"Telemachus" (Joyce), 94
temperance nationalism, 248n45
temporality: in *Anil's Ghost*, 169, 170–171, 177–178; in *The Emigrants*, 137, 145–147, 148. *See also* time
territoriality, citizenship and, 110–111
territorial nationality, 70–71
territorial nativism, 60, 70, 72
Texas Star (periodical), 158
"This Is How It Feels to Me" (Smith), 196, 205
Three Guineas (Woolf), 19
Through Other Continents (Dimock), 170–172
Thucydides, 174
time: anticolonial, 172–174; deep time, 170–174, 257n33. *See also* temporality
time capsule metaphor, in *Anil's Ghost*, 177–178
Times Literary Supplement (periodical), 44
totality, Smith and, 185–186, 208
translatio, 237n40
translation: archival method and, 152; collaborative, 59, 73; as reflections, 55–56, 59; of "The Sunset of the Century," 47, 53–58; Tagore and negotiation of, 37–39, 58; Wells on, 37–38
translation theory, Tagore and, 54–56
transmission, 154, 255n12
transnational blackness, 111
transnational citizenship, 109–110
transnational historical networks, Smith and, 33
transnationalism, state-sponsored, 123
transnational male friendship, *Banjo* and, 132–133
transnational migration, 3
transnational modernism, 235n27
transnational processes of selection, nationalism and, 49–50
transnational upward mobility, 211
Tsing, Anna, 238n61
Turner, Frederick Jackson, 155, 256n16
Twenty Years' Crisis, The (Carr), 10–11

"Two Paths for the Novel" (Smith), 185, 216

Ulysses (Joyce), 32, 94–107, 119; alternating asymmetry in, 76, 96, 97–98; anti-Irish bias in criticism of, 248n45; "Cyclops," 95–105, 106; "Eumaeus," 105; gigantism in, 96–97; Gilbert schema, 96; grotesque in, 76–77; "Ithaca," 105–106; Linati schema, 96, 106
unfinished vs. unfinishable, 21
United Irishman (newspaper), 80, 89
United Nations Conference on Trade and Development, 13
United Nations High Commissioner for Refugees, 219–220, 263n1
United States, response to migrants, 220–221
Universal Declaration of Human Rights, 109, 219
universal humanism, Tagore and, 41
universalism, nation and, 60
universality: Tagore and, 37–38; Wells and, 37–38
university novel, 26
utopia: Adorno on, 264n10; chimera *vs.*, 231
utopian internationalism, Tagore and, 31
utopianism: combined with realism, 12; internationalism and, 11
utopian socialism, 124–125
utopian universalism, Wells and, 37–38, 39

vagabondage, 125; McKay and, 112, 120–124, 133, 147–148
vagabond internationalism, 125
Valente, Joseph, 78
Velody, Irving, 253n3
vernacular, Lamming's use of, 139–141
Visva-Bharati (World-India), Tagore and, 61, 72–73
Viswanathan, Gauri, 44
Vogel, Shane, 117

Wald, Priscilla, 257n29
Walkowitz, Rebecca, 15, 42, 236–237n37
Wallace, David Foster, 216
Wallerstein, Immanuel, 186, 208, 213
Washington Consensus, 261n36
wealth inequality, globalization and, 183–184
welfare state, 263n51; decolonization and, 261n31; global inequality and, 210–211; Smith and, 198–199, 261n32
Wells, H. G., 10, 37–38, 39
Westernization, nationalism and, 48–49
West Indian nationalism, 141–142, 145, 146
West Indies citizenship, Lamming and, 134
West Indies Federation, 137, 147
"What Was Modernism?" (Levin), 14
White Teeth (Smith), 33, 34; causality and, 214–215, 217–218; cricket test in, 217; hysterical realism and, 215–216; root canal metaphor, 184–185, 186–187, 214–215; scalar abnormalities of, 216–217
wholes, relationship between formal and social, 189–190
Wilde, Oscar, 87
Wilder, Gary, 18, 141, 241n18
Williams, Bernard, 211
Williams, Raymond, 5, 26–27, 186
Williams, William Carlos, 15
Williamson, John, 261n36

Wilson, Woodrow, 213
Wilsonian internationalism, 11, 25
Winkiel, Laura, 16
Wollaeger, Mark, 16–17
Wood, James, 185, 196, 215–216, 259n6
Woolf, Virginia, 15, 19
World Bank, 261n36
World Social Forum, 10, 183, 223
world state, internationalism and, 10

Yao, Stephen G., 40
Yeats, W. B., 39, 79, 84
Young Islander Rebellion (1848), 80
youthfulness, *Banjo* and, 121–122